The Public Management and Leadership Se

Series Editor: Paul 't Hart, Utrecht University & Netherlands Sc

CW00336179

Editorial Advisory Group

John Alford (University of Melbourne & Australia and New Zealand School of Government)

Michael Barzelay (London School of Economics)

Geert Bouckaert (K.U.Leuven)

Joanne B.Ciulla (Jepson School, University of Richmond)

Jean Hartley (Open University Business School)

Werner Jann (University of Potsdam)

Per Lægreid (University of Bergen)

Mark H.Moore (Harvard University)

Karen Mossberger (Arizona State University)

Jon Pierre (University of Gothenburg)

Donald J.Savoie (Moncton University)

Mark van Twist (Netherlands School of Government & Erasmus University)

Zeger van der Wal (National University of Singapore)

Kai Wegrich (Hertie School of Governance)

Public management and, more recently, public leadership have over several decades emerged as increasingly central elements in the study and practice of governance, public administration and public policy.

Around them have developed important new strands of research, debate, education and professional formation. And these in turn have informed a wide range of initiatives in many parts of the world to 'modernize', 'reform', 'innovate', 'de-bureaucratize' and 'professionalize' existing institutions and practices.

The *Public Management and Leadership series* aims to provide a set of key texts to meet the changing needs of the growing range of graduate and post-experience courses in this area as well as concise and accessible reading for busy practitioners.

Genuinely international in scope and conception; accessible in style and presentation; and drawing on empirical information and illustrations from a wide variety of jurisdictions and policy sectors, each title will offer an authoritative review of the state of theory and practice in its respective field, and identify the key challenges and the most promising conceptual and practical tools to tackle them.

The Public Management and Leadership series

Series Editor: **Paul 't Hart,** Utrecht University & Netherlands School of Public Administration

Published:

Paul 'T Hart
Understanding Public Leadership

John Alford and Janine O'Flynn
Rethinking Public Service Delivery:
Managing with External Providers

Martin Lodge and Kai Wegrich
Managing Regulation:
Regulatory Analysis, Politics and Policy

Sean Lusk and Nick Birks
Rethinking Public Strategy

Richard Mulgan
Making Open Government Work:
Accountability, Transparency and Public
Management

Mirko Noordegraaf
Public Management:
Performance, Professionalism and Politics

Zeger van der Wal
The 21st Century Public Manager

In preparation:

Political/Administrative Relations
Public Management and Public Finance
Public Management and Collaboration
Public Management and the Media
Public Management in a Digital Age
Strategic Public Management

The 21st Century Public Manager

Challenges, People and Strategies

Zeger van der Wal

First published 2017 by
RED GLOBE PRESS

RED GLOBE PRESS in the UK is an imprint of Springer Nature Limited,
registered in England, company number 785998, of 4 Crinan Street,
London, N1 9XW.

RED GLOBE PRESS® is a registered trademark in the United States,
the United Kingdom, Europe and other countries.

ISBN 978–1–137–50743–3 hardback
ISBN 978–1–137–50742–6 paperback

This book is printed on paper suitable for recycling and made from fully
managed and sustained forest sources. Logging, pulping and manufacturing
processes are expected to conform to the environmental regulations of the
country of origin.

A catalogue record for this book is available from the British Library.

A catalog record for this book is available from the Library of Congress.

Contents

List of Illustrative Material

Boxes

Figures

Tables

Preface

I finished writing this book during a five-week research leave in New York. The apartment we stayed in was located in a 'not so gentrified' part of Brooklyn. Being confronted with the raw side of the metropole – endless piles of garbage, dilapidated housing, poor and homeless people wandering around, migrants selling stuff on the streets hoping to get by – I was strengthened in my resolve to finish this book. I became even more convinced than I already was that the world needs good government, good administrators, and effective public managers; in short: that public management matters. More so, I felt that by offering a book that was hands-on, actor-driven, and speaking to the daily life of public managers who often operate in tough circumstances, my work might even make a difference to some of them, albeit in the smallest possible way.

Back in 2014, I started writing this book for two main reasons. First of all, I was inspired and energized by all the (aspiring) public managers I interacted with during executive programmes, classes, conferences, and research interviews, the vast majority of them working tirelessly every day to create public value in tough circumstances. I have learned much more from them than they could ever learn from me. I continue to enjoy informal interactions and friendships with many alumni from dozens of countries, junior and senior. At the same time, I couldn't help noticing that even the practitioner-oriented and 'down-to-earth' topics, readings, and cases I discussed with them were often too scholarly and too distant from their hard realities, particularly for public managers in developing contexts.

This observation brings me to my second reason. I wanted to write a book that would speak to (aspiring) public managers across the globe. A book that would take their issues, pains, and challenges but also their optimism, clever solutions, and coping mechanisms as a starting point. A book that would categorize and examine current trends and drivers that didn't get the attention they deserved in our conversations as there was always other content that 'had' to be covered. A book, above all, that would take senior practitioners seriously by providing them with examples, perspectives, and strategies grounded in the latest research evidence and best practices while being accessible and actor-driven at the same time. A book, lastly, that would be relevant and timely to public managers in the developing as well as the developed world, in the West and the non-West. Still, all too often – intentionally or not – books and articles propagate views, frameworks, and models that originated in the West but may be less useful in other settings.

At this stage, it is important to say a few things about the nature of this book. This book is not a research monograph reporting in detail on original empirical research, nor a conceptual book propagating one particular theory of or approach to public management (if there even is one). There is no central framework or 'model' guiding the various chapters beyond the notion that 21ˢᵗ century public managers operate in a VUCA world – one characterized by volatility, uncertainty, complexity, and ambiguity. Rather, this book is a timely, practitioner-oriented teaching text for MPA (Master of Public Administration), MPM (Master of Public Management), and executive education audiences across the globe, made up of aspiring public managers who aim to improve their skills and expand their horizons in order to face a 21ˢᵗ century operating environment.

Thus, instead of taking the classical 'topical' textbook approach, with a chapter on performance, another on political-administrative relations, and yet another on accountability or ethics, this book is structured 'the other way around'. It departs from the key trends and demands facing public managers in the years to come, to discuss how existing research and real-life examples help them to make sense of those emerging trends and managerial demands. This was what I had in mind when I started writing and organizing my initial ideas almost three years ago. Now, five versions of the outline and dozens of versions of the manuscript later, the book is finally here. I genuinely hope you will find it helpful, recognizable, and – from time to time – inspiring. I have tried to keep the content and literature up to date until the very last moment.

Finally, I have to thank a number of individuals who played an important role in the process of writing this book. First of all, series editor, colleague, and friend Paul 't Hart has been an amazing support from the early stages onwards. Paul, your constructively critical and always timely feedback has helped a lot to 'keep me going', particularly when energy was low and writer's block was near. Second, Palgrave editors Steven Kennedy and Lloyd Langman, and Assistant Editors Chloe Osborne, and Tuur Driesser (who happens to share a not-so-common first name with my son), have been accommodating, supporting, and pragmatic in their advice and support. I also thank the anonymous reviewer for the valuable comments on my draft manuscript.

Four of my research assistants have contributed immensely to this book – each in their different ways and with their own styles and strengths – and they deserve special mention here. Carolyn Law from Hong Kong, Awa Touray from Gambia, Assel Mussagulova from Kazakhstan, and Aprajita Singh from India: a big thank you! Their diversity in backgrounds is illustrative of the diversity of viewpoints, contexts, and real-life examples and cases I've tried to include in the book, and the diversity in my working environment that I've come to appreciate so much over the past few years. All of you have contributed to realizing my ambition of producing a truly global public management textbook. My colleague and editor Libby Morgan Berri has played a tremendously important role by reviewing and editing each of the chapters. Libby, you have a sharp eye for detail and consistency, and your contributions to this book have been invaluable.

On a more personal note, I would like to thank my three parents, Katie, Gerrit, and Mieke, who raised me well and have always supported my efforts and ambitions, and my brothers and sisters (in law) whom I often miss dearly, being over 7,000 miles apart. Our invaluable nanny Zel deserves special thanks as well: she enables us to work hard while spending enough quality time as a family. But most of all, thanks, love, and appreciation go out to my amazing family. Marjanne, Tuur, and Lauren: you make my life enjoyable and worthwhile every day. I have asked a lot from each of you during the process of writing this book, particularly in the last couple of months. I promise not to start another book project for at least two years!

ZEGER VAN DER WAL
Singapore, 23 September 2016

Chapter 1

Introduction

Being a public manager in a VUCA world

Imagine being a manager in a government agency anywhere on this planet. Your average working day consists of many activities. Organizing meetings and setting agendas to discuss progress on policy and service delivery related activities. Enduring tenured senior staff who are unable to keep up with their rapidly changing environment. Guiding junior staff who need to be carefully managed but don't think they do. Explaining to impatient political masters that complex policy decisions can't be reached within a week's time. Negotiating, communicating, and consulting with stakeholders across sectors on how to jointly design and produce services. Fending off traditional and citizen journalists who scrutinize your performance in catering to a non-stop media environment that feeds off crises and failures.

All these and more may easily fill up your everyday schedule – a schedule that you seem unable to control, let alone direct. Surely, being a public manager has never been easy, but it seems to become more challenging all the time. Four key features seem to increasingly characterize your operating environment.

First, more and more often you and your staff members are confronted with, or rather surprised by, disruptive events, scandals, crises, and shocks. The challenges that you face in such situations are not necessarily hard to understand – you have even planned and practised for some of them. However, their timing and occurrence are seemingly unexpected and their duration unknown. Due to increased interconnectedness, even small events may trigger other disruptive events and crises. The increased occurrence of such events results in larger *volatility*.

Second, you are more frequently confronted with sudden leadership transitions that completely change the outlook of policies and programmes you have been working on for months, sometimes years. You usually understand why the transition happened or why it was inevitable, but you lack crucial information about short-term implications and cues on how to proceed. You and your staff want to develop scenarios and actionables but you have to wait for things to unfold. Because of transitions such as these, you experience more *uncertainty*.

Third, you are increasingly designing and implementing policies collaboratively with a variety of stakeholders, each with their own agenda, worldview, and style. In addition, you have to manage an increasingly diverse workforce, in terms of gender, age, orientation, and background. You proceed based on gut feeling and experience, but you find it hard to effectively engage so many interconnected issues and characters. The increasingly collaborative and intergenerational nature of your work are just two examples of growing *complexity*.

Fourth, you are pressured to implement 'innovative' and untested new solutions as technologies evolve and tech-savvy citizens demand better service. However, as you pilot and experiment, expectations and potential outcomes are completely unclear. Solution providers, political masters, and end users have different, competing objectives, some of which are unclear or unknown to you. Piloting and experimenting is surrounded with *ambiguity*.

Taken together, these four examples illustrate how a 'VUCA world' (Johansen 2007), characterized by *volatility, uncertainty, complexity*, and *ambiguity,* will increasingly shape your operating environment. This operating environment will be to some extent 'unknown', not only in terms of projected outcomes, but also in terms of the required skills, strategies, and parameters. A now famous, but at the time ridiculed, statement by former US Secretary of Defense Donald Rumsfeld at a Pentagon briefing in 2002 nicely captures this feature:

> Reports that say that something hasn't happened are always interesting to me because as we know, there are 'known knowns'; there are things we know we know. We also know there are 'known unknowns'; that is to say we know there are some things we don't know. But there are also 'unknown unknowns' – the ones we don't know we don't know.

As the four features show, VUCA events vary in terms of containing 'unknowns'. Issues surrounded by *volatility* and *uncertainty* are more 'known', but challenging in their own right. They require a certain degree of flexibility and adaptiveness, together with foresight and strategic planning capabilities. Situations characterized by *complexity* and *ambiguity* are least 'known', requiring experimentation, piloting, and the engagement of unconventional expertise. Figure 1.1 displays the key characteristics of a VUCA operating environment.

Twenty-first century public management: more challenging but also more rewarding?

The features illustrate why your VUCA operating environment will be challenging in various ways. Stakeholders, including new generations of employees, act like expert know-it-alls while demanding authoritative leadership and evidence-based solutions at the same time. Media eagerly portray missteps and scandals while being much less interested in steady progress and small yet important wins. Political masters are so demanding and ambiguous that loyally serving them while preserving your values,

FIGURE 1.1   Characteristics of a VUCA operating environment

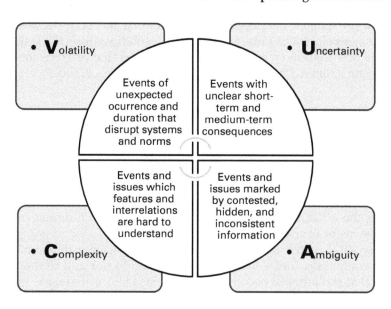

- **V**olatility

Events of unexpected ocurrence and duration that disrupt systems and norms

- **U**ncertainty

Events with unclear short-term and medium-term consequences

Events and issues which features and interrelations are hard to understand

Events and issues marked by contested, hidden, and inconsistent information

- **C**omplexity

- **A**mbiguity

motivations, and neutrality is hardly possible. Unlimited technological opportunities and innovations 'promise the world' but far exceed your human and financial capabilities, let alone your procedural and regulatory space. Sounds familiar, doesn't it?

Certainly, the context in which you operate has its own unique constraints and opportunities. Political environments may be more or less stable, bureaucratic influence on policy outcomes more or less considerable, and change and innovation enthusiastically embraced or fiercely opposed. But, wherever you are, you will share many challenges and frustrations with your counterparts across the globe, just as you will share many passions and ambitions. Such passions and ambitions may have been important drivers to join the public sector workforce in the first place, perhaps in an era quite different from the one today, and you must continue to uphold and nurture them to maintain a sense of professional pride and job satisfaction.

However, emerging developments also provide exciting opportunities for achieving unprecedented levels of public service excellence, together with citizens and vanguards of change from other sectors. In order to be an effective 21st century public manager, you will need to acquire and display a variety of skillsets and mindsets to turn various new challenges into immense opportunities.

If you are an aspiring public manager, things will certainly be more challenging by the time you join the managerial ranks of a government agency. At the same time, managing public agencies and policies in the coming decades will be one of the most exciting, interesting, and rewarding activities you can think of – regardless of whether you're operating in an emerging megacity, a developing country about to join the ranks of developed countries, or a surprisingly resilient developed welfare state that has been declared dead many times before. The same technological revolutions, assertive stakeholders, and new tech-savvy, entrepreneurial colleagues that produce challenges also create unlimited opportunities for public sector excellence.

Preparing for a VUCA world

If you are passionate about creating public value and driven by the intellectual challenges generated by the increasing complexity of 21ˢᵗ century public management, this book was written for you. You may find it inspiring and hopefully even helpful. If you're driven by job security, routine, stability, and predictability of your operating environment, or simply by leaving the office at 5 every day until you retire with a decent pension, you may want to stop reading now.

After all, if there's one thing we know about being a public manager in the coming decades – and there's much we do not and cannot know – it is that the job will become less routinized and demarcated in terms of time, space, task, and policy area, and more complex, risky, multi-faceted, cross-sectoral, and international. A key question in this book is therefore how public managers can prepare for and respond to a VUCA world. Should they do away with current, proven routines and structures – the 'old' – and rush into an unknown future with little guidance other than trying to be 'flexible', 'open', and 'adaptive'? Can new guidelines and strategies be formulated or is it merely 'anything goes', with public managers holding on for dear life?

Above all, public managers should not use the notion of a VUCA world as an excuse to shirk away from the hard and increasingly painful work of strategy and planning (Bennett and Lemoine 2014). Indeed, the VUCA concept first emerged in military circles in the post–Cold War environment of the early 1990s precisely to *stimulate* thinking about planning and preparing for operating environments increasingly characterized by 'wild cards' (Ho 2008, 2010; Petersen 2000). Wild cards are unlikely, high-impact events that are complex, expensive, and seldom politically expedient to anticipate and plan for.

How can public managers begin to think about identifying and responding to the various types of VUCA events? Figure 1.2 outlines basic approaches for public managers to address situations characterized by volatility, uncertainty, complexity, or ambiguity, based on the work of Bennett and Lemoine (2014: 2).

Basic guides like these may aid public managers in making sense of dynamic operating environments. In fact, one could say that being able to operate in a VUCA environment is the overarching 'critical competency' of a 21ˢᵗ century public manager. However, we need to get much more specific about the roles, competencies, and values that public managers

FIGURE 1.2 Identifying, preparing for, and responding to VUCA events

	COMPLEXITY	VOLATILITY
− How well can you predict the results of your actions? +	**Characteristics**: Many interconnected parts and variables. Some information may be available or can be predicted, but the volume or nature of the information can be overwhelming to process. **Example**: You are implementing a new policy strategy across various domains and departments, each with their own rules, values, and operating procedures. **Approach**: Bring up or develop expertise and resources, (re)structure.	**Characteristics**: Challenges are unexpected or unstable and may be of unknown duration, but not necessarily hard to understand. Knowledge is often available. **Example**: You have to respond to a disruptive event, disaster, or crisis that obstructs service delivery and potentially endangers citizens. **Approach**: Build in slack and devote resources to resilience and preparedness – e.g., stockpile inventory or overbuy talent.
	AMBIGUITY	UNCERTAINTY
	Characteristics: Causal relationships are completely unclear. No precedents exist. You face many unknown unknowns. **Example**: You decide to implement a radical and untested new technology to affect client behaviour in healthcare settings. **Approach**: Experiment. Understanding cause and effect requires generating hypotheses and testing them. Design experiments such that broad lessons can be learned.	**Characteristics**: Despite a lack of some crucial information, basic cause and effect are known. Change is possible but not a given. **Example**: A sudden political transition changes the outlook of policies and programs you have been working on over the past two years. **Approach**: Invest in information and scenario building capacity: collect, interpret, and share information. This works best in conjunction with structural changes that reduce ongoing uncertainty.
	− How much do you know about the situation? +	

Adapted from: Bennett and Lemoine 2014: 2.

need to acquire and embody *to successfully perform in this environment –* to create and deliver 'public value' (Benington and Moore 2011: 2) in the 21st century.

This book will critically assess these roles, competencies, and values in the context of various 21st century megatrends – such as economic interconnectedness, demographic changes, and climate change – that will impact public managers no matter where they work. In doing so, this book offers realistic yet promising perspectives for public managers. Such perspectives are now paramount because all too many books and reports offer little more than a 'complaint session' about the inadequacies of bureaucracies in addressing and mitigating 21st century challenges.

Public managers: who they are and what they do

Before we start our journey into the largely unknown world and profile of the 21st century public manager, we should define who and what public managers in the 21st century are. In short: provide some descriptions before we move into predictions and prescriptions. Here, various definitions and typologies float around, from narrow to broad. Noordegraaf (2015), for instance, in his book *Public Management* that is part of this series, defines public managers broadly as 'those who lead in the public domain'.

Similar to 't Hart's book in this series, *Understanding Public Leadership* (2014a), Noordegraaf addresses the debate on how 'managers' differ from 'leaders'. Both assert that the two concepts may denote different roles, activities, and attributes, and therefore justify being analytically distinct. Within the context of this book, however, it is important to emphasize that the focus lies with public managers from a *positional rather than functional perspective* (cf. Noordegraaf 2004). Even though non-managers may very well lead or manage, and managers may not, this book focuses on individuals with managerial positions. In addition, this book does not focus on politicians, one of the three types of public leaders 't Hart discusses (2014a: 23), even though the political dimension of public management features throughout the book.

Thus, this book is written for (future) managers, from mid-level to senior, in public and semi-public sector organizations such as ministries, executive agencies, international, regional and municipal government organizations, statutory boards, public hospitals, universities, state-owned enterprises, and government-linked companies. Such managers can be politically appointed but most of them will be career officials who have risen through the ranks of administrative systems and bear responsibility for policies, programmes, and people (Van Wart, Hondeghem and Schwella 2015). Many of them will have graduate degrees, often of a specialist nature, and participate in leadership development or 'fast track' programmes of various types. Table 1.1 shows four commonly distinguished types of public managers (see also Noordegraaf 2015).

The 'type 1' top manager – or in some countries, executive – is the most senior. However, line managers, programme and project directors, and staff managers exist in many varieties. They range from mid-level managers running one particular policy area, programme, or function with few staff members, to heavyweights who run departments, programmes, or units with thousands of employees and budgets of hundreds of millions of dollars.

Type 1 and type 2 managers engage mostly in strategic policy advice as well as managerial, legislative, and budgetary work, whereas type 3 managers and some type 1 managers conduct more hands-on implementation and service delivery activities, certainly at the local level. Type 4 managers mostly provide operational, legal, and strategic support to the other three types. Increasingly, though, roles, activities, and responsibilities will blur between managerial types. Some suggest future public sectors will consist of a concentrated core of highly skilled strategic policy advisors with most of the implementation and execution of tasks and services outsourced to and shared with other actors (Dickinson and Sullivan 2014; Needham and Mangan 2014).

As such, isn't this rather traditional and seemingly 'neat' distinction between types at odds with the networked and fluid characteristics of the VUCA world? Not necessarily. For decades to come, public managers will have formal job titles, responsibilities, and programmes and departments

TABLE 1.1 Types of public managers according to position

Type	*Activities and responsibilities*	*Examples*
1. Top manager or executive	*Type 1 public managers* are ultimately responsible and accountable for their organizations and departments, both internally and externally (with most formal external communication until now being the exclusive domain of the political boss)	(Deputy) Permanent secretaries and secretary generals, directors and director generals, (deputy) CEOs of agencies, public hospitals and educational institutions, inspector generals
2. Line manager	*Type 2 public managers* are 'regular' managers in ministries, agencies, and other public organizations who bear responsibility for a particular policy directorate, project, and/or unit, accountable to type 1 public managers (and sometimes political bosses)	Policy directors, heads of unit, heads of department, directors of divisions and clusters
3. Programme manager or project manager	*Type 3 public managers* are managers who are responsible for particular policy programmes, taskforces, projects, networks, and collaborative, sometimes temporary structures. They can be accountable to type 1 and type 2 managers (and if a particular programme or issue is of high political salience, to political bosses)	Programme directors, taskforce managers, project managers, strategic planners, network managers, heads of temporary collaborative arrangements
4. Staff manager	*Type 4 public managers* are responsible for managing staff departments in the areas of personnel, information (IT, knowledge), finance, HR, housing, and facilities, usually accountable to type 1 public managers (but seldom to political bosses)	HR and personnel directors, finance directors, communication and public affairs directors, IT directors, facility managers

to run, regardless of the extent of their collaboration with other actors (public, private, and civic). This is the nature of the public sector beast.

However, *what will change* is how *public managers have to simultaneously fulfil sometimes contradictory roles* to survive 21st century operating environments, requiring various traditional, recurrent, and new *skills, competencies, and values underpinning these roles*. The remainder of this book will critically outline and discuss these roles, skills, competencies, and values against the backdrop of global megatrends that place new demands on public managers.

Outline

The outline below specifies how the remaining chapters of this book address these key topics in more detail. Figure 1.3 provides a visual overview.

After chapter '"Traditional" Versus "New"' has positioned public managers across time by providing a critical overview of their traditional, recurrent, and new roles, skills, and values, chapter 'Trends and Drivers' identifies key global megatrends that will affect the organizational environment of public managers in the years to come, such as economic interconnectedness, resource scarcity and climate change, 'ultra-urbanization', and individualism and value pluralism (e.g., Dickinson and Sullivan 2014; KPMG 2013; Needham and Mangan 2014, 2016). Subsequently, chapter 'Demands, Dilemmas, Opportunities' translates these megatrends into seven demands, with associated dilemmas and opportunities.

Chapters 'Managing Stakeholder Multiplicity', 'Managing Authority Turbulence', 'Managing the New Work(force)', 'Managing Innovation Forces', 'Managing Ethical Complexities', 'Managing Short Versus Long Time Horizons', and 'Managing Cross-sectoral Collaboration' are structured around these seven key demands on public managers, illustrating challenges, dilemmas, and opportunities with real-life cases and examples while detailing the competencies and attributes needed to meet each demand and turn challenges into opportunities. Each chapter is structured around a central case featuring a public manager as protagonist. The cases are hypothetical, but all of them are based on real-life events and developments. These chapters make up the core of this book. The last

FIGURE 1.3   Structure and contents of the book

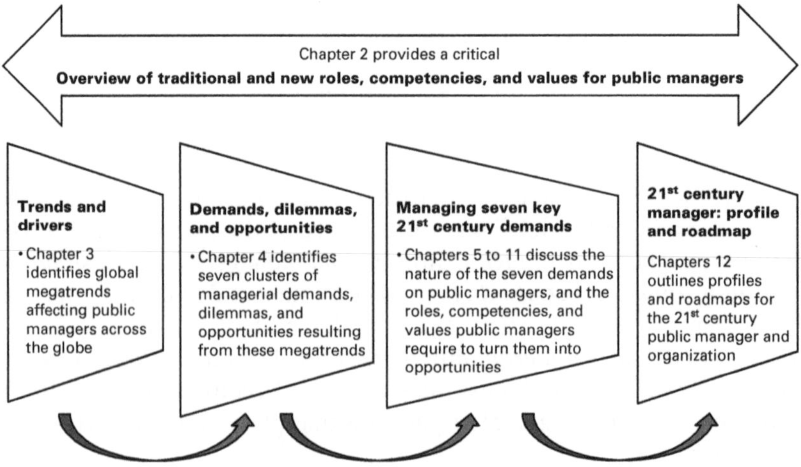

chapter provides a profile of the 21ˢᵗ century public manager, and outlines strategies for making managers and agencies '21ˢᵗ century proof'.

Chapter '"Traditional" Versus "New"', briefly outlines three ideal types of public managers across time as a framework to discuss long-standing, evolving, and new roles, competencies, skills, and values. The chapter argues that effective public managers combine and balance qualities from all three ideal types, dependent on context and setting.

Chapter 'Trends and Drivers', distinguishes various types of change, ranging from gradual to disruptive and unpredictable, before it discusses in detail key 21ˢᵗ century megatrends and how they will affect the lives of public managers across the globe. It provides cases and examples of these megatrends from a variety of geographies and regimes, making the case for a perspective that goes beyond traditional, Western orientations.

Chapter 'Demands, Dilemmas, Opportunities', presents the seven key managerial demands that will structure the remainder of the book, such as 'managing the new work(force)' and 'managing innovation forces'. Subsequently, it translates these demands into seven dilemmas – tough choices reinforced by the ambiguous nature of the demands – and seven unprecedented opportunities for public managers to produce public sector excellence.

Chapter 'Managing Stakeholder Multiplicity', addresses the demand on public managers to serve, respond to, and collaborate with an increasing number of stakeholders, operating in fluid and dynamic networks. The chapter presents tools to map, classify, and engage such networks, arguing that public managers need to develop antennae to anticipate stakeholder dynamics. Competencies such as framing, branding, and storytelling are addressed, along with specific social media and communication skills.

Following on from this, chapter 'Managing Authority Turbulence', discusses fundamental shifts in power structures and traditional notions of hierarchy and authority, even in countries with fairly top-down, authoritative governance structures. Across the globe, assertive, individualized stakeholders question authority, forcing public managers to continuously justify their legitimacy through performance, internally *and* externally. Political astuteness, distributive leadership, and crisis management are key competencies discussed here.

Chapter 'Managing the New Work(force)', critically assesses traits and ambitions of the new workforce amid more fundamental new work practices – the virtual office, blurred lines between professional and personal lives and roles, and 'boundaryless' careers. It will particularly assess effective ways of recruiting, incentivizing, and managing Gen Y and Gen Z, and tapping into their 21ˢᵗ century competencies through reverse mentoring.

Chapter 'Managing Innovation Forces', addresses the balancing act of responding to various (human, natural, technological) pressures to innovate public sector practices amid legal, constitutional, and budgetary constraints. It discusses the 'hard managerial work' of innovation across all five stages of the innovation process: idea generation, selection, testing, scaling, and diffusion. It also addresses ambiguous public expectations of governments to simultaneously experiment, provide stability, and demonstrate 'value for money'.

Chapter 'Managing Ethical Complexities', addresses emerging ethical challenges and rising – sometimes unrealistic and unfair – ethical expectations of public actors, grounded in a discussion on competing values and loyalties for public managers. The chapter argues for an open perspective towards ethical leadership and balanced integrity management systems.

Chapter 'Managing Short Versus Long Time Horizons', addresses the increasingly important issue of managing very short timelines – driven by the never-ending news cycle – and long timelines, amid a context of creating resilient and sustainable solutions for super-wicked problems. Increasingly accessible foresight capabilities may prove to be enablers for public managers to justify long-term decision-making to various constituents. Challenges in preserving institutional memory and 'selling' foresight products to political masters are discussed.

Chapter 'Managing Cross-sectoral Collaboration', outlines the key characteristics of successful network managers who have to operate in a world where public sectors are one of many actors (and sectors) driving collective problem-solving and service delivery. Recent insights about collaborative public management, co-creation, and co-production, and tri-sector collaboration are presented, together with recent, real-life examples.

The concluding chapter 'The 21ˢᵗ Century Public Manager', provides the contours of the 21ˢᵗ century public manager's profile, and assesses the universalism of such a profile. Then, it outlines how governments should start thinking about recruiting, retaining, and developing effective managers by creating 21ˢᵗ century-proof human resource management (HRM) practices and environments. Clearly, 21ˢᵗ century public management behaviour will only come to the fore in enabling organizational environments, ones characterized by entrepreneurialism, adaptation, and robustness.

Key audience and usage

The 21ˢᵗ Century Public Manager focuses on public managers as a *species* rather than public management as a *discipline*. However, I am mindful of the questionable tendency in management and leadership literature to separate the individual from the environment (cf. 't Hart 2014a). Thus, by looking at the interplay between global megatrends (macro), organizational demands in terms of enabling support structures, cultures, and their design (meso), and individual managerial demands in terms of skills, competencies, and values (micro), managers will be constantly viewed in relation to their operating environments.

While grounded in the latest research insights and evidence, and practices from a variety of jurisdictions, this book is a teaching text for graduate and executive classrooms rather than a research monograph written for peers in the field. At the same time, I hope that colleagues in the fields of public management, public administration, and the general management sciences may also find this book interesting and worthwhile.

The book aims to serve three audiences in particular. First and foremost, I hope to inspire a broad international audience of current and future public managers who participate in professional degree programmes and executive education programmes to upgrade their skills and acquire a mindset of change-readiness without accepting overly easy solutions. The overviews of recent debates and state-of-the-art thinking about public managers and their future operating environments, supported by a wealth of real-life examples and cases from across the globe, make this book directly usable in a variety of pedagogical settings.

Second, senior public sector HRM managers and personnel officers may find this book particularly helpful to strengthen and inspire their thinking about the ideal future workforce, and what it takes to recruit, retain, and build such a workforce.

Third, elements in this book may also meet the needs of senior education specialists, trainers, and curriculum developers as they critically examine whether public policy schools, civil service colleges and academies, and think tanks adequately contribute to building the 21st century managerial workforce. More generally, such specialists and developers, including senior peers and faculty members of public policy schools, may find the content and cases in this book useful in their teaching and thinking about 21st century public management education.

The (im)possibilities of a global public management book

Before we start our journey by zooming in on trends and emerging strategic issues and their implications for public managers, let me address one remaining elephant in the room. At the outset of a book with the title *The 21st Century Public Manager,* which aspires to be relevant in educational settings across the globe, I am mindful not to fall into the trap of describing trends or prescribing managerial capabilities that are overly generic, or declaring specific managerial ideas or skills as 'dead' or 'obsolete' too soon. After all, this may be highly dependent on the region or country under scrutiny, and the stage of development and reform.

On the contrary, I would argue that a truly meaningful – and globally relevant – debate on the 21st century public manager needs to take stock of both traditional and novel approaches to public management, carefully weighing prescriptions for good governance and management in various contexts. In fact, this is where 'public management talk' and 'public management practice' meet; they go back and forth, they merge and dilute, they adapt to circumstances and contexts through trial and error, benefiting from a healthy competition of ideas.

Such a healthy, and truly global, competition of ideas is paramount in an era of major power shifts and global change. This is even more important because the vast majority of all public management textbooks currently used across the globe are still Western in origin, in terms of the key assumptions, frameworks, and examples they use. Such misbalance is problematic in a world in which regions that differ from the West in their administrative traditions, political development, and institutional cultures account for much of the economic growth, industrial innovations, and novel governance ideas emerging today. Admittedly, given my own background, the majority of frameworks, evidence, and examples I use in this book still come from Western and Anglo-Saxon countries. However, substantive practices and studies from other governance settings are included, discussed, and contrasted with mainstream examples in their implications for managerial capacity and reform potential.

Indeed, as Fukuyama (2013) suggests, different reform paths may apply to countries in upgrading their governance depending on whether institutions have high capacity: increasing the autonomy of public managers may be desirable in a context of high bureaucratic capacity, yet it may prove disastrous if government capacity is lower. Fukuyama argues that whereas, like Singapore, the US and Germany would benefit from giving public managers more autonomy, public managers in China are given too much discretion (2013: 363). *How* public managers can achieve high capacity in a constantly evolving environment is a key topic in this book.

So, even though many of the developments examined in the book apply to countries across the globe, I will identify and assess them with an eye for local differences and particularities. Therefore, cases, examples, and best practices will be used from different countries and regions. For example, increasing use of social media by well-informed citizens and the emergence of the 'hacktivist' as a criticizing and scrutinizing force of government will be prevalent across continents in the years to come. However, it is evident that these developments impact public managers and their authorizing environments in different ways in the US, the Netherlands, China, and Kazakhstan, to name a few.

Moreover, the 'rise of China' – to name one of the most commonly observed megatrends in this century – will obviously impact public managers in different countries differently, not least those in China. Public managers in dependent emerging countries like Sri Lanka or Myanmar will be affected differently from those in competitive or even hostile countries like India or Japan, with many Western countries somewhere in between. To take another example, there is a tendency in Western democracies to criticize a strict dichotomy between politics and administration as an unproductive and static abstraction of the real world in which political and administrative roles, values, and accountability obligations increasingly blend in to each other. In developing contexts, however, the dichotomy is propagated and even enforced as a means to achieve greater autonomy for public managers.

Clearly, Miles' (1978) aphorism 'where you stand depends on where you sit' remains relevant in a globalizing world. Specific, real-life examples of common trends and their implications are provided for different regions when possible, while realizing that one book cannot cover the entire world and various chapters may be more relevant to some public managers than to others.

I am most aware of the vast socio-economic and cultural differences in status, capacity, and potential impact of public managers in different parts of the world, particularly in well-developed versus 'tough' governance settings. My fascinating experiences as an educator, researcher, and consultant in a wide variety of regions over the past number of years have only strengthened this awareness. This book includes cases and examples from different continents, but for a book like this to be relevant and live up to its promises it also needs to address the normative and empirical contrasts between administrations around the world. In short: in writing a book geared towards the 21st century public manager I realize that *the* 21st century public manager does not exist, even though I titled the book as such.

Chapter 2

'Traditional' Versus 'New'

For things to remain the same, everything must change.

Tancredi Falconeri in Il Gattopardo, 1963

Public management 1990

Imagine being a senior programme manager at a ministry in an Anglo-Saxon country in 1990. In the past few years, you have been involved in various efforts to introduce private sector management techniques in government agencies. These operations have been driven by an urge to cut costs and remove slack from 'dysfunctional, bloated bureaucracies' (in the words of the last two ministers you served).

At this stage, you and your colleagues are preparing for the next, even more fundamental transformation: a series of large-scale privatizations of current government functions, programmes, and agencies. Strengthened by concurrent movements in a number of countries, your political masters are enthusiastic and eager to push through what has been recently referred to as *New Public Management* or *NPM*. In your context, NPM has so far meant a greater disaggregation of policy-making and implementation, competition between agencies and programmes, and more competitive training programmes and remuneration structures for senior management.

Over the past few years, you have loyally contributed to the reform ambitions of your political masters. What they probably don't realize is that in communicating and implementing new measures you got much of your inspiration from rather classical examples, writings, and practices. You remember them well from your days as a graduate student at the country's top school of government, and from workshops over the course of your career.

Indeed, even though you've seen politicians and consultants persuasively propagate new mindsets and values, you increasingly wonder how 'new' they actually are. You remember reading about the American administrative reformers Brownlow and Gulick, who wanted to make government more efficient and effective – more 'businesslike' – in their 1937 report for the Roosevelt administration. In fact, wasn't early 20th century management thinker Frederick Winslow Taylor already stressing efficiency and performance rewards in his 'scientific management' ideas about how operations should be organized? Moreover, the founding father of public administration, Max Weber, emphasized efficiency as a core value of administrative operations, arguing that civil servants should be separated from the political domain.

All of this sometimes makes you cynical about the potential success of yet another big change in public sector operations. If everything had been tried before, why have so many of the clichéd complaints about public bureaucracies remained? Who is to say that new public management – to the extent it is *new* – will solve the pervasive problems of public agencies and their staff? If your government goes further, with the privatization of many core government functions, programmes, and personnel in the next decade, they may regret such drastic steps in the long term, when the pendulum swings back again. You joined the public service exactly because of its public nature. Now you are wondering what will be left of the ethos still characterizing your department a few years from now. Weren't some of the fundamentals of public bureaucracies instituted for good reasons? Perhaps it is only a matter of time before we will 'redis-cover bureaucracy' ….

Now fast forward to the present day. You are that same individual, in your late seventies and reflecting on events since that period in the late 1980s. Were the reforms you implemented at the time indeed that 'new'? Have they grown out of fashion since? Would they nowadays be considered 'old' and perhaps even obsolete? Certainly the public sectors have become more networked and horizontal, and policies much more interlinked and complex, but aren't citizens still expecting the same authoritative perfor-mance and leadership from their governments?

Moreover, when you teach in executive modules offered by your former employer as part of management development programmes, the trainees you interact with still complain about hierarchy and rigidity standing in the way of real innovation and cross-sectoral collaboration. Being more and more reflective about things these days, you close your eyes, smile, and think about a beautiful quote from the classic film *The Leopard*, about the unification of Italy: 'For things to remain the same, everything must change'.

Public managers: three ideal types

As illustrated in the introductory narrative, views on what public manag-ers do and should do evolve across time. At the same time, 'new' ideas are sometimes not new at all, and old ideas resurge every now and again. Therefore, in a book titled *The 21ˢᵗ Century Public Manager,* we have to address the question of how such a public manager will be different from a 20ᵗʰ century public manager.

Dozens of publications structure and sequence key chronological devel-opments in the practice and theory of public management, and define the characteristics of public managers (e.g., Lynn 2006; Noordegraaf 2015; Pollitt and Bouckaert 2011). Over time, we can distinguish three key ideal types of public managers that have emerged alongside changing views of the role of government and concurrent reform movements. The next three sections shortly outline these three ideal types and the roles, competencies, and values they propagate.

Here, I build on recent work of 't Hart (2014b), who speaks about 'administrative craftsmanship 1.0, 2.0, and 3.0'. He emphasizes how these three repertoires blend with and complement each other in the daily life of public managers. In reading these sections, it is important to realize that these three types have not simply replaced each other over time: it is not just 'out with the old, in with the new'. In many ways, ideal type 1.0 still provides the 'foundational software' for the upgraded applications and features of types 2.0 and 3.0.

1.0: The traditional, rule-oriented bureaucrat

In the late 19ᵗʰ and early 20ᵗʰ centuries, the practice of administration and the function of public administrators began to professionalize as bureaucracies grew and became more complex. Although some ancient kingdoms, dynasties, and rulers had long ago developed rather advanced practices of administering territories and institutions (see Rutgers 2005), the common practice in most countries at the time was that one became a public servant by chance or through nepotism, cronyism, or patronage. Two key influential thinkers here were Woodrow Wilson, who later became President of the United States, and German sociologist Max Weber. In their pioneering texts they argued for a separate professional ethos and set of core skills for administrators to detach them from the political sphere (Weber 1921; Wilson 1887).

Weber outlined a set of principles for what became known as the ideal typical bureaucrat. This traditional rule-oriented bureaucrat is loyal to political mandates, neutral in her views of policies and programmes, impartial in executing and administering these policies and programmes, and efficient and lawful in organizing and operating her agencies. She derives her authority from in-depth domain knowledge and legal expertise. Weber's thinking still very much influences how government agencies operate and how public employees are trained and recruited. Many public policies, programmes, services, and goods continue to be realized through the key delivery mode associated with the ideal type 1.0: the hierarchical, formalized, bureaucratic organization. The most commonly used label corresponding with this ideal type is Weberian public administration or *Traditional Public Administration* (TPA).

Weber and his followers spoke of administrators, bureaucrats, or civil servants rather than 'public managers', a label primarily associated with the ideal type 2.0, as the next section shows. At the same time, the ideas on how early bureaucracies had to be organized were also influenced by engineer Frederick Winslow Taylor, famous for his concept of 'scientific management' (1914: 7), which sought to improve the efficiency of factory operations in rapidly industrializing societies. Although Taylor's ideas were primarily oriented towards the private sector, both he and Weber stressed operational efficiency and a belief in technical expertise and 'scientific' methods to manage operations and institutions.

2.0: The 'businesslike', performance-focused manager

The 2.0 public manager is a 'manager' in a more normative sense as she is supposed to embody managerial, private sector-inspired tools, techniques, and values (Lynn 2006; Noordegraaf 2015). This ideal type emerged in the early 1980s in Anglo-Saxon countries such as Australia, New Zealand, the UK, and the US, as the introductory case illustrates. Conservative governments in these countries wanted public sector organizations to emulate practices from the private sector, which they considered superior to the increasingly bloated, unaffordable, and sometimes dysfunctional public bureaucracies. In the 1990s and beyond, governments across the globe pursued reforms that were fully or partly inspired by the notion of 'running government like a business'. A key text here was the bestselling book *Reinventing Government* by consultants David Osborne and Ted Gaebler (1992). They famously declared government had to 'steer rather than row' (1992: 25). In the years that followed, competition, outsourcing, and privatization became key credos of many governments.

The type 2.0, businesslike, performance-focused manager first of all wants to deliver value for money and produce measurable results; thinks in terms of 'clients and customers' rather than citizens; steers and oversees operations that have been outsourced to other actors; and is expected to master managerial competencies rather than domain expertise. While the Weberian quality of efficiency is still emphasized, effectiveness and accountability are more important. Traditional Weberian values such as lawfulness, impartiality, expertise, and neutrality are not as emphasized, and in some ways are even associated with inert, conservative, and dreary bureaucratic mindsets.

The key delivery modes associated with ideal type 2.0 are quasi-markets, contracts, and public-private partnerships (PPPs), considered to deliver cheaper, better, and more responsive public services and goods. The dynamic mix of practices, views, and hypes corresponding with this ideal type has become best known as *New Public Management* or *NPM*, as coined by Christopher Hood (1991) in a seminal article. NPM took shape very differently in various parts of the world.

3.0: The networking, relation-focused collaborator

The 3.0 public manager is first and foremost a networker and collaborator. She operates in a context of 'governance' rather than 'government' (Rhodes 1996), in which the public sector is no longer *the* actor but rather *one of the* actors co-creating, co-designing, and co-producing services in horizontal and vertical networks. This ideal type emerged in the late 1990s and early 2000s alongside the realization that government could no longer 'go it alone' in tackling complex, transboundary policy problems, and that the market was not a panacea either (Agranoff 2006; McGuire 2006). Civil society organizations and NGOs (non-governmental organizations) gained legitimacy and became more powerful and professionalized; citizens became increasingly assertive and educated; and businesses were more concerned with their social and environmental impact. All these 'stakeholders' started to demand a place at the table in addressing as well as *defining* policy problems and solutions.

In this vein, the type 3.0, networking, relation-focused collaborator is a skilled negotiator, communicator, enabler, and energizer who easily operates across sectors and issues while realizing authority and credibility have to be earned time and again from various stakeholders. Classical Weberian qualities are still important, but if emphasized too much, they may get in the way of allowing innovative non-state initiatives to flourish. For a type 3.0 public manager, the objective – the 'what' – is leading, while the exact institutional or legislative configuration through which this objective is met – the 'how' – is contingent and flexible. A key framework here is 'public value', as developed by Harvard Kennedy School professor Mark Moore (1995, 2013), which takes as a starting point the ultimate mission that public agencies and their managers try to achieve. In creating public value, public managers have to get constant buy-in from different and dynamic 'authorizing environments', extending way beyond politicians and voters alone.

As such, the key delivery modes associated with ideal type 3.0 are networks, partnerships, and multi-sectoral collaborations with actors from a variety of sectors and jurisdictions. The term most commonly used for this set of practices and norms is *New Public Governance* or *NPG*, coined by Osborne (2009, 2010).

Figure 2.1 visualizes ideal types 1.0, 2.0, and 3.0 as three interacting clusters of roles, competencies, and values. Successful 21ˢᵗ century public managers will be able to smartly and astutely *combine* sometimes competing roles, competencies, and values depending on the audience, issue, and context at hand, and *add* new ones as operating environments continue to change.

Blending, complementing, and recycling

The previous section presented the ideal types chronologically, as each new ideal type is in some ways a response to its predecessor's shortcomings. However, in reality public management renewal is a process of 'recycling, alteration, and re-balancing', according to leading public management scholar Christopher Pollitt (2011). Indeed, neatly separating and sequencing the types with start dates and end dates, as some textbooks

FIGURE 2.1   Public manager 1.0, 2.0, and 3.0: three interacting modes

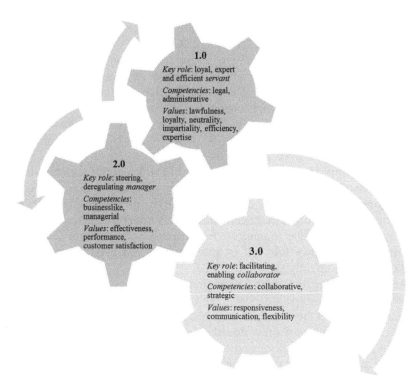

do, glosses over the hybrid realities in which public managers simultaneously employ elements from all three types.

Van der Steen *et al.* (2015: 28) portray this reality as 'sedimentation' to indicate that effective public managers combine the various repertoires in complementary ways. In their prioritization, such public managers are mindful of when repertoires come into or out of fashion, depending on context, key events, and the government of the day. As an example, in the aftermath of the global financial crisis in 2008, many governments re-emphasized the importance of a 'strong state' while pointing at the shortcomings of markets, with some even suggesting that prior privatizations should be undone. Who would dare to display 2.0 behaviour at that stage?

Moreover, viewing 1.0, 2.0, and 3.0 as logically following up on or even replacing each other reveals a strong Western bias. Indeed, what we designate as 'new' or 'change' is highly dependent on a country's contextual and cultural environment and stage of development.

Seemingly similar changes, approaches, and techniques have been implemented quite differently, and with varying degrees of success, in various parts of the world. For example, the ideal type 1.0 is still omnipresent in training programmes and operating cultures across the globe, whereas the ideal type 2.0 still features prominently in public management reform programmes of the World Bank, the United Nations (UN), the Asian Development Bank (ADB), and the Organisation for Economic Co-operation and Development (OECD) (Andrews 2013; Pollitt and Bouckaert 2011). In the West, public management 2.0 – or NPM – has been declared dead many times (Dunleavy *et al.* 2006), but many of its core characteristics are still very much alive in management reforms in countries like China (Christensen 2012). Lastly, in more authoritative settings with largely unquestioned leadership, room for behaviours and competencies associated with type 3.0 may be limited; in fact, they may be frowned upon or even penalized.

Thus, we should refrain from easy generalizations about the components and effects of management reforms, trends, and hypes across contexts. More importantly, we should distinguish 'talk' from 'practice' (Pollitt 2010) in discussing how public management reforms affect the actual behaviours and mindsets of public managers. Any trainer or consultant involved in organizational change will tell us that deep-rooted behavioural patterns and norms change only slowly, if at all.

At the same time, however, we see that all over the world outside events, stakeholders, and expectations – the external operating environment – increasingly affect how public managers (should) behave. This is much more the case now than a few decades ago, when public management was a fairly internalized and 'closed' endeavour (Van der Steen 2015: 263). Whether public managers like it or not, the emerging VUCA world, characterized by increasing volatility, uncertainty, complexity, and ambiguity, will *force* change upon them, necessitating new skillsets and mindsets.

Public managers have to reconcile tradition with innovation

Still, the nature of what makes public managers 'public' implies that changes and reforms may be by definition less radical and drastic than in corporate environments. Indeed, despite decades of discussing new types of public management and public managers, one key aspect in the life of public managers will always differentiate them from business managers. This key aspect is their additional onus of upholding public values and interests, and safeguarding institutional integrity without overstepping the politician's comfort zone (Rhodes 2016; Terry 1995).

No matter how networked, multi-channelled, and innovative the operating environment of 21ˢᵗ century public managers becomes, or how many private sector-inspired tools, techniques, and approaches public managers emulate, they will remain conservators and stewards of the public interest (Watt 2012). Moreover, much of the discourse on private sector-oriented and cross-sectoral network management seems to ignore how legal and constitutional responsibilities and mandates of public managers have remained in place (Rosenbloom 2015; Van der Wal 2011). Indeed, many of the responsibilities and qualities of public managers are *institutional rather than transformational.*

Stressing the uniqueness of these responsibilities and constraints, some have compared public managers to 'gardeners' who require time, patience, experience, and political awareness. They are quiet leaders who are in 'for the long haul' and their craft is compromise (Frederickson and Matkin 2007; 't Hart 2014b). Terry even considers 'the heroic or transformative model of leadership with the great man radically changing the organization and disdaining its existing traditions, a threat to institutional integrity' (1995: 44).

For the remainder of this book, this notion is a crucial one as it illustrates the institutional limits to changes in roles, functions, and values of public managers. Even though 21st century public managers will have to behave differently from their 20th century counterparts, they cannot just 'break free' from the past. 'Creative destruction' (Schumpeter 1942: 90) does not apply to public managers the way it does to business managers, no matter how much some would like to believe it does. Moreover, inherent institutional limits to radical change in public sector settings not only affect which roles, competencies, and values we characterize as new, but also how these have to *be blended with rather than bluntly replace* more traditional ones.

Roles, competencies, and values for a VUCA world

What, then, are some of these new and traditional roles? Dickinson and Needham (2012) identified 11 roles for 21st century public servants in her report for the Future of Public Services commission in the UK, slightly reformulated and reorganized in Box 2.1 for the purposes of this book. On the one hand, she asserts: 'increased involvement of private and third sector providers in the delivery of public services could mean a significant shift in terms of what public servants do, where they do it, what skills they may need and what their career trajectories might look like' (2012: 1). On the other hand, she recognizes that long-standing roles will remain important alongside new and evolving ones, and reiterates that changes in public management are gradual rather than radical, regardless of the nature of their key drivers.

New, evolving, and long-standing roles

As Box 2.1 shows, four *long-standing roles that will remain important* according to Dickinson largely correspond with ideal type 1.0. Here, public managers serve somewhat paternalistically as regulators and protectors of key actors in society, while adjudicating and exercising judgement based on evidence and expertise. Surely, these roles remain important but their legitimacy and credibility will be increasingly contested.

Box 2.1 New, evolving, and long-standing roles for 21ˢᵗ century public managers

Four *new* roles:

Storyteller	A storyteller can author and communicate stories of envisioned new worlds in the absence of existing blueprints, drawing on experience and evidence from a range of sources. It is about fashioning and communicating future options, tentative and experimental as they may be, and engaging service users, citizens, and staff in the project of redesign.
Resource weaver	A resource weaver is able to make creative use of existing resources regardless of their intended or original use, weaving together miscellaneous and disparate materials to generate something new and useful for service users and citizens.
Systems architect	A systems architect is able to continuously describe and compile coherent local systems of public support from the myriad of public, private, third-sector, and other resources, which are likely to vary over time and space.
Navigator	A navigator specifically focuses on guiding citizens and service users around the range of possibilities that might be available in a public support system.

→

The three *evolving roles* clearly combine elements of ideal types 2.0 and 3.0. Public managers increasingly have to act as brokers to align interests, agendas, working styles, and world views of widely different stakeholder networks around issues that such networks seek to address. In smartly exploring and acquiring new pools of outside expertise, skills, and funds, they have to act as reticulists. Public managers as commissioners are able to outsource and oversee a range of processes run by others while keeping long-term public value objectives in mind. A competent commissioner is more than just a type 2.0 privatizer; she takes a holistic and systematic view on which processes and services should be dealt with in-house and which should be outsourced, and when.

Lastly, the *four new roles* Dickinson identifies build on the 3.0 ideal type while adding new elements that emphasize the increasing role of technology and digital resources for public managers. Central to these roles of storyteller, resource weaver, systems architect, and navigator is

→

These new roles sit alongside three *evolving* roles:

Commissioner	A commissioner has the right range of skills to be able to commission services and support on a system rather than service basis.
Broker	A broker is able to work closely with and on behalf of service users to access the appropriate (budgetary) support.
Reticulist	A reticulist focuses on the development and use of collaborative networking skills to identify new sources of expertise and support.

Four *long-standing* roles will continue to be important:

Regulator	A regulator assesses performance of resources against standards.
Protector	A protector intervenes to prevent harm.
Adjudicator	An adjudicator makes decisions on the balance of evidence.
Expert	An expert exercises judgement in decision-making, drawing on relevant skills and experience.

Adapted from: Dickinson and Needham 2012; Dickinson and Sullivan 2014: 26.

the notion that public managers will increasingly act as guiders and facilitators who energize and inspire others, instead of leading and controlling efforts to address policy issues themselves. This implies that they can no longer assume to be the most authoritative experts, with undisputed evidence at their disposal, as prescribed by the traditional roles.

Competing or complementary roles, competencies, and values?

The potential tension between the long-standing role of expert and the new role of storyteller introduces another important element in our discussion of roles, competencies, and values: *the process of blending and complementing is not necessarily harmonious*. Clearly, the Weberian core quality of expertise nowadays competes for attention with other crucial competencies and values. In fact, the very meaning of expertise is subject to debate, not in the least among public managers and their political masters (Van der Wal

2014). Is domain expertise more or less important than more generic management skills in an era where information is widely and readily available to – and more easily absorbed by – non-experts, including many political masters? Should 21ˢᵗ century public managers have both generic skills and domain expertise?

A few years ago, I interviewed Robert Madelin, a seasoned type 1 public manager and former right hand of several European Union (EU) commissioners. He perfectly words the ambiguous stance towards expertise in arguing that effectiveness and responsiveness are ultimately more important (Van der Wal 2014):

> So expertise is a ... necessary, but not a sufficient condition. You absolutely have to be expert. But if you leave things to the experts, and say 'well he's the expert', that's another sort of autocracy. And in this debate about assessing the future, it's very important to be the most expert, but to make sure the experts are not in their white coats in a locked room, but are actually out there listening, not talking, to society. The effective way to design the process is to say, given people are the way they are: how can we deliver the right outcome? And the way you can deliver the right outcome if people are not all equipped with political antennae, is to make sure they talk to each other. If you can create a process that keeps them in the same conversation over a period of 12 to 18 months, even experts who don't like talking to other people will see the way in which the world changes.

Madelin's statement illustrates how various desired competencies and values compete for attention from public managers, making their operating environments more ambiguous and 'charged' than those of their private sector counterparts (De Graaf 2010; Noordegraaf 2015; Putters 2009). Managing such competing values, logics, and pressures will be a core feature of 21ˢᵗ century public management.

Skills, competencies, and values: how do they differ?

The statement of this seasoned public manager also tells us we need to operationalize some of the more general and sometimes abstract 21ˢᵗ century roles identified so far in this chapter into specific skills, competencies, and values. Moreover, we need to assess why and how they're important, and how managers acquire and develop them. Recent reports from government commissions, consulting firms, and public management scholars often interchangeably make reference to or accidentally mix up 'trainable' specific skills, broad competencies, and more 'innate' values.

Box 2.2 defines these three key related concepts featuring throughout this book, and explains how and why they are different. Doing so is not always easy. Is expertise a value, a competency, a cluster of competencies,

Box 2.2 Skills, competencies, and values

Much of the HRM and management literature uses concepts such as skills, competencies, qualities, and values in different and sometimes confusing ways. This book distinguishes between more specific and micro-level *skills* – such as programming, video-editing, or persuasive writing – and more encompassing, overarching crafts or *competencies* – such as social media literacy, political astuteness, and negotiation.

Such skills and competencies are largely 'trainable' – that is, they can be developed before and/or on the job through targeted programmes and mentoring. Some skills and competencies are 'harder' and others 'softer'. In addition, it is common to distinguish between technical, cognitive, and interpersonal skills (Katzenbach and Smith 1993).

More 'innate' and often less tangible *values*, on the other hand, are internalized – personal, professional, and organizational – qualities and behavioural traits. Such qualities and traits can be selected on, recruited for, and nurtured through socialization, mentoring, and some management development features.

A key way in which values differ from skills and competencies, however, is that values have to be already present to some extent in (future) managers at the time of hiring. Moreover, if such (future) managers embrace the wrong values, getting rid of them or replacing them with others just through training, mentoring, and socialization comes close to a mission impossible.

Intriguingly, 21st century skills, competencies, and values may increasingly require 'reverse mentoring', with younger generations bringing older generations up to speed rather than the other way around.

Realizing that these three concepts show interdependence and overlap, they are defined as follows for the remainder of the book:

- *Skill* – An ability acquired through deliberate, systematic, and sustained effort to carry out complex activities and job functions (Baldissin *et al.* 2013).

  Examples: budgeting, persuasive memo writing, programming, stakeholder mapping, and video-editing.

- *Competency* – A cluster of related abilities, commitments, knowledge, and skills (Rosen 2015).

  Examples: collaboration, diplomacy, long-term thinking, negotiation, political astuteness, social media literacy, and stakeholder engagement.

- *Value* – A quality or standard that guides behaviour and decision-making (Van der Wal 2008).

  Examples: agility, empathy, entrepreneurialism, humaneness, neutrality, prudence, and responsiveness.

or all of the above? And what about negotiation? Is this a specific trainable skill or a hard-earned competency requiring many years of experience
and insight? One could write entire books about such definitional issues
alone.

Nevertheless, by distinguishing specific, trainable *skills* – such as video-
editing or memo writing – from broader *competencies* – collaboration
or stakeholder engagement – and *values* – empathy or prudence – the
components of public management repertoires are sufficiently specified
and classified for the chapters that follow.

Skills, competencies, and values: 'traditional' versus 'new'

A dazzling amount of recent scholarly articles and books, along with
consultancy reports and government documents, discuss the *future public sector workforce*. According to such writings, public managers should
be entrepreneurial and locally minded, display interpersonal skills and
commercial savvy, master collaboration and communication, lead and
manage change, deliver projects and programmes, redesign services,
and deliver them digitally (Dickinson and Sullivan 2014; KPMG 2013;
Needham and Mangan 2014, 2016; Alford and O'Flynn 2012; 't Hart
2014b). Clearly, 3.0 skills and competencies are key here. Twenty-first
century public managers should have the ability to operate in increasingly cross-sectoral, international, and co-producing networks in which
citizens manage alongside public managers rather than being managed
by them.

A somewhat more fundamental, macro-level debate concerns the *future
of 21st century work* (Dickinson and Needham 2012; Gratton 2011).
Issues discussed include the emergence of non-routine and spontaneous
teamwork, 'remote' and 'virtual' office settings, and the increase in simu-
lation and experimentation (Melbourne School of Government 2013).
Others emphasize 'social media literacy' and big-data analytical skills
(McKinsey 2013), and the disruptive effects of technology and robotization on the future of work, jobs, and job security (World Economic
Forum 2016).

A contrasting perspective is offered by acclaimed political scientist Rod
Rhodes (2016: 638), who recently suggested that in an era of networked
governance, public managers should retreat from businesslike skills and
approaches to *return to six classical qualities or administrative 'crafts'*.
The six crafts he puts forward are counselling, stewardship, prudence,
judgement, diplomacy, and political nous – referred to by others as political savvy, political antennae, or 'political astuteness' (Hartley *et al.* 2013:
17; Hartley 2015).

In some ways, Rhodes' plea aligns with the perspective put forward
in this chapter that some traditional competencies and attributes remain
important whereas others will become less important, and will be
replaced when external and internal changes and pressures so dictate. He

emphasizes the recovery of 1.0 qualities, arguing they have been under-valued and neglected in recent decades. While that certainly holds true in some cases, I would like to reiterate here that 21st century public managers will have to *combine* 1.0, 2.0, and 3.0 skills, competencies, and values in order to be effective and successful.

Table 2.1 provides a tentative overview of the traditional (but still important) and new (increasingly important) skills, competencies, and values that characterize 21st century public managers. These skills, competencies, and values, and how they compete with and complement each other, feature throughout the rest of this book.

Twenty-first century ethos

Finally, 21st century public managers who want to be effective and successful need more than just a toolbox with skills. They need to operate on the basis of the right values and motivations which, taken together, constitute a so-called *public service ethos* (Horton 2008; Rayner *et al.* 2011). Indeed, two prominent topics in public management research concern the extent to which public employees are driven by altruistic and intrinsic work motivations – a public service motivation or PSM (Perry

TABLE 2.1 Traditional and new skills, competencies, and values

	'Traditional' but still necessary	'New' and increasingly necessary
Trainable skills and competencies Can be acquired through training and development	Political astuteness Counselling Diplomacy Bargaining Domain expertise	Networking Teamwork Stakeholder engagement Collaborating Customer-orientation IT-savviness (particularly social media literacy and big-data analytical skills) Design thinking Storytelling (branding, framing) Navigating
Innate values Can be selected on and nurtured	Judgement Prudence Selflessness Humaneness Neutrality	Innovativeness Responsiveness Agility Ingenuity Courage Entrepreneurialism

et al. 2010) – and by specific public values, such as equity, social justice, and accountability (Van der Wal *et al.* 2015). Many consider such motivations and values – and the public service ethos they are supposed to produce – incommensurable with the traditional private sector ethos characterized by profitability, competitiveness, and innovation (Bovens 1996; Frederickson and Ghere 2005; Jacobs 1992; Pollitt 2008; Van der Wal 2008).

Here, the global perspective and ambition of this book once more complicates things but also leads to fascinating questions and debates. Do public managers across the globe share the same values or motivations? Do they *at all* adhere to an altruistic public service ethos? How will the emergence of a VUCA world affect values and motivations, and their classical differences between public and private sector settings? Will developments force 21ˢᵗ century public managers to simultaneously adhere to a traditional public service ethos *and* display businesslike, 'entrepreneurial', and 'innovative' behaviour? How will they stay grounded and do the right thing?

Indeed, individual public managers will respond differently to developments in their operating environments depending on their personal values, the organizational cultures in which they operate, and above all, their incentive structures and performance requirements (Chen and Hsieh 2015; Van der Wal 2015a, 2015b). Moreover, we may question the applicability and even the very existence of an altruistic public service ethos in developing 'tough governance' settings characterized by endemic corruption, unsafe political operating environments, and ambiguous, often externally enforced reform agendas (Van der Wal 2014: 197).

Perhaps public managers in tough governance settings more closely resemble the traditional, somewhat cynical bureaucrat who is driven by opportunistic, extrinsic motivations such as job security, pension systems, work–life balance, and status and power (Tullock 1976)? Others believe, however, that public managers need even higher levels of PSM to stay motivated and get anything done in such settings (Houston 2014). Most likely, a complex and dynamic mix of intrinsic and extrinsic drivers motivates these public managers.

However, the same may very well apply to developed, Western settings. It is far from self-evident that an altruistic public service ethos is a key driver for many public managers as they go about their daily business. In fact, research shows that many public managers are motivated by more pragmatic concerns, like wanting to be in close proximity to power, having significant work, 'impact', and 'influence' (Van der Wal 2013). Table 2.2 shows an empirical ranking of work motivations of type 1 and type 2 public managers in Western countries, comparing their initial motivations for joining the public sector with their motivations for fulfilling their high-level duties at the present day (Van der Wal 2013: 753–754).

TABLE 2.2 Work motivations of senior public managers

Start of career	*At present day*
1. I want to contribute to, improve, or 'serve' society	1. The function's complexity, challenges, and relevance ('interesting work')
2. The function's complexity, challenges, and relevance ('interesting work')	2. I want to contribute to, improve, or 'serve' society
3. A logical step given my personal background and/or education	3. To operate in close proximity to political power, to have 'influence and impact'
4. A more or less coincidental choice during my first round of interviews	4. Issue-specific but not necessarily related to government
5. 'Government' provides good career prospects and opportunities	5. 'Government' provides good career prospects and opportunities
6. Personal rather than professional reasons and motivations (including work–life balance)	6. I was asked, invited, or 'urged' to do the job
7. Issue-specific but not necessarily related to government	7. A good salary and/or job security
8. I want to be part of something bigger than myself, have a big impact	8. Personal rather than professional reasons and motivations (including work–life balance)
9. I was asked, invited, or 'urged' to do the job	
10. I believe in democracy and the bureaucratic process and I want to do a good job spending public money	

Clearly, a dynamic mix of intrinsic and extrinsic motivations drives these managers, and the composition of this mix develops as their careers progress, with impact and close proximity to power becoming more important. Still, a striking commonality is the emphasis on 'interesting work' as key driver to stay in the public service and work relentlessly within its highest echelons. This work motivation is likely to become ever more important in a VUCA world. A deputy secretary-general reiterates (Van der Wal 2013: 754):

The complexity and therefore the challenge of working in this area is something that motivates me. I find the bottom line complex and therefore much more interesting than the monolithic perspective of a company. It cannot be reduced to a fairly simple calculation. I find the complexity, the necessary trade-offs and the judgments with regard to how do we reconcile all the things that we want in society intellectually stimulating: the 'game of governing'. You have to untie knots and solve complex equations. It is one big intellectual challenge and that is why I like working for the central government so much.

What lies ahead

This chapter has provided the foundations necessary for us to venture into the world of the 21st century public manager. Having identified some key roles, skills, competencies, and values of public managers, we now move to the book's next question: when, where, and why will major changes occur in the managerial operating environment, and what will these changes look like? Chapter 'Trends and Drivers' addresses this question by identifying global megatrends that are impacting managerial work in various, sometimes fundamental ways – no matter where managers are or will be located. Although many of these trends seem fairly continuous and gradual, it is hard to tell what disruptive shocks and events they may set in motion. One thing is clear, however: taken together, these drivers of change will lead to a more volatile, uncertain, complex, and ambiguous operating environment. Let's explore the key drivers of the VUCA world.

Chapter 3

Trends and Drivers

Prediction is very difficult, especially about the future.

Niels Henrik David Bohr (Danish physicist and Noble laureate)

The 3/11 disaster: causes, cascades, and consequences

On 11 March 2011, Japan's Fukushima Daiichi nuclear power plant – operated by corporate giant Tokyo Electric Power Company (TEPCO) – was hit by a tsunami triggered by the magnitude 9.0 Tohoku earthquake. Three of the plant's six nuclear reactors melted down, and the plant began releasing substantial amounts of radioactive material on 12 March. This was the largest nuclear incident since the Chernobyl disaster in April 1986 and the second to measure Level 7 on the International Nuclear Event Scale. To this day, workers continue to mitigate leaking with measures such as chemical underground walls. Although there were no immediate fatalities from radiation exposure, some 300,000 people were evacuated from the area; close to 16,000 people died from the earthquake and tsunami; and 1,600 deaths were attributed to evacuation conditions, such as temporary housing and hospital closures.

The Fukushima Nuclear Accident Independent Investigation Commission found that the nuclear disaster was 'manmade' and that its direct causes were all foreseeable and predictable. Various other inquiries reached similar conclusions. They suggested that 'regulatory capture', collusion, lack of oversight, and corruption were key contributors to the extent of the disaster, resulting from years of close relationships between industry, government, and academia.

International reaction to the disaster was diverse and widespread. The International Atomic Energy Agency (IAEA) halved its estimate of additional nuclear generating capacity to be built by 2035, and anti-nuclear demonstrations were followed by a significant re-evaluation of existing nuclear power programmes in many countries. In June 2011, an opinion poll from Ipsos MORI revealed that 62 per cent of the citizens from 24 different countries were opposed to nuclear energy. Nuclear power plans were abandoned in Malaysia, the Philippines, Kuwait, and Bahrain, and radically changed in Taiwan. China suspended its nuclear development programme, but restarted it on a reduced basis in late 2012.

Germany closed its old nuclear power reactors and decided to phase out all plants by 2022. Although Germany's *Energiewende* ('energy transition') was aimed at moving away from fossil fuels much faster than was previously planned, it resulted in an enormous short-term increase in highly polluting brown coal. In a national referendum in Italy, 94 per cent of voters opposed plans to build new nuclear power plants. The same happened in Switzerland and Belgium. In Japan, however, the government opted to import oil and gas on an unprecedented scale from the Middle East rather than 'going green'. This resulted in massive government borrowing and spending and had unexpected effects on international energy markets.

Clearly, governments responded very differently, sometimes seemingly unintentionally and unexpectedly, to the same 'shock' event. Even today, the Fukushima disaster still affects many regional and global events and decisions. In the years to come, it is difficult to estimate its long-term net effects on global emissions and transitions to a cleaner energy mix, regulations of mining and energy industries, collaborative practices and knowledge transfer between governments, industries, and universities, and so forth.

Trends, hypes, and shocks

The 3/11 disaster and its aftermath powerfully illustrate how events with various interlinked causes and consequences can not only overwhelm government capacity, but also spin off a number of unexpected, perhaps even illogically related, actions by other actors. As 't Hart (2013: 101) argues: 'it is an example of a disaster that turns into a calamity of much bigger temporal, spatial, and political proportions'. Indeed, even when governments have plans in place for events, trends, and drivers that may be foreseeable or preventable, such events may prove hard to manage when they actually happen. Moreover, they may catalyse other events that are much less foreseeable and predictable, and near impossible to plan for.

Even though many designated the 3/11 disaster as a 'once in a lifetime' event, there seems to be a growing recognition that we're living in an era in which continuous complexity and turbulence is the normal state of affairs rather than the exception. 'Something is in the air', as Vielmetter and Sell (2014: 4) assert. Chapter 'Introduction' introduced this sentiment using the VUCA acronym, indicating that volatility, uncertainty, complexity, and ambiguity increasingly characterize operating environments. Others have used the notion of 'chronic turbulence', referring to a situation in which 'complexity and change have escalated to a point at which the adaptive capacities of communities and social institutions are severely challenged' (McCann and Selsky 1984: 465, in 't Hart 2014b: 19). A commonly used metaphor here is that of the 'butterfly effect', coined by Chaos theory pioneer Edward Lorenz in 1969. Gaiman and Pratchett (2006) have beautifully captured its essence:

> It used to be thought that the events that changed the world were things like big bombs, maniac politicians, huge earthquakes, or vast

population movements, but it has now been realized that this is a very old-fashioned view held by people totally out of touch with modern thought. The things that really change the world, according to Chaos theory, are the tiny things. A butterfly flaps its wings in the Amazonian jungle, and subsequently a storm ravages half of Europe.

Clearly, in an era in which events are shaped by unpredictable 'tiny things', we need a fundamentally different approach to public management systems. The traditional approach tends to model operating environments in a 'reductionist' way, assuming we are able to map most of the relevant variables and their interaction effects (Ho 2008). However, alongside those that favour *microtrends* (Penn 2009) as shaping tomorrow's events, various recent reports and writings suggest that *megatrends* (coined by Naisbitt 1988) shape future public management agendas. In many ways, thinking in terms of megatrends like urbanization, climate change, or ageing almost seems reassuring: more gradual, long-term processes allow us to plan ahead and anticipate new demands on public managers, adjusting along the way.

For the purposes of this chapter and the book that lies ahead of us, I argue that we need to consider both gradual megatrends and less predictable microtrends in order to identify 21st century demands, together with the capabilities they require. Indeed, the 3/11 example shows how megatrends and microtrends can interrelate in unexpected ways. Moreover, we need to be able to distinguish hype and fad from the undeniable and unstoppable. How else can we begin to prioritize?

Box 3.1 introduces us to *four different categories of change*: (1) trend, (2) gradual discontinuity, (3) hype or rage, and (4) abrupt discontinuity.

This vocabulary allows us to distinguish between trends and gradual discontinuities on the one hand, and shocks, disruptions, and abrupt discontinuities on the other, and to understand their implications for public managers. Clearly, category 3 and 4 changes can transform, accelerate, or redirect category 1 and 2 changes – think of housing bubbles or stock exchange crashes and their long-term, rather linear effects on public debt ratios, or tsunamis causing nuclear meltdowns causing fundamental, long-term shifts in energy policy as in the 3/11 example.

Thus, gradual versus disruptive changes require partly different attributes and capabilities – planning, forecasting, and scenario-building versus resilience, agility, and experimentation. Yet, taken together they necessitate the inculcation of an anticipatory mindset into civil servants, according to Singapore's former Head of Public Service Peter Ho (2010: 2):

> The skill-sets needed for long-term policy planning are different from those needed to deal with more immediate volatility and crisis. Both are important. But those charged with thinking about the future should be given the freedom and allocated the bandwidth to focus on this important role without getting bogged down in day-to-day routines.

Box 3.1 A vocabulary to discuss and assess change

In order to determine which changes are likely to occur, we have to assess if and how particular issues are already taking place, and how they may lead to the occurrence of other issues in the future. Such an assessment is aided by a common language or vocabulary about change. The nine patterns divided into four categories distinguished by Van Rijn and Van der Burgt (2012: 32–42) provide a vocabulary to determine action perspectives. Examples from across the globe are included.

Category 1: Trend

Definition: a repetitive pattern that evolves when (long-term) data is taken into consideration

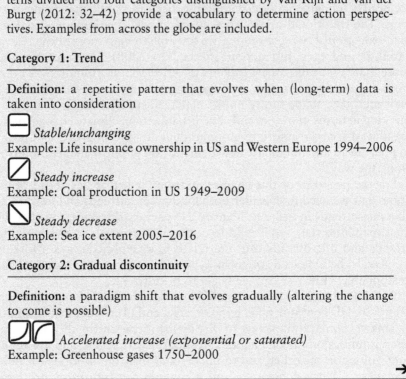 *Stable/unchanging*
Example: Life insurance ownership in US and Western Europe 1994–2006

Steady increase
Example: Coal production in US 1949–2009

Steady decrease
Example: Sea ice extent 2005–2016

Category 2: Gradual discontinuity

Definition: a paradigm shift that evolves gradually (altering the change to come is possible)

Accelerated increase (exponential or saturated)
Example: Greenhouse gases 1750–2000

→

However, as unknowns are unknowns, it is difficult to write a chapter about them. Indeed, I don't have a crystal ball and I can't predict the occurrence of 'black swans' (Taleb 2007) – rare, extreme, unpredictable events – and 'wild cards' (Petersen 2000) – low-probability, high-impact events. Moreover, strategizing based on 'predictions' is not only impractical, but perhaps even outright dangerous (Kuah 2015). Rather, in laying the groundwork for upcoming chapters about emerging managerial demands and dilemmas, and the skills, competencies, and values they require, this chapter outlines widely recognized, interrelated megatrends.

The global ambitions of this book necessitate that we identify trends with global reach, ones that 'affect all regions and stakeholders' (Vielmetter and Sell 2014: 6). Still, these 'long-term, transformational processes with global reach, broad scope, and fundamental and dramatic impact'

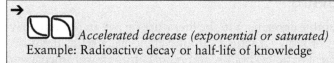 *Accelerated decrease (exponential or saturated)*
Example: Radioactive decay or half-life of knowledge

Category 3: Hype or rage

Definition of hype: a development of which people have far too high expectations
Definition of rage: a product or lifestyle that is temporarily fashionable

Temporary increase
Example: Dotcom bubble 2000 or subprime housing bubble 2007–2008

Temporary decrease
Example: E. coli outbreak Germany 2011 or SARS outbreak Asia 2003: consumption and travelling

Category 4: Abrupt discontinuity

Definition: a paradigm shift that evolves so fast that a system becomes unstable (altering the change to come is not possible)

Abrupt increase
Example: Earthquake and tsunami Japan 2011

Abrupt decrease
Example: Financial crash Dow Jones September 2008 or Shanghai Stock Exchange early 2016.

Source: Foresight Cards, https://foresightcards.com/background-information/patterns-of-change.

(Z_punkt 2008: 1), and their often mutually reinforcing character, point towards the same VUCA world-proof competencies. Many of these trends are already in full force (Compston 2006; OECD 2009, 2005), with some taking the shape of gradual discontinuities (Box 3.1).

I treat trends, drivers, and forces of change as interchangeable concepts, as they all refer to the same macro-level, relatively gradual and continuous factors that will affect the way we live and work in the decades to come. At the outset, it is important to realize once again that the megatrends identified here can be perceived *as constraints as well as enablers*, depending on how they're addressed by public sectors and the managers who populate them. This, in turn, will depend on the manager's competencies and overall mindset – whether they take a leap into a 'crafted future' or passively accept a 'default future', as Gratton (2011: 16) puts it.

Global megatrends

Given the considerable agreement in the literature on key trends and drivers, this chapter is broadly structured around eight megatrends identified by a variety of recent articles, books, and reports from governments and consulting firms (CSIRO 2013; Dickinson and Sullivan 2014; Dobbs *et al.* 2015; Gratton 2011; KPMG 2013; McKinsey 2013; Needham and Mangan 2014, 2016; Roland Berger 2011; Vielmetter and Sell 2014; 't Hart 2014b). The trends show remarkable similarity and overlap. Moreover, the 3/11 disaster illustrates how these trends operate in clusters, and how abrupt increases and shocks can further reinforce their effects. Using KPMG's (2013) classification, these eight trends can be broadly grouped into trends related to *individuals* (trends 1–3), the *global economy* (trends 4–6), and the *physical environment* (trends 7–8), with 'technology' and 'globalization' often identified as key overarching factors (Gratton 2011; Jones 2013). KPMG (2013: 8) asserts:

> Global megatrends are highly interrelated. While the individual trends won't play out to the same degree in each country, the resulting consequences are inevitably interconnected and reinforce each other in terms of impact. This relationship is evident when considering, for example, the nexus of issues around changing demographics, resource stress and climate change [the same goes for rise of the individual, enabling technology, and economic power shifts and interconnectedness].

This chapter focuses on how these trends impact public sectors around the world, albeit differently according to economic and political context and stage of development. The remaining chapters zoom in on how they impact the individual public manager.

Trend 1: 'All is networked': enabling technology, social media, and big data

Obviously, a key overarching factor here is technological advancement. Rapid technological evolutions of the past few decades have led to a world in which many gadgets that appeared in science fiction films in the 1980s and 1990s are now reality; in fact, they have even been surpassed. When I ride the subway to work every morning I am increasingly surprised that nearly everyone's attention is captured by that small smart device in the palm of their hands. It makes the subway scenes from Verhoeven's famous 1990 film *Total Recall* look outdated.

Indeed, it seems hard to imagine nowadays that smartphones didn't even exist less than a decade ago; currently, the 'global app' economy is estimated to be worth US$151 billion in 2017. Smartphones with mobile internet are transforming the way we work, live, and communicate on a daily basis, and the 1,000-fold increase in speed of the mobile internet when 5G replaces 4G around 2020 will accelerate this beyond imagination (Dean 2014). Increasingly, we are living in a 'network society' (Castells and Cardoso 2005) that leads to global economic interconnectedness, the fourth megatrend in this chapter.

By its very nature, technology accelerates the changes it sets in motion and exponentially increases available data and information. In 1965, future Intel founder Gordon E. Moore famously predicted that the capacity of microchips would double every two years. This observation, dubbed 'Moore's Law', was adjusted a decade later by Intel executive David House to 18 months. It appears that the rate of growth will begin to slow (as chip capacity is not infinite), one consequence of increasing computer processing and storage capacity is an increase in the *production* of data, or the 'creation of knowledge'. It is estimated that around 90 per cent of the digital data in the world today was created in just the past two years (IBM 2013).

The implications of recent extrapolations of the 'knowledge doubling curve', initially created by US architect and futurist Buckminster Fuller (1982), are almost unimaginable (see Figure 3.1). This is an example of the exponential increase identified in Box 3.1.

Much has been written about the implications of 'big data' for business, government, and society (Schönberger and Cukier 2013). Less explored are the potential effects on public sectors, in areas such as the information processing capabilities of systems and managers, performance management information use (Meijer 2015; Moynihan and Pandey 2010; Van Dooren 2013), and public service delivery (Barber, Moffit, and Kihn 2010). Already, the key issue facing public decision-makers is an *over-abundance rather than a shortage* of relevant policy and performance data. Most current public managers who are not heavily specialized in IT

FIGURE 3.1   Exponential growth of information: 1900–2020

1900	1950	2000	2020
Until 1900, human knowledge doubled approximately every century	By 1945 knowledge was doubling every 25 years	Currently, on average human knowledge is doubling every 13 months	It is estimated the "internet of things" will soon lead to the doubling of knowledge every 12 hours (IBM 2013)

lack even a basic understanding of what this overabundance means, let alone the skillset and mindset required to leverage this data.

Many citizens, particularly younger generations, already far outperform the existing stock of public managers in this area. This fact, in conjunction with citizens' increasing demands for transparency in how governments use data to plan and justify their decision-making, puts immense pressures on public managers. One such threat is the increasing incidence of cybersecurity threats, including the rise of 'hacktivists' (RAND 2013). These pressures, in turn, require management development (MD) and human resource management (HRM) strategies to attract and train future public managers who can live up to the standards and demands of external stakeholders.

Trend 2: 'Great expectations': individualism and demands for unlimited transparency

A second trend, reinforced by technological advancements, is captured by labels like the 'rise of the individual' (KPMG 2013), 'great expectations' (Melbourne School of Government 2013), and 'individualism and value pluralism' (Vielmetter and Sell 2014). The thrust of this trend is that technology and education have empowered individuals, and younger generations in particular, with massive improvements in literacy (now at a global rate of 84 per cent), participation of women in the workforce, and a rapidly expanding middle class (KPMG 2013; UNDP 2013; UNESCO 2011). By 2030, the global middle class will double from around 30 to around 60 per cent of the population, with 80 per cent residing in the developing world, particularly Asia (Kharas and Geoffrey 2010; Mahbubani 2013; OECD 2010).

This increasingly empowered, vocal, participatory, and critical middle class, armed with high-speed, internet-powered smartphones, will keep governments on their toes, or ultimately remove them from power. This dynamic is particularly prominent in more hierarchical and authoritative cultures and regimes – think of the Arab Spring in 2011 or Occupy Central in Hong Kong in 2014 – where social media play a role in three key dynamics: organizing protests, shaping the narrative, and putting pressure on the international community (Boyd 2011; KPMG 2013).

Such dynamics will fundamentally change the way in which regimes and the public managers that represent them have to interact, communicate, and collaborate with stakeholders and citizens. In short, governments need to become 'more open, more innovative, more responsive, and smarter' (Deloitte 2010: 38). Are 'great expectations' a hype? No, events that have been unfolding for some time now rather point at a steady decrease in the self-evidence of (traditional) authority, with the backlashes and defensive responses of authoritarian regimes being a natural reaction.

Indeed, Box 3.2 illustrates how China, with the fastest-growing middle class on the globe (Kharas and Geoffrey 2010), is experiencing dynamics

Box 3.2 Social media and civic engagement in air quality issues in China

In February 2015, the documentary *Under the Dome* – about the health impact of China's smog, and made by former state media investigative journalist Chai Jing – went viral on Chinese websites, just days before the country's ruling party hosted its annual top-level meetings. It is estimated to have been viewed more than 200 million times in the week following its release, before it was eventually blocked from Chinese video sites. The 104-minute film is a rather basic compilation of TED talk excerpts, video footage from polluted cities, charts, and figures, with the red thread being the personal drama of Jing, who found out that her baby was carrying a tumour she claims was caused by pollution.

Before the film was taken down, China's newly appointed Environmental Minister Chen Jining praised the video, saying it reflected 'growing public concern over environmental protection and threats to human health'. Even after it was removed, however, video and commentary continued to spread. Li Yan, the head of Greenpeace's energy and climate change campaign in Beijing, says: 'The discussion on social media triggered by Chai Jing's film has been very vivid. Very lively. It has already taken on its own life.' But the issue is nowhere to be found on major Chinese media outlets. Yao Bo, a well-known commentator on Chinese social media, dismissed the idea of internal conflict between China's leaders about how to respond: 'The censors eventually acted as expected, after going through this bureaucratic process that is always half a step behind.'

The massive online debate on pollution and air quality, often neglected and countered by the mainstream media in the country, is far from being an isolated event. In fact, studies show social media have drastically increased citizen awareness of air quality issues, which many consider the most serious problem resulting from modernization.

In the years to come, an empowered citizenry will continue to participate in public debates and scrutinize public policy, and public managers will have to decide how to position and conduct themselves amid this trend. How can they engage citizens without obstructing political masters? What kind of communication, media analysis, participatory, and negotiating skills are needed to do so? How can training programmes for public managers be reinvigorated to produce such skills and values given China's governance context?

*Sources:*CNN2015;*TheGuardian,*https://theguardian.com/world/2014/mar/05/china-pollution-economic-reform-growth-target; Phillips 2015.

in government–citizen interaction relative to its government's ability to control and direct information flows. It also illustrates once again how various megatrends – in this case all is networked, great expectations and more with less – interact with and reinforce each other.

Trend 3: 'Forever young': demographics, fertility, and ageing

A third cluster of trends related to individuals has to do with demographic dynamics. Birth rates throughout the developed world are going down and individuals are ageing. It is estimated that in 2030, 13 per cent of the world's population will be aged 65 or above, compared with 8 per cent today; by 2050, one in five persons will be elderly (INIA 2013, 2015). Population ageing is mainly caused by two factors. First, birth rates on average declined from 37 per 1,000 in the early 1950s to 22 in the late 1990s, and are projected to fall to 16 per 1,000 by 2035 (UNPD 2013). The United States is a notable exception to most developed countries in this regard as its population is still expected to increase for decades to come. However, as the vast majority of new births takes place among immigrants, this trend poses its own political and policy-related problems (in a sense, many European countries face an exaggerated version of this problem as their 'indigenous' population is ageing and shrinking even more rapidly, exacerbated by the current refugee crisis).

Second, individuals are living longer. The EU, Australia, the US, and Russia are expected to see a dramatic increase in the number of 65+ year olds and 80+ year olds between now and 2040, when most of these countries will peak (Rodrigues *et al.* 2012; UNDP 2011). To illustrate: 174 million people in Europe and North America are now aged 65 years or older, 40 million more than 20 years ago.

A further increase of about 93 million people is expected within the next 20 years, pointing towards an acceleration of population ageing (Rodrigues *et al.* 2012: 24). And increasing and accelerating improvements in healthcare technology will push up this number to heights that are hard to predict today. Will the elderly be 'forever young' (Melbourne School of Government 2013) just a few decades from now?

The developing world shows a completely different dynamic. Ninety per cent of the global youth lives in developing countries (ILO 2013; KPMG 2013), and a rapidly developing country such as India is estimated to add 1 million people to its labour force *every month* between now and 2030 (ADB 2011). It goes without saying that the implications for governments across the world are immense. Clearly, the developed world has already started to fundamentally rethink its pension systems, elderly care arrangements, housing, and overall fiscal policies, and how and by whom these should be financed and delivered (Alford and O'Flynn 2012; Dickinson 2012; KPMG 2013). In a way, this process was aided and accelerated by the global financial crisis in 2008 and 2009. However, in the developing world the key issue is achieving economic growth levels that allow the economy to absorb ever-growing numbers of youths looking for jobs, in conjunction with upgrading the educational backgrounds and skills needed for 21st century jobs. This struggle is experienced by many countries across Africa, Asia, and Latin America (and increasingly, Southern Europe as well).

So, while the overall global workforce will be shrinking, this process will be very unevenly skewed towards the developed world. Beyond the obvious consequences for healthcare, housing, and healthcare policies, public sector organizations, in HRM terms, will witness unprecedented 'Star Wars': wars for talent between organizations to prevent a much-feared 'leadership cliff' (Vielmetter and Sell 2014: 108). Public managers play a key role here in managing and balancing the expectations of external stakeholders and political actors amid painful choices and reforms, and in formulating dynamic, complex policy architectures to mitigate these trends. In addition, public managers themselves will be subject to, increasingly international, Star Wars.

Trend 4: 'Economic interconnectedness': convergence, contagion, and regulation

Moving from megatrends in the individual domain to the global economic domain, a key issue is how technology and the rise of the individual affect the nature, shape, and size of the global economy, which in turn largely determines the agendas and playing fields of international and domestic governance actors. KPMG (2013: 26) labels this trend 'economic interconnectedness'. Free trade and international investment have seen an immense surge in the past few decades: global trade as share of GDP increased from 40 per cent in 1980 to about 60 per cent in 2014 (Economist 2014; World Bank 2014). Moreover, global growth in trade is expected to continue at about 5 per cent annually between now and 2030 (HSBC 2015; KPMG 2013), with 80 per cent of the current trade agreements in force having been introduced since 1990 (Arestis *et al.* 2012). The Trans-Pacific Partnership (TPP) and the proposed Transatlantic Trade and Investment Partnership (TTIP) ... whose implementation may be stalled and/or amended given recent election results in the Western world ... will add an estimated US$357 billion to global GDP annually (Brookings 2014; Francois *et al.* 2013). Mahbubani (2013) suggests that increasing economic interconnectedness will also lead to a 'great convergence' of cultural and political discourse, management thinking, and educational strategies across the globe and between the East and West in particular.

Again, there are stark differences between countries and regions here, as the next two megatrends will show. In addition, as with most of the trends identified here, risks and opportunities go hand in hand, as KPMG (2013: 26) concludes:

> There are also new challenges as economies are increasingly connected to risks beyond national borders. These risks not only move quickly, they also defy the scope of national regulation, demanding international cooperation. As the trend toward increased economic interconnectedness is expected to continue, governments throughout the world will need to ensure that they have the policy frameworks in place to capture the benefits of trade and manage the risks.

The global economic shocks caused by the bankruptcy of one large US bank in 2008 are a case in point. In response to the crisis, countries around the world have introduced similar economic regulations, showing regulatory convergence that was unthinkable before the crisis. In addition, Foroohar (2015, 2016), Sitglitz *et al.* (2015), and others have shown that the 'enabling technology' and 'economic interconnectedness' this chapter discusses increasingly benefit the top and bottom of the labour market rather than the entire population; in fact, the rise of the middle class in many developing countries will go hand in hand with the decline of the traditional middle class in Western countries.

Moreover, growth in some of the emerging economies that were predicted to dominate the world economy just a decade ago – some of the BRIC countries (Brazil, Russia, India, China), for instance – has stalled dramatically in recent years. At the same time, global interest rates seemed to have reached a historic low that has been perpetuated for an unusually long period of time, with rates even being negative in large parts of the developed world where low growth seems to be the new normal (Foroohar 2016). In an increasingly connected world, penetrating new markets that are immune to these developments becomes increasingly hard, if not impossible.

The impact on politics and policy is evident. Public managers will play a key role in mitigating the protectionist and nationalist frustrations of citizens and preventing their elected bosses from caving in to such demands.

Trend 5: 'More with less': public debt and fiscal pressures

One of the most profound public sector trends in the developed world has been the massive growth of public debt and the resulting fiscal pressures; just between 2007 and 2014, net debt to GDP ratios in developed countries ballooned from 46.3 per cent to almost 80 per cent (IMF 2014). The demographic trends discussed earlier will only exacerbate public debt and accompanying fiscal pressures, and the increasing demands by citizens on their governments to 'deliver' (Noordegraaf 2015; 't Hart 2014b) will make it harder to postpone or mystify fiscal decision-making. In short: governments will permanently have to do 'more with less' (Needham and Mangan 2014). In fact, given the investments in capacity-building that many of the other trends require to make public sectors and their managers 'future proof', they will face severely constrained investment potential. The 1980s were also marked by similar issues as a consequence of post-WWII welfare state expansion, with massive budget cuts, management reforms and privatization, and unemployment and social unrest (see Ferrera and Hemerijck 2003; Pollitt and Bouckaert 2011). However, economists are now much less optimistic that the current period of austerity will be followed by a 1990s-like boom in the developed world, as demonstrated before.

In a way, this trend seems puzzling given the projections of growing global trade also presented in this chapter. However, once again striking differences exist between countries. For instance, Europe, the US, Australia, and Japan are growing modestly and will see their ageing-related public expenditures alone increase by 4.4 per cent of GDP between now and 2030 (IMF 2013). In contrast, parts of the developing world, where most of the global growth will be achieved in the next two decades, and where populations are much younger, will not see such dramatic increases in public spending.

These observations bring us to the megatrend on global power shifts, including the much-discussed emergence of a 'new Asian hemisphere' (Mahbubani 2008), the 'rise of Asia' (Vielmetter and Sell 2014), the 'Asian century' (Gillard 2012), 'the silk highway' (CSIRO 2013), or most provocatively, in the form of a book title, *When China Rules the World: The End of the Western World and the Birth of a New Global Order* (Jacques 2009).

Trend 6: 'Global power shifts': the Asian century and the multi-polar world

To start with, the estimate that 57 per cent of global GDP will be generated by developing countries in 2030 (OECD 2010), with the BRIC countries amounting to 36 per cent (compared with 18 now) and averaging annual growth rates of 8 per cent (Roland Berger 2011), are amazing facts as such. However, these numbers pale in comparison with the economic rise of Asia, and China and India in particular. For example, just 35 years ago, the US share of global gross national product (GNP) in purchasing power parity (PPP) terms was 25 per cent while that of China was 2.2 per cent; by the end of 2014, the US share stood at 16.2 per cent and China at 16.4 per cent (IMF 2014). This is the first time in 200 years that the largest economy in the world has been non-Western (Mahbubani 2015: 17). The middle class in Asia is expected to explode in less than a decade, from 500 million people in 2015 to 1.75 billion around 2020, with China's middle class expected to double to 1.1 billion people (Roland Berger 2011). These are tectonic economic power shifts. Much of the economic growth, trade, and traffic of goods and services in the next decades will take place on the new 'silk highway' (Melbourne School of Government 2013: 4).

It goes without saying that these economic shifts will lead to political, diplomatic, cultural, educational, and military power shifts as well, many of which are occurring as we speak. For instance, between now and 2020, acquisitions of foreign companies by Chinese firms are set to quadruple (Wolf 2011). In early 2016, the China-initiated Asian Infrastructure Investment Bank (AIIB) took off, supported by various European countries but not joined by the US. China will own 30 per cent of the shares. The AIIB is seen as an important tool for China to further enlarge its influence and interests in the region. As we speak, one country after the other is signing up to support and participate in AIIB while the US remains a staunch and increasingly isolated adversary. The US position provoked unusually sharp remarks from China's Finance Minister, Lou Jiwei, when he outlined the AIIB proposal in 2015: 'For decision-makers in the United States, they really have to be reminded that if they do not jump on the bandwagon of change in time, they will soon be overrun by the bandwagon itself.' With new economic and political ties being forged and broken faster than before, and old powers moving up and down the global economic and diplomatic food chain, the world is now more 'multi-polar' than it has been in the past two centuries (see Kaplan 2009).

Clearly, the impacts of these shifts for governments and public managers depend on their locus and focus. However, I would challenge the notion that global economic trends and international developments only affect those working in foreign relations and trade departments. In fact, it is likely that *all public management work will internationalize and globalize in the decades to come* (cf. KPMG 2013; 't Hart 2014b), whether public officials like it or not. Governments in the West will increasingly have to get accustomed to a new normal in which Asian (and to a lesser extent African and Latin American) forces are driving their agendas, rather than the other way around.

For public managers in Asia, and particularly in countries whose economic and political clout is rapidly increasing, these developments imply they have to facilitate their governments to lead rather than follow, to create rather than obstruct global agendas, and to obtain and maintain the roles and capabilities their new status requires: 'noblesse oblige'. An inward-looking and protectionist mindset is the last thing that public sectors should develop, but this is exactly what is happening in many parts of the world.

Trend 7: 'Ultra-urbanization': megacities as nodes of growth and governance

A trend resulting from socio-economic and physical dynamics and technological developments is rapid urbanization. Emerging 'megacities' are sprawling out and expanding into autonomous centres of economic activity and governance, with 80 per cent of urbanization between now and 2030 taking place in Africa and Asia (UNDP 2006). In 2030, 60 per cent of the world's population will live in cities (compared with 50 per cent now), and more than 90 per cent of the developed world will live in cities. Simultaneously, the world's population will grow by more than 1 billion (KPMG 2013), with obvious consequences for economic development and disparity between rural and urban areas.

Economic interconnectedness and enabling technology act as accelerators here. Already, just 600 cities house around 20 per cent of the world's population and generate 50 per cent of global GDP (McKinsey 2012). In addition, the number of so-called megacities with populations of over 10 million will double to around 40 in 2030. Such developments have immense consequences for infrastructure investment, social inequality, crime, and liveability – with no change in policy, the number of people living in slums will double from 1 billion today to 2 billion in 2030 – and pressures towards sustainable development (Doshi *et al.* 203; KPMG 2013; OECD 2008).

Less resourced and developed 'secondary' or second-tier cities (Storey 2014) are also emerging. Indeed, in the coming decades, much of the economic development in developing countries will happen here: China already has 135 such cities with populations between 1 and 10 million (Storey 2014). Increasingly, mayors and city managers of such cities take the stage and drive policy and management agendas, often in competition with and to the displeasure of national governments. Some observers suggest that policy innovations and experimentation, and the creative leadership and collaborations they require, increasingly take place at the city level. Others have speculated about what would happen *If Mayors Ruled the World*, as the much-hyped book by Benjamin Barber (2013) is titled (with the telling subtitle *Dysfunctional Nations, Rising Cities*).

Box 3.3 sketches some key issues governments face in managing and 'directing' the emergence of secondary megacities, and highlights how these affect public managers.

Like most of the other megatrends, 'ultra-urbanization' creates as many risks and threats as opportunities. As cities increasingly attract populations and economic growth, but central governments continue to hold and distribute the majority of government budgets, public managers will have to bargain and broker. They will have to align 'the resource demands of their jurisdictional responsibilities, rights to revenue and incentives', and 'formulate cross-jurisdictional and cross-governmental planning forums and mechanisms that support integrated planning' (KPMG 2013: 48).

Trend 8: 'More from less': resource stress, environmental depletion, and climate change

In many ways, climate change and resource stress can be perceived as downsides of the previous trends. As phrased by the Melbourne School of Government, we have to get 'more with less' (2013: 3). A recent ADB report (2013) predicts the 'rise of Asia' alone means the region's oil consumption will double, natural gas consumption will triple, and coal consumption will rise by 81 per cent by 2035. In turn, 75–80 per cent of the costs of adaptation to climate change will be shouldered by the developing world, with East Asia and the Pacific region bearing most of these expenses (World Bank 2010).

Box 3.3 'Secondary megacities': emergence and government response

'Secondary cities are the emerging engine of the rapid-pace urbanization the world will experience in the forthcoming decades. Already in Latin America, secondary cities represent close to 25 per cent of the country's GDP. Some of these cities are off springs of large metropolises such as Mexico City, São Paulo, and Buenos Aires that have encountered serious constraints in accommodating urban growth.' *Ellis Juan, General Coordinator of the Emerging and Sustainable Cities Initiative (ESCI).*

Much of the future economic growth and innovation in the developing world will take place as secondary cities turn into thriving and bustling 'megacities', with new secondary cities as offsprings. Governments across the world, particularly in Asia and Latin America, struggle with the rapid and chaotic growth of these urban monsters. In terms of policy design and governance, governments are trying out different approaches, which can be grouped in three main categories (based on the work of Cities Alliance 2014):

- *Decentralization and devolution of politics, policy, and management*

Many decentralization initiatives are ambiguous because central governments often strongly influence resource allocation and planning. Substantive delegation sometimes occurs, but often national, regional, and local actors confront each other rather than collaborate.

- *Special spatial planning policies*

  - 'New towns': belt of secondary cities around megacities to disperse population

  →

Global warming has become the key frame in recent discussions about the environment but still seems 'far off' and far away to many public managers, although things are beginning to shift after a historic global agreement to substantively cut back emissions was reached at the COP21 meeting in Paris in December 2015. However, what is already directly and significantly affecting their operating environments is the intertwined dynamics of environmental depletion and resource scarcity.

For instance, as global energy consumption will increase by around 25 per cent up to 2030 and total annual water demand will increase more than 50 per cent, even the most positive scenario in terms of renewable energy use and technological advancement cannot prevent almost half of the world's population from living in 'areas of high water stress' (Roland Berger 2011). Global demand for food will rise while growth rates in global agriculture will fall, exacerbated by the depletion of clean water needed to support increasing agricultural efficiency. Raw materials such as indium and gallium, which are needed for the technologies to mitigate

→

- 'Satellite towns': expansion of primary cities often tied to specific economic needs
- 'Industrial zones and business parks': production hubs aided by tax incentive schemes
- 'Growth poles': politically motivated development hubs in under-developed areas
- 'Technopoles': planned concentrations of R&D and high-end business activities
- 'Urban revitalization': often centrally directed rejuvenation and stimulation attempts

- *New urbanism ideas*

Increasingly, certain industries, technologies, and sections of society are clustering together in (virtual or physical) 'networked' cities, with or without explicit government support.

Questions facing public managers at various levels include the following. Should central actors lead the way in terms of designing models or 'blueprints'? If local actors feel empowered to experiment, lead, and grow, should central actors facilitate and enable local success through more decentralization and devolution? How do cities create sufficient managerial and political capacity to meet the needs of business – local governments are often considered the weakest link in public service delivery (Roberts 2014)? In particular, how do cities attract 21st century public management talent while they know most 'high flyers' enter government at the central level, as most of the resources, (perceived) career opportunities, and talent and trainee programmes are situated there?

the above-mentioned developments, will most likely decrease (Roland Berger 2011). Like many of the other trends discussed here, numerous dynamics interrelate and accelerate each other, leading to immense challenges for governments in mitigating, planning for, and adapting to a world in which 'more from less' will coincide with 'more with less'.

Surely, 'technophiles' like Apple CEO Tim Cook, Tesla CEO Elon Musk, or *New York Times* journalist Thomas Friedman argue, ongoing technological revolutions and advancements will help us in overcoming most of these problems. Indeed, a hopeful sign is that investments in renewable energy and 'clean tech' have gone up dramatically in recent years, surpassing investments in fossil fuels for the first time ever in 2015 (FS-UNEP 2016).

However, for many governments, particularly those in underdeveloped settings, acquiring – let alone leveraging – these technologies (if they can even deliver as promised), requires massive upgrading of human capital and management development and training systems. Even more important, acquiring and leveraging them will require shifts in current attitudes towards organizational and individual learning and cultures of experimentation.

What lies ahead

The megatrends identified in this chapter impact governments across the world in ways imaginable and unimaginable. Chapter 'Demands, Dilemmas, Opportunities' will address these impacts in terms of the demands, dilemmas, and opportunities they produce for public managers across contexts and settings. While I am mindful of the importance of *what* governments need to change in terms of specific policies in the areas of pensions, healthcare, environment, and education, the key focus of this book lies with *how* governments need to change; specifically, I explore which roles, competencies, and values public managers need in order to enable changes in strategies and structures. The demands placed on public managers to drive and accommodate these changes are manifold, but they are not necessarily as neatly and harmoniously aligned as some (perhaps unintentionally) would suggest. As public managers prioritize and manage these demands, they face a variety of dilemmas as well as unprecedented opportunities. How these play out in the daily life of public managers will become clear in the next chapter.

Chapter 4

Demands, Dilemmas, Opportunities

There is no dilemma compared with that of the deep-sea diver who hears the message from the ship above, 'Come up at once. We are sinking.'

(Wisconsin seminary Professor Robert Cooper, 1979)

Public management 2025

Imagine you are the Deputy Secretary of the Ministry of Planning and Infrastructure in a rapidly developing middle-income country in the year 2025. Your key priority in the next ten months is to develop a comprehensive policy framework for how the recently elected government has to facilitate and manage emerging 'secondary cities'. Such cities will be the main engines of economic growth in the years to come and will house over 80 per cent of your country's population before 2050, half of which currently lives in rural areas in traditional and sometimes backward communities. Not only will millions of citizens move to these emerging urban areas, either temporarily or permanently – these areas are also expected to attract large numbers of blue collar and white collar workers from neighbouring countries.

In addition, your minister has tasked you to incorporate the latest thinking on 'smart' cities. He urged you to be as ambitious and bold as possible in your proposals for leveraging the latest technologies, including artificial intelligence in driverless cars, digitally managed smart and 'green' electricity grids, use of cloud computing and dashboard technologies in setting up citizen registers and service delivery frameworks, and robotic technology in designing housing projects for the elderly and vulnerable. He's made it clear that key international and regional players and financiers such as the World Bank, UNDP, New Development Bank (NDB), and the Asian Infrastructure Investment Bank (AIIB) are eager to assist in the long-term development of these smart cities, provided your policy framework proves viable and sustainable over time. These financiers want to showcase their role in upgrading urban environments in a developing country. Currently, the secondary cities in your country suffer massive environmental degradation due to aged factories in the middle of residential neighbourhoods (which were industrial outskirts just 15 years ago), continuous traffic jams, and overreliance on cheap fossil fuels imported from neighbouring countries.

However, at this stage it is completely unclear how much – if any – financial support and enthusiasm you can expect to receive, making it hard to add a realistic budget in support of your framework. Your minister is an ambitious and eager 'street fighter'-type politician whose support base mainly consists of blue collar workers in emerging cities and the working poor in rural areas. He has staked much of his political future on the promotion of secondary cities. At the same time, he lacks the expertise – and the patience – to be of much help in the mission impossible he tasked you with. So far, he has consistently denied your requests to engage external consultants, hire new, young, tech-savvy staff, or incorporate new ways of working to operate more flexibly and virtually, arguing that existing government budgets are already insufficient to meet various stakeholder demands. You see many opportunities here to drastically improve citizens' lives, but you don't know how to grasp them.

While planning and deciding based on imperfect information is inherent to the nature of your job, increasingly your problem is having *too much* rather than *not enough* data. Moreover, your sources of high-quality information are not 'neutral': in fact, many of them are actors with considerable stakes in this issue, not in the least the private sector, profit-oriented 'pushers' of smart city technologies. You feel a desperate need to tap into the reservoir of expertise outside of your ministry, but you lack the time to reach out to various potential collaborators, and your co-workers and their managers lack the mindset and skillset to build collaborative capacity. To make things worse, some of them have a history of collusion with private sector vendors. The new government got elected on a strong 'ethics in public office' platform – a key concern among the new, rising middle-class electorate – and your minister emphasized the need for your department to adhere to the highest ethical standards in his first major address to you and your colleagues.

At the same time, many young 'Gen Z' citizens are more than eager to voice their opinions and provide suggestions for what their ideal future city should look like. Being tech-savvy and skilled at finding and processing information about global best practices – much more so than the majority of your own team – they provide daily policy suggestions through the interactive online platforms established by the new government as part of their 'citizen-centric' campaign branding. As creative and inspiring as some of these citizen contributions are, they lack any basis in reality, or even a basic understanding of affordability and implementability. Because of this, you're increasingly annoyed by how your minister brings up their ideas in meetings, seemingly criticizing you and your team for lack of progress.

Can you look at other developing countries in the region for advice or best practices? Not really, as they've recently radically reversed their immigration and urban development policies due to political backlash against overcrowded and oversized cities, adopting a 'back to basics' political discourse opposite to that in your country. The recently elected prime minister of a neighbouring country that's just ahead of yours in development even declared the smart city concept dead in a newspaper interview last week titled 'Dumb cities: road to nowhere'. All this is part of a political agenda aimed at restoring the primacy of political decision-making at the national instead of the local level. You want to avoid the mistakes made in other countries and you believe in the immense importance and opportunities of smart secondary cities for the economic future of your nation, yet sometimes you can't help but think that the plans are 'too big to fail' before you've even started to draw them.

Your next meeting with the minister is in two weeks. Several questions keep you awake at night:

- *At what stage* do I engage various actors to assist me in developing my policy framework while remaining 'in charge' at the same time?
- *Which actors* do I engage and how do I manage them in a collaborative fashion?
- If I engage private sector stakeholders *now*, will I be able to exclude them again *later*?
- How do I *process* all available data and available ideas?
- Can I ignore some of the 'fantasies' of voters without coming off as an inward-oriented bureaucrat or antagonizing my minister?
- How do I even *make sense of the overabundance of data out there* without having the technological savvy or personnel capacity to leverage useful information?
- What kind of a delivery process can I *design* given the disparities between political ambitions, available budget, and staff capabilities?
- How do I even *determine the right course of action* in a region and domain that is changing so rapidly that smart city plans of today may indeed create dumb cities ten years from now?

Megatrends and managerial demands

This case captures just some of the key demands and dilemmas that public managers in a rapidly developing country in 2025 will most likely face. Many of the megatrends distinguished in chapter 'Trends and Drivers' all come into play here at the same time: technology and big data, demographic changes, urbanization, environmental issues, fiscal constraints, and assertive citizens participating in policy planning and demanding the highest ethical standards. The protagonist in the case is not only confronted with her own inadequacies and unknown unknowns, but constrained by organizational and human capabilities in her department. Moreover, she needs to forecast various scenarios to tap in to the expertise of potential collaborators, and to create and maintain trust in what will be a complex long-term process. If these were subsequent, linear demands she would at least be able to meet them in due course based on her considerable experience and skillset. She could prioritize and sequence 'actionables'.

However, the key issue here is that she has to make various interrelated hard choices at the same time while confronting and persuading competing stakeholders, amid an ambiguous and unreliable political operating environment with unpredictable horizons. In short, our case protagonist is faced with a 'cascade' (Noordegraaf 2007) of *multi-faceted and contradictory demands* which, in turn, result in complex *public management dilemmas*. A key question here is to what extent public managers are actually able and capable to affect – let alone drive – these dynamics. Often, they will feel as if these demands are simply placed upon them by 'higher powers' and 'larger forces', including political bosses and their electoral pressures and promises, or international market and governance actors. How can they move from default to crafted mode (Gratton 2011)? How can they ensure they are 'at the wheel' rather than 'under fire' (Noordegraaf 2004) and turn demands and dilemmas into opportunities?

Not all of these demands and dilemmas are necessarily unique or new. Indeed, the observation that 'competing values' (Cameron and Quinn 1989: 32) and 'competing logics' (Noordegraaf 2015: 64) dominate managerial environments has been around for quite some time. Various authors have addressed the 'multiplicity' and 'ambiguity' of public sector settings before (March and Olsen 1989; Brandsen *et al.* 2007: 1). However, the magnitude and interrelatedness of 21ˢᵗ century trends and drivers means that new demands and dilemmas will be:

- the *norm* rather than the exception;
- mutually *reinforcing and exacerbating* (with decreasing predictability);
- affecting *all types* of public managers rather than just those at the very top; and
- affecting the *nature and practice and not just the content* of (public management) work.

The megatrends identified in chapter 'Trends and Drivers' have a variety of consequences for managers. Vielmetter and Sell (2014: 141) use the concept of *reinforcers* in pointing out 'powerful consequences that result from – and are thus reinforced by – two or more megatrends in tandem. The nature of these reinforcers is such that they are intimately linked and therefore overlap to a degree.' Their reinforcers show a remarkable overlap with future challenges for public managers identified in various recent writings, with different authors adding their own flavours, accents, and priorities (e.g., Dickinson and Sullivan 2014; Melbourne School of Government 2013; Needham and Mengan 2014, 2016; 't Hart 2014b). Box 4.1 lists a number of commonly observed consequences and challenges produced by global megatrends.

Staying true to the global ambition and scope of this book, I formulate my own final set of seven specific – interrelated and partly

---

Box 4.1 Global megatrends: consequences for public managers

- **stakeholder dynamics,** a multiplication of – more ambiguous – interests that must be taken into consideration;
- **collaborative modes of working** in co-producing stakeholder networks requiring power sharing, use of new media, and open innovation;
- **power shifts away from traditional to new authorities,** and more frequent and sudden authority shifts from one leader or constituency to another;
- **increased legitimacy and performance requirements** towards an increasingly assertive, savvy, and scrutinizing array of stakeholder networks;
- **new working practices, the emergence of new types of work, working, and workers** due to technological revolutions, changing attitudes towards work, and new generations of employees;
- **pressures for smarter organizing and budgeting** due to scarcity of talent and natural resources and the use of advanced technology in an era of low growth and austerity;
- **ethicization,** a demand for the highest ethical standards from organizations and their leaders.

Sources: Dickinson and Sullivan 2012; Needham and Meegan 2014; 't Hart 2014b; Vielmetter and Sell 2014.

---

overlapping – demands applying to public managers that structure the remainder of this chapter. They apply to public managers in both developed and developing, and more or less democratic settings. I realize such a list is always arbitrary and may look different five years from now. However, given the aspiration for a longer shelf life for this book, the demands are broad and universal in nature, and their salience is broadly shared among experts and scholars. Their specification and contextualization takes place in the next seven chapters, each of which is dedicated to one demand.

When navigating the map of megatrends and the managerial demands they produce in Figure 4.1, five 'navigational instructions' should be kept in mind:

- Each of the demands is a consequence of multiple – usually three or four – megatrends taken together, with technological revolutions ('all is networked') and increasing citizen demands ('great expectations') playing a key nodal role as they appear across almost all demands.
- Due to their evolving and multiple nature, megatrends cannot always be neatly separated from each other, their causes, and their – often unpredictable, non-linear, and disruptive – consequences.

FIGURE 4.1   Map of megatrends and managerial demands

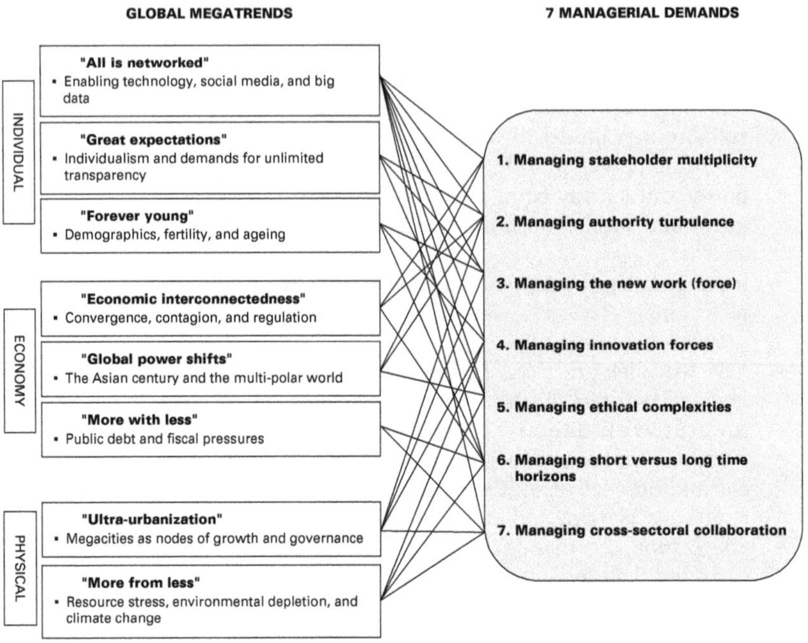

GLOBAL MEGATRENDS   7 MANAGERIAL DEMANDS

INDIVIDUAL

"All is networked"
• Enabling technology, social media, and big data

"Great expectations"
• Individualism and demands for unlimited transparency

"Forever young"
• Demographics, fertility, and ageing

ECONOMY

"Economic interconnectedness"
• Convergence, contagion, and regulation

"Global power shifts"
• The Asian century and the multi-polar world

"More with less"
• Public debt and fiscal pressures

PHYSICAL

"Ultra-urbanization"
• Megacities as nodes of growth and governance

"More from less"
• Resource stress, environmental depletion, and climate change

1. Managing stakeholder multiplicity

2. Managing authority turbulence

3. Managing the new work (force)

4. Managing innovation forces

5. Managing ethical complexities

6. Managing short versus long time horizons

7. Managing cross-sectoral collaboration

- Megatrends 'trickle down' to the micro-level operating environment of public managers and have meso-level implications for how public organizations, regulations, and policies should be organized; these will be discussed in the next seven chapters, in which each demand is deconstructed.
- Obviously, some megatrends impact certain types of managers more than others: macro-economic shifts and developments only indirectly affect the operating environments of the majority of public managers.
- Demands are phrased in terms of 'managing' rather than merely 'dealing with', to emphasize that various publics will expect – and legislation and policies demand – that public managers will take active control.

Indeed, a key message here is that *the crafting 21st century public manager* will manage demands whereas the *default public manager in the 21st century* will be managed by them (cf. Gratton 2011). The chapters on demands will provide public managers with ideas, best practices, and tools to seize the opportunities that emerge alongside the demands.

Table 4.1 breaks down the seven demands in specifying *who should be managed* – various, sometimes interlocked stakeholders and players who have different roles and wear several hats at the same time like in our

TABLE 4.1 Demands, subjects, and objects

Demand	*Manage* who?	*Manage* what?
1. Managing stakeholder multiplicity	• Fluid stakeholder networks • Multiple publics • Advocates and adversaries	• Multi-faceted, volatile communication processes • Various media platforms and dynamics • International, regional, and local agendas and arenas
2. Managing authority turbulence	• Concerned, cynical, and impatient citizens • Frequent new bosses • Individualized, assertive workforce	• Anti-collectivism and anti-authoritarianism • Crises, emergencies, and revolts • Participatory policy process designs • Performance (rankings, branding)
3. Managing the new work(force)	• Individualized, selective workforce • New generations • Near-retirees • (Reverse) mentors	• Mobile and virtual work(places) • Protean careers • Blurred work–life boundaries • Anti-collectivism and anti-authoritarianism
4. Managing innovation forces	• Critical, tech-savvy, and ambiguous citizenry • Pressured, impatient politicians • 'Pushy' tech companies and solution providers	• Disruptive technologies • Talent and skills shortage • 'Smart' networks, policies, and solutions • Arms race for innovation • Rare specializations
5. Managing ethical complexities	• Critical, tech-savvy, and ambiguous citizenry • New generations • Individualized, assertive workforce	• Value-based practices and reputations • (International and networked) ethical frameworks, codes, and rules • Sustainable models and performance • Social media and 24/7 'glass house'
6. Managing short versus long time horizons	• Planet • Future generations • Ageing populations • Pressured, impatient politicians	• Foresight tools and scenario-planning • International agendas, treaties, and arenas • Looming disasters, crises, and scarcity • Contested budgets
7. Managing cross-sectoral collaboration	• Diverse and diffuse sets of colleagues and clients • Autonomous co-producers • Non-governmental funders	• Co-production and co-creation networks • Outsourcing of key functions • Complex supply chains • Private sector contracts, morals, and interests

case – and *what should be managed*, in terms of actions, practices, technologies, policies, and sentiments (cf. CSIRO 2013; Vielmetter and Sell 2014). Obviously, subjects and objects overlap across the seven managerial demands.

Often, these demands create various dilemmas and paradoxes for public managers, as illustrated by the introductory case. In this light, Noordegraaf (2004: 26) uses the concept of 'intervention trap' to typify the simultaneous demands and constraints on public managers to 'act firmly', perform, and make decisions. At the same time, savvy, entrepreneurial, and eager public managers will have unprecedented opportunities to improve public sector performance. They can overcome restraints by embracing technology and engaging an ever-wider range of stakeholders. In fact, this is what makes them 21st century public managers. So, rather than focusing on problems and challenges alone, we choose to distinguish seven *clusters* of demands, dilemmas, and opportunities.

Seven clusters of demands, dilemmas, and opportunities

Demand 1: Managing stakeholder multiplicity

The Deputy Secretary in the case faces a multitude of stakeholders, each with multiple – and ambiguous – demands, attitudes, and styles. In addition, as the case aims to illustrate, stakeholders will increasingly form ever-changing allegiances. Potential supporters such as the international financiers and the new tech-savvy citizens may turn into adversaries almost overnight if they are not constantly courted and included in important practices and processes (Bryson 2004). Managing such increasing stakeholder multiplicity not only requires extraordinary communication and collaboration skills and a responsive mindset, but also antennae and astuteness to separate claimants from influencers (Mitchell *et al.* 1997: 859). What may appear to be a 'dormant' or 'dependent' stakeholder one day can turn into a 'dangerous' or 'dominant' one almost overnight (1997: 875–876). The newly elected prime minister in the neighbouring country serves as an example here.

In fact, *stakeholders themselves will often be the antennae of public managers.* Public managers will need to leverage their positions in large, complex, international networks of other stakeholders. Two different types of such groups in the case are the migrant workers who will be drawn to the urban clusters as they emerge, and the citizen groups engaging in the online policy process. Each of these groups will have different preferences, and 21st century public managers will need antennae in their networks to proactively manage them.

Box 4.2 shows the key dilemma and opportunity, and the potential trade-offs, resulting from demand 1.

Box 4.2 Demand 1: Managing stakeholder multiplicity

Dilemma: Delivering a clear, consistent message to an increasingly disparate set of audiences with different and inconsistent demands.

Opportunity: Leveraging unlimited channels, audiences, and supporters to 'brand', communicate, and propagate policy goals, and channel fit between supply and demand through targeted messaging.

Potential trade-offs:

- Balance resources between ensuring support of current stakeholder allegiance and scanning and courting potentially supportive (but currently opposing or indifferent) stakeholders.
- Balance the risk of overlooking future 'main players' and that of losing key supporters.
- Focus on policy quality first and on framing and branding later, keeping stakeholders at bay during the process; or involve them in formulating the message from the start.
- Uphold message consistency and integrity while adjusting content and framing for various audiences with potentially conflicting demands.

Demand 2: Managing authority turbulence

Our case protagonist has formal authority and power but her actual ability to influence decision-making seems limited. In addition, her operating environment is characterized by assertive stakeholders demanding visible performance and delivery amid political dynamics at home and abroad. These characteristics allude to a broader global phenomenon. Both more traditional, hierarchical societies and advanced democracies experience a decrease in the self-evidence of authority and seniority: *authority will increasingly have to be earned through performance and delivery* ('t Hart 2014b). Increasing individualism, value pluralism, and the rise of the 'assertive citizen' are key here (Needham and Mengan 2014). This cluster of trends has three consequences for public managers as shown in the case:

- *Citizens and other stakeholders* – the Gen Z 'netizens' and international investors and vendors – will demand ever more insights into and transparency about policy choices and delivery.
- *Colleagues and subordinates* – the team members who lack 21st century skills but see themselves as important collaborators anyway – will demand to be managed in a participatory manner and through informal leadership rather than hierarchy and seniority.
- *You* will have to account for your performance any time of day, without being able to hide behind rank, role, or rationale. Just as your

---

Box 4.3 Demand 2: Managing authority turbulence

Dilemma: Displaying collaborative leadership by handing over power while projecting authority and control.

Opportunity: Overcoming hierarchical restraints and structures by sharing accountability to unleash potential for collective and collaborative ownership of programmes and policies.

Potential trade-offs:

- Hand over power, authority, and responsibility to co-workers, subordinates, and external stakeholders to increase ownership and diversity of viewpoints at the risk of being outplayed, outnumbered, or perceived as inaccessible or old-fashioned.
- Treat stakeholders as equals and make structural and serious efforts to incorporate their information, 'knowledge', and viewpoints into your decision-making, or limit their participation and engagement to the advisory and evaluation phase.

---

colleagues eschew traditional bureaucratic structures, you will most likely be reluctant to accept such traditional bureaucratic behaviour from *your superiors*. Think about the interplay between you and your minister with his lack of expertise and his erratic decision-making behaviour.

Authors have used concepts such as 'distributed leadership' (Gronn 2002: 423) or 'altocentric leadership' (Vielmetter and Sell 2014: 162) to indicate behaviours associated with managing employees more horizontally. However, such perspectives sometimes underestimate the ever-present pressures on managers to appear 'in control' and 'at the wheel' (Noordegraaf 2015), as illustrated in the case. Box 4.3 shows the key dilemmas and opportunity, and the potential trade-offs, resulting from demand 2.

Demand 3: Managing the new work(force)

The Deputy Secretary is forced and pressured to adopt new ways of working and accommodate world views and attitudes of newer generations in both her internal and external operating environments. Indeed, various reinforcing megatrends have created a new 'class' of employees who will make unprecedented demands on employers and ask 'what's in it for me?' (Deloitte 2016; Holmes 2012; Twenge and Campbell 2012) Indeed, much has been written about the changing workforce, consisting increasingly of Gen Y or even Gen Z individuals, as well the changing *nature of work itself* (Gratton 2011; McKinsey 2013). New generations and new ways of

> ### Box 4.4 Demand 3: Managing the new work(force)
>
> *Dilemma:* Accommodating the changing nature of work and workers while controlling, monitoring, and ensuring delivery.
>
> *Opportunity:* Getting 'the job done' 24/7 while saving on office space, costs, red tape, and procedural constraints, to create truly post-bureaucratic environments that engage and retain new generations for public sector work.
>
> *Potential trade-offs:*
>
> - Manage, motivate, and retain newer generations of employees with 'protean' career ambitions and blurred boundaries between personal and professional lives in a resource-constrained environment, while maintaining a certain level of control and bureaucracy.
> - Closely manage and mentor incoming employees at the risk of alienating and demotivating them, or give them maximal freedom and autonomy at the risk of delays and failures (with you taking the blame).
> - Allow co-workers to work outside the office, minimizing meetings and physical interaction to maximize performance and work–life balance while risking continuance of delivery, or maintain traditional office behaviours even though technology will eventually make these behaviours obsolete.

working may immensely improve public sector performance. As the case illustrates, however, it is far from evident that bureaucracies will accommodate or are able to fund newer generations' demand for more flexible, mobile, and techy work environments. Moreover, public personnel systems ensure that tenured senior employees with potentially very different preferences will remain in service for many years to come.

Concomitantly, a young, educated, assertive, and tech-savvy citizenry wants to see its complaints and requests heard, and its ideas and viewpoints incorporated in policy proposals regardless of whether they're implementable or affordable, as the case illustrates. Like our Deputy Secretary, public managers will have to find ways to meaningfully integrate new ways of working and new types of workers while maintaining key structures and obligations. Box 4.4 shows the key dilemma and opportunity, and the potential trade-offs, resulting from demand 3.

Demand 4: Managing innovation forces

Back again to the Deputy Secretary in the case, who has to substantively upgrade the entire system with which cities will be governed and maintained in the decades to come. While developing these ambitious plans, she is constantly told to be as bold as possible and incorporate new, ever-developing and improving technologies, while being constrained by budgetary and capability factors. Moreover, the costs of some resources and materials may explode while continuously developing technologies make others more affordable, depending on the moment of adoption of the innovation. This produces 'innovator's dilemmas' (Christensen 1997: 1). She can't even imagine how to process, budget, or incorporate many of the technologies and applications needed 15 years from now to enable these urban centres to function and thrive. More fundamentally, however, she experiences tensions between the need for bureaucracies to provide stability, legality, and predictability (see Van der Wal 2008), and external pressures to innovate (Hartley 2015; Hartley *et al.* 2013). Perhaps public agencies cannot really innovate *by nature*?

Moreover, only some of her current staff and team leaders have the capabilities and skills to practise collaborative and entrepreneurial public management (De Vries *et al.* 2016; Vij and O'Leary 2012) in order to leverage the 'crowdsourcing' (Meijer 2014) of ideas from tech-savvy citizens. So, she is caught between a rock and a hard place: in order to innovate, she would have to invest in technology, training, and recruitment, and promote adaptability and courage. However, as this will take time and her minister is impatient, she may as well decide to spend the country's sparse means on external support and 'hard' infrastructure. Box 4.5 shows the key dilemma and opportunity, and the potential trade-offs, resulting from demand 4.

Box 4.5 Demand 4: Managing innovation forces

Dilemma: Being adaptive, entrepreneurial, and experimental amid severe limitations and ambiguous expectations.

Opportunity: Piloting and experimenting with new policies, programmes, and tools faster, cheaper, and easier than ever before within increasingly agile, enabling environments.

Potential trade-offs:

- Blend the roles of entrepreneur, regulator, expert, and institutional preserver in addressing 'disruptive' innovations and innovation pressures.
- Prioritize IT resources over human resources with long-term investment strategies from the viewpoint that the latter can increasingly be automated, while risking long-term, irreplaceable loss of institutional memory.
- Heavily invest in employee skills and capabilities through lifelong learning strategies with little short-term pay-off to show to political masters.
- Continue to apply traditional budgetary strategies amid volatile electoral, innovation, and budgetary cycles, or budget more adaptively and experimentally.

Demand 5: Managing ethical complexities

The case illustrates that the demand for ethical governance is a global phenomenon (Cooper and Menzel 2013). The combination of meg-atrends will continuously enhance this demand, also within fairly closed, top-down, or authoritarian governance regimes, enforced by electoral promises from politicians who may be ethically ambiguous themselves as shown in the case. Moreover, the increasing transparency requirements of citizens, combined with their savvy to turn over every (digital) stone to find compromising information about public leaders, create more pres-sures for leaders, such as our Deputy Secretary, to pass various ethics tests convincingly (Lawton *et al.* 2013). How will she be able to pass the famous 'front page test' (Kaptein 2006) when evaluating or assessing her decisions, when citizens create their own version of the front page on a daily basis, for everyone to see?

More fundamentally, as she is simultaneously pressured by her politi-cal master, citizen aspirations, international competition, and various innovation forces, the Deputy Secretary's operating environment will be characterized by constant conflict between key values such as privacy, equity, accountability, and sustainability (Van der Wal *et al.* 2011, 2015). New technologies provide unlimited innovation potential, but should she necessarily pursue everything that becomes technologically possible?

Box 4.6 Demand 5: Managing ethical complexities

Dilemma: Leading and managing ethically amid and in front of ever more scrutinizing publics with competing value sets.

Opportunity: Becoming a role model by going beyond the legal and ethi-cal minimum; and engaging social media and citizenry proactively and openly to (re)gain legitimacy.

Potential trade-offs:

- Exceed demanded ethical standards and lead by example through continuous upgrading and enforcement of ethics policies, while risk-ing a decrease in efficiency and effectiveness.
- Meet ethical demands of key stakeholders strategically and selectively to maximize efficiency and effectiveness, with the risk of being 'too late'.
- Select collaborators and colleagues based on 'values fit', ethical atti-tudes, and image rather than capabilities and added value, to maintain values, standards, and culture that will withstand ethical scrutiny of a network, chain, or agency.

How can she stand firm against eager private sector solution pushers if their interests clash with those of needy citizens? How can she remain politically neutral when she engages the skills, capital, and ideas of so many different stakeholders, while loyally serving her new political boss as well as her country?

Although some of these questions need to be addressed in the political arena, they also affect her. After all, the various publics involved will formulate positions, sometimes too hasty and too harsh, towards these ethical issues, and will demand a clear position from her and her team. To complicate matters further, the international financiers, the smart solution providers, the blue collar and the tech-savvy, educated citizens, will each have different, competing, and sometimes unfair stances on ethical issues; each and every one of them will scrutinize our Deputy Secretary with an ever-increasing toolbox at their disposal. Box 4.6 shows the key dilemma and opportunity, and the potential trade-offs, resulting from demand 5.

Demand 6: Managing short versus long time horizons

The case illustrates how our lead character has to manage short-term timelines – 'get me a comprehensive policy proposal in two weeks!' – alongside long-term horizons – 'project the characteristics of a smart city 20 years from now in a rapidly developing context'. Public managers have always had to balance short-term and long-term planning and performance. However, this demand will become more critical but at the same time more paradoxical, as turbulence will continue while foresight tools and methods to deliver solutions and run predictive models will rapidly develop. To meet the demand, our pressured Deputy Secretary needs to combine various skills and logics: enabling the politician to score and appear to be 'doing something' amid a never-ending news cycle, along with planning ahead, preserving a policy legacy, and preparing successors by preserving institutional knowledge and overall resilience.

In this light, Ho (2010: 6) suggests that in addressing wicked problems, public managers 'face a choice of either becoming de facto insurers of the worst outcomes resulting from inaction in these areas, or addressing these challenges ahead of time with the boldness, exploratory mindset and innovation of an entrepreneur'. However, how much room does our lead character really have to be entrepreneurial and explore long-term scenarios and experiments, given her critical audience, timelines, and budgetary constraints? Box 4.7 shows the key dilemma and opportunity, and the potential trade-offs, resulting from demand 6.

> ## Box 4.7 Demand 6: Managing short versus long time horizons
>
> *Dilemma:* Integrating and balancing long-term thinking and planning with the immediacy and volatility of the digital era and of politics.
>
> *Opportunity:* Anticipating and operationalizing future challenges and outcomes better than ever before with accessible foresight and scenario-building techniques, aided by big-data analytics and open software.
>
> *Potential trade-offs:*
>
> - Prioritize short-term deliverables and quick wins as they will produce maximum credit, even though the VUCA environment may render current plans obsolete or undesirable in just a few years.
> - Clearly contrast between managerial and political roles and objectives, trusting that political masters will ultimately appreciate that public managers advocate the 'long view'.
> - Adjust the planning to the politics and media rather than the other way around, or focus on well thought-through, evidence-based strategies first and garner support from key players later.

Demand 7: Managing cross-sectoral collaboration

To meet the various and demands and pressures facing our Deputy Secretary of Planning, she is forced to collaborate extensively with a variety of stakeholders: to attract additional financial resources, to tap into innovative ideas and external expertise, to get buy-in from unfamiliar stakeholders, and to roll out large-scale implementation and delivery chains. Indeed, the case reiterates what most colleagues in our field have established for some time now: 21st century public service delivery will be co-created and co-produced in cross-sectoral networks of public, semi-public, private, and civic actors (Agranoff 2006; Alford and O'Flynn 2012).

Government is no longer *the only actor*, but merely *one of the actors* producing public services and outcomes (Rhodes 2016). Because of this, the public manager in our case will have to master networking and teamworking skills (Klijn *et al.* 2010) along with abilities to manage high-risk, partly unpredictable 'complex contracts' (Malatesta and Van Slyke 2015: 665) with both the international financiers and the private players involved.

From extensive research on networks and public-private partnerships of various natures (Boyer *et al.* 2015; Greve and Hodge 2011; Bouckaert and Halligan 2008), we know she is most likely to encounter classical principal-agent problems alongside disputes about objectives and outcomes. Obviously, trust is a factor that is as intangible as it is hard to manage, particularly in the context of past collusion between public sector colleagues and private sector actors like in our case. At the same time, tackling wicked management and policy problems collaboratively seems the only viable way forward. Box 4.8 shows the key dilemma and opportunity, and the potential trade-offs, resulting from demand 7.

Box 4.8 Demand 7: Managing cross-sectoral collaboration

Dilemma: Managing horizontal partnerships while balancing trust, contracts, power relations, and information asymmetry.

Opportunity: Enabling stakeholders to participate throughout the policy cycle with huge potential for shared ownership, bottom-up governance, complementary capabilities, and creative solutions.

Potential trade-offs:

- Find ways to educate assertive citizens and political bosses that public managers are no longer the *only* but rather *one* among many governance actors, each with their own strengths and authoritative positions, or argue for a resurgence of political-administrative leadership in driving policy solutions.
- Talk the collaborative talk but walk the hierarchical walk by anchoring relations through contracts, building in safeguards, checks, and balances, and making sure partners are 'dispensable'.
- Build expertise and capacity internally by enhancing knowledge management systems and recruitment and remuneration strategies to remain a key player at considerable cost, or operate a lean and flexible core agency while maximizing relations with external partners, contractors, and consultants.

What lies ahead

Public managers and the organizations they run require a variety of traditional, upgraded, and new roles, attributes, and competencies to turn the demands and dilemmas outlined in this chapter into opportunities. Chapters 'Managing Stakeholder Multiplicity', 'Managing Authority Turbulence', 'Managing the New Work(force)', 'Managing Innovation Forces', 'Managing Ethical Complexities', 'Managing Short Versus Long Time Horizons' and 'Managing Cross-sectoral Collaboration' will discuss these roles, attributes, and competencies, structured around the seven key managerial demands discussed here. Each chapter starts with a central case that illustrates the demand and the tough questions it produces for public managers. We begin our discussion of demands in the next chapter by unravelling the issue of *managing stakeholder multiplicity* while proposing and evaluating tools, platforms, techniques, and competencies to bind and communicate to diffuse stakeholder networks.

Chapter 5

Managing Stakeholder Multiplicity

Find the appropriate balance of competing claims by various groups of stakeholders. All claims deserve consideration but some claims are more important than others.

(Warren Bennis, leadership guru)

Who deserves to be a claimant?

Imagine being a senior manager at Shell UK, part of Royal Dutch Shell, one of the largest corporations in the world, in 1991. You have just decided to decommission the massive oil platform Brent Spar, positioned in the North Sea. After conducting around 30 different studies, and engaging various local governments and NGOs, you and your team decide that sinking the platform in deep water is the *Best Practicable Environmental Option (BPEO)*, as opposed to horizontal decomposition on land. Due to the platform's size and the damage to some of the storage tanks, moving the Brent Spar to shore for decomposition on land would be complicated, costly – US$69 million versus US$18 million for the sinking option – and potentially damaging to the environment.

Convinced you have adequately compared the options, you send a BPEO concept to the UK Department of Trade and Industry (DTI), which licenses the operation in February 1995, after consulting the other four governments in the Associations of Nations around the North Sea and the European Commission, none of which object. You and your bosses are mindful of the sensitivities surrounding this decision given that no one has ever decommissioned a platform this way. However, you have gone out of your way in doing your due diligence.

Now imagine you are an ambitious campaign manager at Greenpeace, the largest lobby movement for environmental preservation, with a global membership of over 3 million. Eyeing the Brent Spar process very carefully, your colleagues sent a report to DTI in September 1994, titled *No Ground for Dumping*. You support the report that claims sinking the Brent Spar will set a dangerous precedent for the planned decommissioning of 130 other platforms in the North Sea, and the environmental damage will be much larger than Shell suggests. Despite various attempts to participate, you and your colleagues were not actively involved in Shell's decision-making process. You feel it is about time for someone to stake a claim in the issue on behalf of the environment, a stakeholder in her own right. On 30 April 1995, four of your colleagues enter the platform from the ship *Altair*. They start broadcasting from the platform, with mainstream media eagerly jumping in. Immediately, public opinion begins to shift.

Now imagine you are the communications director at the German Ministry of the Environment, Nature Conservation, and Nuclear Safety (BMU). On 9 May 1995, your minister announces she feels she has to publicly speak out against Shell's decision; one week later, the entire opposition in the UK Parliament denounces the plan; followed by all European ministers of trade, foreign affairs, and the environment just one day later. You are taken aback by the sudden change of views. Didn't all governments involved sign off on the decision a few months ago after two years of careful examination and reporting by Shell UK? Hadn't all sorts of stakeholders been involved in the process?

While Shell UK engages in legal procedures against Greenpeace and starts to tow away the platform to North Feni Ridge, the situation deteriorates rapidly. Petrol station revenue in Germany declines by 50 per cent, and 50 stations are damaged, two are bombed, and one is shot at. Greenpeace occupies the platform a second time in June 1995, and simultaneously publishes the results of its sampling of the platform, which show that it contains 5,000 tons of oil and a large number of toxic substances. On 20 June 1995, Shell UK revokes its decision to sink the platform. Greenpeace calls the decision 'a victory for everyone, a victory for common sense and a victory for the environment'. Shell, on the other hand, speaks of 'a victory of the heart over the head', insisting that sinking remains the best environmental option.

Now imagine you are a senior public manager with the DTI in the UK. You most likely feel overwhelmed and perhaps even betrayed. You advise your minister to warn Shell that approval of the decomposition is no longer guaranteed, and demand additional explanation and study. Indeed, Shell requests the Norwegian consulting firm DNV to audit the platform in July and check its earlier findings. To your surprise, however, the audit shows that the measures Greenpeace used were inaccurate (it had taken samples from the top of the pipelines and not the supply tanks), resulting in another shift in public opinion, particularly in conservative media, this time away from Greenpeace. What was happening here?

On 5 September 1995, Greenpeace apologizes to Shell UK for its sampling errors, admitting its claims were incorrect. The reputed British newspaper *The Guardian* – a staunch ally of Greenpeace during the affair – publishes a comment two days later, stating that almost all of the scientists it had interviewed considered sinking to be the least damaging decommissioning option. In January 1998 Shell decides to decompose and recycle the platform on the Norwegian coast. In the end, the costs of the operation amount to US$100 million. Shell President Cor Herkströter proclaims that global companies will increasingly need a 'licence to operate' from society to be able to conduct their business.

All managers involved in the affair are likely to be dazzled, frustrated, and perhaps even angry at this stage. Can they still rely on evidence and data in deciding the best way forward in future decisions? Can they afford to act decisively at all, or should they become much more careful in anticipating public opinion and powerful minority views? Apparently, long-term allies can turn into adversaries in just a few weeks. Indeed, how can they ever be sure again in determining who make up their *authorizing environment*? (Disclaimer: *This case description is based on actual events. The managers described, however, are fictional, and any feelings or actions attributed to them are completely hypothetical.*)

Now fast forward to today's social media environment, where small players amplify their claims to global reach. This environment further intensifies the key issues in the Brent Spar case. How do public managers define who has a 'stake' in their strategic objectives and operations, legitimate or not? How do they determine who may become crucial allies or adversaries, if not today, maybe just two weeks from now, and how do they prevent staunch allies from walking over to 'the other side'? How do they establish the dominant frame instead of finding themselves on the defensive? Are agencies adequately equipped to develop antennae for assessing stakeholder dynamics, especially in an era of social media, big data, and a never-ending news cycle? Do they invest in new skills and capabilities like stakeholder analysis, storytelling, framing and branding, and video-editing and production?

Managing stakeholder multiplicity

The case dynamics between businesses, NGOs, and governments powerfully demonstrate why managing an unpredictable landscape of stakeholders – and one that is constantly changing in terms of prominence, allegiance, and stance towards policies, programmes, and objectives – will be a key demand of public managers in the 21st century. It is useful to note that even without Twitter and Facebook, Greenpeace managed to damage Shell's reputation in just a few weeks and alter a major public-private collaborative decision-making process. Stakeholders have added a wide range of media tools and data collection opportunities to their arsenals since the Brent Spar affair, further enhancing their abilities to support and obstruct managerial objectives. Vielmetter and Sell (2014) recently introduced the term 'stakeholder proliferation' to point out these increased stakeholder communication abilities, the growing number of stakeholders that organizations have to deal with, and the increased frequency of interactions they will face.

But there is more to it than just growing numbers, frequencies, and means. *Stakeholders themselves, and the networks in which they operate, are increasingly fluid, dynamic, and ambiguous.* New technologies and social structures allow stakeholders to take on many, often seemingly contradictory, roles at the same time. Today, environmental NGOs may partner up with business interests to fight public managers on regulation they perceive to be in the way of collaborative partnerships to promote sustainability. The next week, the same NGO may advocate for other policies proposed by the same public manager. Just think back to the European governments in the case who moved from supporting and collaborating with Shell to being adversaries within three weeks, all due to a clever 'branding' campaign by Greenpeace, taking in *The Guardian* and other reputed media. In a sense, stakeholder behaviour increasingly reflects the ambiguity and multiplicity characterizing managerial work in the public domain (Brandsen *et al.* 2007; Chun and Rainey 2005; Noordegraaf 2015).

Furthermore, the technological and societal revolutions presented in chapter 'Trends and Drivers' not only diffuse stakeholder networks, allegiances, and needs; they also provide even the smallest, underfunded, minority stakeholder with powerful weapons to win the war for public opinion and information framing. A single, savvy individual may prove as powerful as Greenpeace in the years to come. As a result, public managers will have to manage a manifold variety of stakeholders, with multiple allegiances, multiple agendas, and multiple means to make their claims. Moreover, multiplicity implies that public managers have to be able to combine a variety of roles and skills to assess and co-opt divergent and opportunistic claimants. In short: *managing stakeholder multiplicity* will be a key 21ˢᵗ century managerial demand.

Mapping, prioritizing, engaging

How can public managers effectively map, classify, and prioritize in this dynamic stakeholder environment? This is a critical question, as classification and prioritization decisions largely determine engagement and participation strategies (Bryson 2004, Fung 2015; Nabatchi and Leighninger 2015). However, many of the existing tools for 'separating claimants from influencers' (Mitchell *et al.* 1997: 859) are fairly static, as they only allow for determining the power or position of particular stakeholders at a given point in time. Indeed, to explain from a managerial point of view why sensible European governments and reputable newspapers were quick and eager in supporting Greenpeace's scientific claims over Shell's (derived through over 30 studies), we need to better understand stakeholder dynamics.

Mitchell *et al.*'s (1997) seminal article proposed a typology of seven stakeholder types, which allows managers to map and assess salience dynamics depending on shifts in *power, legitimacy*, and *urgency*, as shown in Figure 5.1. Key here is the managerial perspective: stakeholders may very well consider themselves powerful, urgent, and legitimate claimants, but what matters is that public managers assess who deserves prominence and attention, now and in the future.

FIGURE 5.1   Stakeholder typology: one, two, or three attributes present

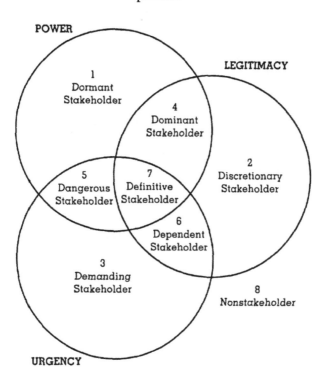

Reprinted with permission from Mitchell *et al.* 1997: 874.

Back to the case now. In the early days of the conflict, Shell managers most likely perceived Greenpeace as a discretionary stakeholder – one bearing some legitimacy but lacking the power and urgency to deserve a spot at the decision-making table. At that stage, managers may have not believed it important to reciprocate attention. In the course of just a few weeks, however, and aided by media, public opinion, and independent research capabilities, Greenpeace transitioned into a dominant stakeholder by acquiring negotiation *power*. Then, when popular and political pressures – and in some cases threats – towards Shell started to mount, they became a definitive stakeholder in Shell's operations by leveraging a sense of *urgency*. Towards the end of the process Greenpeace's *legitimacy* took a hit, propelling them back to the dangerous category. After the episode, however, Greenpeace purchased half a million Euros worth of shares in Shell so it could attend and vote at shareholder meetings, turning them back into definitive stakeholders (it sold them off again a few years later).

Clearly, 21st century public managers will have to develop a high level of sensitivity for assessing how stakeholders move across the map displayed above, *and* how they can influence the movement of stakeholders in the desired direction and acquire *exchange legitimacy* and *influence legitimacy* (Suchman 1995). Moreover, stakeholder multiplicity in a VUCA world implies that stakeholders will operate in groups and networks, sometimes being interconnected – even without intent or knowledge – around specific issues or problems.

In a useful article on stakeholder analysis, Bryson (2004) presents a variety of practical tools and visuals for analysing and engaging stakeholders, including the *stakeholder-issue interrelationship diagram*, shown here as Figure 5.2. Public managers can use this diagram to map which groups of stakeholders have an interest on certain issues, how they are related, and whether they see eye-to-eye on the issue. Bryson (2004: 37) explains:

FIGURE 5.2   Stakeholder-issue interrelationship diagram

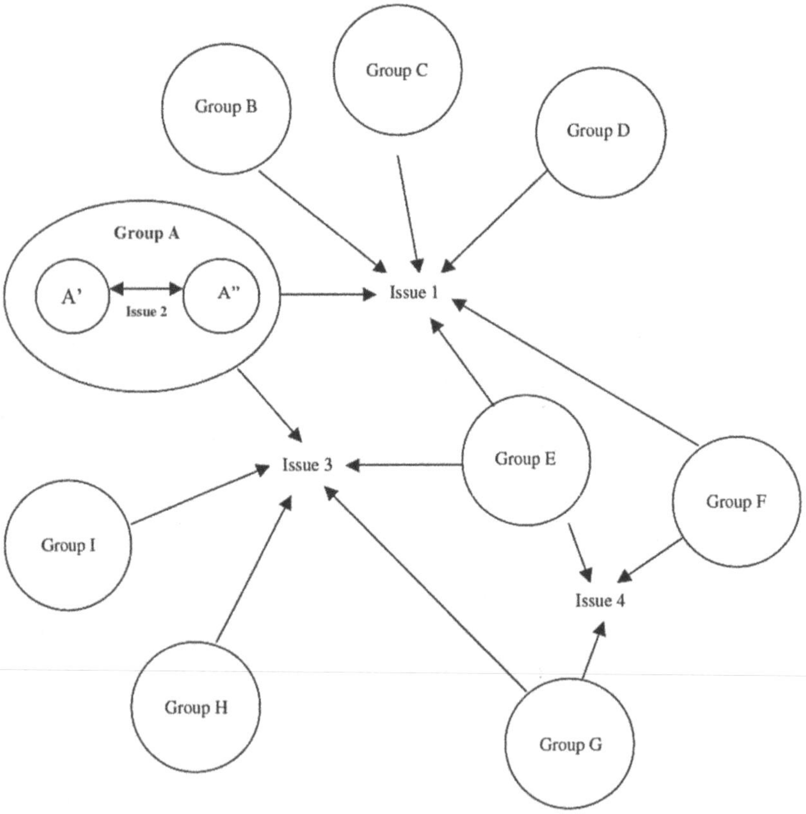

Reprinted with permission from Bryson 2004: 38.

Stakeholder-issue interrelationship diagrams help show which stakeholders have an interest in different issues, and how the stakeholders might be related to other stakeholders through their relationships with the issues. The resulting diagrams help provide some important structuring to the problem area, in which a number of actual or potential areas for cooperation – or conflict – may become apparent. An arrow on the diagram indicates that a stakeholder has an interest in an issue, though the specific interest is likely to be different from stakeholder to stakeholder, and those interests may well be in conflict. The arrows therefore should be labelled to indicate exactly what the interest is in each case.

After mapping stakeholder dynamics and interrelationships, public managers need to come up with strategies to manage their stakeholder allegiances; they need to enlarge their support base while minimizing both the number of adversaries and the adversaries' powers to derail strategies and decisions. Strategic stakeholder management ultimately aims to grow allegiances by convincing adversaries to become followers or even advocates. Table 5.1 provides a basic stakeholder allegiance worksheet that shows how managers can manage and engage stakeholders at various levels of allegiance. Interestingly, much of the 'traffic' is likely to take place towards the Indifferent category, where public managers may have to compete with other actors seeking to co-opt these stakeholders into their sphere of influence and support.

TABLE 5.1 Stakeholder allegiance worksheet

Level of allegiance	*How to manage*
Advocates	• Keep on side through active management • Use input directly in policies and proposals
Followers	• Increase understanding of their benefits • Avoid temptation to exploit or take support for granted
Indifferent	• Identify and address knowledge gaps • Keep informed and updated • Maximize efforts to prevent them from becoming blockers
Blockers	• Court and convince of mutual interests and agendas • Use conflict management techniques • Explain and frame to overcome fears
Adversaries	• Counter frames and arguments • Develop deep understanding of their values and interests

Adapted from: Manchester Metropolitan University, *Stakeholder Analysis Toolkit*, http://www2.mmu.ac.uk/media/mmuacuk/content/documents/bit/Stakeholder-analysis-toolkit-v3.pdf.

In order to maximize allegiances amid diffuse, scattered operating environments, 21st century public managers not only have to develop 'antennae' for stakeholder dynamics, they also have to become gifted storytellers and persuasive, seductive communicators. These new competencies will have to complement, and in some cases replace, more traditional ones such as 'hard' bargaining and negotiating, as governments can no longer assume they start from a position of superior authority, power, and information. Moreover, communication between public managers and stakeholders will increasingly consist of bi-directional exchanges, with public managers having to monitor, respond, and adapt, rather than simply broadcast their points of view (Mergel 2010, 2011). The remainder of this chapter unlocks these two related sets of competencies by discussing how narrating, framing, and branding are crucial in winning over and binding stakeholders, and how mastering social media is increasingly crucial in doing so successfully.

Framing, branding, storytelling

Public managers will increasingly need to develop the ability to convincingly construct and communicate a narrative about the public value they are trying to achieve, in order to persuade, rope in, and 'seduce' the stakeholder groups they want on their side. In his seminal work on public value, Moore (1995: 39) argued that constructing *a powerful narrative or story of the mission of public agencies and policies* – the public value they seek to produce for society – may be the most important aspect in ensuring that relevant authorizing environments continue to legitimize and support that mission.

Fast forward 20 years, and we're living in an era in which most teenagers are more skilled than public managers at constructing narratives suitable for current platforms. Moreover, it is ever more difficult to establish what public value looks like in a VUCA world. The *authorizing environment* that Moore (1995, 2013) argues is crucial for gaining and retaining legitimacy and support is more dynamic and unpredictable than ever before. Therefore, public managers must frame policy objectives and proposals effectively in order to win over and bind stakeholders.

Framing for public managers

In political science and the communication sciences, the topic of framing has received ample scholarly attention (e.g., Chong and Druckman 2007; Jacoby 2000), dating back to McLuhan's (1967) seminal work *The Medium Is the Message*. More recently, public administration scholars have started to show interest in framing (e.g., De Bruijn 2012; Sels and Arensman 2007). Even though most of their examples concern politicians – after all, the majority of public managers seldom engage in front-stage policy communication – their work offers useful lessons for public managers. Indeed, public managers in their various capacities prepare speeches for their political masters, formulate policy options and evaluations, and have to persuade other public, private, and civic actors to support their policies, programmes, and proposals. Moreover, the nature of the trends and demands discussed in chapters 'Trends and Drivers' and 'Demands, Dilemmas, Opportunities' will pressure public managers to engage in policy-framing and communication more directly in the years to come, resulting in a number of conflicts and dilemmas, as argued in Box 5.1.

In trying to establish effective policy frames, many public managers will continue to weigh stakeholder demands based on political guidelines or mandates in remaining *loyal and serviceable to the political leadership rather than outside parties*. Yet stakeholder dynamics will make it increasingly difficult for public managers to hide behind this rather traditional view of their role. A deputy secretary-general of a social affairs department I interviewed a few years back forcefully illustrates this dilemma (Van der Wal 2014: 1035):

> You know, I don't mind to meet wishes of stakeholders but it is up to the politicians which wishes and demands should ultimately be prioritized. For me, I have to be careful to make decisions 'wearing the right hat'; maintaining intimate and frequent ties with certain stakeholders may impede the job of a civil servant. Frankly speaking, I loathe the current 'crying with the wolves' mentality of some politicians. Organizational effectiveness and policy effectiveness are way more important than pleasing everyone.

Why is framing useful and how does it work? De Bruijn (2012) provides five key lessons.

- An effective frame sticks around, it absolves us from tough dilemmas, and we intuitively agree with it because it activates underlying core values.
- An effective frame is hard to refute, forces the opponent to go on the defence, and requires lots of evidence from the opponent but little evidence from the introducer of the frame.
- When going against a dominant frame, reframing the debate is key, using different language while building up a frame of your own.
- Effective framing is an absolute necessity for managing stakeholders in a VUCA world, characterized by policy complexity and managerial pressures that are simply too technical, apologetic, or 'boring' to explain to the average constituent or stakeholder.
- It becomes increasingly impossible and meaningless to distinguish content from frame; the frame is the content and determines the debate.

Box 5.1 Public managers as front-stage policy-framers?

Politicians engage in front-stage framing on a daily basis. Public managers, however, with the exception of key frontline actors such as police chiefs, usually communicate and 'frame' behind the scenes unless a crisis or scandal requires them to 'show up' in front of angry client groups or inquiry committees. Increasingly, however, stakeholders will demand real-time policy communication and 'storytelling' from busy and inadequately informed politicians, pressuring public managers to take up more front-stage roles during 'peace time' as well. As such, they will fulfil multiple roles and wear multiple hats.

Most governments, however, legally and politically discourage and restrain direct communication between public managers and stakeholders, particularly members of parliament or ministers from other departments. They don't speak directly to journalists, and the increasingly open media environment can be risky for public managers. A recent gag order from the UK government, for instance, prohibits civil servants from making public statements without prior consent from their minister; this event sparked outrage from the usually calm union for senior civil servants, FDA. Conversely, in the Netherlands most actors advocate loosening of existing constraints. Countries with a long-time majority political force, such as China or Singapore, also profess that administrators are politically neutral. However, public managers in such settings run much less risk of mistakenly 'advancing' one particular political ideology over others.

Most likely, communicating to stakeholders directly while maintaining political neutrality will present a continuous stream of dilemmas and conflicts for public managers, who traditionally emphasize the neutrality, impartiality, and legality of their role. Surely, new and recurrent roles discussed in previous chapters challenge traditional notions, but the question remains whether public managers can engage in strategic stakeholder communication and policy-framing without compromising important traditional roles and values. At the same time, new technologies and citizen demands mandate public managers to speak out from time to time, urging them to develop new mutual communicative rationalities with their political masters.

Sources: Baetens 2013; *The Guardian*, https://theguardian.com.

Going back to the Brent Spar case, we see now how a framing lens allows us to explain much of the case dynamics. The initial Greenpeace frame – Shell as a typical greedy corporation that makes decisions based on financial instead of environmental criteria, and opportunistically uses data and research to achieve its aims – became almost impossible to counter or refute, even when it turned out that Greenpeace had done much of the same to advance its own organizational interests. If Shell had predominantly referred to technical research processes and outcomes in order to win back support, emotional and impatient stakeholders may have perceived this as boring. This would be even more the case today.

How, then, can managers use framing tools and techniques? Table 5.2 operationalizes De Bruijn's (2012) five lessons into managerial objectives and actions that help public managers manage stakeholder multiplicity more effectively.

From framing to branding

If used effectively, framing can help public managers to dominate and direct stakeholder discourse and shift stakeholder dynamics. However, in an era of joint, cross-sectoral meaning-making, greater dependency between stakeholders and partners, and the demands of popular culture

TABLE 5.2 Framing to manage stakeholder multiplicity: objectives and actions

Managerial objective	Actions
1. Activating underlying values of different stakeholder groups	• Find out what makes multiple stakeholder groups tick • Target groups separately with frames playing into their beliefs and agendas
2. Defining debate content by setting the frame	• Approach complex issues from the start by identifying frames for different groups expected to engage in debates around the issue • Refrain from viewing framing as a 'post hoc' or even 'inferior' activity that is left to communication professionals
3. Quickly and accessibly explaining positions to stakeholder groups	• Clearly define mission and public value objectives for each programme and policy proposal (and how they advance even sceptical, opposing groups) • Develop abilities across agencies to explain objectives and decisions in one or two sentences
4. Forcing adversary stakeholder groups to go on the defensive	• 'Be first' by maintaining a continuous and active presence in relevant forums and outlets • Play into key weaknesses of opposing groups (in terms of arguments, expertise, and alliances)
5. Refuting a dominant opposing stakeholder frame	• Work with different scenarios to have frames and narratives 'shelf ready' if needed • Anticipate frames by organizing 'mock' policy debates and stakeholder dialogues (learning from the political sphere)

and media, public managers also need to utilize other communicative tools (Eshuis and Klijn 2012: 11–12). One crucial tool is the ability to successfully *brand* policies and programmes as the key products of public management. Branding involves using signs, symbols, and labels such as 'smart nation', 'smart city', 'big society', or 'joined up government' that aim to evoke a sense of belonging, positive association, and identity in various stakeholders. According to Eshuis and Klijn (2012: 3):

> Brands, being symbolic constructs that add value or meaning to something in order to distinguish it from its competitors, are increasingly used in strategies for managing perceptions in the public sector. Branding has been used to influence public perceptions of persons, places, organizations, projects, and physical objects such as transport infrastructure and buildings (see e.g., Eshuis and Edelenbos 2009; Evans 2003; Pasotti 2010). In particular, political branding and city branding are applied rather widely.

Branding has long been a successful tool in the private sector, helping distinguish successful businesses from their less successful competitors. Nowadays, it is becoming a crucial public management instrument for at least three reasons. First, public agencies need to counter existing (often negative) frames about government or bureaucracy, often associated with inertia, dysfunction, and lack of responsiveness (cf. Eshuis and Klijn 2012; Lynn 2006). For instance, right after he took office in January 2009, US President Barack Obama vowed to 'make government cool again'. The Singapore government refers on a daily basis to labels as 'smart governance' and 'smart city' to emphasize the use of big data and technology in improving the lives of citizens.

Second, public agencies are beginning to realize they can do a much better job in selling their policy proposals *and* successes in a rapidly changing media landscape where traditional 'no news is good news' media compete with highly individualized, 24/7 social media outlets. Such outlets allow public managers and politicians to obtain direct feedback from (future) policy consumers and to share success stories. In order to do this well, they have to speak the multiple languages that fit such media.

Third, successful branding positively *activates* and *binds* a wide range of stakeholders (Eshuis and Klijn 2012: 71). Images and symbols communicate the values, identities and aspirations that the brand represents (Batey 2008) rather than rational arguments, and use classical negotiation and persuasion techniques to win over stakeholders. Brands bind because they create loyalty among actors and networks (Eshuis and Klijn 2012). Therefore, branding constitutes a key competence for managing stakeholder multiplicity.

Box 5.2 identifies the components of successful policy branding by the Singapore government. The 'city in a garden' brand successfully activates and binds multiple stakeholders to contribute to the vision of Singapore

Box 5.2 Branding to bind stakeholders: Singapore as 'city in a garden'

In thinking about how to attract multinationals, foreign investment and tourism to Singapore after its independence in 1965, founding Prime Minister Lee Kuan Yew realized he could distinguish the young city state from its regional competitors by creating what he called a 'garden city'. His vision that a green and clean environment would signify that Singapore was a well-organized city, conducive to tourism and foreign investments, was a great example of early city branding.

Initially, the 'garden city' vision mostly consisted of an intensive tree-planting programme spearheaded by the Parks and Trees Unit. To involve various communities, the government introduced Tree Planting Day in 1971 as an annual event where the Prime Minister planted a tree simultaneously with students, residents, and grassroots groups across the nation. In 1975 the government enacted the Parks and Trees Act, mandating both government agencies and private developers to allocate fixed amounts of space in housing and infrastructure projects to greenery. Clearly, these stakeholders have competing interests on a range of issues, but all of them developed an affective attachment to the 'garden city' brand. Today, almost 50 per cent of Singapore's space consists of greenery, even as the city state is one of the most densely populated nations in the world. Moreover, Singapore is home to more plant and tree species than the entire USA.

In recent years, amid increased competition from other emerging Asian cities such as Hong Kong, Bangkok, and Shanghai, the government felt it had to go even further: Singapore had to become a 'city in a garden' rather than just a 'garden city'. The new vision is enacted through a set of integrated policy initiatives in the areas of mobility and sustainability, including stimulating cycling over driving, and green energy usage in office buildings. Indeed, the brand is used to 'tie together' such initiatives. In 2014, the brand got a big boost when UNESCO (the United Nations Educational, Scientific and Cultural Organization) declared Singapore's Botanic Gardens a World Heritage Site.

Clearly, various agencies and managers within the Singaporean government undertake concerted efforts to introduce and streamline policies and programmes, and constantly engage citizens and grassroots organizations through nationwide branding. Thus, successful branding is not mere 'window-dressing' or 'greenwashing'. On the contrary, effective branding by public managers serves the purpose of 'selling' policy plans and successes to multiple stakeholders with varying interests. The 'city in a garden' brand both stimulates 'whole of government' behaviour – various government agencies collaborating for shared public policy goals – and generates buy-in from a wide variety of stakeholder groups.

Sources: EResources, http://eresources.nlb.gov.sg/history; Ministry of National Development, https://app.mnd.gov.sg; National Parks, https://www.nparks.gov.sg.

as a green, clean, and well-maintained city through individual and collaborative activities, even though some of these stakeholders do not see eye-to-eye on other policy issues.

The example shows how clear public sector goals can coincide with active citizen participation and engagement to overcome the unidirectional, reactive, and control-oriented kind of policy communication, which Eshuis and Klijn (2012: 68) argue has for long been the modus operandi:

> Communicating policy was still seen as something predominantly rational, unidirectional (from government to citizens), and preferably as precisely defined and coherent as possible (clear goals and instruments). This seems not very effective in a governance context where various stakeholders have to be seduced to participate, and networks of actors have to be built and sustained. Co-production, communicating, and joint action have become more important in governance processes at the expense of implementing preformulated goals.

Indeed, others have also shown how traditional means of communication by government departments (some of which are still widely used) tend to be highly formalized, standardized, and one-directional, using 'gatekeepers' and emphasizing damage control (Meijer and Torenvlied 2014; Perrow 1986; Yates 1989; Weber 1968).

Nowadays, however, pressures from multiple, diffuse authorizing environments force governments to become more networked and multichannelled in their communications with stakeholders, using Facebook, Twitter, Google+, and other social media platforms. Such platforms provide enormous opportunities for improving the narrating, framing, and branding potential of public managers, and tailoring branding efforts to address multiplicity. The key here is being one step ahead of stakeholders – or at least moving at the same pace. Doing this requires a high level of savviness in social media and an understanding of how these platforms can both serve and obstruct their goals. In other words, it requires that public managers master social media.

Developing social media-literate managers

In just the past five years, social media have dramatically changed the landscape of public management and policy-making in at least three ways:

- Citizens and other stakeholders have an unprecedented array of means at their disposal to follow, scrutinize, examine, and constantly feed into what governments are doing.
- In turn, governments and individual public managers have an unprecedented array of means at their disposal to obtain information about

stakeholders, to collect and easily analyse big data on their behaviour and attitudes, and to communicate and frame proposals, objectives, and positions.

- As a result of the first two dynamics, policy-making is by definition 'too slow' to keep up with real-life developments: the classical cycle from formulation to implementation easily takes years. To remain relevant, not least in the eyes of their political masters, public managers will have to 'make policy' in real time, at least symbolically, to convince stakeholders they are 'on it'. In doing so, however, public managers are pressured in three ways: they will encounter *resistance*, face new types of *risks*, and have to carefully manage *reputations* (Noordegraaf 2015: 166). Box 5.4, later in this chapter, illustrates these pressures.

These dramatic changes will continue to unfold with ever-increasing speed, in ways unknown to us today. We don't know what the next Twitter or Facebook will look like, nor how such platforms will both frustrate and enable effective public management. What we do know, however, is that public managers will be unable to manage stakeholder multiplicity if they do not drastically improve their mastery of social media. Here, some governments do better than others. The US (see Mergel 2014), the UK, and Australia, for instance, have recently begun to appoint social media directors in government departments. In countries such as Estonia, Ireland, the Netherlands, New Zealand, and Singapore, public agencies maintain a very (pro)active presence on social media (OECD 2015), aiming to directly influence policy debates by 'being first' and setting the narrative. It can hardly be a coincidence that the public sectors in these countries consistently rank in the top ten on various governance indicators, including e-government, citizen trust, policy effectiveness, and adaptiveness (Van der Wal 2016).

Monitoring social media

One oft-heard complaint from public managers nowadays is: 'How do I make sense of all the noise on social media platforms, how do I know which data are useful, and how can I avoid spending too much time and effort on the complaints of a potentially negligible (yet loud) stakeholder minority?' One key skill here is effectively monitoring social media platforms. Mergel (2014), who has done a lot of pioneering work on social media, transparency, and public managers, recently produced a guide to social media monitoring for public managers. Some of the social media monitoring tools that Mergel discusses are shown in Box 5.3. Such monitoring is useful in managing stakeholder multiplicity because it allows public managers to keep track of the different priorities and connotations displayed by groups with respect to their agency, and its policies and (perceived) performance. How do different stakeholders perceive these

Box 5.3 Four social media monitoring tools for public managers

Socialmention.com

This free tool aids public managers to search and analyse aggregate user-generated content from social media platforms, including Twitter, Facebook, YouTube, Google+, or Digg. Public managers can key in specific Twitter hashtags, social media account names, or general keywords. The result is a list of the most recent mentions of the search item across all social media platforms, together with a sentiment analysis (positive, negative, neutral mentions), the top related keywords used in the social media updates, and the top users referring to the search term.

Tweetreach.com

This tool analyses the activities of individual Twitter accounts. For example, using the US Department of Interior account (@interior), the tool provides insights into how many Twitter accounts are reached by the agency's updates. In addition, the tool provides public managers with data about exposure as calculated by the number of Twitter users reached through retweets of @interior's followers and a breakdown of the most retweeted content, among other insights.

Topsy.com

This free tool allows social media directors and public managers to compare the attention that different government-related issues receive online. As this tool only allows public managers to monitor the attention to different Twitter hashtags over a certain period of time, and not the nature of that attention, it may be useful to use it in combination with one or more of the other tools listed here.

TweetDeck

This tool provides a quick review of the number of retweets or shared updates occurring in other social media accounts. TweetDeck's main purpose is to compose and schedule social media updates and organize feeds by hashtags. Public managers can use this tool to save time and focus efforts in more effectively monitoring updates across various social media accounts they find relevant.

Adapted from: Mergel 2014: 7–8.

features online, how consistent are those perceptions, and which outputs from the manager and the agency side actually affect such perceptions?

However, as platforms and monitoring tools are constantly changing, public managers cannot just become skilled monitors and recipients of social media feedback data: they need to become active architects, apprehenders, and producers of social media content.

Social media literacy

Building on the concept of digital literacy (Hargittai 2002; Van Dijk 2005), Deiser and Newton (2013) emphasize 'social media literacy' as a key competency for 21st century managers. They identify six social media roles and skills that guide social media-literate leadership. Three of these roles concern *individual* behaviour (2013: 4–8):

1. *Producer* – Developing authentic storytelling abilities and honing new communication skills (particularly video-editing).
2. *Recipient* – Making sense of the noise through intelligent filtering, and creating resonance by selectively linking and replying.
3. *Distributor* – Understanding cross-platform dynamics and what makes content go viral, and building a sustained body of followers (i.e., a digital stakeholder allegiance).

In addition, they identify three *organizational* capabilities necessary to maximize social media opportunities (2013: 8–12):

4. *Advisor* – Enabling and supporting a 360-degree environment in social media usage while coordinating and bundling organizational efforts.
5. *Architect* – Balancing vertical accountability and horizontal integration, leveraging social media for key functions while retaining focus.
6. *Analyst* – Monitoring social media industry dynamics closely (through specific functionaries or departments), gaining deep understanding of the social and behavioural impacts of platforms on stakeholders and own employees.

To what extent are public agencies and public managers already social media-literate? Large differences exist between agencies and between countries. One public sector domain in particular has served as a key testing ground for trial and error in social media usage: the police. Box 5.4 presents some of the less successful episodes of Twitter use by police departments and individual officers.

Ironically, while social media are considered by many commentators, and younger generations in particular, to provide opportunities to highlight successes (Grimmelikhuijsen and Meijer 2015) and strengthen capacity to shape public relations (Campbell *et al.* 2014), the attempts displayed here achieved the exact opposite. In a sense, they exemplify how public officials, in their usage of new media, are in themselves 'multiple' actors, confusing and conflating their personal and professional role and presence. The examples also illustrate the challenges that public actors face in controlling the brand and limiting unintended effects of social media behaviour (Braun 2012; Karens *et al.* 2015).

Indeed, in their study of Twitter use by the Dutch police, Meijer and Torenvlied (2014: 16) emphasize the challenge of managing communicative

Box 5.4 Twitter use by cops: enticing or antagonizing stakeholders?

Police forces around the world have started to experiment with the use of Twitter for three main reasons: to quickly broadcast information to citizens; to receive information from bystanders and witnesses to better investigate and apprehend offenders; and to enhance stakeholder trust by being more transparent about methods and operations. Has this third objective been met so far? The results are mixed, to say the least. Various scandals have attracted substantial media attention and have illustrated the volatile nature of bi-directional communication and the challenges of blurred boundaries between private and personal behaviour on social media.

In 2014, a Dutch police officer was heavily criticized after tweeting the following post with a picture of his new police-issued weapon: 'my new best friend for the remainder of my career. Don't f..k with the neighbourhood cop!' The officer's Twitter account displayed his real name in combination with 'neighbourhood cop'. Responses from the general public evoked sentiments of fear about police officers in their neighbourhood being emotionally unstable and trigger happy.

In April 2014, the New York Police Department (NYPD) launched the Twitter campaign #myNYPD to boost its image, asking citizens to post friendly pictures of their encounters with NYPD officers. The hashtag was quickly hijacked by users posting images of police aggression, accompanied by cynical tweets such as 'Here the #NYPD engages with its community members, changing hearts and minds one baton at a time.' The NYPD's response was somewhat reserved, arguing it would

→

risk but also downplay the transformative effects of social media on communications. Their findings show that a minority of the police officers studied use professional, formal Twitter accounts (and don't use personal names) for external communication purposes, alongside a variety of classical communication methods. Other studies corroborate the somewhat limited reach of communication using Twitter thus far, emphasizing its usefulness in targeting specific audiences who are already active on social media (Grimmelikhuijsen and Meijer 2015: 598). This suggests that tools such as Twitter are helpful in managing multiplicity, at least partly. However, these authors conclude that the dominant effect of such targeting is *transparency*, resulting in an increase in perceived legitimacy, but *not necessarily in active citizen participation*. Also, although such communication methods provide many opportunities for managers to manage internal stakeholder multiplicity, their use in intra-organizational communication has been rather limited.

Clearly, the organizational roles of architect and analyst outlined in Box 5.4 are not yet very well developed. Indeed, in many ways the organization of social media communication is hybrid rather than radically different from the classical 'bureaucratic' model, as Meijer and Torenvlied

> continue to pursue new ways to engage with the community, with open, uncensored dialogues being good for the city.
>
> There has since been a surge in the use of social media and smartphone video recordings to scrutinize alleged racial violence by police officers, resulting in violent protests (again, amplified by social media) and the resignation of various officers across the US in recent years.
>
> The examples show that social media interactions are hard to reg- ulate, control, and direct, suggesting that they should be architected intelligently to meet stakeholder outreach objectives. Police forces in Canada, the Netherlands, and the UK, among others, have started to issue social media guidelines to their officers, and the Toronto Police Force even provides mandatory communication training for all its offic- ers. One key element is online risk awareness and the need to separate professional accounts from personal accounts. These are much-needed initiatives, as many public actors are still a long way from being social media-literate.
>
> The same applies to intra-organizational campaigns, which are increas- ingly employed by managers to create buy-in for organizational reforms from multiple internal stakeholders. Both internal and external communi- cation campaigns using social media run the risk of increasing rather than decreasing 'us versus them' sentiments.
>
> *Sources*: BBC, https://bbc.co.uk/news/technology-27126041; Elsevier, https://www.nrc.nl/ nieuws/2014/04/02/dont-f-with-the-wijkagent-en-een-foto-van-je-wapen-dat-kan-echt- niet-a1426074; Gray 2015, http://connectedcops.net/the-toronto-police-service-launches- social-media-program.

(2014: 15) assert: 'The hybrid nature of the organization of social media communication can be regarded as a reaction to the changes in the outside world that require government organizations to be both central- ized, formalized, and closed off from its environment and decentralized, personalized, and open to its environment.'

For now, perhaps the hybrid model is a logical structure for many government organizations. The question is whether such a model will be sufficient five to ten years from now, as media innovations continue to put pressure on stakeholder communication.

Producing 'public managers 2.0'

Having discussed current and emerging demands and challenges for public managers in effectively communicating with various stakeholder networks, together with the tools, skills, and mindsets needed to aid such effective communication, the question remains how to best develop social media-literate public managers. Social media and public management scholar Ines Mergel (2012) has outlined the elements of a course titled

'Government 2.0', which was aimed at producing 'public managers 2.0'. She argues (2012: 471):

> Public managers need to be equipped with an understanding of how their diverse set of stakeholders view the usefulness of interactions with government and use engagement channels that support the agency's mission to accomplish these goals. The existing methods and instruments out of the e-government era no longer support the use of social media and tasks, and resources have to be changed to address these challenges.

Mergel suggests that in being able to equip public managers with such understanding, public affairs and public policy programmes need to innovate and provide more venues for informal and online learning, sharing, and networking between public managers; their formalized organizational structures often do not facilitate 'out-of-the-box' discussions. To achieve this goal, 'public affairs programs need to provide skills that include:

- new forms of digital competencies,
- new forms of collaborative capacities, and
- new forms of social and digital awareness to mitigate the risks for each participant not just individually but also for the organization as a whole.' (2012: 472)

In particular, courses should be designed to develop individual skills and prepare students for their future networked workplace, and should include pedagogical elements for applying social media on three different levels (2012: 468):

- *Informal networking*: social media tools directly connect students to practitioners and learn from first-hand accounts in real-life situations.
- *Class participation* elements include the use of social media tools to collaboratively co-create content.
- *Social media services* are used to create a culture of constant engagement and social awareness between weekly face-to-face meetings.

Mergel urges us to rethink how 21ˢᵗ century public managers can be trained and developed to meet the demands discussed in this chapter. She provides a detailed course design with attention to topics like barriers and drivers for social media adoption, records management and risk mitigation, information reuse and mobile applications, design elements of social media campaigns, and measuring social media impact, In my own teaching, I have started to challenge aspiring public managers to communicate their analysis of key policy and management issues in more effective ways, following Deiser and Newton's (2013) argument that managers should become skilled producers of (social) media content.

For example, I have introduced video production assignments in addition to policy memo writing. Box 5.5 displays how such assignments may, and in my view should, become more prominent in educating and developing public managers with the ability to manage stakeholder multiplicity.

Box 5.5 Producing videos: a key component of management training in 2025?

Given the content, structure, and delivery mode of most degree programmes and executive courses in public management, it seems hard to imagine that we will train students to become skilled editors and producers of video content rather than masters in memo writing anytime soon. But perhaps we should become much more imaginative, and rapidly so. Younger generations are increasingly developing and mastering video production skills in their private time; they will be challenged to hone those skills in school assignments and projects from primary school onwards. Indeed, schools are already using iPads as key teaching tools. Why not further develop and specify those skills, and direct them towards specific policy-framing and branding objectives?

If public policy schools and civil service colleges want to remain relevant, they may have to drastically rethink their curricula and pedagogy. Given the speed with which information travels and stakeholders consume and co-produce such information, we should not underestimate how stakeholders (including political masters) will increasingly be unreceptive and impatient when confronted with dozens of pages of materials, or even with concise memos and briefs. From a framing and branding perspective, the short, cleverly edited two-minute video that can be disseminated to millions in a matter of minutes has unlimited potential. Moreover, to manage stakeholder multiplicity and thus target recipients of the same policy or programme with very different messages, public managers will have to become more versatile in the range of communication tools they use. In recent years, governments have started to increasingly use video as a communication tool, but production is still largely entrusted to highly specialized departments or outsourced to commercial parties.

With little extra effort, however, future generations can be trained and encouraged to master this process themselves, aided by increasingly accessible and user-friendly technology. At the same time, they will have to be made aware of the risks involved in distributing videos easily and informally, consonant with the broader risks of employing social media.

Perhaps the most urgent issue is how training programmes can be reformed to urge Gen X-ers, making up most of the managerial workforce in public sectors in the next five to ten years, to actively embrace tools and techniques they find intimidating and sometimes even frustrating and annoying. One way to address this issue is through facilitating reverse mentoring of seniors by juniors in addition to classical mentoring seen in current trainee programmes (further discussed in chapter 'Managing the New Work(force)').

What lies ahead

The demand that 21ˢᵗ century public managers manage stakeholder multiplicity emerges in conjunction with various other demands and pressures. As we've seen before, megatrends – and their consequences for public managers – do not operate in isolation: they arrive in clusters, exacerbating each other as they unfold. Whether public managers will be successful in managing complex stakeholder networks will partly depend on their abilities to manage the other demands outlined in this book, most prominently managing the new work(force), managing tri-sectoral collaboration, and managing innovation pressures.

One overarching challenge for public managers, however, will be how to perform and display leadership in an era where traditional notions of authority are eroding, even causing alienation and revolt among younger generations. How can you be 'at the wheel' and display the strong leadership that stakeholders demand, as these same stakeholders, pro-active, assertive 'experts', resist any form of top-down leadership, particularly from government? In addition to mastering the new communication methods, tools, and styles discussed in this chapter, public managers will have to experiment with various types of participatory governance and citizen engagement techniques. In a way, they will need to become 'anti-leaders' to lead 21ˢᵗ century crowds. The next chapter explores what such leaders and crowds may look like.

Chapter 6

Managing Authority Turbulence

One of Galileo's followers: 'Unhappy the land that has no heroes!'

Galileo: 'No, unhappy the land that needs heroes!'

(Life of Galileo, Bertolt Brecht)

Of revolutions, silent and loud

Imagine being a public manager in a Middle Eastern or North African (MENA) country. The collective, rapid, and impactful outburst of civil unrest you've witnessed in recent years was an unprecedented, highly unexpected VUCA event given the traditional, top-down, and closed, governance culture that characterized your region for centuries. You had no idea what the self-inflammation of Tunisian fruit-seller Mohamed Bouazizi on 17 December 2010, after a municipal inspector confiscated his wares, would trigger. A year later, four long-time heads of state – with over 120 years of uninterrupted tenure combined – had been removed from power. Simultaneously, popular uprisings and protests had occurred in half a dozen other MENA countries. The initial violent responses of many governments, displayed across the globe within seconds on social media, exacerbated the mass rallies, strikes, demonstrations, and social media campaigns, and the overall feelings of oppression and neglect among the citizenry. The common slogan of the protesters, empowered by the regional resonance of their movement, became *Ash-sha`b yurid isqat an-nizam* ('the people want to bring down the regime').

Since that December afternoon, new leaders and structures have emerged across the region. However, many of the protesters proved to be highly ambitious in their search for new figures and structures of authority. Some wanted tribal rule or self-rule to fulfil revolutionary governance ambitions, while others just wanted stability, peace, and quiet. Many of the elections following the outburst produced the same 'alpha-male' authoritarian leadership that protesters wanted to get rid of in the first place. Still, you feel that new authoritarian leaders will have to continuously gain their legitimacy much more than they used to, not only from citizens but also from you and your colleagues.

Now imagine you are a public manager located about 6,000 miles to the east, in Hong Kong, operating in the tense aftermath of the Occupy Central with Love and Peace movement (*OCLP* or 和平佔中). Citizens in the long orderly port city seemed increasingly weary with the relationship with China, having been reunited with the mainland as a special administrative region (SAR) in 1997. The OCLP started in 2014 when students and young professionals occupied the 'Central' area in Hong Kong's business district, after the Chinese government was unwilling to let Hong Kong citizens directly elect its Chief Executive in future elections. Protesters camped in tents while making music and discussing politics, demanding talks with the government. They were afraid that authorities would shut down the web, so they used the FireChat app, which allows smartphones to connect within a 75-yard radius through Bluetooth, thus exponentially increasing the number of connected users. After several weeks, the OCLP surrendered without achieving its aims. Tensions and protests, however, continue, and the atmosphere is tense. You are still taken aback by the unusual outburst of civil disobedience in Hong Kong given the law-abiding Confucian mindset of Hong Kong people, who tend not to visibly challenge authority.

If you are a public manager in the West, you have long been used to citizen protests and a certain degree of defiance of authority, in both your external and internal operating environments. Still, you also experience various subtler and 'silent' revolutions that have eroded traditional notions and structures of authority. Globalization, new (social) media, and initiatives such as WikiLeaks have bred – and created demand for – increased government transparency and scrutiny of public sector performance from different classes of citizens.

In addition, authority vacuums have emerged *within* organizations, with newer generations being much less inclined to respond to – let alone incentivized by – top-down leadership behaviour. 'Playing the seniority card' will most likely not be an effective management strategy in 21ˢᵗ century public agencies. However, it is much less clear what successful management *will look like* in workplaces characterized by authority turbulence.

Moreover, as said before, stakeholder views of authority are themselves highly ambiguous. Even in critical, plural Western democracies with highly dispersed leadership, a large majority of citizens are happy to quickly return far-flung powers and authority to their rulers in the wake of attacks and crises, demanding the strong leadership they previously resented. This 'double-edged sword' feature of authority turbulence results in a variety of tough demands and dilemmas for public managers and requires a dynamic skillset.

How do public managers maintain at least some authority and legitimacy in the eyes of ever more assertive stakeholders? Should they advocate more or less transparency, more or less collaboration and participation, and more or less crowdsourcing of policy and management ideas? Should they reinvest in domain expertise – the traditional underpinning of the senior civil service's authority and legitimacy vis-à-vis political masters and external stakeholders? What kind of leadership, if any, fits an era characterized by authority turbulence? How do public managers deal effectively with rapid turnover in political and administrative bosses? How do they maintain bureaucratic consistency and political neutrality in such an unpredictable operating environment?

Authority turbulence: cause and consequence

The introductory examples signify how empowered, assertive stakeholders no longer accept authority (or seniority) just for the sake of it, both in more traditional, hierarchical societies and in developed democratic states. At first glance, one might argue that traditional societies are just following the pattern taken by most Western democracies: *tradition-based* authority is gradually succeeded by *legal-rational* authority, with people subscribing to leaders and institutions based on long-established legal, bureaucratic, and democratic procedures that prove to work well (cf. Weber 1919), interrupted from time to time by unconditional loyalty to *charismatic* authority figures – for better or for worse.

However, legal-rational authority is no longer the 'normal', or even the desired, end state for many high-trust Western democracies (see Box 6.1). These countries have also experienced an increase in authority 'shocks', with assertive stakeholders asking, 'What have they done for us lately?' ('t Hart 2014b: 22). In an era of increasing transparency demands, public actors and institutions will need to continuously acquire and consolidate *performative* authority, making their legitimacy *consequential* (Scott 1992; Suchman 1995) and far from self-evident.

In recent years, high-trust societies with long-term stable and predictable governance cultures, like Denmark, the Netherlands, or the UK, have experienced how fragmented, volatile, and disloyal electorates no longer produce traditional majorities or coalitions, or grant governing elites their votes and confidence. As a result, we have seen new modes of governance, electoral reform, and cabinet formation. However, stable countries with less competitive electoral systems are also experiencing increasing scrutiny of their public sector's performance by media and citizens.

For some time now, we have seen a steady *decline in authority* of traditional political and administrative institutions. These institutions are no longer seen as adequately representing the wants and needs of – increasingly cynical and distrusting – citizens (Van de Walle *et al.* 2008; WRR 2012). However, what is new is increased *authority turbulence*: unpredictable, rapid dynamics in how public leaders and institutions 'acquire, consolidate, and lose' authority (Breslauer 2002: 13). This turbulence is incited by technological tools and empowered citizens who think they know better than their leaders but are unclear about what they want.

A rather extreme manifestation is the subversion of thousands of Western teenagers to the simple yet powerful message of Islamic State (IS), travelling off to desert warzones to fight to the death. Here, the classical pattern is reversed: youngsters cultivated in modern, developed societies

Box 6.1 Five features of declining democratic involvement in Western democracies

In his book *Ruling the Void,* the late political scientist David Mair (2013) identifies five key features of the withdrawal from and revolt against traditional governance institutions and democratic engagement starting in the 1980s.

- **Citizen disengagement from conventional politics**: There are fewer spaces in which citizens and their representatives can interact, resulting in greater weight accorded to non-democratic governance institutions.
- **Declining electoral participation**: There has been a fairly consistent decline in electoral participation, particularly among younger generations who seem to have never been politically engaged to begin with.
- **Increased electoral volatility**: The distribution of partisan preference is increasingly inconsistent and unstable, with voters switching parties from one election to the other across ideological fault lines.
- **Declining party loyalties**: Alongside increased electoral volatility, voters no longer identify as strongly with a particular party or ideology, implying they don't feel represented by one particular political class.
- **Declining party membership**: There is a significant, consistent decline of party membership across all long-established democracies, accompanied by rapidly rising NGO membership numbers; these trends signify citizen identification with concrete issues rather than broad ideologies.

Based on: Mair (2013: 17–44).

denounce legal-rational authority in favour of a mix of traditional and charismatic authority, branded with modern technology.

Clearly, managing the external and internal dimensions and implications of authority turbulence will be a key demand for public managers in the years to come. This chapter will explore both the challenges and the opportunities produced by authority turbulence.

Diffuse causes and manifestations

As with all the demands highlighted in this book, increased authority turbulence results from various related developments exacerbated by technology and globalization. A key influential cluster of trends here is 'power to the person: individualism and value pluralism' (Vielmetter and Sell 2014: 57), 'great expectations' (Dickinson and Sullivan 2014), and the 'rise of the assertive citizen' (Needham and Mangan 2014). Box 6.2 lists five key manifestations of authority turbulence occurring across the globe, albeit in different forms and with different speeds.

Box 6.2 Authority turbulence: five manifestations

- Individuals no longer (just) accept formal, traditional authority structures

  Culturally, historically, or ancestrally established authority structures no longer guarantee allegiance.

- Individuals decouple 'authority' from 'function' and 'position'

  Increasingly, public sector leaders are *formal but not necessarily material* representatives of authority. Stakeholders pledge allegiance to other high-profile icons – in fields including sports, entertainment, and technology – who *may not be formally in charge but are seen as leaders with authority* (cf. Heifetz 1994; Rothkopf 2008). In *Never Mind the Bosses*, Ryde (2012) propagates the 'death of deference' in the workplace.

- Individuals follow only those who can satisfy their immediate needs and priorities

  Stakeholders grant authority to those who can directly satisfy their own short-term interests, while no longer subscribing to a broader philosophy, ideology, or political conviction (a key difference from the anti-authoritarian movements of the 1960s and 1970s). They engage with small, ad-hoc civic movements instead of traditional political and administrative institutions (cf. Dalton 2004; Mair 2013).

- Individuals expect government to deliver and perform 'on the spot'

  Stakeholders scrutinize and monitor public sector performance impatiently and often unrealistically (Baetens 2013).

- Individuals experience 'demystification' of governance institutions and public leadership

  The inevitable dirtiness, irrationality, and incompetence of public actors and institutions are more easily displayed out in the open ('t Hart 2014b). The glass house has become 'real', permanent, and digital – a process further aided and accelerated by phenomena like WikiLeaks.

Overall, the assumption that increased transparency will lead to increased legitimacy has turned out to be naïve: authority will increasingly have to be earned through performance and delivery ('t Hart 2014b). However, various publics each have their own reasons for legitimacy claims and scepticism about performance. Indeed, to further specify authority turbulence we need to distinguish sentiments displayed by different clusters of citizens with their own reasons, lifestyles, and aspirations. One particularly useful typology has been developed by

TABLE 6.1 Specifying authority turbulence: three stakeholder classes

Stakeholder class	Sources	Manifestations
'The concerned citizens'	• Feelings of abandonment and misrepresentation • Perceived lack of (progressive) opportunity	• Complaining, protesting, and revolting (physically and electorally) • Turning away altogether from political-administrative institutions and services
'The enthusiastic self-sufficient'	• Perceived incompetence of public action and actors due to increased visibility • Ever-increasing abilities to access data, expertise, and best practices	• Demanding far-reaching involvement in co-production of policies and services • Competing for policy solutions with traditional institutions through 'crowd-based' initiatives
'The indifferent consumers'	• Perceived public sector encroachment on 'hard-earned' freedoms and rights • Negative attitude towards any type of large-scale interference or intervention	• Assertively yet selectively defending freedoms and rights (physically and legally) • Viewing institutions and elites with suspicion and distrust

Motivaction (2013) and SCP (2015). They distinguish three citizen clusters, displayed in Table 6.1.

The first group, *the concerned citizens*, are cynical, agitated, and often less educated. They feel overwhelmed and 'taken' by globalization and internationalization, distrusting elites and experts as a result, while believing that expertise and 'wisdom' are equally distributed between scientists and taxi drivers (cf. Baetens 2013; Bovens and Wille 2010; Schnabel 2015). They are the 'netizens', Tea Party supporters, or *wütburger*, a term coined by Kurbjuweit (2010) to describe angry, middle-aged, white Germans turning to conservative and nationalistic ideologies in their (mostly online) protests. This group feels alienated, abandoned, and unrepresented, and engages in aggressive rather than constructive civic action – often online and sometimes in real life – or withdraws from civic spaces and public services altogether.

The second group, *the enthusiastic self-sufficient*, are mobile, self-confident, and often highly educated. Many of them belong to the so-called 'creative class' (Florida 2012: 67). They feel they can deliver many things better and faster than their government, empowered by technology and expertise. They are still politically and societally active, albeit through NGOs, social entrepreneurship, and crowd-based initiatives rather than political parties.

The third group, *the indifferent consumers*, are tech-savvy and generally optimistic. However, in contrast to the second group, they do not really care that much about public participation, or public policy for that matter. As long as their lifestyle choices are not restrained by others, and certainly not by government, they don't cause trouble. They will rise up to authority, however, when they feel 'shortened' – although they will not make the effort to acquire deep knowledge of the issue at hand or devise well thought-through alternatives.

In addition to acting on their own, all three groups can also join forces – each for their own reasons and in varying compositions – to rise up against allegedly illegitimate authorities, creating existential trouble for public institutions and officeholders, as the Arab Spring and Occupy Central illustrate. In their own way, all three groups act like they 'know better'. In order to secure their buy-in and tap into their expertise while mitigating their revolt, public managers need to employ different responses.

Internal and external managerial implications

The features of authority turbulence translate into various demands and dilemmas in the internal and external operating environments of public managers, five of which are listed below. As a result of authority turbulence, public managers:

- Will have to deal with leadership change and legitimacy shifts more frequently, and much faster, than before, with political masters becoming more frantic and impatient than they already were.
- Will need to effectively manage teams of different generations and different types of professionals with their own views about how work should be organized and how they should be managed – if at all (Noordegraaf 2015; Ryde 2012; Weggeman 2007). The new workforce seems no longer inclined to simply accept authority and seniority. At the same time, many Gen Y-ers and Gen Z-ers do appreciate clear and inspirational leadership to incentivize or motivate them (Holmes 2012; Lyons and Kuron 2014).
- May increasingly need to publicly account for their actions. Performative pressures on many public agencies mean that these agencies no longer operate behind the scenes (Jacobs and Cuganesan 2014; Schillemans 2011, 2015), and public managers may need to brand their performance externally to retain or regain legitimacy and authority.
- Will have to smartly design and be involved in new ways of participatory governance and policy co-production that reach both highly educated, socially engaged citizens and the disenfranchised (Alford and O'Flynn 2012; Fung 2015; Nabatchi *et al.* 2015).

- Will have to meet and manage ambiguous stakeholder demands when turbulence actually visibly occurs, triggering authority vacuums (Boin and 't Hart 2000). When faced with an emergency or crisis – external, institutional, or both – stakeholders may demand strong, directive, 'law and order' leadership again, as long as it does not inhibit their own ambitions and possibilities (Boutellier 2004). For example, in the wake of recent terror attacks, citizens have called on public authorities to protect 'us' against 'them', curbing civil liberties and disregarding privacy concerns if necessary. However, these same citizens all too easily complain or resist when such authorities subjugate them to enhanced border controls or airport security checks. This produces a key dilemma for public managers: if authority turbulence increases, in some cases leading to revolutions and uprisings, they need to appear tough and 'in control' but simultaneously realize that this same turbulence renders such postures nearly impossible (Noordegraaf 2015; 't Hart 2014a).

Eight managerial responses

Translated to managerial practice, these demands prompt responses from public managers in the process of *managing up* towards administrative and political bosses, *managing down* towards different types of staff and teams, and *managing out* towards a variety of external stakeholders (cf. Moore 1995). The remainder of the chapter discusses eight potential responses that public managers can make in situations of authority turbulence. These responses, outlined in Figure 6.1, highlight some of the tough choices and paradoxes they involve, along with the skills and mindsets needed to turn these choices and paradoxes into opportunities.

FIGURE 6.1   Potential managerial responses to authority turbulence

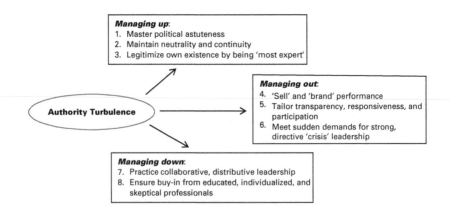

Managing up:
1. Master political astuteness
2. Maintain neutrality and continuity
3. Legitimize own existence by being 'most expert'

Authority Turbulence

Managing out:
4. 'Sell' and 'brand' performance
5. Tailor transparency, responsiveness, and participation
6. Meet sudden demands for strong, directive 'crisis' leadership

Managing down:
7. Practice collaborative, distributive leadership
8. Ensure buy-in from educated, individualized, and skeptical professionals

When *managing up* towards administrative and political bosses, three types of responses, involving a variety of skills and values, may prove helpful in navigating through authority turbulence.

Response 1: Master political astuteness

First of all, 21st century public managers have to be *politically astute*. This competency, explained in Box 6.3, is relevant to managerial work across sectors, particularly for those in more senior positions (Gandz and Murray 1980; Hartley *et al.* 2015: 197). Being neutral about political outcomes, political astuteness pertains to both 'small p' and 'big P' politics – both the informal and the formal, according to Hartley *et al.* (2015: 197). Although it is evident that the use of 'political' extends to political interactions across a wide range of issues, arenas, and stakeholders, the *importance of reading and accommodating the styles, agendas, and stakeholder allegiances of administrative and political bosses* cannot be stressed enough here. This applies particularly if such bosses replace each other ever more frequently due to authority turbulence, leaving authority vacuums as a result. Being able to read and accommodate requires antennae acquired through experience, patience, and an open mind rather than concrete training programmes.

In their famous article 'Managing Your Boss', first published in 1980, Navarro and Kotter emphasize how gaining a good understanding of one's superiors, oneself, and their mutual dependencies is crucial for success as a manager. They stress cooperation, reliability, and honesty rather than simply 'sucking up' to superiors. The advice of 'speaking truth to power' (Rustin 1955) is effective if done prudently and aimed at achieving solutions. In a similar vein, McCreary (2014) gives five tips for handling a new boss:

- Ease into the relationship;
- Observe her style;
- Consider others' claims on her attention;
- Collaborate;
- Be honest.

Response 2: Maintain neutrality and continuity

An ever important responsibility of public managers is to 'keep their head cool' amid political and societal turbulence, to maintain the long view, and to ensure a degree of institutional continuity and policy consistency. It is far from easy to successfully enact this response to turbulence. Just imagine being a department head in the justice or internal affairs ministry in Egypt, Libya, or Syria these days. You've spent the past few years ensuring the very survival of the state, pressured and guided by a variety

Box 6.3 Political astuteness as key 21ˢᵗ century competency

Jean Hartley and colleagues have done valuable conceptual and empirical work into *political astuteness,* which they define as (2013: 24):

'Deploying political skills in situations involving diverse and sometimes competing interests and stakeholders, in order to achieve sufficient alignment of interests and/or consent in order to achieve outcomes'.

Related terms include:

- *political savvy* (Ferris *et al.* 2005)
- *political acumen* (Perrewé and Nelson 2004)
- *political nous* (Rhodes 2016)
- *socio-political intelligence* (Burke 2006)
- *political antennae* (Benington and Moore 2011)
- *political sensitivity* (Page 2012).

As a competency, political astuteness can be broken down into five more specific skillsets:

- **strategic direction and scanning** – strategic thinking and action in relation to organizational purpose (see also chapter 'Managing Short Versus Long Time Horizons');
- **building alignment and alliances** – detailed appreciation of context, players, and objectives of stakeholders in relation to the managerial goal;
- **reading people and situations** – analysing or intuiting the dynamics that can or might occur when stakeholders and agendas come together (see also chapter 'Managing Stakeholder Multiplicity');
- **interpersonal skills** – 'soft' skills: ability to influence the thinking and behaviour of others;
- **personal skills** – self-awareness of one's own motives and behaviours.

According to Hartley and Fletcher, mastering political astuteness requires competence in each of these skillsets, with some of them being more salient for certain activities and contexts (2008: 2014). Arguably, political astuteness has always been a key competency of successful public managers. Still, increasing authority turbulence further enlarges the importance of political astuteness for public managers – not only to be effective, but to survive in the first place.

For further reading, see: Hartley *et al.* 2013, 2015; Rhodes 2016.

of old and new leaders who were elected, arrested, ousted, or murdered, along with international communities with their own views on your country's future.

However, even in less troubling governance settings, leadership dynamics will bestow increased responsibility upon public managers to maintain a sense of continuity and neutrality in managing institutions and policies. This applies to situational 'emergency management' as well as institutional 'crisis leadership' ('t Hart 2014b: 137). In other words, being politically astute does not mean public managers can neglect to safeguard important institutional qualities and values in times of turbulence.

At the same time, frequent leadership shifts provide opportunities for maximizing *bureaucratic power and influence* (Frederickson 2006; Partridge 1974) by consistently pushing sound policy proposals and maintaining order, continuity, and collegiality in turbulent times. These are qualities that superiors with short tenures and big ambitions will gratefully appreciate. However, maximizing such powers requires being skilled at organizing expertise in an environment of various competing information actors and claims.

Response 3: Legitimize own existence by being 'most expert'

Public managers have always derived much of their legitimacy and authority from domain knowledge and experience. Indeed, studies also show that 'expertise' is among the values considered most important by public managers in various countries (Van der Wal 2008; Van der Wal and Yang 2015). Politicians, often lacking such expertise, depend on public managers for authoritative advice and support (Aberbach *et al.* 1981; Nieuwenkamp 2001; Weber 1919), and political executives eagerly outsource the organization of sufficient expertise to their administrative apparatus (Van den Heuvel *et al.* 2002; Van der Wal 2014).

However, the importance of policy expertise and domain knowledge for public managers has somewhat depreciated in the past 20 years as a consequence of increasing job rotation and emphasis on managerial skills within senior executive services across the globe (Bekker 2009; 't Hart and Wille 2006). This, in turn, may have weakened the positions of authority that public managers hold vis-à-vis political bosses. In addition, political and administrative bosses have greatly expanded their knowledge base. They can turn to paid consultants who are often keen to provide the desired or 'right' facts and outcomes, solicit free advice from international agencies like OECD and the World Bank, and encounter lobbyists and interest groups who eagerly provide expertise free of charge, even without being asked. Moreover, within organizations, various clusters and 'camps' of public managers and their constituents will always compete for attention and authority. Finally, the abundance of publicly available data, made accessible by information brokers with more or less altruistic intentions, and institutionalized links with universities, think tanks, and entrepreneurial professors complete the picture of today's competitive public sector information landscape.

As a result, competing streams of information and policy advice find their way up to the highest echelons (Pollitt and Bouckaert 2011). Table 6.2 lists four key challenges for public managers aspiring to become authoritative experts, and suggests actions and approaches for mitigating these challenges.

TABLE 6.2 **Public managers as authoritative experts: challenges and strategies**

Challenges	Strategies
Open data Most data are now publicly available and easily accessible.	Master the process of filtering, translating, and brokering public data to political and administrative masters.
Competitive advice Consultants, international agencies, interest groups, lobbyists, and colleagues eagerly offer expertise to political and administrative bosses.	Collaborate with but set conditions and guiding frameworks for external advisors to your masters, and penalize non-compliance.
Counter frames and counter narratives Media and stakeholders will scrutinize and assault your claims and facts.	Place framing, branding, and storytelling 'front and centre' in the policy process, establishing first mover advantage.
'Politics of expertise' Political and administrative bosses and professional groups are increasingly contesting the 'right' expertise.	'Organize' your own channels and allegiances of expertise, rather than losing energy over continuous battles (see also the final response in this chapter).

Clearly, both expertise and managerial skills are important, but the importance of being 'most expert' should not be underestimated if public managers want to remain relevant, legitimate, and authoritative when managing up.

One final aspect of managing up that acts as a precondition for successfully managing out is exerting some influence and control over *how* and *why* performance criteria are established, *who* establishes performance criteria, and *what* these criteria are in the first place (Behn 2008, 2014; De Bruijn 2012). After all, it is hard to sell and brand your performance if the criteria to assess and measure that performance lack salience or even fairness in the first place. De Bruijn (2012: 55–56) has identified three principles for effective performance systems that maximize buy-in and meaningful measurement (see also Noordegraaf 2015: 135):

- *Interaction* – managers and professionals should be involved in designing key performance indicators (KPIs) and performance measures.
- *Variety* – trade-offs, multiplicity, and value conflicts should be acknowledged and not neglected.
- *Dynamism* – performance measurement should be a lively and challenging activity.

These three responses aid public managers in managing bosses; however, managing out towards assertive constituencies requires a set of complementary responses and skills.

When *managing out* towards stakeholders, three types of responses may prove helpful in navigating through authority turbulence.

Response 4: 'Sell' and 'brand' performance

In the old days, 'being most expert' also was a prudent strategy for remaining authoritative in the eyes of external stakeholders. Not any more. Nowadays, external stakeholders focus on tangible performance in their assessment of whether public managers can be considered 'authoritative'. Whereas chapter 'Managing Stakeholder Multiplicity' discussed how public managers can strategically employ brands and labels to reach multiple stakeholder networks and win them over for plans and proposals, in the context of authority turbulence *branding and selling past performance* are absolutely crucial to maintain and regain legitimacy and buy-in from stakeholders.

Selling performance is no longer just the responsibility of politicians during election time. Public agencies will have to account for the 'what' and 'how' of the public value they produce; they have to strategically practise accountability. Various studies show how some public managers have moved beyond 'suffering' from accountability obligations to leverage them as opportunities for displaying and explaining performance success, and if necessary, failure (cf. Schillemans 2008, 2015). Indeed, the capacity to prioritize obligations and strategically anticipate and combine accountability cycles is an asset, with inventive public managers restructuring internal information to communicate performance at any time to a variety of stakeholder forums (Schillemans 2015: 439).

Effective 21st century public managers are able to continuously prove they deliver 'value for money', communicating public value in laymen's terms to any type of audience. Some of the skills discussed in chapter 'Managing Stakeholder Multiplicity', such as maintaining a pro-active social media presence or framing, branding, and producing videos, will help to retain some authority in changing times. Still, it has proven challenging to explain tough decisions to the disenchanted, even though governments have more past achievements and innovations to boast than they get credit for (see Mazuccato 2013). Social media forums frequented by concerned netizens are one venue in which to communicate such successes with the public. However, as the previous chapter shows, it is crucial to strike the right tone. Box 6.4 displays a successful example of a public agency proving *and* advertising its legitimacy to the outside world.

The SKAT example shows how different groups of stakeholders need to actually see, feel, and experience that *they are part of the policy-making process*, and that programmes and policies *explicitly take their interests into account*. Key public values of transparency, responsiveness, and participation are enacted to increase legitimacy of public action. The question is, however, whether we can assume such a relation to work in all more contested policy-making contexts that involve joint meaning-making and

---

Box 6.4 SKAT: selling public value to (re)gain legitimacy

No one likes to pay taxes. They are unavoidable, but the process of filing and administering taxes is often cumbersome. However, an effective tax base determines the government's fundamental capacity to authoritatively make budgets and policies; it determines its 'state power'. Danish tax authority SKAT has undergone a major transformation in recent years, widely advertised across the globe. By creating a highly interactive, 24/7 online portal for all tax matters, it has:

- Drastically *lowered the bar for all citizens* to ask questions about taxes, how they are filed, and what they are spent on – almost all taxpayers now file their taxes online by themselves;
- *Enhanced its legitimacy* by showing (and advertising) that public agencies can keep up with the latest developments and technologies, be user-friendly and responsive, and increase effectiveness, even while reducing expenditures on salary (SKAT reduced its number of employees by almost 40 per cent between 2005 and 2015);
- Allowed SKAT employees and other public servants to exchange questions, solutions, and dilemmas 'out in the open', *showing the public that government employees* do not always have all the answers but *are willing to learn*;
- *Documented, branded, and advertised their innovative service delivery process* in various ways across continents, turning it into a widely known, 'standard' case study on smart government.

Sources: Copenhagen Capacity, http://copcap.com; KSAP 2012; SKAT, http://skat.dk.

---

communication. 'Tailoring' the extent of transparency, responsiveness, and participation may be required in such cases.

Response 5: Tailor transparency, responsiveness, and participation

In 2009, President Obama took office in the United States vowing to increase the transparency of the federal government's actions and decisions. Soon, however, his 'open government initiative' was clouded by unexpected events and the tough realities of public office. When WikiLeaks, Bradley Manning, and Edward Snowden revealed secretive government documents, they showed that the administration may not have been as transparent (or honest) as it had claimed to be. Moreover, their actions more fundamentally displayed the limits to and dangers of 'too much' unguided public sector transparency, where raw data is provided to stake-holders who interpret those data selectively (cf. Etzioni 2010; Margetts 2011; Roberts 2012). In this context, a permanent secretary I interviewed a few years ago when WikiLeaks revelations were making headlines actually *advocated more secrecy* (Van der Wal 2014: 1030):

> Procedural openness and transparency are not necessarily functional. Of course, outcomes need to be clear as well as division of responsi-bilities and accountability, but a certain degree of secrecy is an abso-lute necessity. At the moment, I am involved in a major governance process: I cannot tell you what kind of process because it is highly secretive. And please, no transparency at this stage because it will in-evitably lead to immediate failure! Secrecy – or perhaps exclusiveness of information is a better term – is not such a big issue as such as long as you do not lie to people. And even that is not really a crime as long as you're acting in the public interest, right?

The majority of political executives I interviewed for the same study saw transparency as subordinate to efficiency and effectiveness. According to them, transparency in every phase of the decision-making process is not conducive to increased public value. Output transparency: yes, process transparency: no. Indeed, only a small minority of political and adminis-trative elites considered transparency to be a key value (Van der Wal 2014: 1040). Carefully pitching the right level and 'type' of transparency to the issue, process phase, and stakeholder at hand is of key importance here.

In this light, Meijer *et al.* (2015) distinguish between political and administrative evaluation criteria for assessing transparency, with trans-parency serving different means and values in each sphere. The authors find some cases in which more administrative transparency results in increasing engagement with stakeholders and a better relationship with the media (see also Hazell and Worthy 2010). However, transparency can also amplify risk (perceptions) and 'underperformance'. If perfor-mance reporting of individual organizations takes place too frequently or is devoid of context, it may trigger self-fulfilling prophecies where citizens move out of poorly performing schools, neighbourhoods, hospitals, and so forth (Meijer *et al.* 2015: 14).

To some extent, studies show similar sentiments regarding responsive-ness: public managers are fearful of being too responsive and prioritizing certain interest groups over others, and argue they should be responsive to the minister and not the outside world. Their political masters, on the other hand, struggle in determining how to meet the wishes and demands of various stakeholders – some loud, some silent – while applying their own critical filter to evaluate public needs (Van der Wal 2011, 2014). Some scholars argue that public sector *legitimacy decreases as process transparency increases*; if citizens see up close 'how the sausages are made' they often don't like what they see ('t Hart 2014b).

So, is the appropriate response to be less transparent about processes of public management and public policy, and less responsive to stakeholder demands? It's a tough call. On the surface, this approach seemed to have worked for many decades in some of the Arab countries discussed at the start of the chapter. Ultimately, however, citizens find ways to get informed about what their governments produce, and scrutinize them. Increasingly, governments and individual public managers will have to become more skilled in explaining *why* they make certain choices, and *how* these result in the 'greatest good for the greatest number' in the long term, 24/7, and on a variety of platforms.

Ultimately, assertive stakeholders will pressure public managers to move beyond just being responsive and transparent and to let stakeholders physically and virtually participate in public decision-making and policy-making. The evidence on whether this will lead to 'better' public policy and more policy legitimacy is mixed (Fung 2015). Table 6.3 shows some of the trade-offs involved.

Involving various stakeholder groups during the policy-making process may prove a viable strategy to enhance legitimacy and trust, but *only* if participatory processes are designed such that *all groups* can be nudged to meaningfully participate. In order to 'deliver what they promise', interactive forums, events, and dynamics have to be very carefully planned and designed, tailored, and targeted to different stakeholder classes (Fung 2006; Nabatchi 2012, 2014). Harvard professor Archon Fung has done much acclaimed work on public participation processes and civic engagement in recent years. He identifies three key design choices (2006, 2015):

- *Selection and recruitment of participants* – Participants can range from nearly everyone to elite expert administrators, with in-between categories of targeted, well-prepared (stratified or randomly selected) 'mini-publics' occupying different positions often resulting in the most meaningful outcomes (Fung 2015: 2).
- *Modes of communication and decision* – Participants can just listen as spectators, express and formulate preferences, or be actively involved

TABLE 6.3 Traditional vs participatory policy-making: trade-offs

	Traditional	*Participatory*
Speed	Usually low	Often even lower
(Technical and legal) quality	High	Undetermined
Legitimacy	Low, unless success is proven	Mixed; input has to materialize
Stakeholder engagement	Low	High

in negotiating and bargaining policy outcomes. Not all participatory processes should aim to produce high-level deliberation, according to Fung (2006: 68); sometimes the opportunity merely to voice complaints will produce more satisfied stakeholders.

- *Authority and power* – The key question here is: 'How is what participants say linked to what public authorities or participants themselves do?' (Fung 2006: 69) Options range from merely allowing participants to provide suggestions to giving them direct authority or binding decision power, like in the case of citizen juries. Local governments across the world have successfully experienced with giving citizens full authority over budget decisions or local policing (Peixoto 2014).

Evidence shows that some clichés indeed hold true: quite often, deliberative forums are mostly attended by highly educated, well-spoken citizens who are already politically engaged (Nabatchi 2012). At the same time, different classes of citizens who are less used to expressing themselves in such forums may engage each other in ways that are far from constructive. Recent municipal council hearings over plans to build refugee centres in various European countries are a telling example. In some cases, they were attended by organized pockets of trouble-makers, and riots broke out with police forces having to secure mayors, council members, and fellow citizens who spoke out in favour of admitting refugees. In the years to come, public managers will have to smartly design such meetings to ensure that various citizen types feel involved in controversial issues and decisions. Table 6.4 contrasts two design approaches, each with different implications for legitimacy.

Often, (local) politicians will decide on the contours of participatory forums. However, the public managers tasked with designing such forums, weighing competing values such as public safety, feasibility, legitimacy, and transparency, have important choices to make. They need to think carefully about who they invite, how much actual influence they grant participants, how information provided prior to the event has to be structured, and, most importantly, what happens with stakeholder input afterwards when they have to formulate choices, actions, and measures. After all, there's probably nothing more detrimental to trust and legitimacy than being given the impression they would have a voice, only to see later that this was just an illusion (cf. Fung 2015). One promising development is the recent growth in co-production and co-creation, alongside demands from different stakeholder classes to be more involved. These are discussed more extensively in chapter 'Managing Cross-sectoral Collaboration'.

Response 6: Meet sudden demands for strong, directive 'crisis' leadership

In some instances, turbulent VUCA times call for strong leaders who speak in simple prose, distinguish between good and bad, and provide

TABLE 6.4 Designing participation to enhance legitimacy: open vs tailored

	Open	Tailored
Invitation	Open announcement; no targeted or stratified selection and recruitment takes place; participants self-select. Example: recent municipal hearings on refugee centres in Europe, allowing all inhabitants to participate. Concerned citizens were given a rare platform, but it proved difficult to provide a safe environment for all in some cases.	Selective or random recruitment, allowing for control over diversity of backgrounds and viewpoints and/or size of crowd. Example: recent electoral reform committees in Canada and the USA made up of selected, small groups of citizens, like the British Columbia Citizens' Assembly or the California Citizens Redistricting Committee (see Fung 2015).
Preparation	Participants attend forum based on topic or agenda items; organizers have little control over the data and information they consume beforehand. Example: participants in these hearings on refugee centres attended without receiving clear information beforehand about the how and why of decisions (including policy trade-offs).	Participants attend one or more (pre-arranged) physical and/or virtual information session(s), being provided with carefully crafted yet neutral information. Example: these electoral reform committees met regularly over a year, being facilitated by experts while provided with detailed yet accessible documentation (see Thompson 2008).
Decision-making	Participants listen, absorb information, and express views and preferences, but the exact influence often is not clear. Example: in most cases, hearings on refugee centres provided an opportunity to 'blow off steam', express concerns, and share viewpoints without clear outcome parameters. In one case, a mayor postponed a planned centre and offered apologies for not engaging local citizens earlier in the process.	Participants know beforehand what exact influence and authority their input yields; this may range from little to considerable. Example: reform committees were explicitly charged with investigating and recommending changes to improve the electoral system; proposals were put up for referendum, assembly vote, and supreme court decisions, resulting in both victory and defeat (Sonenshein 2013).

clear, top-down directions. In a way, the erosion of citizen trust in public institutions and office holders is *in itself* a creeping institutional crisis, triggering sudden situational crises like collective outbursts of violence and protest (cf. 't Hart 2014b: 130). At first glance, collaborative, 'servant' approaches to leadership outlined in other sections leave public managers fairly empty handed when events demand strong, directive leadership. Indeed, much of the literature on crisis management seems to emphasize leadership behaviour characterized by immediate, 'tough' action, clearly delegating responsibilities and tasks, and overriding normal procedures, and asking for legitimacy and approval afterwards (cf. Boin *et al.* 2009; Brecher 1993; Keeler 1993). A majority of anti-authoritarian stakeholders will initially appreciate public managers who establish the dominant frame while projecting strength, control, and certainty. However, as 't Hart (2014a: 141) asserts: 'Stress and arousal can easily lead to the messages of leaders being misinterpreted and distorted – especially among those parts of the audience who do not see government as their ally. Pre-existing opposition and distrust do not simply disappear just because a crisis has arrived on the scene.'

Such dynamics raise the question of to what extent it is possible to appear authoritative and 'in control' while being mindful of an ever more sceptical and scrutinizing public. Here, some of the other competencies and responses come to the fore, such as branding, framing, and developing stakeholder antennae. Moreover, recent evidence suggests that media-savvy publics can be of great help in co-producing crisis communication and solutions.

A powerful example is the use of Twitter and Facebook to coordinate aid relief in the aftermath of the April 2015 Nepal earthquake. The government remained silent in the early days, but social media forums exploded to provide support to remote areas with hard to reach victims, amid weak administrative capacity. Spontaneous networks of victims, volunteers, and various aid agencies, including foreign military assistance, emerged, setting up apps, chat groups, and websites to direct and prioritize resources to locations that needed them most. Intriguingly, even while working in a highly mobile, decentralized mode, the various actors involved still managed to establish central, authoritative mapping sites and aftershock monitors that were used and updated by thousands of stakeholders.

Finally, research tells us that the internal dynamics of effective crisis leadership have always been much more collective and facilitative than myths would have us believe, corroborating the importance of delegation and teamwork in decentralized networks of well-trained professionals ('t Hart 1993, Boin *et al.* 2009). The final two responses discussed here emphasize such collaborative approaches, particularly when managing 21st century professionals.

When *managing down* towards employees and co-workers, two types of responses may prove helpful in navigating through authority turbulence.

Response 7: Practise collaborative, distributed leadership

Dealing with intra-organizational authority turbulence in a networked world may very well require 'less' leadership and more frequent and meaningful involvement of employees. As management guru Simon Caulkin (2015) asserts, 'if good leaders are so rare, the solution is to build organizations that need them less. Over time resilient systems outperform collections of individualistic stars.' In a similar vein, Needham and Mangan (2014: 18) stress in their interview study *The 21st Century Civil Servant*:

> The traditional individual leader approach is not one that will be effective in the context of complex, adaptive problems facing society. The skill sets of leaders in the future need to be different, and the type of leadership approach also needs to change ... The 21st century public servant rejects heroic leadership in favour of distributed and collaborative models of leading.

Needham and Mangan build on work done by the Virtual Staff College in the UK (2012) and argue that collaborative, distributed leadership has to replace traditional images of leaders 'as the sole source of power and authority reflecting the complexity of modern society and the decline of deference'. Somewhat similarly, Dickinson and Sullivan (2014: 12) conclude:

> Hero-leaders aren't the answer. When leadership is spoken about in the media and in the literature it is often focused on individual heroes. However, the evidence suggests that there is a need for a new kind of public sector leader to respond to the changing context, in which leadership beyond boundaries and beyond spans of authority will become important. Rather than focusing on individuals we will need to think about forms of distributed or dispersed leadership.

Vielmetter and Sell (2014: 166) introduce the concept of 'altocentric leadership' as an alternative to the egocentric leadership that is aimed at making headlines. Although altocentric leaders are confident, skilled individuals with strong, charismatic personalities, their 'defining characteristic is a primary focus on and concern for others rather than themselves' (166), resembling what scholars have labelled post-heroic, humble, or servant leadership (Collins 2011; Greenleaf and Spears 2002). The common argument is that traditional 'big-man' alpha-male leadership contains significant performance risks as it tends to neglect the complex, multifaceted character of VUCA issues. In addition, individualized, empowered citizens are 'less inclined to tolerate coercive leaders' (2014: 166). Finally, such leadership does not sit well with emerging work practices where increasingly mobile individuals and teams work remotely and online in autonomous and decentralized settings.

Unleashing and maintaining loyalty and followership in collaborative settings requires five key tactics, according to 't Hart (2014a: 95):

- Motivate participants by reminding them of the stakes involved and their mutual interdependence.
- Keep the conversation flowing, and focus on listening.
- Make it possible for participants to 'move' and 'learn' by creating 'offline' venues with limited visibility and pressures.
- Nudge parties to shared understanding (rather than enforcing a dominant frame).
- Take the time for relationships to build, while realizing that collaboration is neither a linear nor a heroic process.

Box 6.5 provides public managers with suggestions for building and managing collaborative, effective teams.

To sum up, although command-and-control, big-man leadership still is omnipresent in the public domain, and is often rewarded by current performance appraisal systems (Needham and Mangan 2014, 2016), the question is whether such leadership is really '21st century proof', especially when crises occur. Moreover, the louder that politicians and public managers become in their attempts to regain and restore declined legitimacy and authority, the more difficulty they will experience when accounting for their almost inevitably disappointing performance later on (Trommel 2009). As tempting as the 'strongman' response may seem, it lags way behind the interconnected, multi-sectoral, 'flat' organizational cultures we see emerging in many public agencies (Osborne *et al.* 2013; 't Hart 2014b).

Response 8: Ensure buy-in from educated, individualized, and sceptical professionals

In 2007, former knowledge worker turned academic Matthieu Weggeman published a book with the telling title *Managing Professionals? Don't Do It!* His key argument was that managing, let alone controlling, the knowledge workers who increasingly make up the majority of employees in public and semi-public services is not only difficult (as any public manager will recognize) but often counterproductive (see also Noordegraaf 2015). Indeed, traditional professionals like lawyers, judges, professors, and doctors have powerful positions within organizations, characterized by high levels of autonomy, formally and externally recognized expertise, and legal decision-making space, backed up and 'defended' by professional associations and diplomas (Freidson 1994; Scott 2008).

Arguably, many newer 'professionals' such as welfare case workers, policy analysts, IT systems managers, and even public managers themselves (Noordegraaf 2007) may be equally challenging to motivate and

---

Box 6.5 Building and managing teams: lessons for public managers

In 1993, McKinsey consultants Jon R. Katzenbach and Douglas K. Smith published a classical article, 'The Discipline of Teams'. Although their work dates back a while and is focused on the private sector, their key insights bear relevance for public managers seeking more collaborative, shared leadership. Three contextualized and updated lessons are offered here:

- **'Managers have to make clear what teams are and why they exist'**

  Most committees, focus groups, and advisory councils are not teams (1993: 112), but taskforces, units, and programme directorates with collective goals, accountability, and performance structures are. Rather than inflating the label, managers should advocate and train team-work competencies. Teams are not just groups doing things together, they are established with a clear performance purpose in mind, requiring both individual and mutual accountability (1993: 112) to prevent free riding and stimulate collaboration. Ideally, performance evaluation includes individual and collaborative components, although such evaluation is rare in reality.

- **'Teams do need to be carefully composed and managed; they don't function by themselves'**

  An oft-propagated assumption is that teams can only build a common commitment if they are 'left alone' to function organically and autonomously (1993: 113). Entrepreneurial start-ups notwithstanding, this assumption may prove false, particularly in public sector settings. Teams only start to perform successfully and 'own' their (politically mandated) purpose if managers define, update, defend,

  →

---

manage authoritatively, even though their professional habitus is not yet as well established. Surely, the broader individualization and empowerment trends highlighted in this chapter make it hard to get even less self-confident and educated professional staff 'behind you'. How do public managers ensure buy-in from such colleagues to realize managerial objectives? Can they be 'most expert' not only while managing up but also while managing down?

To avoid getting entrenched in unproductive battles over authority, Weggeman (2007) suggests managers should entrust professionals with maximal responsibility since they are well prepared and intrinsically motivated to do a good job due to extensive educational (peer) socialization. By emphasizing facilitation rather than control, managers and professional

→ and incentivize that purpose. Moreover, managers need to carefully assess (and advise political masters on) the complementary skillsets required for realizing the team's public value mission. Teams need a combination of three skillsets: technical or functional expertise, problem-solving and decision-making skills, and interpersonal skills (1993: 115–116). Managers should be forthcoming in acknowledging their own skill gaps.

- **'Teams and good performance can't exist without each other'**

  Without good performance, there is no reason for a team to exist (1993: 4). However, public sector teams are much less pressured by ruthless market discipline: 'There's nothing as permanent as a temporary government organization.' Keeping teams functional requires continuous personal attention by public managers, 'smart' design of incentives and of remuneration and performance structures, frequent rotation of positions and responsibilities, and exit of non-performing team members.

The authors conclude that four key elements make teams function effectively (1993: 111):

- common commitment and purpose
- performance goals
- complementary skills
- mutual accountability.

Collaborative public managers will not only have to passionately profess these elements but also recruit, hire, and develop staff members and managers able to make up effective teams.

Source: Katzenbach and Smith 1993.

staff can collectively pursue ambitions and share accountability (see also Box 6.5). Such advice strongly resonates with the collaborative leadership advocated in response 7.

At the same time, we should not be naïve. Public managers have responsibilities and targets to reform, report, and budget, making clashes and power struggles with assertive knowledge workers unavoidable from time to time. Box 6.6 displays four different approaches to managing professionals. Doing so successfully will often require a delicate mix of these approaches, depending on the situation (and profession) at hand. In the years to come, managing new generations of workers in increasingly autonomous, 'remote', and virtual office settings will create additional challenges and opportunities.

Box 6.6 Managing professionals authoritatively: a mission impossible?

As a public manager, one of the toughest parts of the job is nudging individualized, well-educated professionals to contribute to organizational goals and vision. How will they take you seriously? Will they even do what you say and how do you know? How can you get them 'in line', or even get rid of them if needed, without undermining your own authority across the organization? There are roughly four things that public managers can do, although none of them is a panacea for all situations.

- 'Co-manage, and do so from the start'

  This is easier said than done, but evidence shows that involving professionals in all stages and aspects of management processes is conducive to buy-in and continued motivation. Taking the time to convince knowledge workers that certain plans and decisions are necessary and meaningful – also to organize *their work more effectively* – requires effort and energy but may pay off immensely.

- 'Show them who's boss (when needed)'

  For various reasons, managers may feel the need to put stubborn, hard-to-control professionals in their place from time to time. Some even argue that professionalism is best understood as a power struggle (Kirkpatrick 2007; Scott 2008). Showing professionals 'who's boss' may prove necessary from time to time, but to maintain rather than lose authority, you should choose your battles wisely.

- 'Delegate, trust, and (largely) leave them be'

  To reiterate Weggeman's provocative claim, one way of managing professionals is simply not to manage them at all. Let them decide on targets, performance criteria, peer evaluation, division of labour, and reporting structures. Public managers only intervene when things get really out of hand. Such a 'hands off' approach minimizes grunt work for both sides and prevents (even avoids) conflict, though with obvious risks in terms of managerial accountability and oversight when problems occur.

- 'Teach them (about) the importance of management'

  Recently, Noordegraaf (2015) has stressed the relevance of 'organizing professionalism': teaching professionals how to collaborate, work within frameworks and constraints, and detect and manage risks. This is a long-term strategy as it requires tailored, often brand new modules and programmes being incorporated in both graduate training curricula and management development (MD) programmes. Approach 1 can be a follow-up to, or 'on-the-job' component of, such learning.

Further reading: Barber 2015; Freidson 1994; Noordegraaf 2015; Weggeman 2007.

What lies ahead

Indeed, concomitantly with authority turbulence, new forms of work and new types of workplaces emerge, as younger generations of employees move up the managerial ranks and new technologies disrupt traditional boundaries between work life and private life, and between countries, cultures, and time zones. Managing the new work and the new workforce will challenge public managers but also provide them with unprecedented opportunities for leveraging the energy, drive, knowledge, and 21st century skills of new workers.

In addition, enabling new ways of working will attract a more diverse workforce and entice them to produce public value from a variety of locations, and in a variety of ways, without having to sacrifice work–life balance. At the same time, many managers currently experience difficulties in managing so-called Gen Y-ers or millennials. Are they a blessing or a curse? And what are the key characteristics of Gen Z, who will start to enter the public sector workforce just a few years from now? These and other questions will be addressed in the next chapter on *managing the new work(force)*.

Chapter 7

Managing the New Work(force)

*Caricatured as navel-gazers, millennials are said to live for their
'likes' and status updates. But the young people I know often
leverage social media in selfless ways.*

(Chelsea Clinton, Board Member, Clinton Foundation)

Managing clouds rather than agencies?

Imagine being a public manager heading the Prime Minister's (PM's)
communications department in a country with a young population that's
recently gone through a series of cutbacks and austerity measures. In the
years to come, you will most likely be tasked with refreshing your teams
– largely consisting of middle-aged and older public servants – while
keeping costs down by making work processes and employment contracts more flexible. Doing this will allow you to secure funding from the
Treasury for a systems upgrade needed to realize the PM's communication ambitions – to 'future proof' the way in which government engages
stakeholders. You are keen to kill two birds with one stone here: make
room for newer generations of employees who will seize the opportunities provided by the latest communication technologies and social media
platforms, and leapfrog into a near future in which you manage your
resources and reservoirs – both human and physical – through flexible
'clouds' rather than rigid, bureaucratic practices.

Recently, technology giants have started to offer services like GovCloud
that allow governments to store, move, and process sensitive information
24/7. Such services would allow you to cut back on hardware and paper,
tools that are perceived as near obsolete anyway by the graduates you plan
to hire. However, you want to do more than just use cloud services for
information. What if you could set up online pools and reservoirs of flexible, part-time contractors who would be readily available when needed
– during peak times such as annual debates about the federal budget or the
opening of the parliamentary year – and disengaged right after peak times
ended? Making large parts of your workforce flexible would allow you to
achieve tremendous savings on employee benefit expenses. In part, these
savings would help you to achieve austerity targets while being able to
pay the substantial hourly fees needed to contract high-quality new media
specialists during peak times. The millennial workers you need to fulfil the
ambitions of your political boss are said to value flexibility and multi-job,
protean careers above stability and security. Moreover, defiant of authority
as they are, they prefer to manage their own time instead of taking orders.

112

However, the first time you share your draft work plan, *Government Communication 3.0*, with the PM's Chief of Staff, his response is sceptical. Although he agrees that public sector job security is a thing of the past, he considers this a grave concern rather than an opportunity. He stresses how the PM has pledged to increase the retirement age, suggesting that room for hiring new graduates may be limited. He even mentions how his teenage kids who are about to enrol in college hold pessimistic views of their own future and would love the prospect of a stable job after they graduate. The meeting leaves you with various tough questions to ponder.

Are decreasing job security and increasing flexibility commensurate with the aspirations of newer generations? How can you be so sure what they look for in a job, diverse as the available jobs will be? Will increasingly flexible, remote, and part-time jobs lead to less commitment and cohesion of your teams, outweighing the benefits of cost-effectiveness and adaptiveness? How can you transition towards a more fluid work environment with new types of workers while maintaining the expertise and ethos of your current, more senior employees?

Questions such as these illustrate how *managing the new work(force)* is becoming a key managerial demand. The demand is a result of various related developments that are emerging alongside the authority turbulence elicited in the previous chapter. Three megatrends in particular are changing the ways in which public sectors and employees *work*, new generations *view work*, and public managers *need to organize new ways of working and manage new workers*: 'all is networked', 'great expectations', and 'forever young'. More indirectly, 'ultra-urbanization' and 'economic interconnectedness' also play a role, as they affect labour market dynamics. Table 7.1 lists five key manifestations of the demand for managing the new workforce occurring across the globe, albeit in different forms and with different speeds, and identifies challenges and opportunities for public managers.

Evolving types of work, working, and workers

Table 7.1 reflects the mushrooming literature that has developed in recent years on two – partly related – clusters of issues:

- New types and generations of *workers* and their effects on public sector employment and management, with key topics including: the millennial workforce and Gen Y; future Gen Z employees; cultural and generational diversity; recruitment, retention, and remuneration policies; and (reverse) mentoring and coaching practices (Bozeman and Feeney 2007, 2008, 2009; Chaudhuri and Ghosh 2012; Dickinson and Sullivan 2014; Dill 2015; Ng *et al.* 2010; Johnson and Ng 2015; Parry *et al.* 2012; Twenge and Campbell 2012).

TABLE 7.1 Managing the new work(force): challenges and opportunities

Manifestations	Challenges	Opportunities
1. **Influx of new generations and large-scale retirement of senior managers** Bozeman and Feeney 2007, 2009; Chaudhuri and Ghosh 2012; Hamidullah 2016; Lewis and Frank 2002; Ng *et al.* 2010; Twenge and Campbell 2012.	• Preserving institutional memory • Creating meaningful (reverse) mentoring and coaching practices • Ensuring organizational socialization and safeguarding key values • Meeting high expectations and demands of new generations of employees	• Engaging active and eager retirees as mentors and advisors • Changing archaic structures and mindsets • Making perpetual innovation more self-evident • Encouraging continuous intergenerational learning and knowledge exchange
2. **Increasing workplace diversity** Groeneveld 2015; Guillaume *et al.* 2014; Pitts and Wise 2010.	• Balancing conflicting views, backgrounds, and lifestyles • Managing political and ideological polarization on the work floor • Ensuring a commitment to shared culture, language, and communication modes	• Building more wide-ranging antennae and networks for recruiting new employee types and reaching non-traditional stakeholders • Operating with more confidence and skill in international arenas
3. **Versatile, unpredictable, and boundaryless careers** Briscoe and Hall 2006; Gratton and Scott (2016); Morgan 2014; Parry *et al.* 2012.	• Planning ahead and building loyal and long-lasting teams • Preserving institutional memory • Building and implementing long-term HRM and MD strategies	• Recruiting and incentivizing by emphasizing non-financial rewards and development-focused careers • Poaching private sector talent
4. **Virtual and remote offices, teams, and contractors** Caillier 2016; Ferrazzi 2012; Gratton 2011; Green and Roberts 2010; Mahler 2012.	• Minimizing workforce divide and isolation • Finding effective communication and engagement styles to maintain cohesion and collegiality • Rethinking responsibility and accountability structures	• Realizing productivity, efficiency, and sustainability gains • Increasing job satisfaction and improving work–life balance • Unlocking new reservoirs of potential employees
5. **Disappearance of traditional job security** Dickinson and Sullivan 2014; Dill 2015; PSA 2015.	• An increasing portion of the workforce working temporary, part-time, 'multi-jobs' – the 'uberization' of the workforce • Decreasing loyalty and commitment	• Increasing both flexibility and resilience of agencies • Managing agencies and programmes from 'cloud-like' structures with readily available resources that can be easily shifted

- New ways of *work* and *working* and their organizational and managerial implications, with key topics being: virtual offices and teams; long-distance work; increasing portions of temporary, non-unionized, and multi-job public sector employees – the 'uberization' of the public sector workforce; and dynamic, protean careers characterized by job-hopping and sector-switching (Briscoe and Hall 2006; Briscoe *et al.* 2006; Caillier 2016; Ferrazzi 2012; Gratton 2011; Green and Roberts 2010; Lyons *et al.* 2015; Mahler 2012; Watkins 2013).

This chapter will first identify characteristics of new types and generations of workers and how they affect public management and managers. In discussing these effects, we devote one key section to recruiting and incentivizing new generations of workers and one section to (reverse) mentoring and coaching practices, and organizational socialization. The second part of this chapter discusses the implications for public managers of increasingly virtual and remote office settings – partly as a response to changing needs and desires of new generations – alongside more fundamental developments like robotization and automation of white collar jobs, and decreasing legal protection of public sector labour.

Because of its focus on work and the workforce, this chapter will address HRM issues such as recruiting, incentivizing, and training more explicitly than some of the other chapters. After all, addressing this demand requires managers *not just to upgrade their own* skills, competencies, and conceptions of their role. It also requires them to rethink how new types and generations of employees have to be recruited, incentivized, managed, and tied to functions and jobs in increasingly virtual, remote, decoupled, and insecure employment settings. Moreover, many of these new employees will themselves attain managerial responsibilities as their careers progress.

New types and generations of workers

Generation Me, Generation Next, Gen Y, or the millennial generation – roughly those born between 1980 and 1995 – is probably the most studied, written about, and stereotyped generation to date. Governments, academics, consultants, and companies trying to define new markets and customers have produced hundreds of books, reports, and workshops, often without much empirical support (Twenge and Campbell 2012). Gen Y-ers have been accused of being over-confident, entitled, narcissistic, lazy, impatient, 'high maintenance', and 'emotionally needy' and praised for being socially engaged, competitive, solution-focused, 'fast', and tech-savvy (Durkin 2010; Pew 2010; Twenge 2006; Twenge and Foster 2010). Although these characteristics may resonate with public managers working with this generation, we should be careful not to overstate their 'uniqueness', as cohort differences may be a function of age as much as generational demarcation.

Indeed, some critique the existence of common and generalizable traits across a cohort that is as heterogeneous as any, suggesting that previous generations were also more entitled, self-centred, deferent towards authority and status quo, and socially and ideologically engaged than their parents, simply because they were young (Lyons and Kuron 2014; Twenge and Campbell 2012; Van Doorn 2002). If this holds true, older public managers 'can understand younger workers simply by remembering what it was like when they were young' (Twenge and Campbell 2012: 2). Still, most public managers will agree that cross-generational understanding is not that easy. Something is 'different' about these newcomers, although some of the megatrends in chapter 'Trends and Drivers' may better explain their traits than specific birth year cut-offs. After all, pervasive changes in culture produce generational change at least as much as specific events like 9/11 or the Asian financial crisis (Twenge *et al.* 2016).

Indeed, the largest cultural change in the West – and increasingly, in the East – is individualism (Myers 2000), which in turn has produced increasing self-confidence, narcissism, expectations, diversity, and value pluralism, labelled together in this book as 'great expectations'. Technological revolutions commencing in the 1990s have exacerbated some of these traits, shaping the values of a generation that feels 'very comfortable in a fast-paced online world with instant access to information and constant social networking and communication' (Pew 2010; Twenge and Campbell 2012: 3). These individuals are often called 'digital natives' (Shaw and Fairhurst 2008), although the emerging Gen Z (for want of a better term) has started to claim that label recently, as Box 7.1 shows. Gen Z also seems to be more conscious of economic volatility, as it is coming of age in a period characterized by the megatrend 'more with less' – with ballooning public debt and modest economic growth in many parts of the world, particularly in the West, where Gen Z data have been collected.

Stereotyping aside, 21ˢᵗ century public managers must anticipate the needs, skills, and levers of incoming cohorts of employees. All too often, however, worries, problems, and challenges dominate the discussion. Some have noted the decline of public service ethos among upcoming generations of public managers (Lyons *et al.*, 2014), along with their tendency to value quality of life over hard work (Twenge and Campbell 2012). Others emphasize increasing personnel problems that public sectors may expect due to the rapid ageing of their workforce amid the ongoing global 'war on talent' (Beechler and Ian 2009; Lent and Wijnen 2007; Lewis and Frank 2002).

At the same time, however, Gen Y and Gen Z employees may – by default – meet some of the demands and possess some of the attributes outlined in previous chapters. Indeed, they are said to be entrepreneurial and energetic, care less about formal hierarchy, network easily, and take

---

Box 7.1 Gen Z: 'millennials on steroids'?

Public managers looking ahead strategically to the next wave of graduates entering the public sector workforce may want to shift their focus from Gen Y to Gen Z – those born from 1995 onwards. They are 2 billion and growing worldwide. In countries such as India, Indonesia, and Iran they make up the majority of the population – and future workforce – but even in countries such as the US and Brazil they make up around 25 per cent of the population, more than millennials and baby boomers. Empirical research on Gen Z is sparse. However, initial surveys and anecdotal evidence from the West point to some intriguing features:

- Gen Z is the first truly digitally native generation, born after the World Wide Web took off. This provides Gen Z-ers with unprecedented capabilities to master the 21st century work environment; some have even suggested that their brains are wired differently, making them more suitable for multi-tasking and digital navigation but potentially also less social and intelligent.
- They do not just enthusiastically embrace technology, due to privacy concerns; in fact, they are highly conscious, smart, and somewhat conservative in their online behaviour.
- Having been brought up surrounded by modern technology and affected by global economic uncertainty and insecurity (the VUCA world), Gen Z seems to be more conservative, health conscious, and focused on job security, educational choices, and parental advice than millennials.
- Gen Z-ers are curious and socially engaged but much less optimistic about their own future than those who were growing up during the economic boom of the 1990s. As a result, some suggest they more closely resemble their parents (and their parents' parents) rather than resembling Gen Y-ers.

In a public sector working environment where job security is in decline, incentivizing and managing the expectations of Gen Z-ers may prove even more difficult for public managers than managing millennials. But these individuals will shape the future of work and inject unparalleled innovation capacity into public agencies. In adapting government to changing times, they will lead public managers as much as being led by them.

Sources: Bauerlein 2008; Dill 2015; Turkle 2012; Williams 2015.

---

into account technology implications in everything they do (Holmes 2012; Ng *et al.* 2012; Twenge and Campbell 2012; Williams 2015). When these traits are perceived as an opportunity, the question then becomes: how can incoming generations be recruited, retained, enticed, and incentivized so that public sectors can maximize their potential to create public value?

Recruiting and incentivizing the new workforce

Real-life data and HRM literature on the professional needs and career preferences of newer generations, and how organizations and managers attempt to address those needs and leverage those preferences, are abundant. It is far from clear, however, to what length public managers should go in accommodating the ever-expanding needs of newer generations, given their own personnel needs and organizational objectives. 'We're not interviewing them; they're interviewing us' is a common observation from hiring managers (Kyle 2009). Two interrelated 'public management puzzles' will be discussed here:

- anticipating and accommodating increased sector-switching and protean careers;
- devising effective compensation, motivation, and talent management strategies.

Sector-switching and protean careers

Recent years have seen an acceleration of a longer-term shift in career progression, as traditional, linear careers within few organizations have been replaced by boundaryless and self-directed careers characterized by a greater number of job and organization changes (Lyons *et al.* 2012, 2015; Briscoe and Hall 2006; Parry *et al.* 2012). Although traditional bureaucratic careers have remained more linear and conservative than those in companies and NGOs, this shift increasingly characterizes public sectors as well (Hansen 2014). Moreover, younger generations in different parts of the world display increasingly *protean* career orientations with a desire for interesting and meaningful work, personal growth, developing new skills, and high materialistic rewards rather than a specific sector preference (Gratton and Scott (2016); Ng *et al.* 2010; Tschirhart *et al.* 2008; Twenge and Kasser 2013; Van der Wal 2015b). Indeed, the proliferation of management degrees that emphasize transferable skills and cross-sectoral problem-solving may increasingly produce 'sector-agnostic' graduates who self-direct their careers to jobs and organizations matching their needs and values (Ng *et al.* 2016; Rose 2013; Van der Wal 2015b).

Public managers with limited abilities to offer competitive financial compensation packages have to search for other ways to attract and retain new workers. An emerging body of work on different types of 'sector-switchers' provides insight into their motives and characteristics (Bozeman and Ponomariov 2009; De Graaf and Van der Wal 2008; Hansen 2014; Johnson and Ng. 2015; Su and Bozeman 2009). Such empirical insights assist public managers in devising actions for attracting, retaining, and re-employing talent, focusing here on switches towards and away from the public sector, as shown in Table 7.2.

TABLE 7.2 **Managing motives for sector-switching**

	Push factors	*Pull factors*	*What managers can do*
Public to private	• Lack of career progress	• Better pay and compensation	• Increase 'cost of leaving' • Maximize flexible pay opportunities
Public to non-profit	• Lack of career progress • 'Entry shock' (disillusionment with lack of opportunities to actualize values and motivations)	• Advancement opportunities • Better value fit	• Provide opportunities for mission-intensive, street-level projects • Enable cross-sectoral work and volunteer opportunities
Private to public	• Downsizing or outsourcing	• More meaningful work • More managerial responsibilities • Better value fit	• Strategically recruit from private sector by emphasizing mission and social innovation opportunities • Create lateral entry roads while providing senior-level coaching about the 'public sector ways'
Non-profit to public	• Declining values fit due to 'mission drift' • Lack of self-development opportunities	• Better pay and compensation • More job security	• Emphasize how realizing public missions is supported by better career opportunities • Illustrate how public sectors are crucial in scaling up and diffusing social innovations

Overall, research evidence provides three key take-aways for public managers.

- They have to differentiate between senior employees and junior employees without supervisory responsibilities, as well as between university-educated and non-university-educated employees. Managers and graduates are both more likely to switch between different sectors than non-managers and non-university-educated individuals, with pay being an increasingly important factor (Hansen 2014; Johnson and Ng. 2015).
- Millennials with unrealistic expectations towards making promotion and getting more opportunities are pushed out from the public sector by a perceived lack of career opportunities and advancement (Foster *et al.* 2003; Ng *et al.* 2010). For senior managers, disappointment with a perceived lack of trust in their abilities to run large-scale policy programmes and departmental operations may be a key reason to leave government (Su and Bozeman 2009). We should note, however, that pay for senior executives varies considerably across countries, and this also may affect switching considerations (Brans and Peters 2012).
- Values and ethos are important pull factors, but, more importantly, experienced 'values misfit', let alone demotivating or unethical environments and superiors, can quickly push out employees with a strong sense of mission and public service motivation (De Graaf and Van der Wal 2008).

Compensation, motivation, and talent management

This observation on values and motivations brings us to an increasingly crucial issue in public sector HRM. How can public managers maximize the intrinsic, mission-oriented character of public sector work to attract and retain talented employees with a calling for public service (Perry *et al.* 2010; Vandenabeele 2008), while offering realistic compensation and advancement opportunities (Twenge and Kasser 2013; Van der Wal 2013)? As shown, millennials and Gen Z-ers are motivated by a complex and dynamic mix of intrinsic and extrinsic motivators (listed in Table 7.3). Public managers and personnel directors have to offer balanced packages and opportunities that speak to both types of motivators. Indeed, salary and monetary benefits remain important components of competitive compensation packages, no matter how important intrinsic levers may become (Andersen *et al.* 2012; Hamidullah 2016; Pink 2009).

However, studies on sector-switching dynamics suggests that while opportunities to make fast promotions and acquire heavier responsibilities are important early in careers, competitive compensation is more

TABLE 7.3 Intrinsic versus extrinsic motivators

Intrinsic	*Extrinsic*
• Job content	• Pay and other benefits
• Self-development	• Job security
• Autonomy	• Career perspective
• Interesting work	• Position and power over other people
• The chance to learn new things	• Work–life balance

Sources: Buelens and Van den Broeck 2007; Houston 2000; Khojasteh 1993.

important later, and investment in training and development is increasingly important throughout a millennial's career (Hamidullah 2016; Lyons *et al.* 2015; Terjesen *et al.* 2007). Moreover, contrary to what private sector-inspired wisdom suggests, some surveys suggest the new workforce prefers more base pay rather than performance pay 'given the weak achievement-reward link that they exhibit and their sense of entitlement' (Ng *et al.* 2010: 290).

However, the public sector has a unique selling point that goes beyond these more general offerings. It offers new generations who want to change the world and do meaningful work the best opportunities to do just that. Indeed, governments have increasingly started to brand the public sector as an exciting and intellectually stimulating employer by advertising how opportunities to work on the most complex societal issues satisfy more intrinsic drivers and values.

A proliferating body of work examines such drivers and values through the concept of *public service motivation* or *PSM* – 'an individual's predisposition to respond to motives grounded primarily or uniquely in public institutions and organizations' (Perry and Wise 1990: 368). PSM consists of four main dimensions, as shown in Box 7.2. Evidence shows that public sector and non-profit employees generally have high levels of PSM, certainly when compared with private sector employees. PSM, in turn,

---

Box 7.2 Dimensions of public service motivation (PSM)

- attraction to policy-making
- civic duty and commitment to public interest
- compassion
- self-sacrifice

Sources: Perry 1996, 2000.

relates positively to job performance, job satisfaction, organizational citizenship, and public sector career choices (Perry *et al.* 2010; Wright and Grant 2010; Kim *et al.* 2013; Ritz *et al.* 2016). Some regional differences exist, with Asian public workers – including millennials – being somewhat more extrinsically motivated as they emphasize a 'love for money' and a desire for success and (financial) achievement compared with their Western counterparts (Chen and Hsieh 2015; Liu and Tang 2011; Perry *et al.* 2012; Van der Wal 2015a, 2015b).

Branding activities alone are insufficient, however, as idealistic employees with high levels of PSM may get disappointed when the first few years of public sector employment turn out to be less rewarding and exciting than they envisioned (Kjeldsen and Jacobsen 2013). Thus, HRM practices need to be *commensurate with public service values and motivations*, and reward and promote those with talent for creating public value. Partly, this is a matter of constructing meaningful performance measurement criteria, increasingly alongside employees and stakeholders (De Bruijn 2012; Noordegraaf 2015). Newer generations are keen to co-create solutions in teams but also highly value work autonomy. In fact, a constraining boss is considered one of the main reasons for quitting a job, and millennials are more loyal to their teams and networks than to agencies and sectors (Adams 2000; Hamidullah 2016).

More than this, however, public managers need to offer opportunities and autonomy so that new employees can directly contribute to public value creation and experience meaningfulness up close. One seemingly counterintuitive attribute of millennials, given their desire for autonomy, is their need for constant feedback and affirmation, and for clear supervision and guidance in the early years of their career. In fact, unsuccessfulness sometimes results in overreaction, aggression, and anxiety (Twenge *et al.* 2012; Bushman *et al.* 2009; Silverman 2011). So, how do public managers nurture somewhat narcissistic employees who all want to be leaders while only few will?

Most importantly, public managers will have to ensure that those in the new workforce continue to feel that they are taken seriously by providing them with constant feedback, training and learning opportunities, and individualized career perspectives. As a result, public managers need to tailor their HRM and talent management practices much more than in the past. One way of doing this is through appointing chief talent officers rather than personnel directors, and not just as a semantic exercise (see Box 7.3). More structurally, however, public managers will need to engage in a variety of mentoring practices and programmes. Such programmes have to:

- socialize and groom new generations for successful public service careers;
- be honest about expectations that may *not* be met;
- maximize public service ethos and PSM in newcomers;
- keep their own managerial skillsets up to date.

Box 7.3 Chief talent officers

Traditionally, HR managers and personnel directors are associated with fairly boring, routine activities, like salary administrations and annual performance reviews. This goes in particular for public sector organizations, whose personnel policies are constrained by labour regulations, tenure, and seniority structures. Moreover, the HR office is often joked about as 'the employee's version of the principal's office': a place that they want to avoid as much as they can.

Since the early 2000s, however, there has been a surge in so-called *strategic* HRM practices, consulting, and scholarship that connect the HRM function more explicitly with leadership objectives and executive decision-making. One product of strategic HRM thinking has been the so-called chief talent officer (CTO).

Initially, CTOs were met with scepticism. Despite the C in front of their title, the first cohorts of CTOs seemed to lack authority and seniority and were not really 'chiefs' of anything except the same old personnel management routines. In recent years, however, urged by personnel shortages, a baby boom cohort retirement wave, and an international, cross-sectoral war for talent, CTOs and the strategic importance of human resource development they signify are increasingly integrated in broader organizational strategies.

Maximizing the CTO function requires a continuous, future-oriented assessment of needs and shortages, a long-term view of succession planning and leadership development, and perhaps a fundamental overhaul of HRM practices, with the recent abolishment of performance reviews by consulting giant Deloitte as an example. It is no coincidence Deloitte employs one of the world's most well-known CTOs.

So far, the CTO has been an exclusively private sector phenomenon. What is the potential for the CTO function in 21st century public agencies, and how can public managers reform rigid HRM systems and practices? Senior executive services in some countries have institutionalized a more tailored approach to leadership grooming (see also Box 7.4) – often at considerable cost, and with varying success. Newer generations, however, will demand such an approach, even if they are not part of an elitist high-potential class. Increased investment and effort into talent management at all levels will have to accompany increased flexibility and mobility to enable public managers to incentivize employees within budget constraints.

Sources: Fast Company, https://fastcompany.com/3002275/leveraging-power-chief-talent-officer; Forbes, https://forbes.com/sites/jacobmorgan/2016/03/01/the-chief-talent-officer-of-deloitte-on-the-future-of-talent.

(Reverse) mentoring

Public management mentoring of new employees has only recently attracted attention from scholars and practitioners. That goes even more for 'reverse mentoring', where older members of the workforce less accustomed to new ways of working are mentored by younger, tech-savvy employees. Both types of mentoring serve at least four clusters of managerial objectives:

- They *increase organizational socialization and acquiescence of social capital by newcomers*, they help preservation of institutional memory and culture, and they instil a sense of public service ethos and PSM in new employees (Bozeman and Feeney 2008, 2009; Paarlberg and Lavigna 2010; Wright and Grant 2010).
- They *increase workplace diversity and mutual understanding between generations and employees with different backgrounds*, and empower traditionally disadvantaged and underrepresented groups (Barrett and Greene 2008; Ehrich and Hansford 2008; Ragins 1997; Riccucci 2002).
- They *help build a pipeline of future managers and leaders* with enhanced career potential amid a rapidly ageing managerial class (Hamidullah 2016; Barrett and Greene 2008; Schall 1997).
- They *prolong the productivity, skillset, and sense of belonging of older workers*, who will retire later than before but may experience reduced commitment and motivation (Chaudhuri and Ghosh 2011; Harvey *et al.* 2009; Lancaster and Stillman 2002).

In their study on public management mentoring, Bozeman and Feeney (2009) present the potential outcomes of public management mentoring at three levels: the organization, the mentee, and the broader public service (displayed in Figure 7.1).

FIGURE 7.1   Public management mentoring outcomes at three levels

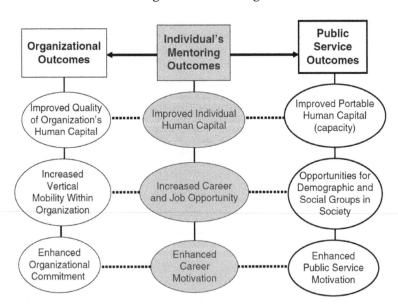

Reprinted with permission from Bozeman and Feeney 2009: 144.

Managing traditional mentoring: issues and benefits

Indeed, mentoring – if executed well – can aid public managers in addressing various HRM issues discussed in this chapter. In thinking about initiating or institutionalizing mentoring practices in their agencies, however, public managers need to manage and make choices on a number of issues:

- Should programmes be formal or informal?
- How should they set expectations and objectives?
- How actively should they be involved in coupling mentors and mentees?
- Should they be from the same organization or not, and have a formal working relationship?

Table 7.4 addresses these four key questions and outlines issues public managers should consider (see Bozeman and Feeney 2008; Godshalk and Sosik 2003), along with strategies to manage them.

It is very possible that public managers and their employees alike will recognize that much of the successful mentoring they've experienced takes place through organic and informal rather than formal programmes and practices. Evidence is somewhat inconclusive as to which approach produces the most effective outcomes in terms of employee satisfaction, promotion, psychosocial support, and managerial objectives and costs (Bozeman and Feeney 2008; Chao *et al.* 1992; Noe 1988; Tepper 1995). Ideally, public managers will employ both informal and formal approaches; support organizational cultures in which employees learn from each other and share insights, skills, and social capital across generations and hierarchical fault lines; and design smart, targeted programmes for specific socialization, succession, and empowerment purposes.

To what extent are public agencies already engaging in formal mentoring, and are current programmes successful? Various agencies across the globe have started formal mentoring programmes in recent years (Bozeman and Feeney 2009; Ehrich and Hansford 2008; McKinsey 2013), having lagged behind the private sector for decades (Eby and Allen 2002; Fox and Schuhmann 2001). Box 7.4 identifies commonalities from a number of successful recent initiatives. It shows that the duration of mentoring programmes, ranging from a few months to several years, should be contingent on the programme's key purpose.

Managing reverse mentoring: issues and benefits

Most mentoring programmes have a fairly classical structure: a senior manager shares strategies, networks, and 'war stories' with a mentee to prepare her for a great future within the organization. However, to meet 21st century demands, senior public managers will increasingly need to be mentored by Gen Y and Gen Z employees who can intuitively explain

TABLE 7.4 Four mentoring questions and strategies for public managers

Key questions in public management mentoring	Potential issues	Managerial strategies
Should public managers emphasize formal programmes or informal, organic practices?	• Formal programmes tend to constrain choice and may not emphasize the quality of the mentoring relationship • Informal practices, on the other hand, are hard to manage and outcomes may not be comparable or measurable	• Create tailored formal programmes for newcomers, middle managers, and top leadership succession • Support and enable informal practices throughout careers by giving seniors time and responsibility for mentoring
How do public managers set and communicate objectives and expectations?	• Objectives and expectations should clearly match programme purposes to avoid disappointment or 'absence' of outcomes • At the same time, mentoring programmes for newcomers may serve various purposes and should not be overly straightjacketed	• Formalize expectations in outcome targets with mentor and protégée while allowing protégées some flexibility in defining needs and expectations • Organize in-between assessments to modify and improve process if necessary
How do public managers devise criteria and procedures for coupling mentors and protégées?	• Highly popular, motivated, and networked mentors and protégés will self-select their relationships, with uneven mentoring outcomes as a result • Too much involvement, however, will lead to a 'forced' relationship	• Diversify and steer coupling to ensure a mix of gender, experience, character, and background • Match identified gaps and needs rather than personalities and 'stars'
Do public managers assign internal or external mentors?	• Internal mentors are likely to meet more frequently with protégées, comply with programme objectives, and ensure better organizational socialization • External mentors, on the other hand, may be more natural (and long-standing) partners, provide a wider network, and have no formal authority relationship with the protégée	• Assign internal mentors for newcomers with concrete socialization and networking objectives • Allow and support informal external mentoring by former colleagues, teachers, and coaches • Create formal external mentoring opportunities as part of leadership programmes

---

Box 7.4 What successful public sector mentoring initiatives share

- A very **clear sense of programme purpose**: Public managers need to be very clear about whether the programme's objective is (a) to socialize newcomers into the organization's ways – requiring no more than a few sessions during a three-month period – or (b) to be a competitive succession management programme aiming to produce a pipeline of future leaders, which may take years and various rounds of training, assignments, and mentoring. Examples include senior leadership programmes from the Department of Defense (DOD) and the National Security Agency (NSA) in the US, which cultivate selected employees long before they reach the senior level, and combine experiential with formal, academic leadership training.
- A **continuous, self-accelerating dynamic**: Public managers and employees valuing the outcomes of the coaching and mentoring they receive often become coaches and mentors themselves. An example is a recent initiative in Newcastle in the UK where 100 public managers are coached before enrolling in an advanced leadership and performance coaching degree programme, initiating and building a perpetual internal mentoring capability. Ultimately, the aim is to make the public sector self-sufficient in coaching provision while providing public managers with opportunities for self-development *and* the chance to 'give back' their experience and energy to future generations.
- A **forward-looking approach**: Regardless of whether successful mentoring programmes are aimed at socialization, coaching, or succession, they are characterized by a forward-looking approach. An example is the Internal Revenue Service (IRS) in the US, which runs various annual individual assessments by managers and agency reviews of potential future leaders linked to emerging leadership needs. Managers and employees sit down every year to make a development plan. This has led to a situation where the IRS has between three and ten candidates 'shelf ready' for various managerial positions, from frontline to senior.

Sources: McKinsey Global Institute 2013; Partnership for Public Service 2013; *The Guardian* 2013; *Washington Post* 2013.

---

technological innovations and other emerging workplace trends to them. The term 'reverse mentoring' was coined for this inverted mentoring relationship in 1999 by the notorious CEO of General Electric and leadership guru, Jack Welch (Chaudhuri and Ghosh 2012). It is a fairly new phenomenon, particularly in the public sector. However, private sector evidence provides public managers with four key lessons, particularly for using reverse mentoring as a tool to keep new generations committed and older workers engaged.

First of all, public managers will have to overcome a sense of reluctance to introduce reverse mentoring. After all, reverse mentoring challenges many normative expectations and perceptions of traditional mentoring in terms of age suitability for a productive mentor–mentee relationship (Noe 1988). At first, many older employees may feel uncomfortable, or even offended, when assigned a junior mentor. Private sector experience shows the key here is to remove age and experience stipulations by emphasizing skills such as technology and (social) media competence instead (Kram and Ragins 2007).

Second, once public managers decide to initiate reverse mentoring programmes, however, they may find older employees keener to participate than they expected. Partly, this may be explained by a concept known in the management sciences as *perceived organizational support* or *POS* (Eisenberger *et al.* 1986). Older employees who are not part of management development programmes may be plateauing in terms of job content, intellectual challenges, and career opportunities; this process is exacerbated by a general lack of professional development initiatives for mid-level employees (Allen *et al.* 1998; Chaudhuri and Ghosh 2012: 62). Indeed, they perceive a lack of organizational and managerial support, and experience declined commitment and satisfaction as a result (Keene 2006; Taylor and Urwin 2001).

Box 7.5 illustrates how some of the stereotypes of older workers can be addressed. Participating in reverse mentoring programmes may reduce insecurities that senior managers have about skill obsolescence and their future in the organization (Armstrong-Stassen and Ursel 2009; Charness and Czaja 2006).

Third, millennials and the emerging Gen Z may be equally keen to respond to the call of public managers to participate in such mentoring programmes, albeit partly for different reasons. As they enter organizations that operate based on long-established values, rituals, and assumptions of older generations occupying key positions (Schein 1992), they may have difficulty socializing (Myers and Sadaghiani 2010). Giving them opportunities to share their skills and feel recognized as useful contributors from the start will not only improve fit but meet some of the key work motivators of new generations identified earlier in this chapter.

Fourth and finally, public managers may particularly satisfy such drivers if they pitch these programmes as mutually beneficial by emphasizing social affiliation and embeddedness with other generations. In a way, assigning older employees who do not occupy very senior roles in the organization – and may therefore be more keen to participate anyway – will pre-empt normative role expectations, as young entrants will be less intimidated and older protégées may feel less 'behind schedule' in their careers (Chaudhuri and Ghosh 2012: 64; Finkelstein *et al.* 2003). It will be important, however, for public managers to introduce the senior protégée to the young mentor as someone with proven value and experience, to ensure mutual respect and prevent the perception of the mentee as a 'has been'.

Box 7.5 'Greyglers' and millennial beards

In a 2015 *TIME* magazine article with the title 'The millennial beard: why boomers need their younger counterparts. And vice versa', Susanna Schrobsdorff describes how middle-aged workers are increasingly insecure when it comes to anything that concerns content or technology, and enthusiastically embrace almost any idea coming from a millennial. The most telling example she gives is how Google – with a median employee age of 29 – has started a support group for people over 40 – called 'Greyglers' – that hopes to promote 'age diversity awareness' and foster the success of its 'elders'. Supported by the notion that young people are smarter and faster, many technology and social innovation-oriented agencies deliberately aim for a young workforce. This is increasingly the case in the public sector as well, as the next chapter will show.

Indeed, with newer generations of workers rapidly entering organizations and moving up the managerial ranks, they may soon outnumber employees currently in their 40s and 50s. However, the notion that such older employees will increasingly become redundant, obsolete, and 'useless' may be mistaken. Public managers need to realize that for organizations to be successful they will have to leverage the strengths of increasingly co-dependent generations. They should also communicate the benefits of generational interdependency to their successors, who will in turn be 'old' themselves one day.

Young entrants need older, experienced employees to provide guidance and feedback for improvement, and senior employees need millennials and Gen Z-ers to get their ideas across to multiple stakeholders in 21st century ways. Moreover, senior employees who have 'seen it all' and 'tried that before' have an important role to play in mentoring millennials' high expectations, also when it comes to balancing family life with a demanding career – something youngsters greatly aspire to but hardly know how to manage.

Gen Y and Gen Z employees can aid more senior workers in transitioning into office cultures where landlines, voicemails, nameplates, and private offices may soon become obsolete. They can also re-energize older colleagues by showing how ideas that didn't work in the past are easily achievable with the help of technology. Positioning junior employees as mentors who have skillsets that matter will also boost their morale and create a win-win dynamic. Sharing is key here; subordinate–manager relationships should be avoided here even more so than in traditional mentoring programmes. Lastly, reverse mentoring programmes should address more than just technology and include broader lifestyle issues such as the changing nature of office work.

Sources: Biggs 2016; Earle 2011; Schrobsdorff 2015.

Managing newcomer socialization through networks

Finally, public managers need to position the various (reverse) mentoring efforts they employ within existing internal and external networks. Indeed, evidence shows that using such networks effectively is crucial for learning, adjustment, and rapid integration, which ultimately ensure successful socialization and person–environment fit (Fang *et al.* 2011; Hatmaker 2015; Morrison 2002). Socialization also requires pro-active behaviour on the part of the newcomer; successful socializers will quickly cease to be newcomers and even reshape network ties. However, to allow newcomers to ease in and feel comfortable admitting a lack of knowledge and asking questions (Borgatti and Cross 2003), public managers need to explicitly point out the various types of networks that exist and clarify their functions. Hatmaker (2015: 1153) identifies five important network types:

1. *advice networks* for advice on task performance, decision-making, and problem-solving;
2. *organizational information networks* for knowledge about goals, norms, politics, structure, and history;
3. *friendship networks* for support, and sense of belonging and identity;
4. *social support networks* for discussing sensitive matters and to rely on in a crisis;
5. *developmental networks* for career development, consisting of individuals and developers.

Managing flexibly, virtually, and remotely

Managing changing views and nature of work

The need for mentoring, coaching and personal development, and flexible work options supporting the desire for work–life balance – a deciding factor for newer generations when taking a job (Burke and Cooper 2004) – signifies that there is a broader, more fundamental phenomenon affecting public sector workplaces than just generational changes. There is a shift in the nature of work itself and the thinking about the role and importance of work – and how and where it is carried out – in our societies. This shift will be central in the remainder of the chapter.

Indeed, organizations across the globe have not only started to offer benefits like parental leave for young dads – a much desired and utilized feat of employment packages in recent years (Vielmetter and Sell 2014) – but also flexitime, telecommuting opportunities, and room for pursuing additional education, volunteer work, or other personal and professional development opportunities (Johnson and Ng 2015; Ng *et al.* 2010). All such offerings reflect a world in which boundaries between public and private life are increasingly blurred. As the introductory examples in this chapter illustrate, more flexible, remote, and virtual work settings are emerging, aided by technological revolutions that allow individuals and teams to work, network, and interact anywhere and everywhere.

In the same vein, various thinkers have recently produced fascinating scenarios about the changing nature of work – how, where, and when it is done – and changing views towards work and careers, including their overall importance and their position vis-à-vis private life (see e.g., Gratton and Scott (2016). In such scenarios, work will be increasingly non-routine, spontaneous, and experiential, with policies and programmes being 'experienced' and co-created together with stakeholders (Dickinson and Sullivan 2014; Levy and Murnane 2004). The consulting firm Deloitte (2010, 2016) has produced various reports on this issue, introducing the concept of the 'corporate lettuce' to replace the 'corporate ladder', and illustrating a working world that is increasingly flat, flexible, remote, intuitive, and blurred: 'work is what you do' rather than 'work is where you go'.

Public managers will have to move along with – and shape – such developments while maintaining a sense of structure, accountability, and stability. A key way to do this is by providing teleworking opportunities (Green and Roberts 2010; Mahler 2012). How can public managers do so effectively?

Managing teleworking teams

Clearly, managing employees, teams, and bosses of various generations and backgrounds in a classical office setting is hard enough as it is. Managing them in increasingly scattered, diffuse, and 'virtual' workplaces requires additional communication, coordination, and motivational skills to maximize the opportunities such settings provide. In fact, remote work has been with us in various shapes and forms for a few decades now (Cascio 2000; Fiol and O'Connor 2005), with public sector organizations being somewhat slower in its adoption than their private sector counterparts (Overmyer 2011; Mahler 2012).

However, despite the promises of reductions in cost, travel time, and environmental footprint, and of improved productivity, efficiency, employee wellbeing, and work–life balance, various long-standing organizational and managerial concerns remain (Caillier 2012; Crandall and Gao 2005; Green and Roberts 2010; Johnson 2010). Such concerns continue to hamper wide-scale implementation of remote work-enabling practices even though technological developments and workforce characteristics will urge public sectors to drastically expand and maximize such practices. One emerging concern is the so-called 'telework divide' (Mahler 2012: 408), described in Box 7.6, which highlights how less digitally skilled managers and employees struggle with operating effectively in such settings.

Box 7.6 Telework divide

Governments across the world have adopted a variety of long-distance work practices, aided by teleworking and telecommunicating technologies, jointly labelled as the 'virtual workplace'. Such efforts, however, have paid little attention to potential downsides of further dividing an already inequitable workforce into 'teleworkers' and 'non-teleworkers', creating an increasing telework divide. Whereas some employees and functions may simply not be eligible for remote working, other employees may be prevented from engaging in potentially advantageous ways of working because of management resistance or distrust in their capabilities.

Evidence from various large-scale surveys within the US federal government suggests a telework divide exists:

- those who are not allowed to telework feel they have fewer opportunities to improve their skills, feel their talents are less well used and they are less empowered, and receive less supervisory support for work–life balance;
- those who are not allowed to telework have higher turnover intentions, perhaps because they feel a lesser obligation to remain;
- those who choose not to telework show consistently higher levels of satisfaction than those who are not allowed to do so; and
- those who frequently telework report higher levels of public service motivation (PSM) than those who telework up to one day a week.

The findings seem to corroborate the view that public sector employees increasingly demand autonomy, opportunity, and support for collaboration from their managers. Public managers, in turn, need to devise and communicate clear standards for flexi-work eligibility, utilize such standards consistently and fairly, and carefully explain decision outcomes about who is entitled to more flexibility and why.

Sources: Caillier 2011, 2016; Mahler 2012; Government Office of Personnel Management (OPM) 2011; Government Merit Systems Protection Board (MSPB) 2011.

One way of addressing the telework divide and other risks and weaknesses of telecommuting is by applying what we know about effective teamwork to the emerging virtual workspace. Managers need to compose virtual teams – of on-site and remote employees in various configurations – rather than simply outsourcing and isolating individual functions (Green and Roberts 2010). Bridging on-site, remote, and virtual worlds, practices, and skills is key here. Indeed, we can identify a number of common concerns and success factors in creating such bridges and making virtual teams work, from the viewpoint of both team members and their managers (Caillier 2016; Ferrazzi 2012; Watkins 2013), shown in Table 7.5.

TABLE 7.5 Managing virtual teams: concerns and success factors

	Members	*Managers*
Common concerns	• Unequal opportunities to participate in remote working practices ('telework divide') • Unclear and unpredictable communication and meeting patterns • Alienation and isolation • Free-riding behaviour • Lack of training and skills	• Reduced employee oversight and accountability • Lower employee productivity • Less direct interpersonal contact • Fewer team-building opportunities • Risks of virtual micro-managing
	Green and Roberts 2010; Mahler 2012; Watkins 2013.	Green and Roberts 2010; McDonald 2004; Watkins 2013.
Critical success factors	• Commitment to a communication and scheduling charter • Negotiated agreement on shared language and norms • Pro-active stance and added, continuous investment in maintaining group cohesion	• Remote *and* physical spaces devoted to team-building and trust-building (particularly early on) • Careful design and tracking of tasks and commitments (e.g., through 'deliverables dashboard') • Leveraging the most enabling and robust technologies rather than the newest or most advanced
	Cascio 2000; Ferrazzi 2012; Mahler 2012; Watkins 2013.	Ferrazzi 2012; Mahler 2012; Offstein *et al.* 2010; Watkins 2013.

Many of these factors hark back to those generally identified in chapter 'Managing Authority Turbulence' when we discussed effective teams. However, the additional challenges of remote and virtual teams amplify critical traits such as trust-building; coordination and predictability of communication; a shared understanding of tasks, goals, and responsibilities; and the need to recruit for a complementary variety of behavioural attributes and skillsets (Green and Roberts 2010; Katzenbach and Smith 1993). In the same vein, Kossek and Thompsom (2015: 5) argue that managers can avoid various 'workplace flexibility traps' by using flexi-work as a systemic empowerment tool and not just to accommodate changing employee demands.

Managing computerization and robotization

Being mindful of how interpersonal skills and collective performance management will mitigate common issues in virtual and remote teamworking settings will aid public managers in making such settings work. Still, in the years and decades to come, 'virtual' and 'remote' will take on new meanings, some of which may be hard to imagine at present, thus exerting new pressures on managers aiming to maintain a 'human touch' in virtual settings. Already, advanced e-governance solutions (to be discussed extensively in the next chapter) have entirely replaced the physical and human elements of public service delivery. In addition, managers and employees who collaborate across time and space will increasingly use highly sophisticated joint-authoring and co-creating tools in the cloud, as illustrated in this chapter's introduction, rather than just long-distance meeting and communication devices. Such tools require more advanced technical competencies.

An even more fundamental development, however, is the fact that software and robots are predicted to take over up to 45 per cent of current jobs and functions in a variety of sectors between now and 2035 (Elkins 2015; Frey and Osborne 2013). Box 7.7 outlines the potential implications of computerization and robotization for the public sector workforce and public managers.

Managing workforce uberization

Some of the new public sector employees already seem to have adapted to a working environment characterized by less job security. They increasingly accept part-time, temporary, multi-job, and non-unionized modes of employment that do not provide the traditional protection and security of public sector tenure (Dickinson and Sullivan 2014; Kingston 2014). Some speak of increasing 'uberizing of the government workforce' (Kellar 2015), making reference to taxi industry disruptor Uber, which allows part-time individuals to offer taxi rides through Uber's app-based client network without receiving any employee benefits or employee protection.

However, the job security and stability emphasized by the next generation of Gen Z workers (based on the evidence we have so far), and their concomitant worries and pragmatism about their own economic future, distinguish them from the Gen Y employees currently rising through the public sector ranks. A resurgence of the classical bureaucratic motivator, 'job security', may create new pressures and challenges for public managers when the demand for secure and predictable work environments far exceeds supply. Also, pension and labour market reforms that are under way in many countries will force individuals to work longer and longer, potentially beyond the age of 70, a few decades from now. All this urges public leaders to fundamentally rethink the types of careers and security that public sectors have to offer, as illustrated in Box 7.8.

In a way, these developments fit with a public management reform trend that started in the early 2000s in countries such as New Zealand and Sweden, and has trickled down to various other OECD countries. Their governments have fully or partially abolished the special, legally protected status of civil servants through a normalization process that aims to harmonize civil servants' rights and duties with those of their

Box 7.7 Computerization and robotization: workforce implications

Since the 1980s, large-scale IT developments have led to increasing automation of jobs. In the years to come, however, automation will most likely no longer be confined to 'blue collar' jobs. A variety of medium-skilled to high-skilled tasks are at risk of being automated, including financial analysis, paralegal research, skills training, and communication and recruitment. Certain managerial work itself may ultimately be outsourced to automated intelligence. The 'relentless rise of automation' and 'robotics' were key themes at the World Economic Forum in 2016.

Discussions about the end of work are reminiscent of economist John Maynard Keynes' famous predictions during the Great Depression in the 1930s: that technological progress would allow for a 15-hour work week with abundant leisure time by 2030. Current predictions should be therefore be viewed with a healthy dose of scepticism. In particular, senior managers practising political management will not see their masters or adversaries being replaced by machines and software anytime soon.

Moreover, optimists emphasize the creation of possibilities and jobs that we do not know of today, just as the first machine age was spurred by the industrial revolution, and the internet economy has created many new opportunities. Like other critics in the past, they dismiss the end-of-work argument as 'Luddite fallacy', referring to 19th-century British hand-weavers ('Luddites') who destroyed textile-making machines, fearing they would rob them of their jobs. Moreover, innovations already destroy 15 per cent of all jobs each year in developed countries, with recent predictions about robots adding to those numbers perhaps being rather marginal.

Still, regardless of whether the 'fourth industrial revolution' or 'second machine age' will produce as many new jobs as it eliminates, it has at least three implications for public managers. It reinforces the importance of reverse mentoring and skills programmes to prevent less adaptable workers from lagging behind. At the same time, it provides public managers with a hiring advantage in the nearby future, given the rising number of underemployed and unemployed graduates. Finally, it may increasingly render the closed and seniority-based tenure systems that still characterize many public sectors unworkable as they prevent public managers and politicians from upgrading and adapting at reasonable costs.

Sources: Elkins 2015; Frey and Osborne 2013; WEF 2016; Worstall 2013; *The Atlantic*, https://theatlantic.com/magazine/archive/2015/07/world-without-work/395294/.

private sector counterparts (Lavelle 2010; Pollitt and Bouckaert 2011; Van der Meer, Van den Berg, and Dijkstra 2013; Van der Wal 2016). Taken together, these developments pressure public managers to become more flexible, inventive, and ad hoc in their job design and hiring practices while providing enough opportunities for employees to remain mobile.

Box 7.8 The end of job security: threat or opportunity for public managers?

Traditionally, public sectors have been able to offer the most stable and secure types of careers. Job security and stable benefits and work environments have been key bureaucratic job motivators for over a century, and still are in many countries with career-based rather than position-based systems. Increasingly, however, governments hit by austerity measures and cutbacks are offering temporary, sometimes part-time contracts for a variety of functions, just like businesses that have to downsize and rehire almost continuously. Those supporting smaller government laud, and even promise to stimulate, such work-force uberization.

At first glance, governments appear to lose a key competitive advan-tage in terms of employer attractiveness for those who value job security. On the other hand, not all future employees may desire stability and secu-rity. Various public managers are already adjusting to this new reality. For example, HR managers of Coconino County in the US state of Arizona chose to provide job-sharing, phased-retirement options, telecommuting, and flexible scheduling to retain employees when it could not offer salary increases. Employees responded with great enthusiasm. As a result, the county was awarded the Center for State and Local Government Excel-lence (SLGE) 2011 Workforce Award and a 2012 American Psychological Association (APA) Psychologically Healthy Workplace Award. City man-agers in other cities and counties in the US are following suit.

It is hard to predict what future generations may demand from public managers and agencies. Twenty-first century public managers, however, have to look ahead and anticipate what is most likely to be more rather than less uberization. They have to start branding public sector employ-ment differently by emphasizing flexibility instead of stability, changing bureaucratic mindsets as they go along. They may even attract a more dynamic, entrepreneurial type of employee. Isn't that exactly what 21ˢᵗ century public agencies need?

Sources: Governing, http://governing.com/columns/smart-mgmt/col-government-workforce-temporary-contract-employees-millennials-flexibility.html; Vox, https://vox.com/2016/3/4/11162514/republicans-love-uber.

Public managers will need to make choices here. Implementing general training and advancement programmes is important, but evidence shows employees easily feel excluded from such programmes if their direct man-ager simply doesn't care that much about their development (Dickinson and Sullivan 2014: 44). Twenty-first century public managers can show they have their workforce's best interests in mind by being honest and direct about opportunities and their limits.

What lies ahead

If public managers can *adequately address new ways of working* and *accommodate and enable new workers with widely divergent attitudes towards work,* they may 'kill two birds with one stone' in meeting some of the key demands in this book. Indeed, Gen Y and Gen Z employees embody many of the skills, competencies, and values called for by a VUCA world. Mentoring newer additions to the public sector workforce to acclimatize them to public sector ways without curbing their enthusiasm and entrepreneurialism is key. Public managers' ability to be 'vulnerable' and open enough to allow juniors to mentor seniors may very well prove a crucial component in creating 21st century public organizations. As such, managing the new work(force) effectively also mitigates some of the forces causing authority turbulence within organizations.

Alongside the influx of new types and generations of workers, technological developments will increase both demands and opportunities for flexible and innovative public service delivery. These demands and opportunities will pressure public managers to respond to increasingly disruptive and radical innovations, and advocate and enable innovative practices within government. How public managers choose to respond, and build a culture of innovation and learning within agencies while overcoming traditional public sector barriers to renew and experiment, will be addressed in the next chapter: *managing innovation forces.*

Chapter 8

Managing Innovation Forces

The innovator has for enemies all those who have done well under the old conditions and lukewarm defenders in those who may do well under the new. This coolness arises partly from fear of the opponents, who have the laws on their side, and partly from the incredulity of men, who do not readily believe in new things until they have had a long experience of them.

(Machiavelli, Il Principe, 1532)

Operating amid disruptions

Imagine being a public manager with the Ministry of Commerce in Beijing, tasked with regulating companies like app-based taxi firm Didi Chuxing, which are part of the rapidly expanding 'sharing economy'. This new economic mode emerged out of an era of economic uncertainty, as it allows unemployed or underemployed individuals to make earnings by leveraging their time, expertise, or personal assets, at any time of day. Didi Chuxing, much like its Indian corollary Ola Cabs, was inspired by the success of San Francisco start-up icons Uber and Airbnb and has managed to increase its value to tens of billions of dollars even faster than they did. *Uberization* – denoting the process where a high-tech middleman replaces past intermediaries with little more than apps and peer feedback systems – has now entered the lexicon. Clearly, a game-changing phenomenon was evolving here and your ministry would need to stimulate such economic innovation to enable Chinese start-ups to develop and compete globally.

At the same time, you and your colleagues struggle with finding the appropriate balance between regulating emerging industries and technologies and protecting existing industries, often with long-standing and deep ties to political and administrative elites. Moreover, there is somewhat of a rift between younger colleagues who are enthusiastic adopters and consumers of these new technologies, and older colleagues who hardly see the significance of them and even seem fearful of how they will affect their long-established ways of working.

Clearly, disruptive innovations like those brought about by the sharing economy create regulatory dilemmas for public managers across contexts. They have to balance existing labour laws, consumer protection, and quality control with the emerging economic opportunities and customer demand to create a conducive rather than stifling climate for entrepreneurship. Moreover, they must not make implicit decisions about which firms fail or succeed, with regulations being perceived by some to favour incumbent firms.

As they respond to disruptions in industries and markets, public managers also have *to innovate their own policies, practices, and assumptions* in responding to assertive stakeholder demands and technological developments, such as cybersecurity threats, social media, and big data. However, public managers aspiring to innovate have to justify investing taxpayers' money in experiments with uncertain outcomes. Moreover, they have to overcome pervasive institutional and individual forces constraining change and renewal, as Machiavelli already observed almost five centuries ago. Institutions and their constituents simply like doing things the way they're used to, even more so when their environment is characterized by uncertainty.

As the new workforce described in the previous chapter is said to be tech-savvy, entrepreneurial, and defiant of traditional bureaucratic hierarchy, it may act as a bottom-up innovation force. However, how do we know it will live up to these promises? After all, resorting to comfort zones and work avoidance rather than adaptation, self-reflection, and the acceptance of responsibility for error characterizes human behaviour across age groups and generations. Either way, it is evident that public managers operating in a VUCA world have to become more skilled at recognizing and adjusting to trends and developments early on, while realistically weighing risks, values, costs, and benefits. This demand of *managing innovation forces* produces tough questions for public managers.

When do they 'move in'? What is 'too early' and what is 'too late', and why? How far can public managers push boundaries in terms of experimentation and piloting by 'trial and error' without risking wasting massive amounts of taxpayer money and losing stakeholder legitimacy? How do they weigh and assess risks? How much innovation is 'enough'? How do public managers nurture a culture of learning, creativity, and adaptation; how do they attract innovators; and how do they become innovators while preserving what works well? More fundamentally, can public managers innovate *at all* given the tense relation between innovative and entrepreneurial behaviour and the key values associated with the long-established bureaucratic ethos, such as stability, predictability, impartiality, and frugality?

Managing innovation forces

Four megatrends in particular are forcing public sectors to change the way they *think, operate, respond, facilitate, and produce* (Tully 2015: 4–5): 'all is networked', 'great expectations', 'more from less', and 'more with less'. Indeed, increasing fiscal, technological, and environmental pressures will render traditional reflexes of slashing budgets and out-sourcing public services insufficient (Hartley *et al.* 2013; Pollitt 2010a). Moreover, as discussed in previous chapters, stakeholders increasingly question the legitimacy of political and administrative decision-making, certainly if public policies fail to effectively tackle wicked problems. In a VUCA world, governments are increasingly confronted with the question of whether their policies, programmes, and processes have evolved in tandem with the complexity of issues, and indeed *whether their existence matters at all*.

To address this question, public managers must fundamentally rethink roles and values, engage in continuous organizational learning, overcome deep-rooted defensive routines and institutional barriers, and adopt new types of management and leadership (Argyris and Schön 1996; Hartley 2015a; Hartley *et al.* 2013; Osborne and Brown 2011). Moreover, when confronted with innovation forces and pressures, they will continuously have to ask themselves whether adopting and implementing innovations will *actually produce public value for citizens* (Moore and Hartley 2008). Indeed, they will have to determine for whom, at what stage, and for which reasons existing policies, practices, and programmes should change.

This chapter suggests ways for public managers to overcome barriers by unlocking opportunities to stimulate, implement, and perpetuate cultures and practices of innovation, illustrated by examples of success and failure from across the globe. It outlines these barriers and opportunities using the five main stages of innovation: idea generation, idea selection, idea testing, idea scaling up, and idea diffusion.

Ranges and types of innovation

However, before we go into the managerial practices and styles needed to manage innovation forces effectively, we have to clarify what 'public sector innovation' means, and whether different types and scales can be distinguished. Like many buzzwords, the 'innovation' label is sometimes too easily used. Most authors insist that innovation involves not only the creative generation of ideas but also *the practical realization, translation, and implementation of those ideas*, emphasizing a certain achievement of results, successful or not (Bessant 2005; Damanpour 1991; Hartley 2015a; Nasi 2015). As such, public sector innovation is commonly under-stood to involve the introduction of new knowledge, processes, skills, services, or policies that transform – sometimes radically or fundamen-tally – current ways of doing things, forging breaks with the past (see De Vries *et al.* 2016; Moore and Hartley 2008; Wynen *et al.* 2013; Zhu 2013).

At the same time, public managers constantly 'work on change' with varying degrees of disruptiveness and radicalness. They engage in small, targeted, sometimes temporary interventions and improvements to make government 'smarter' and keep it 'up to date' alongside more fundamental

FIGURE 8.1   A continuum of renewal

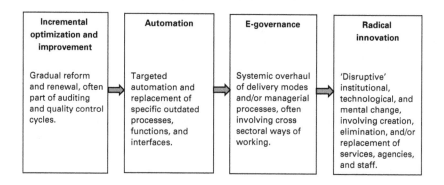

Incremental optimization and improvement	Automation	E-governance	Radical innovation
Gradual reform and renewal, often part of auditing and quality control cycles.	Targeted automation and replacement of specific outdated processes, functions, and interfaces.	Systemic overhaul of delivery modes and/or managerial processes, often involving cross sectoral ways of working.	'Disruptive' institutional, technological, and mental change, involving creation, elimination, and/or replacement of services, agencies, and staff.

reforms and overhauls. Clearly, radical innovations are most complex as they often involve transformation of managerial beliefs and practices. Figure 8.1 displays these different ranges of change and renewal as a continuum, ranging from incremental optimization to radical, transformative innovation (see also Christensen and Laegreid 2001; Hartley 2011; Lekhi 2007).

In addition, we can distinguish different *types* of public sector innovations according to the objectives they serve and the levels at which they operate. Box 8.1 lists five types with an example of each type. Public managers will often be directly involved in the first three types of innovations, whether they are construed 'in-house' or through inter-organizational, inter-sectoral, or 'open' innovation processes (Hartley *et al.* 2013). Conceptual innovations often involve outsourcing to or receiving unsolicited input from external actors, ranging from consultants, design thinkers, and increasingly frequently, citizens, through to the process of 'crowdsourcing' (Crosby and Bryson 2010; Meijer 2014), while rhetorical innovations may involve public managers as co-conspirators in feigning substantive innovation and reform.

Innovating to create public value

Many real-life public sector innovations constitute a combination of types and scales as they unfold over time. They may start as a radical service delivery innovation while simultaneously changing systems and mindsets more fundamentally in the long run, resulting in continuous upgrading and improvement (and ultimately, a new status quo) if they succeed, or the other way around. The example of 'one-stop-shop' Huduma centres in Kenya and similar initiatives across the globe in Box 8.2 illustrate how basic innovations can combine objectives and outcomes. They can improve service delivery and cut red tape while transforming a deeply ingrained mindset of monopoly and corruption at the same time.

Box 8.1 Five different types of public sector innovation

1. **Process innovation:** directed at enhancing the calibre and efficiency of internal and external –administrative, managerial, and technological – work processes.
   Nature: often internally oriented (at least initially) reforms and upgrades, consisting of IT solutions and staff training to reduce 'red tape', speed up procedures, and introduce new ways of working.
   Example: merging and automating interdepartmental authorization cycles to cut down decision layers from five to just two, reducing approval time by 80 per cent.

2. **Product or service innovation:** aimed at developing new public service amenities, services, and products.
   Nature: external, citizen- and customer-oriented e-government solutions often involving automation, outsourcing, and/or collaboration.
   Example: delivering tailored elderly care solutions 'at home' and 'real time' using online consultations and mobile teams of healthcare professionals.

3. **Governance innovation:** focused on the creation of new forms and processes to tackle particular societal issues, often involving cross-sectoral initiatives.
   Nature: often externally oriented (at least initially) and cross-sectoral initiatives to address wicked problems more effectively through new types of policy creation or shared authority and accountability.
   Example: combining public, private, and civic capacity to police unsafe neighbourhoods, using local stakeholder expertise while providing technology and incentives.

4. **Conceptual innovation:** aimed at refashioning and reframing ideas, frames, references, or paradigms about the character of problems as well as their solutions.
   Nature: often creative, disruptive, and radical at the start, while 'toned down' when reaching the implementation stage (if the idea or frame is transformed into a service, process, or skill at all).
   Example: the concept of 'smart city' has reshaped debates about how rapidly growing urbanizing areas can leverage new technologies and big data to address and even pre-empt a variety of urban issues.

5. **Rhetorical innovation:** serving the purpose of convincing stakeholders that reform is under way and government stays up to date, in some cases even to mask cutbacks or lack of 'real' progress.
   Nature: largely symbolic and semantic, sometimes quasi-renewal and reform announcements that may produce actual change when followed through by entrepreneurial individuals and agencies, but may often not.
   Example: rebranding a ministry of environmental affairs into 'the green department', with accompanying new logos and websites, while the core functions and bureaucratic routines stay exactly the same.

Based on: De Vries *et al.* 2016; Hartley 2005, 2015; Newman and Clarke 2009.

Box 8.2 Huduma centres in Kenya: 'taking out the middleman'

After taking office in April 2013, Kenyan President Uhuru Kenyatta declared war on the inefficiencies of the public service. For example, citizens losing their ID card had to secure a sampled abstract from the police – if it was available at all – obtain certifications from chiefs and district officers, have two sets of fingerprints taken, fill out various forms, have photos taken, and then wait endlessly. According to Kenyatta, 'this inefficiency bred corruption, initiating a cycle of vice which tormented many and cost the country billions'.

The introduction of the first one-stop-shop *Huduma centre* in Nairobi in November 2013 allowed people to digitally access and pay for government services ('huduma' translates as 'service' in Swahili). Kenya, one of Africa's most technologically forward countries – famous for its start-ups and online banking innovations – had yet to transfer these capabilities to the public sector. Now, the renewal of an ID card simply required one to report its loss and apply for a replacement. The system's linkage to a government database makes it unnecessary to undergo repeated bouts of fingerprinting and photo-taking.

The initial goal was the provision of 18 services from 10 government agencies, including duplication of National ID cards, drivers' licence renewals, National Health Insurance Fund registration and claims, business name registration, and student loan applications. To date, over 50 established centres attend to over 12,000 people daily and have served millions of Kenyans. The centres brought efficiency and convenience to citizens and government by streamlining government services using a central platform. These gains led to Kenya being awarded the prestigious United Nations Public Service Award in 2015.

In recent years, various other countries have introduced similar service delivery innovations. In Singapore, automated self-service kiosks (AXS and SAM) allow users to pay bills and fines to over 600 public and private institutions, in addition to purchasing a variety of their services. India has introduced the Andhra Pradesh (AP) Smart Card initiative to enhance access to banking and financial services, diminish fraudulent payments, and enable efficient delivery of public services to poor segments of society. Kazakhstan has an e-government web portal, synchronizing all government services into one place to enhance inter-agency linkage and increase convenience to citizens. Now, anyone can register their business online within 15 minutes.

These innovations created public value for citizens through simultaneous service delivery improvements, curbing corruption, and stimulating inclusion and entrepreneurship. Bypassing street-level bureaucrats where they did not add value, they took out the middleman who is a major source of corruption in developing countries.

Sources: Africa Review, http://africareview.com; BBC, http://bbc.co.uk; AXS, http://axs.com.sg; E.gov, https://egov.kz; Ministry of Devolution and Planning (Kenya), http://devolutionplanning. go.ke; Jomo Kenyatta University of Agriculture and Technology, http://Jkuat.ac.ke; Government of Andhra Pradesh, Department of Rural Development, http://rd.ap.gov.in; Standard Digital, https://standardmedia.co.ke.

These examples are successful attempts by public managers to increase public value and respond to stakeholder needs through the use of technology because:

- they are *citizen-centric and user-centric* innovations that are designed with one objective only: to make life easier for average citizens;
- they *leverage technology, not to be 'techy'* but to improve processes of service delivery and eliminate deficiencies in the system;
- they *engage in strategic mimicking of existing best practices* – so-called 'recombinant innovation' through knowledge brokering (Hargadon 2002) – rather than attempting to reinvent the wheel, thus minimizing potential costs, risks, and delays.

Clearly, not all usage of technology to tackle policy problems is successful. Failures occur for a number of reasons, but the dynamics of large-scale failures of public sector IT projects point to a number of commonalities (Commission Elias 2015; Gauld and Goldfinch 2010; Goldfinch 2011). Pushy consultants and solution providers, and impatient political masters – pressured to show they are 'doing something' – dominate the external innovation force field rather than stakeholder aspirations. Moreover, political and administrative elites may also introduce innovations mainly for rhetorical or reputational reasons (Hartley 2005), or even to pursue personal, sometimes narcissistic hobbies or aspirations (Camm 2014; Kets de Vries 2003). As a result, the focus can shift from what is operationally feasible and useful to what is technologically possible, and what 'looks good'.

The example of a public innovation failure in Box 8.3 illustrates what happens if such external innovation forces overwhelm public managers, and private actors capture the collaborative process and exploit it to their own advantage. This highlights the contrast between public value- and private value-seeking behaviour (Hartley *et al.* 2013: 826). Such behaviour is well documented in the literature on public-private partnerships (PPPs) and complex contracting (Boyer *et al.* 2016; Hodge *et al.* 2010; Teisman and Klijn 2002). For partnerships to work, partners need not only networking skills but also smart contracts that distribute risks in a context of information asymmetry and moral hazard. Clearly, public managers should consider 'where, when and how they might best engage the private sector to use their particular skills and expertise' (Cook *et al.* 2009: 1).

The case also shows why public managers need to open up parts of the innovation process as much as possible to include end users and stakeholders. Doing so turns innovation into a collaborative as well as user-centric endeavour, rather than an in-house activity of public and private sector managers (Collm and Schedler 2013: 141; Hartley *et al.* 2013), unless circumstances necessitate secrecy. Different stages of the innovation process may call for varying degrees of openness and collaboration, however, as the next sections will argue.

Box 8.3 The US 'virtual border fence': innovation disaster?

Illegal immigration and border security have been a contested policy issue in the United States for many years. President Bill Clinton's tactic was to build a wall along part of the Mexican border, which was completed only partially. President George W. Bush, on the other hand, sought to address the issue through technology. In 2005, the Department of Homeland Security (DHS) introduced a programme that aimed to secure the 2,000-mile border with a high-tech 'virtual fence'. The Secure Border Initiative Network programme would enable visual monitoring of the border through a network of electronic observation posts on 80-foot towers. The towers would be equipped with cameras and sensors designed to detect movements up to seven miles away and transmit an alert to a Border Patrol station.

However, severe heat and inclement weather conditions disrupted the equipment: if the wind blew the leaves on a bush, the cameras would home in on the activity. The sensors meant to track humans often tracked animals instead. Moreover, many promises made by Boeing, the equipment manufacturer, never materialized. The failure of the system was partially attributed to its complexity. However, the biggest issue was that neither DHS nor the engineers at Boeing bothered to consult the customers – in this case, Border Patrol staff who would actually use the surveillance system – about their needs. As often happens, the employees involved were *confronted with the innovation rather than involved in making the innovation a success*.

Given its $1 billion price tag, the project has been deemed a failure despite some arrests and busts over the years. Professor Wayne A. Cornelius of the University of California contends that 'it's a great deal for Boeing and its subcontractors. It's a bad deal for the taxpayers.' The programme was cancelled by the Obama administration in 2011. It was revived in 2014 when an Arizona House panel approved a plan to develop 350 miles of virtual fence on the southern part of the border. Learning from past experience, DHS used prevailing technology as opposed to the previously used custom-built solutions. More recently, 'building a wall' featured prominently again in the presidential campaign of Donald J. Trump, with various experts disputing the feasibility of his proposals.

This case shows that innovations are trial-and-error endeavours, with failures providing important learning experiences that may prevent future failures. The case also reveals a lack of research, scrutiny, and consultation on the technology's viability and end users' needs. Clearly, public managers need to install (financial) risk mitigation mechanisms to safeguard taxpayers' money, and recognize, correct, or halt initiatives altogether if they are failing. However, public leaders seldom accept 'sunk costs', with prestige and fear of 'losing face' often playing a big role.

Sources: Kroft 2010; Longmire 2015; Medrano 2014; CNN, http://cnn.com; CBC, http://cbc.ca; Fox News, http://foxnews.com.

Managing innovation stages effectively

Before the benefits of successfully implemented innovations are reaped, public managers will have been involved in a painstaking iterative and incremental (rather than disruptive) process of generating, selecting, testing, scaling, and diffusing new ideas (Meijer 2014). This process of innovation has been conceptualized and visualized as a cycle (Hartley *et al.* 2013), a series of analytical phases (Meijer 2014), resembling the well-known policy cycle (Howlett and Ramesh 1995), or a process consisting of loops, jumps, and detours (Mulgan 2014). Experts stress the complex, iterative, and often chaotic nature of innovation. Phases are bypassed or repeated as new ideas are 'shot down' by risk-averse politicians, overturned by electoral results, and made redundant by accelerating technologies (Bason 2010; Hartley 2015a). Moreover, Boxes 2 and 3 show that innovations consist of not just the generation of original ideas and inventions, but also the effective adoption or adaptation of others' innovations (Damanpour and Schneider 2008). Strategic mimicking can also realize innovation.

This brings us to the various roles played by individual public managers during the innovation process. Authors like Hartley *et al.* (2013), Heifetz *et al.* (2009), and Meijer (2014) debunk the notion that innovations are created by brilliant, creative geniuses or 'hero-innovators' (Roberts and King 1996) who work long hours, take risks, and skilfully and confidently persuade politicians to implement their proposals. Although certain traits are associated with successful innovators – including autonomy, risk-taking, entrepreneurship, creativity, and competitiveness – public managers with other skillsets may be highly effective in later stages of the innovation process.

Indeed, conceptual, subversive thinkers creating bold new ideas have very different qualities than the conservative, cynical managers required for testing and re-testing those ideas; and these individuals, in turn, differ from relentless implementers who focus on monitoring and delivering the new idea (Barber 2015). The same applies to teams and organizations: smaller teams work better for generating out-of-the-box ideas, whereas larger organizations are better at scaling up and implementing innovations (Hage and Aiken 1967).

Based on Meijer's (2014: 201–203) work, Figure 8.2 identifies five managerial roles and types in relation to five commonly distinguished stages in the innovation process. These stages will structure the remainder of the chapter.

Managing idea generation and sourcing

Not all public managers are creative, intellectual geniuses – and they don't have to be. They *will* have to be skilled at consulting, hiring, and locating creative types where they add most value, and soliciting ideas through a

FIGURE 8.2   Stages of the innovation cycle and managerial roles

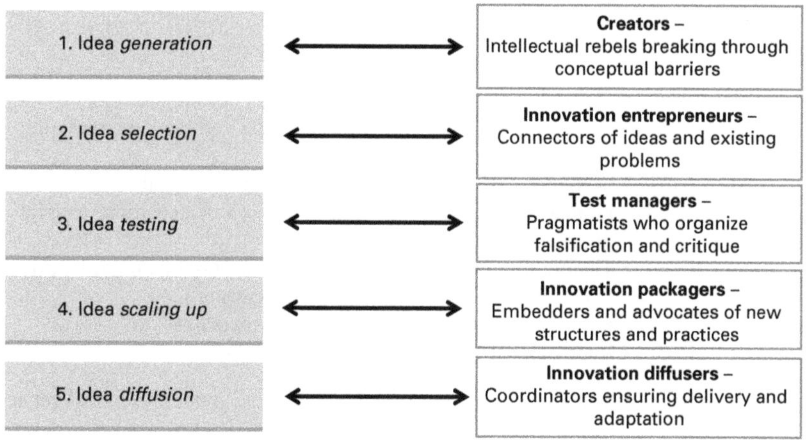

1. Idea *generation*	←→	**Creators –** Intellectual rebels breaking through conceptual barriers
2. Idea *selection*	←→	**Innovation entrepreneurs –** Connectors of ideas and existing problems
3. Idea *testing*	←→	**Test managers –** Pragmatists who organize falsification and critique
4. Idea *scaling up*	←→	**Innovation packagers –** Embedders and advocates of new structures and practices
5. Idea *diffusion*	←→	**Innovation diffusers –** Coordinators ensuring delivery and adaptation

variety of channels. 'Scouting' innovators with great ideas is as important as facilitating innovations within the organization (Meijer 2014: 211). In addition, innovative ideas often reach public managers unsolicited through creative (or annoyed) employees, pressured politicians, peer organizations and networks faced with similar issues, and stakeholders proposing improvements in the way services and programmes are delivered. As such, innovations are also a critical method or tool for public managers to improve performance and enhance legitimacy with stakeholders (Moore and Hartley 2008), an issue addressed in chapter 'Managing Authority Turbulence'. Indeed, drivers for public managers to innovate emerge from various levels: the external operating environment, the organization itself, and individual employees. Table 8.1 outlines a variety of drivers on these three levels.

To leverage such drivers to turn them into opportunities, 21st century public managers will need to pursue two things in particular. First of all, they will need to create a strong innovation culture – one that is positive towards new ideas and supports challenging existing ways of doing things while channelling new ideas from a variety of sources (Hartley 2015b; Kanter 1984; Richards 1996). Contrary to popular belief, evidence is mixed on whether public organizations are less supportive of such cultures than private sector organizations, or whether public managers are less receptive to innovation, reform, and organizational change, or more risk-averse, than their private sector counterparts (Bozeman and Kingsley 1998; Rainey and Chun 2005).

What is important, however, is that public managers introduce incentive structures that stimulate innovative behaviour – smart mixes of awards, bonuses, and other types of recognition (Cankar and Petkovsek 2013). In addition, they need to create innovation-conducive, decentralized

TABLE 8.1 Drivers for public sector innovation

Level	Drivers
Environmental	• Technological breakthroughs • Disruptive industries (e.g., social media and big-data analytics providers) • Demands and wishes from media, politicians, and various publics (due to perceived lack of public value creation or fiscal pressures) • The number of compatible organizations taking on innovation ('peer pressure' and 'benchmarking pressure') • Public-private collaborations and partnerships • International best practices and rankings
Organizational	• 'Slack resources', including people, time, money, technical capacity, political backing, and contacts • The existence of incentives for innovation • Flexibility and capacity of bureaucratic and organizational structures • Amendment of regulations • Reputational concerns at the agency level
Individual	• Level of autonomy and standing of employee • Financial, career-related, and other individual incentives to innovate • The ability to take risks, solve problems, and explore new ways of working • The extent to which employees can freely express opinions and ideas

Sources: Cankar and Petkovsek 2013; De Vries *et al.* 2016; Gilad *et al.* 2013; Leon *et al.* 2012; Maor *et al.* 2013; Tully 2015.

internal environments that provide a sense of ownership and autonomy for employees and managers (Bysted and Jeperson 2013; Wynen *et al.* 2013).

Second, in the years to come public managers will need to maximize 'open innovation' (Chesbrough 2003; Hartley *et al.* 2013; Von Hippel 2005). This occurs when innovative ideas are co-produced and co-designed with external stakeholders, partner organizations, and individual employees. However, just as with other participatory processes, public managers will need to be selective in whom they involve in idea generation. Some stakeholders will have the interests of others in mind, but many will try to pursue their own motivations and needs (Hartley *et al.* 2013). The same goes for politicians who may not always see the 'big picture' in terms of what is administratively feasible and desirable. Although political will and backing are crucial in making public innovations succeed, public managers may also have to educate their political masters in the extent – and the amount – of reform that their agency and staff can bear. They need to protect and support their innovators, acting as 'sponsors', 'advocates', or 'standard bearers' (Meijer 2014; Osborne and Brown 2005, 2011). Inspired by the work of Hartley *et al.* (2013) and others, Table 8.2 provides four catalysts or sources of innovation and suggests enabling managerial strategies.

Clearly, many of the trends described in this book create an environment in which crowdsourcing and co-creation of ideas will become the norm. In many cases (if managed well), these processes will result in meaningful and valuable innovations that are citizen-centric and user-friendly, as Box 8.4 illustrates.

At the same time, public managers will always be faced with the choice of which ideas to select and which to dismiss, and how to actually implement suggestions. This is where the second stage of the innovation cycle comes in.

TABLE 8.2 Catalysts of innovation and enabling managerial strategies

Catalysts of innovation	*Enabling managerial strategies*
Managers and employees (bottom-up)	• Create an environment where idea sharing is appreciated, rewarded, and nurtured • Be realistic about the extent and speed with which ideas will be actually selected and implemented • Free up employees and teams to spend time on idea generation (create slack resources) Borins 2012; Newman *et al.* 2001; Rashman *et al.* 2005.
Networks	• Create systems for knowledge sharing and transferring • Address competition between agencies, sectors, and countries by creating incentives for sharing and trust-building • Let partner and peer institutions and their managers benefit from innovative ideas on a reciprocal basis Hartley and Downe 2007; Inkpen and Crossan 1995.
Users of products and services	• Enable and stimulate crowdsourcing • Help build trust between employees and their external clients and partners • Be aware of, and selective in, who is involved • Emphasize collective public value objectives Hartley *et al.* 2013; Meijer 2014.
Elected politicians (top-down)	• Provide realistic organizational and professional responses to plans ('speaking truth to power') • Distinguish (implications of) rhetorical innovation from approved and mandated policy and legislative innovation Considine *et al.* 2009; Moore and Hartley 2008.

Box 8.4 The Wellbeing Project

At first glance, the coastal city of Santa Monica in California seems to have it all: long stretches of coastline with beaches accessible to everyone; picturesque mountains and striking architecture; top-notch schools, police, and firefighters; and a world-famous pier. In light of the city's stability and success, it could be assumed that there is a high level of societal wellbeing. However, to measure whether Santa Monicans truly have high-quality lives, the city started the Wellbeing Project. It is part of the Bloomberg Philanthropies first Mayor's Challenge, an initiative aimed at stimulating innovative ways of tackling urban challenges.

In order to measure wellbeing, the project uses a Wellbeing Index that measures quality of life based on six categories: outlook, community, place, learning, health, and opportunity. The Wellbeing Index uses information collected from three sources: a 2014 survey of 2,200 Santa Monica residents, administrative data of the city, and opinions of Santa Monicans as expressed on social media.

The project identifies aspects of life, and policies and public services, that Santa Monicans are more or less satisfied with, thus providing a means of actively engaging them to elucidate their concerns and challenges and identify areas of improvement. This allows officials and residents to work to actively enhance the wellbeing of local residents.

The aim is to leverage the power of data to advance a shared understanding of the city's strong suits and needs and to promote collaboration among city leaders, local organizations, and residents to enhance the city's collective wellbeing. Ideally, the data will be harnessed to stimulate discussion and source solutions. As always, the challenge lies in translating the data into meaningful action. Which ideas will public managers of the city government use, and how will they justify to residents that certain suggestions were dismissed?

Source: The Wellbeing Project, http://wellbeing.smgov.net.

Managing idea selection and dismissal

It is one thing to create a conducive environment for new ideas to be generated and shared. Effective public managers, however, may need to be fairly ruthless in dismissing unrealistic and unfeasible ideas, on the one hand, and entrepreneurial and daring in selecting ideas that merit testing and piloting on the other. Indeed, innovation implies by definition a venture into the unknown, meaning that public managers have to estimate future public value creation without 'the benefit of hindsight' (Hartley 2015b: 90). It is estimated that 30 to 45 per cent of private sector innovations fail and half overrun their budget or timeline (Tidd and Bessant 2009), whereas as much as up to 90 per cent of all start-ups do not succeed. For public sector innovations, failure estimates run up to 70 per cent (Cucciniello and Nasi 2014). As media and political opposition members are always ready to eagerly exploit misappropriation of public budgets, overt failure produces considerable political and managerial costs. So, early dismissal of poor ideas is crucial.

Thinking back to the successes and failures displayed in Boxes 2 and 3, public managers have to strike a balance here between what they think is feasible – keeping in mind technology will enable ever more innovation in just a few years – and what will actually improve the lives of stakeholders in the near future. A certain degree of risk-taking is involved, and managers need to develop archiving systems that can quickly revive dismissed ideas later in the process, if necessary. Indeed, selecting and dismissing new ideas is about finding a fit between the solutions that new ideas provide and real policy problems (cf. Kingdon 1995; Mintron 1997). This is where the innovation system is more cyclical and iterative than linear.

At the same time, public managers will need to both *act* entrepreneurial and *attract and nurture* entrepreneurs to ensure that ideas with potential for public value creation do not die somewhere in the bureaucratic system. A key question for public managers seeking to expand their recruitment pool is what type of organizational characteristics appeal to creative individuals. Hunter *et al.* (2012: 315–316) distinguish six organizational features that attract innovators, largely resembling those recently suggested by Needham and Mangan (2014, 2016) and Dickinson and Sullivan (2014). These are displayed in Box 8.5.

Box 8.5 Organizational features that attract innovators

- **Autonomy** – Creative staff react poorly to micro-management by superiors, so significant levels of autonomy are required to produce an innovative workforce.
- **Support for risk-taking** – Creative individuals typically like to attempt new and different things. If they feel their ability to explore original ideas is hampered, they will move on to another organization that doesn't stifle their creative capacity.
- **Promoting diversity of expertise** – Innovative individuals want fresh experiences and knowledge, and are attracted to organizations that support broad collaboration and sharing (internally and externally).
- **Passion for work** – Intrinsic motivation is an important predictor of creative capacity. Consequently, creative people want to work in an environment characterized by enthusiasm and passion for innovation.
- **Recognition** – Organizations that highlight both innovation successes and failures signal that original thinking is valued as a means of solving problems, and learning from mistakes is seen as valuable.
- **Right rewards** – While pay matters in terms of recruitment, the previously discussed factors are more important in drawing creative talent. In fact, too much emphasis on extrinsic motivations such as pay may hinder creativity, because hiring those who are motivated by money will impede organizational creativity and innovation in the long term.

Source: Hunter *et al.* 2012: 315–316.

As previous chapters have shown, public agencies attract individuals with a complex mix of motivations, drivers, and values; some of these individuals resemble traditional bureaucrats, and others resemble entrepreneurs. Public managers need to be able to *be both* and *recruit both*; they need to be able to embrace a certain degree of role ambiguity (Noordegraaf 2015). Figure 8.3 contrasts these two sets of competing values as the conservative ethos of the traditional bureaucrat vis-à-vis the businesslike ethos of the innovator (cf. Jacobs 1992; Van der Wal 2008).

Note that the bureaucrat's ethos is not necessarily 'less' or 'worse' than the innovator's ethos. Each brings strengths and weaknesses to different stages of the innovation process. However, it is clear that they generate tension during the testing and dismissal stage, and public managers have to ensure this tension is creative.

Managing idea testing, piloting, and experimentation

Once public managers have rallied their employees and political masters behind a selected innovation idea, the idea needs to be tested and piloted. Not all external stakeholders may be involved at this stage; in fact, some piloting and experimentation may have a better chance if it is conducted with a certain degree of secrecy (Hartley 2015b). Different practices to test and pilot ideas exist, including soliciting competitions and awards to showcase or stimulate pilots and experiments; setting up innovation labs and special teams and agencies; institutionalizing regulatory flexibility and 'buy-outs'; and creating special experimentation zones with diminished accountability and transparency regimes. Box 8.6 shows four different concrete innovation initiatives, with examples of each type.

However, either during or towards the end of the testing and piloting stage, stakeholders and end users will need to be engaged and involved.

FIGURE 8.3   **Managing creative tensions between two value systems**

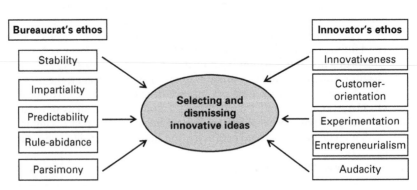

Box 8.6 Four different innovation initiatives

1. **Awards and competitions** (e.g., crowd innovation) – Awards are an increasingly employed tool to promote innovation.
   - *The Harvard Kennedy School innovation competition* offers practitioners a means of publicizing their efforts, providing them with significant exposure and giving peers the opportunity to learn.

2. **Public Sector Innovation labs (PSIs) and pilots** – provide physical spaces that offer staff an environment different from the conventional routine of government to experiment with and alter the way government operates in terms of administrative and political procedures and practices.
   - *The Barcelona Urban Lab* in Spain undertakes tests and pilots using the city as an urban laboratory, with the goal of making it easier to use public spaces.
   - *MindLab Denmark* represents one form PSI labs can take. Spanning across key ministries and operating at both state and local levels, it is a medium for cross-governmental collaboration with the aim of seeking out 'new insights, new solutions and new understandings'.
   - *The Centre for Public Service Innovation* in Pretoria, South Africa aims to cultivate the culture and practice of innovation throughout the public sector through a host of mechanisms.

3. **Legal and regulatory initiatives** – laws and regulations exempting pilots and experiments from the usual scrutiny, transparency, and accountability obligations for a period of time.
   - A *'right to challenge' mechanism* proposed by the European Commission Expert Group gives organizations and EU member states the ability to apply for an exemption from an existing regulation as long as there is 'proof of concept', illustrating how the exemption would allow for better innovation.

4. **Public sector-wide movements** – 'whole of government' movements that stimulate the piloting of new practices and policies, staffed and driven by young public servants, interns, and consultants from outside government.
   - *Public Service 21 (PS21)* was set up by the Singaporean government in the late 1990s as an 'internal change movement' located directly under the Prime Minister's Office. The goal was to promote change and improvement in the daily work of public servants, and constantly rethink public service practices in light of future developments.
   - *Obama's 'stealth team'* (see Box 8.7) was a taskforce of young 'whizz kids' from the tech industry given access to federal government institutions with the aim of fundamentally rethinking the way government operates.

Sources: Borins 2014; Christiansen and Sabroe 2015: 4–5; Droll 2013: 7; Puttick *et al.* 2014: 15; Public Service Division, Singapore, http://psd.gov.sg.

Here, collaboration comes in once more. The primary aim of such engagement should be to improve public managers' understanding of how regulations, programmes, and interventions suit stakeholders, ultimately to ensure they are devised *with* rather than *for* them (Bason 2010: 2–4). Evidence shows that encountering first-hand what potential recipients of innovations go through is usually an enlightening experience for public managers, as they seldom use the services they deliver or regulate (Alford and O'Flynn 2012). European Commission officials, for instance, are required to spend an entire week at a private organization each year in order to get a sense of the daily life of those types of organizations that they regulate and support (Bason 2010).

Indeed, evidence from cases ranging from user-led mental health services to nursing–family partnerships and prisoner councils in the public sector indicate that co-production leads to enhanced innovation outcomes (Alford and O'Flynn 2012; Damanpour 1991; Prahalad and Ramaswamy 2004). In addition, stakeholders are also valuable sources of falsification and critique during this stage (Needham and Mangan 2014; Hartley *et al.* 2013; Meijer 2015). They can aid managers in adjusting features of the proposed innovation before scaling and implementation begins – in other words, before it's too late.

For public managers, peer institutions and peer networks through which they can share and acquire testing experiences are also key stakeholders during this stage (Cankar and Petkovsek 2013). Such institutions and networks include parent and sister agencies, communities of practice, professional associations, senior executive services, practitioner and academic conferences, and policy supply chains (Birkinshaw *et al.* 2015; Hartley and Downe 2007; Noordegraaf 2015). They provide avenues for public managers to share best practices, and perhaps even more important, lessons provided by common failures. At this stage, public managers are not incentivized to keep innovations confidential, as their counterparts in the private sector are (Hartley 2015b), although they may have to temper the urge to compete for reputation. Table 8.3 provides an overview of stakeholders and suggests ways that public managers can engage them in the testing and piloting stage.

Managing idea-scaling and initial implementation

Not every pilot or experiment can be scaled up, given the limited financial and personnel capacity of most governments, so public managers will want to play safe here as much as possible. Considerable financial and political risks are involved with innovations, and personal reputations are at stake. Evidence suggests a new managerial type or role is needed at this stage: an *idea project manager* rather than generator or tester (Meijer 2014: 212). Such a manager is driven by the prospect of successfully managing complex projects rather than by the desire to innovate. Managers who excel at this stage need to advocate and package the innovation

TABLE 8.3 Stakeholder engagement during the testing and piloting stage

Key stakeholders during testing and piloting phase	Why they help public managers	How public managers should engage them
Peer institutions and networks	• Their previous pilots and tests may provide comparable insights	• Being open and reciprocal rather than competitive
End users and clients (including public sector professionals)	• Their first-hand experience may point out flaws and avenues for improvement and refinement	• Being honest about what is ultimately possible and centred on their needs
Political masters	• They may specify initial cost projections and risk assessments	• Being strategic about risks but explicit about political gain while negotiating budgetary space
Private sector solution providers	• They can point out (im)possibilities and tailor final needs	• Fill skills gaps and acquire service and technology needs while being somewhat careful regarding their promises of what is possible
Consultants	• They may provide an extra set of (external) eyes, being able to benchmark against peers	• Being thankful for suggestions without implying open-ended involvement

while being 'capable of doing the bureaucratic fighting that is needed to protect the innovation against external threats' (2014: 212).

One initial way of scaling up labs and pilots is the creation of entirely new agency types and project structures that operate outside the regular bureaucracy, as shown in Box 8.7. These may be particularly useful if public managers want to overcome traditional barriers and bring in new types of employees with tailored incentive structures. With sufficient political will and proven performance, managers can then roll out such initiatives to entire organizations and sectors to enforce more permanent change.

Creating a truly autonomous facility with its own building, technological support, operating structure, and hiring and remuneration policies is one way of mitigating traditional barriers and creating a 'different' entrepreneurial culture. On the other hand, a parallel structure or agency is

Box 8.7 New agencies and 'geek teams'

Obama's 'stealth team'

During his second term, US President Barack Obama quietly started to recruit a number of senior 'techies' from leading firms such as Google, Amazon, and Hulu. Called to a roundtable in Washington DC on a hot summer day, various high flyers from the tech world were surprised to find the President himself in the room. Urging them to postpone their careers and take pay cuts, he managed to amass a sizeable team with one mission: to 'reboot' government. The embedded 'stealth team' is tasked with fundamentally rethinking how government works, acts, and thinks in order to make it 21st century proof. This team, among other achievements, managed to quickly fix the disastrous healthcare.gov website that tainted Obama's signature healthcare legislation.

Future administrations may not continue this experiment. Regardless, the effort will have an effect on existing structures and mindsets. Perhaps even more important, it energizes talented young people with innovation skills to devote those skills to the public interest. Many stealth team members were sceptical at first, but have begun to appreciate the nature and complexity of government work and its higher purposes.

'Hive' in Singapore

In July 2015, the newly created Government Digital Services division of the Singapore government became part of Hive, a team of 90 data scientists, coders, and engineers who continuously monitor and update government websites and apps to keep up with rapidly changing citizen wishes and demands. Hive is housed in a space that has all the features of a Silicon Valley-style start-up office: open spaces, high ceilings, couches, and a ping-pong table, located in technology and biotech hub one-north. In order to keep digital government services up to date, interactive, and engaging, they are not only improved based on user feedback and interaction, but citizens are regularly invited to Hive's design experience lab. The culture at Hive aims to enable creativity and innovation, rather than emphasizing procedures, hierarchy, and meetings.

There are also examples of less successful attempts to create such groups outside of the bureaucratic structure. In 2011, the US Consumer Financial Protection Bureau (CFPB) was set up to be a data-hungry, self-innovating, start-up-like agency, hiring spirited, creative millennials. But it failed miserably, slowed by overhead, red tape, political assaults, and overall slow decision-making. Having rapidly transgressed into a 'classical' bureaucracy, employees got frustrated and left for the private sector.

Sources: Fast Company, https://fastcompany.com; Government Technology Agency of Singapore, https://ida.gov.sg; *Straits Times*, 28 December 2015; Stephen Lurie in the *Washington Post*, 18 June 2014.

hardly a permanent solution, and may even be a way to institutional-ize 'work avoidance' (Heifetz *et al.* 2009: 84) or 'kill off' the new ways of working at a later stage. The most difficult managerial and leader-ship work comes when innovations have to be diffused and disseminated across agencies and branches, and have to become the new operating status quo. The key issue here is to make innovations and change 'stick'.

At this stage, initial innovators may sometimes become barriers to change. Their rebellious nature and eccentric mindset were needed at the start to push through new ideas. However, the project manager types may now need to push initial innovators aside to enable implementation. As argued before, managers need to transition between different roles to bring the innovation process to a good end. Not all public managers will be capable of mastering each role. They may even want to appoint an *idea fighter* (Meijer 2014: 212) to protect the implementation process against external threats from conservative forces, allowing them to focus on institutionalization.

Large bureaucracies can act as enablers as well as constraints here. On the one hand, the size and complexity of many public agencies, coupled with accountability pressures, tend to produce risk-averse silo mentalities, keen to avoid public criticism (Droll 2013: 22; Hartley 2015b; Meijer 2015: 199). On the other hand, public managers are well placed to lev-erage the fact that large, bureaucratically structured organizations are particularly successful in scaling up and exploiting innovations regard-less of whether they are located in the public or private sector (Hartley 2015b).

Still, the mindsets and routines they produce are notoriously hard to change, particularly given the fact that most meaningful public sector innovations concern service innovations or process innovations rather than product innovations (Walker *et al.* 2011). In addition, they often require behavioural change not only on the part of public managers and agencies but also on the part of external stakeholders in their roles of citizens, clients, and end users. As a result, managing idea diffusion and dissemination may be the hardest stage of all.

Managing idea diffusion and dissemination

Harvard Kennedy School's Ronald Heifetz, one of the world's most sought-after speakers and consultants on leadership, is known for his realistic views on what leaders can (and sometimes cannot) accomplish. Together with his colleagues, Heifetz developed a body of work on adaptive leadership practices to guide managers through tough pro-cesses of change, learning, and adaptation. Taking their inspiration from biology, history, business, and politics, they outline six features of adaptive leadership as a successful practice to aid organizational change. These are translated in Box 8.8 to the operating environment of public managers.

Box 8.8 Six features of adaptive leadership

- **'Adaptive leadership is specifically about the change that enables the capacity to thrive'**

  To allow organizations to thrive in new circumstances, the leadership must wrestle with normative, sometimes painful questions of value, purpose, and process. Public managers have to mobilize and orchestrate multiple stakeholder priorities, but they cannot please everyone if adaptation is necessary.

- **'Successful adaptive leadership changes build on the past rather than jettison it'**

  A managerial challenge here is to engage an organization to identify what is essential to preserve from its heritage and what is expendable. Heifetz *et al.* (2009: 15) label successful adaptations as both conservative and progressive. Preserving institutional history and memory (including people) is particularly important in public sector contexts, as so many drastic – and private sector-inspired – reforms have destroyed the institutional heritage that proved useful again at a later stage.

- **'Organizational adaptation occurs through experimentation'**

  Evidence suggests many public and private sector innovations fail. Some innovations may be too radical to survive. Particularly when taxpayer money is involved, public managers need to carefully weigh up when they need to step in and scale up, learn to improvise as they move along, and buy time and resources to invest in the next wave of experiments and trials.

  →

Viewing managerial 'innovation work' as adaptive leadership explains why many of the proponents of radical, disruptive innovation who dismiss all other change as real innovation may overlook how actual public sector change happens. This reasoning harks back to Figure 8.1, in which gradations of renewal are visualized as a continuum, and the more general argument developed in this book that radical, destructive 'big-man' change may often fail in public sector contexts, even if such change may be necessary to ensure survival. Moreover, diffusion understood as gradual adaptation has an important (political and managerial) risk management function, as it mitigates implementation uncertainties by adapting and mimicking what other organizations have done, and allowing peer institutions to do so (Hartley 2015b; Hartley and Benington 2006).

Still, displacing routines and assumptions is painful and creates resistance. Public managers tasked with institutionalizing and distributing new ways of doing things across their organizations and teams are forced to engage in what Argyris and Schön (1978: 2–3) famously labelled 'double-loop

- **'Adaptation relies on diversity'**

  For adaptation to succeed, managers need to build a culture that appreciates a diversity of viewpoints and expertise, and let go of some of their urges to 'plan everything'. Cloning and copying may be less suitable for creating environments for innovations to thrive, according to Heifetz *et al.* (2009: 16). However, in public sector contexts, strategic copying of best practices – rather than being the early adapter in all cases – may be cost-effective and realistic in terms of risk management.

- **'New adaptations significantly displace, reregulate, and rearrange some old DNA'**

  Learning and loss, including letting go of loyal employees who suited past environments, are painful. One manager's or employee's innovation can make others feel incompetent, redundant, or outdated. Skilful public managers are able to recognize when to 'take' losses, and detect and counteract predictable defensive and avoidance patterns that people display when they need to change their mental models and usual ways.

- **'Adaptation takes time'**

  Progress may seem radical *over time* but is incremental *in time*, particularly in public sector contexts. Significant change only occurs in such contexts as a product of incremental changes and adjustments. Cultures and assumptions change slowly, as the seminal works of Argyris and Schön (1978, 1996) and Senge (1990, 1999) have shown us.

Sources: Heifetz *et al.* 2009: 14–17.

---

learning'. Single-loop learning is a continuous process in which goals, values, and frameworks are taken for granted. The emphasis is on 'techniques and making techniques more efficient' (Usher and Bryant 1989: 87). Double-loop learning, in contrast, involves questioning the role of the framing and learning systems that underlie actual goals and strategies. In short, single-loop learning concerns the question: 'Are we doing *things right*?', whereas double-loop learning is concerned with answering the question: 'Are we doing the *right things*?' (Romme and van Witteloostuijn 1999: 452).

Single-loop learning is less risky for the individual and the organization, and affords greater control of the change process. Double-loop learning is more creative and reflexive, and involves consideration of routines that have evolved unquestioned for some time: 'the basic assumptions behind ideas or policies are confronted; hypotheses are publicly tested; processes are disconfirmable and not self-seeking' (Argyris 1982: 103–104). The difference is visualized in Figure 8.4.

FIGURE 8.4   Single-loop learning and double-loop learning

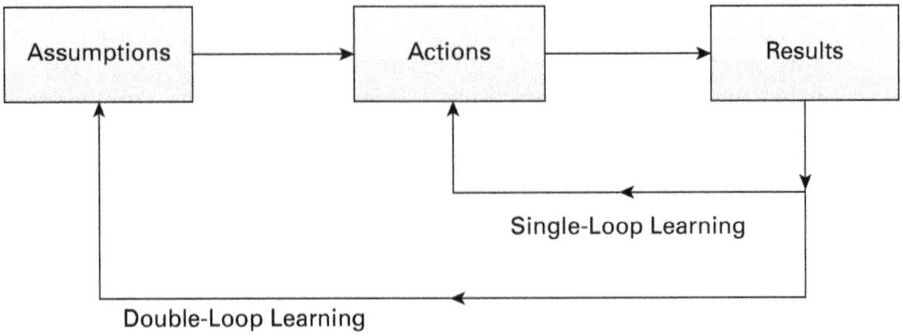

Reprinted with permission from Hargrove 2008: 115.

In the process of double-loop learning, organizations and teams are forced to question their 'shared basic assumptions', the deepest layer of prevailing organizational cultures that organizational members tend to defend as they have invested heavily in them (Schein 1992: 22–23). Public managers have to orchestrate a process of 'unlearning' shared rules, routines, metaphors, values, and behaviour patterns (1992: 10), and turn sceptics into followers, one by one if necessary. This causes anxiety and anger, and may even lead to letting go of long-valued employees as Box 8.8 suggests.

Think back here to the scenario at the beginning of the chapter – the public manager in China who was used to regulating friendly, predictable, well-known industry partners in a team of regulators with long-established collegial and relational routines. New economic dynamics and players began to challenge such long-held routines, and even though the manager recognized the opportunities provided by economic developments, it was a difficult and daunting task to convince his colleagues of those opportunities. Contrary to what popular opinion may suggest, evidence shows that such learning and adaptation is just as painful for public organizations as it is for private sector organizations: the latter are not necessary 'better' at learning or innovating (Hartley *et al.* 2013; Heifetz *et al.* 2009; Senge 1990).

Various scholars have built on the seminal work of Argyris and Schön to pursue the idea of 'triple-loop learning' (Flood and Romm 1996; Hargrove 2008; Swiering and Wierdsma 1992; Yuthas *et al.* 2004), shown in Figure 8.5. This denotes even higher-order processes of learning: learning about learning itself (Tosey *et al.* 2012). Some radical or disruptive innovations in the operating environments of public managers may indeed require them to question the very context and systems through which their organizations and their predecessors have chosen to learn and reform in the past.

FIGURE 8.5   Single-loop, double-loop, and triple-loop learning

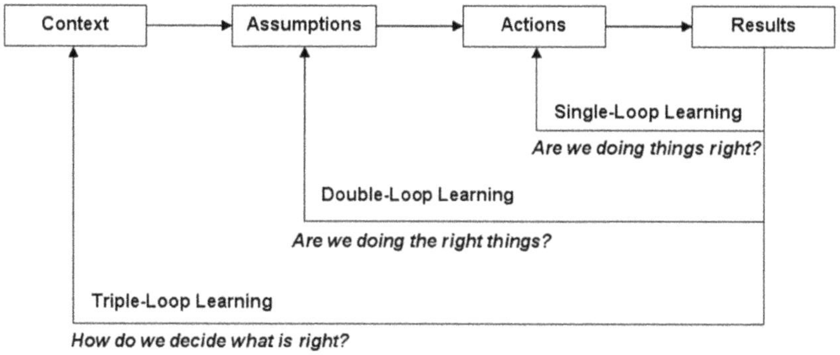

Reprinted with permission from Hargrove 2008: 116.

In addition to forcing behavioural change upon their *internal operating environments*, public managers have to diffuse and disseminate new ways of doing things to *external stakeholders*. One key question here is how they assess their stakeholders in terms of their readiness and willingness to adopt innovations, and how they advocate those innovations to heterogeneous social groups. Remember the different citizen categories distinguished in chapter 'Managing Authority Turbulence': the 'enthusiastic self-sufficient' may be more inclined to buy in to and collaborate on a different range of untested innovative public service ideas than the 'concerned citizen'. For example, the former may be more than willing to participate in a pilot that tests app-based medical records that patients and doctors can access 24/7, whereas the latter may find the idea that large institutions can now more easily access their personal data frightening. Stakeholders may not only demand different types of innovations, with varying degrees of radicalness, but may also adopt innovations very differently, if at all.

A useful frame for public managers to assess adaptation and diffusion is the famous innovation diffusion curve, developed in 1962 by marketing expert Everett Rogers. Rogers classified adopters of innovations into five categories, ranging from risk-taking 'early adoptors' – those individuals and groups with high social status, financial resources, and expert knowledge who are close to the source of innovation – to 'laggards' – who are change-averse, sceptical individuals who operate in more narrow social circles. He emphasized the role of opinion leaders in propagating novel ideas, while advocating that managers forge ties between homogenous and heterogeneous social groups – the diffuse stakeholder networks described in chapter 'Managing Stakeholder Multiplicity' – for innovations to spread widely.

FIGURE 8.6   'Crossing the chasm' on the innovation diffusion curve

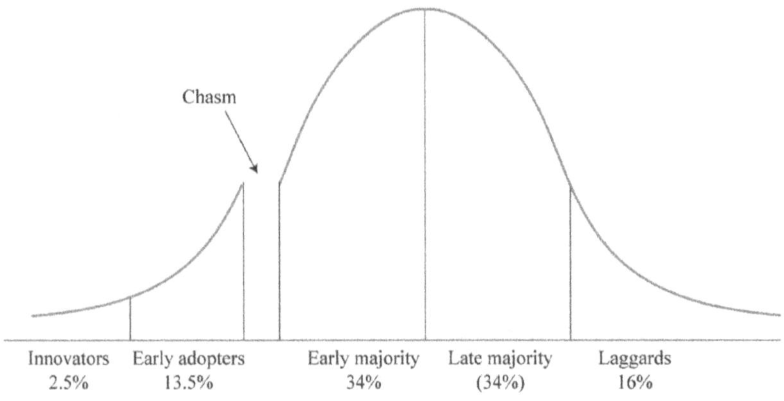

| Innovators
2.5% | Early adopters
13.5% | Early majority
34% | Late majority
(34%) | Laggards
16% |

Based on: Moore 2014: 21.

Building on Rogers' work, Geoff Moore (2014) developed the notion of a 'chasm' – the transition that managers need to make to entice not just visionaries but also more pragmatic stakeholders, shown in Figure 8.6.

To 'cross the chasm', public managers will need to advocate and disseminate innovations to widely different external and internal publics *and* decide whether their agencies can afford to be laggards in adopting the latest technological tools and capabilities, or if they need to move in early with all the potential risks and costs involved. In a similar vein, Harvard's Clayton Christensen (1997) famously wrote about the 'innovator's dilemma', referring to the tendency of managers to keep investing in proven technologies for big markets rather than chasing smaller, untested markets with less chance of success. Evidence suggests that managers reach a turning point when they manage to convince around 20 per cent of a given population to buy in to the innovation (Moore 2014). Moreover, recent studies show how organizational reforms are more likely to be enthusiastically disseminated by employees if managers explicitly involve them in the early stages of the process: *understanding* the need for change is at least as important as *agreeing* with the change itself (Van der Voet and Vermeeren 2016; Van der Voet *et al.* 2016).

Three enduring questions for public managers

Is innovation necessarily a collaborative process?

It follows from the examination of managerial roles and behaviours during the various innovation stages that innovation is a collaborative process only to the extent that it suits managerial objectives. End users and citizens should take precedence over other actors with potentially ambiguous agendas. At the same time, innovation processes are not easily straightjacketed: ideas and technological opportunities flow in and out of public agencies and programmes. Moreover, the megatrends producing an increasing multitude of innovation forces will 'thrust' collaboration upon public managers in the years to come.

Clearly, public managers need to accept that innovation processes are increasingly collaborative, but will this benefit the outcomes? According to Ansell and Torfing (2014), public value-creating innovation is almost by definition collaborative, as in-house innovations may intentionally or unintentionally neglect potential beneficiaries. Putting the user first is also central to the increasingly popular 'design thinking' approach (Bason 2010), in which stakeholders are directly involved in idea generation and prototyping of services and products.

Indeed, various examples suggest collaborative innovation produces more effective and legitimate outcomes (Osborne and Brown 2013; Hartley *et al.* 2013). For instance, governors in the US who involved various stakeholder groups in crafting vision statements for the future of state-based education, after failing to pass reform bills, found that a year-long collaborative process managed to yield results, even though proposals were less radical than the governors had hoped for (Roberts and Bradley 1991). In the same vein, evidence from urban renewal networks and habitat protection initiatives in the US and Europe show that long-lasting, diverse networks tend to produce innovations with higher feasibility and legitimacy than when governments 'go it alone' (Dente *et al.* 2005; Steelman 2010). At the same time, long-established networks may capture innovation processes and become conservative over time, urging public managers to frequently 'refresh' such networks (Hartley *et al.* 2013).

Based on a variety of recent studies, Table 8.4 identifies the benefits and constraints of collaborative approaches to innovation, and suggests managerial actions and roles to overcome constraints and maximize benefits.

Can innovation performance be evaluated?

How and when will public managers know their innovation has succeeded, and who decides? Impact evaluation is important, as it allows public managers and their masters to portray and celebrate success, and make the case for additional investments in future innovations. However, many public sectors lack a culture of innovation evaluation (Cucciniello and Nasi 2013: 92). And, given the nature of the beast, it may be virtually impossible to *measure innovation at all*. In contrast to the private sector, a common output measure like sales revenue cannot be used, and quantitative output measures are often sector-specific – successful innovation in hospitals will look very different from successful innovation in schools.

TABLE 8.4 Managing the benefits and constraints of collaborative innovation

Common constraints	Potential benefits	Public managers need to:
• Political preference for confidentiality and seclusion. • Policy areas with deep-seated ideological conflict. • Large power imbalances between stakeholders. • Private sector opportunities for exploitative capture. • 'Group think' by usual suspects in closed, stable networks who may collaborate but still stifle innovation.	• Diverse actors can help assess gains and risks. • Partners can test in environments not burdened by public sector constraints. • Networks of public managers, professionals, and experts can identify innovations with most potential. • Collaboration can provide ways to address the lack of public resources, budgetary cutbacks, and policy deadlocks.	• Act as *conveners* to bring together actors, set the agenda, and create and frame the interactive arena. • Act as *mediators* to create or clarify interdependencies, resolve disputes and remove barriers, and build trust. • Act as *catalysts* to encourage out-of-the-box thinking, and explore and advocate opportunities. • *Reformulate traditional role perceptions* between public, private, and civic actors.
Ansell and Gash 2008, 2012; Hartley *et al.* 2013; Skilton and Dooley 2010.	Benington and Moore 2011; Gray 1989; Moore and Hartley 2008; Pollitt 2010; Torfing *et al.* 2012.	Ansell and Gash 2008; Crosby and Bryson 2010; Hartley *et al.* 2013; Newman 2011; Page 2010; Straus 2002.

Moreover, it is problematic to pinpoint indicators for collective services that are neither consumed by nor provided to an individual (2013: 92–94). Most evaluations focus on efficiency or reductions in red tape, waiting time, and so forth, while innovations often aim to produce more than just time or cost savings. Other internal and external indicators could be the organization's image, customer satisfaction, awards received, or enhanced motivation and commitment among employees (2013: 91).

Like many policy interventions, innovations often produce indirect, sometimes unintended spill-over effects, with significant time lags between expected and actual change. Failures are often swept under the rug, making it hard to compare and substantiate the actual public value created by innovations. Moreover, as Hartley (2015b: 84) argues:

Service innovations typically have high levels of ambiguity and uncertainty since they are affected by the variability of the human characteristics of both service giver and service receiver (the latter, in some cases, as co-producer). The innovation is often not a physical artefact at all, but a change in service (which implies a change in the relationship between service providers and their users) and many features are intangible, with high levels of tacit knowledge.

Still, governments across the globe have launched initiatives to map innovation readiness, promote innovative behaviour, and measure and compare innovation impact, as shown in Box 8.9. The efforts illustrate

---

Box 8.9 Attempts to measure innovation capability and impact

OECD's Observatory of Public Sector Innovation: A detailed database with hundreds of successful cases from around the world, illustrated with videos, data, and personal stories from managers and stakeholders involved. The focus lies with experienced stakeholder improvements and cross-governmental learning.

UK's National Endowment for Science Technology and the Arts (Nesta): Headed by Geoff Mulgan, the former 'strategy guru' under prime ministers Tony Blair and Gordon Brown, Nesta develops innovation indices, training programmes, and cross-sectoral partnerships spurring innovation. It moved out of the public sector in 2012 and is now a charity.

South Korea's Government Innovation Index (GII): An auto-assessment web-based tool developed in the mid-2000s to evaluate how organizations innovate. Organizations can use the index to score their own capabilities, identify weaknesses and barriers, create action plans, and benchmark against sector averages. Conducting diagnostic analyses, the GII is more supportive in overcoming barriers than most other indexes used worldwide.

Canada's Employee Innovation Program: More individual and bottom-up than most other programmes, the Employee Innovation Program allows individual public servants to propose innovations through an online portal with the aim of collecting new ideas in a cost-effective way.

Australian Public Sector Innovation Indicators (APSII): The APSII project provides indicators in eight areas for public agencies so they can report their progress annually against national innovation priorities established by the Australian government. In addition, it provides an online platform for agencies to share experiences.

United States' President's Evidence and Innovation Agenda: In 2013, the Office of Management and Budget (OMB), part of Obama's 'West Wing', produced a memo for agency heads, urging them to continuously improve and innovate without expecting (much) additional budget. It suggests five strategies: harnessing data to improve agency results; high-quality, low-cost evaluations; rapid, iterative experimentation; using innovation-outcome grant designs; and strengthening agency capacity to use evidence.

Based on: Nasi 2013; OECD, oecd.org; Office of Management and Budget, Executive Office of the President 2013.

that governments try out both quantitative and qualitative methods, sometimes engaging external evaluators, while involving public servants and end users to different extents. Whatever measure public managers choose, it has to go beyond just organizational performance metrics and include public value estimates, consisting of both what the public values and what adds value to the public domain (Benington and Moore 2011; Hartley 2015b).

In recent years, the former head of the famous Delivery Unit under the Tony Blair administration in the UK, Michael Barber, has developed the concept of 'deliverology' to emphasize the relentless real-time and data-driven monitoring of delivery performance (Barber *et al.* 2010). In his view, public managers and their political masters can only achieve their goals if they set a small number of priorities; translate those priorities into measurable stretch targets; and develop frequent routines for data collection, tracking performance, and adjusting priorities (2015: 1–25). In a way, Barber's focus on 'boring' routines (in his own words) seems counterintuitive to the routine-disrupting nature of innovation. However, the anecdotal evidence presented in his books shows that many innovations fail to deliver because governments tend to show little interest in the actual delivery of promised reforms, busy as they are with announcing the next big reform proposal.

Barber has established delivery units within governments across the globe, often consisting of a diverse team of less than 40 junior and senior public employees supplemented with some consultants and analysts whose sole responsibility is to track the effects of reform implementation. He mandates that these units have full power to request data from the highest echelons any time of day – in fact they are often backed by prime ministers themselves – and his delivery units have proved to be highly successful in bringing innovations to a good end.

Is innovation always 'good'?

A final issue that merits attention is whether innovation is always a good thing. Perhaps public managers should ask themselves from time to time: how much innovation is enough? Indeed, the 'innovation imperative' may unintentionally imply that managers must pursue entrepreneurial ventures in order to be perceived as doing well even if these ventures are invalidated or eventually harmful (Jordan 2013: 20). In a way, public sector innovations are experiments where the citizenry acts as players, financiers, and potential beneficiaries. As such, innovation produces considerable dilemmas for public managers: they must ensure safety and evaluate risks, but a context of disruptive innovation renders it impossible to make guarantees.

There are also more fundamental dangers and risks in unbridled technological innovation and 'revolution'. In 2000, a former chief scientist at Sun Microsystems, Bill Joy, wrote a provocative article titled 'Why the Future Doesn't Need Us'. Joy's key argument was that 21st century technologies such as robotics, genetic engineering, artificial intelligence (AI), and nanotechnology could produce a 'robot rebellion' from technological entities more intelligent than humans yet lacking abilities for moral reasoning. Such reasoning is reminiscent of James Cameron's blockbuster 1985 film *The Terminator*, in which the self-learning computer system Skynet unleashed an unstoppable – and far from virtual – war against mankind.

In 2015, dozens of tech giants and AI experts including Stephen Hawking and Elon Musk wrote an open letter in which they expressed similar fears, suggesting that we are at a turning point in artificial intelligence and need to institute mandatory research on the pitfalls and risks of new projects. Stressing the absence of solutions for the 'control problem', Microsoft's Eric Horvitz ends the letter with a telling statement:

> We could one day lose control of AI systems via the rise of superintelligences that do not act in accordance with human wishes – and that such powerful systems would threaten humanity. Are such dystopic outcomes possible? If so, how might these situations arise? ... What kind of investments in research should be made to better understand and to address the possibility of the rise of a dangerous superintelligence or the occurrence of an 'intelligence explosion'?

In the same vein, *The Guardian* published a somewhat chilling piece in 2016 about the founder of Google-owned AI-company DeepMind, Demis Hassabis, questioning whether he would ultimately lose control of his self-taught AI agents, which now match human-level performance in various games and tasks. Recent breakthroughs published in *Nature* show that Hassabis' agents are capable of 'mimicking intuition' in solving the most complex puzzles and problems, a feature most experts believed would take many more years to develop. Hassabis describes his mission as no less than 'solve intelligence, and then use that to solve everything else'. In a somewhat more down-to-earth fashion, Mayer-Schönberger and Cukier (2013) elicit a variety of risks of technological transformations in their widely acclaimed book *Big Data*. They put forward three strategies as a foundation for 'effective and fair governance of information in the big-data era': shifting privacy protections from individual consent to data-user accountability; enshrining human agency amid (data and computer generated) predictions; and inventing a new caste of big-data auditors the authors call 'algorithmists' (2013: 184).

What lies ahead

As the previous section shows, disruptive innovations and technological revolutions may produce a variety of ethical dilemmas for public managers. Such dilemmas add to existing value conflicts produced by decades of ambiguous, sometimes treacherous management reforms. These reforms have pressured public managers to be more business-like, networked, and citizen-centric yet still adhere to the traditional ethos and high standards of legality. In the years to come, the demands described in this book will lead to an accumulation of often unrealistic and ambiguous ethical expectations from assertive stakeholders towards public managers. In short, in navigating through various moral minefields to get their job done, 21ˢᵗ century public managers will have to become skilled at *managing ethical complexities*. How such conjectures emerge and how public managers can address them, acting on the proper values, morals, and motivations, is discussed in the next chapter.

Chapter 9

Managing Ethical Complexities

Action indeed is the sole medium of expression for ethics.

(Jane Addams, social worker and first female Nobel Laureate)

Easy to go wrong, hard to stay right

Imagine you are a senior HR officer at the police department of a major metropolitan city. Recently, your officers have started to experiment with the use of social media like Twitter, Facebook, and Ubideo to share and solicit information from the general public. Initiatives range from asking citizens to share pictures, videos, and live streams of small violations so that officers can follow up immediately, to distributing information about felonies to citizens and asking for assistance. The impact so far has been mixed. Some officers seem to enjoy using the new tools and apps while others struggle and resist; citizens feel empowered by the opportunity to collaborate on safety, but often find their input neglected. More worrisome, however, are several recent complaints from citizens about police officers sending inappropriate messages and materials to their personal accounts after they had shared information with the officers.

Alongside these developments, you are dealing with various internal ethics and compliance issues. First of all, two female junior officers have charged a well-connected senior lieutenant with a history of misconduct including harassment and discrimination. In addition, there has been an incident between a newly recruited IT staffer from a religious minority group who demanded separate prayer and bathroom facilities, and one of your colleagues who accused her of being privileged and – when things got heated – even extremist.

You're especially frustrated with this incident given the enormous efforts you've put in to create a diverse department that is more representative of the city's population; the mayor has exerted pressure on your commissioner regarding this issue. Moreover, you are about to hire various new colleagues from minority groups, together with two near-retirees, as part of a municipal reskilling programme coinciding with a nationwide two-year increase in the retirement age. As a result, you expect more turmoil and inappropriate conduct. Then, there's the contractor leaking information to regional TV channels to point at neglected flaws in the department's outdated IT infrastructure. He first shared his concerns with the confidentiality officer in your office, but he was told, in an intimidating way, to hold off. At least, that's his version of the story ...

The current departmental ethics guidelines date back almost 15 years and are hardly known among employees. Vague as they are, they are not of any value to you in deciding at what stage disciplinary steps need to be taken or when legal charges need to be pursued. However, an opportunity has emerged to improve things. You have been asked to join a departmental taskforce to update current ethics policies to better tackle these pervasive, newly emerging ethics issues. The taskforce will assess the department's ethics code, training needs, whistleblowing regulations, and administrative and legal procedures to determine when violations occur.

You see this as an opportunity to fundamentally revise and update policies, and make them 21ˢᵗ century proof. Moreover, you feel the discussion should be broadened to include the department's core values and aspirations, and how they relate to its overall mission. Having a uniform, up-to-date, and attractively packaged value statement should also help your office in recruiting and retaining high-quality personnel with high moral standards.

However, taskforce members display contrasting views on the core values of the department – identified long ago as service, courtesy, integrity, and respect – and also on the key integrity risks, and indeed whether 'there is a problem at all'. Many are reluctant to respond to increasing stakeholder demands, some of which are indeed unrealistic and even treacherous, but you feel there isn't much of a choice. Operating in the public eye, the department has to exceed even the highest ethical expectations. How can you create sufficient buy-in for ethics reform before embarking on the painstaking journey of designing – let alone implementing – comprehensive new guidelines?

To complicate matters further, you are facing a personal dilemma. A young officer has requested to take some leave days on short notice. You have known for some time she is struggling to become pregnant, and you want to support her visit to a popular fertility clinic with a year-long waiting list. However, the commissioner has made it clear no leave is to be granted in this quarter, except for extraordinary circumstances. Yesterday, you decided to slightly alter the administrative code accompanying her request, indicating that a close family member is terminally ill. Technically, you are not lying: her mother has been hospitalized for some time, even though doctors disagree on the seriousness of her illness. You are experiencing first-hand the difficulties of separating professional norms from personal loyalties. All this leaves you stressed and insecure on how to proceed.

Moreover, you can't even imagine how your life will look five years from now with rapidly increasing diversity (pressures) – and the resistance this creates among more traditional colleagues – and technological developments forcing robotics, big-data analytics, and artificial intelligence onto the department's policing practices. Many colleagues are far from ready for these developments. If mishandled, they could put your department at risk.

The demand of *managing ethical complexities* creates a variety of tough questions for public managers. Which values are supposed to guide decision-making, whose values are they, and what do managers do when they conflict? How can managers guide their employees and stakeholders by displaying ethical leadership? Can cultural contexts be used as an 'excuse' to display minimal ethics, or to set aside certain core public values? How can increasingly unrealistic and unreasonable stakeholder expectations of public officials' ethics be managed? And, finally, how do public managers keep ethics guidelines and regulations up to date in an era of hypertransparency, technological innovations, and assertive stakeholders?

Recurrent and new ethical dilemmas for managers

The introductory case displays various ethical challenges occurring in the daily life of public managers, albeit with varying intensity depending on role and context. In many ways, the 21st century trends and demands discussed in previous chapters amplify various classical dilemmas for public managers. These include managing conflicts of interest between and loyalties towards internal and external stakeholders, getting things done without compromising key principles (the 'dirty hands dilemma'), and punishing wrongdoing without creating a culture of fear and retaliation.

In addition, they create entirely new – and partly unknown – managerial dilemmas. Such dilemmas include managing employees' (online) behaviour outside of work without trampling on legal boundaries and privacy rights, and counterbalancing accusatory media and stakeholder frames while maintaining sometimes unrealistic accountability postures in an era of contracting out and co-production. Twenty-first century ethical dilemmas therefore become increasingly complex: they create treacherous minefields in which public managers have to operate, balancing unrealistic expectations and scrutiny with high ethical standards *and* high performance. They have to do good *and* do well (De Graaf and Van der Wal 2010).

This chapter examines these complexities, and highlights key values, policies, and strategies to manage them, or at least *keep them manageable*. First, we discuss how public managers have to adhere to various clusters of competing values to operate ethically and effectively, and meet obligations towards various masters, domains, and principles. Subsequently, we classify traditional types of unethical behaviour that will take on new shapes and forms in the 21st century. The core of this chapter examines how mitigating and managing such behaviours creates complexities for managers in three key areas: political-administrative relations; HRM and diversity management; and social media and big data. Real-life examples are provided, along with recent examples of updated ethics guidelines from across the globe. Finally, we discuss how public managers can effectively manage ethics in various settings.

Competing values and obligations

As previously, values are defined here as qualities or standards that guide behaviour and decision-making. Which values should guide public managers as they make decisions? In the last two decades, there has been a surge in publications about 'public values'. These publications are largely a response to worries about public values being crowded out by private (or business) values as a result of public management reforms in the 1980s and 1990s (Van der Wal *et al.* 2015).

Increasingly, however, scholars acknowledge that what makes values 'public', and according to whom, is a disputed issue (Beck Jørgensen and Rutgers 2015; Rutgers 2008, 2015). Public values can be realized by public, private, and non-profit actors. Moreover, public managers now operate in a hybrid organizational landscape consisting of many organizations that are neither fully public nor fully private (Bozeman 2004; Moulton and Wise 2010). And, aren't they supposed to focus on efficiency and effectiveness, regardless of where they operate? Still, many agree that certain traditional legal and institutional values – including lawfulness, predictability, neutrality, and impartiality – are crucial for public managers, and distinguish some of their key responsibilities from those of their private sector counterparts.

In his seminal article 'A Public Management for all Seasons?', Christopher Hood (1991) outlined three partly competing sets of core values for public managers, each with its own standard of success and failure. His sigma-type values, theta-type values, and lambda-type values are elaborated on in Table 9.1. Hood's overview is powerful because it shows why the daily life of public managers is characterized by constant value conflict, prioritization, and trade-offs in policy, administrative, and managerial decisions (Koppenjan *et al.* 2008; Stewart 2006; Thacher and Rein 2004). Public managers have to adhere to key legal, moral, and constitutional values; keep things efficient and effective; and simultaneously worry about long-term adaptiveness and resilience.

Value conflict, prioritization, and trade-offs

Unfortunately, while agency core values statements – like good governance codes – often list laudable qualities that everybody would support, they seldom make mention of conflict or trade-offs, or even prioritization. As such, they are somewhat unsatisfactory, and in some cases even annoying for public managers (Van der Wal *et al.* 2011). Indeed, they are often of limited use for solving actual dilemmas like those in the introductory case, except for the rare codes that include contextualized guidelines and cases. But before we begin to discuss codes and

TABLE 9.1 Three sets of core values in public management

	Sigma-type values *KEEP IT LEAN AND PURPOSEFUL*	Theta-type values *KEEP IT HONEST AND FAIR*	Lambda-type values *KEEP IT ROBUST AND RESILIENT*
STANDARD OF SUCCESS	*Frugality* (matching of resources to tasks for given goals)	*Rectitude* (achievement of fairness, mutuality, the proper discharge of duties)	*Resilience* (achievement of reliability, adaptability, and robustness)
STANDARD OF FAILURE	*Waste* (muddle, confusion, inefficiency)	*Malversation* (unfairness, bias, abuse of office)	*Catastrophe* (risk, breakdown, collapse)
CURRENCY OF SUCCESS AND FAILURE	*Money and time* (resource costs of producer and consumers)	*Trust and entitlements* (consent, legitimacy, due process, political entitlements)	*Security and survival* (confidence, life and limb)
CONTROL EMPHASIS	Output	Process	Input/Process
SLACK	Low	Medium	High
GOALS	Fixed/Single	Incompatible 'Double bind'	Emergent/Multiple
INFORMATION	Costed, segmented (commercial assets)	Structured	Rich exchange, collective asset
COUPLING	Tight	Medium	Loose

Reprinted with permission from Hood 1991: 11.

guidelines, we have to examine what public managers actually value most, and how they prioritize. Empirical studies are sparse, but they provide useful directions.

Figure 9.1 presents a public-private value continuum with a core of shared values based on a series of studies comparing how public and private executives rank values in organizational decision-making (Van der Wal 2008). The continuum displays a fairly traditional and consistent value orientation in both sectors. Public managers prioritize theta-type values lawfulness and impartiality over sigma-type values efficiency and

FIGURE 9.1   **What public and private sector managers value most**

PUBLIC SECTOR

Lawfulness
Incorruptibility
Impartiality

Accountability
Expertise
Reliability
Effectiveness
Efficiency

Honesty
Innovativeness
Profitability

PRIVATE SECTOR

Source: Van der Wal 2008: 167.

effectiveness, even though these values conflict constantly as explained by a director-general (Van der Wal 2008: 96):

> I work in the domain of planning and housing and I can never let go of lawfulness, because there is a considerable chance that you will meet yourself at a later stage. Then you have a huge problem and, moreover, a greater loss of time. So, in a conflict situation, lawfulness is always – well, I hesitate to say always – superior to efficiency. After all, when you end up having legal problems, it will be at the cost of your ability to be efficient.

Accountability is another key value because it serves various countervailing functions (Bovens *et al.* 2008; Bovens *et al.* 2014). Indeed, accountability is considered of overarching importance in decision-making, particularly in relation to the other values (Koppell 2005; MacCarthaigh 2008). In circumstances where other values have to be compromised or cannot be fully realized, public managers will always have to *account* for such compromise, at some point, to some stakeholder (Van der Wal 2011: 652). In the words of a director of an education agency (Van der Wal 2008: 97):

> I think that accountability is the most important. Do we want to abide by the rules, yes; do we want to produce efficiently, yes; we want it all,

but when push comes to shove, we want to be able to be accountable, even though things have been less transparent and less efficient than they should have been. Integrity and responsiveness remain; they do not conflict. But I consider accountability to be the most important.

At the same time, public managers enact accountability with gradations: its importance and actualization depend on who is addressed (audience), at what time (timing), and on which topic (content) (Mulgan 2003: 22; Van der Wal 2011: 651). This gradual and realistic perspective on accountability may also explain why public managers do not consider honesty to be that important (see also De Vries 2002). Public managers see considerable leeway for secrecy and framing *during* decision-making processes as long as the *outcome* is beneficial to stakeholders.

Clearly, the daily life of public managers is characterized by the management of competing values. So, how can they best deal with this? Koppenjan *et al.* (2008) provide three useful approaches for dealing with competing values, illustrated with examples in Box 9.1.

Although public managers do not have the luxury to simply 'pick' one approach over the other, with politicians heavily affecting value trade-offs at the policy and legislative levels, it is evident that the stakeholder approach will become increasingly prominent. Assertive stakeholders will no longer simply accept a given value constellation, and value prioritization in managerial decision-making will increasingly be a product of constant negotiation. Moreover, public managers will not just be involved in managerial and institutional value trade-offs and negotiations. From time to time they will struggle immensely with meeting conflicting obligations and loyalties towards clients, colleagues, friends, family, professional standards, the law, religious vows, personal beliefs and principles, and society at large.

The personal, the professional, and the managerial

Indeed, as the introductory case illustrates, public managers do not only enact and balance macro-level 'organizational' and 'managerial' values. They also have to balance a range of personal, professional, and organizational obligations and loyalties (De Graaf 2010; O'Leary 2010). Suppose a public manager is pressured by her permanent secretary, who is pressured by his minister, to quickly implement a drastic reform proposal that will almost certainly lead to valued colleagues being outsourced, clients being disappointed, and key public interests being neglected. To whom is the public manager most obligated in such a situation? What kind of ethical obligations can we distinguish? Foundational public administration scholar Dwight Waldo (1988: 103) distinguished 12 ethical obligations for public servants and emphasized the impossibilities of prioritizing one over the other (Figure 9.2).

Box 9.1 How public managers can deal with competing values

- The *universal approach* views value trade-offs as zero-sum game. Public managers are responsible for safeguarding key values through formal laws, procedures, and accountability mechanisms.

  Example: A welfare agency safeguards the impartial and equal treatment of clients through a legal provision that allows clients to file a complaint about the treatment of their case, and mandates the agency head to follow up with the official in question and report back to the client within four weeks.

- The *stakeholder approach* considers the creation and meaning-making of values as a dynamic and political process involving various actors. Here, public managers have to produce workable trade-offs through a mix of legislation, markets, and networks.

  Example: A city manager of a major metropole wants to be more innovative, effective, and efficient in her use of municipal funds for infrastructure projects. Many local stakeholders seem to support this approach, but certain legal provisions will have to be minimized or scrapped. Public managers will need to design more efficient stakeholder forums, and to educate stakeholders by explaining that hearings will be organized differently in the future, or not at all.

- The *institutional approach* sees the institutional context as affecting the prioritization of values and how they are translated. Public managers have to stay true to their institutional context and historical practices without assuming a generic approach.

  Example: The CEO of a large public hospital, in a developing country with a long history of community-driven reform and collusion with powerful local politicians, wants to overhaul existing accounting and budgeting systems to enforce greater transparency. As reforms cannot succeed without buy-in from powerful, long-term stakeholders, whose influence is likely to decline, the CEO will have to redefine the institutional character of the hospital while creating a new space for historically important players.

Based on: Charles *et al.* 2007: 7; De Graaf *et al.* 2011; Koppenjan *et al.* 2008.

Clearly, ethical dilemmas emerge when two or more of these obligations and the loyalties they evoke clash. Such dilemmas often go beyond the rather analytical and political trade-offs discussed before. They are what Harvard professor Joseph L. Badaracco (1997: 1) famously called 'defining moments': 'right versus right' or 'wrong versus wrong' choices that keep managers up at night. What is expected from public managers in such situations?

FIGURE 9.2   Waldo's 12 ethical obligations to public servants

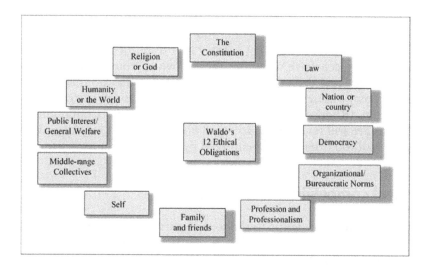

Reprinted with permission from O'Leary 2010: 11.

Formally, their key moral obligation has always been 'obedience to the mandates of law and policy mediated by the elected and appointed officials of democratic regimes' (Dobel 2005: 159). However, such passive, obedient, amoral notions of 'bureaucrats' have since long been disputed (Adams and Balfour 2009; Arendt 1963). Indeed, classical texts illustrate how frontline workers and street-level bureaucrats need to display considerable discretion and creativity to do their job (Kaufman 1960; Lipsky 1980). Some have argued that the constitution or the 'law of the land' should serve as a moral compass in case mandates seem to go against key public interests or universal ethics standards (Cooper 2012; Rohr 1992). Others suggest that public managers may be forced to be more activist, and nurture an 'ethics of dissent' if their agencies deal with unethical political masters (O'Leary 2005, 2010: 8).

Public managers as active moral agents

In a similar vein, O'Flynn (2009: 2) has argued that public managers are more than classical bureaucrats: 'the public manager [is] an active and motivating agent, rather than an actor that passively executes the will of their political masters'. As such, labelling senior public servants 'public managers' is more than a positional or semantic decision: it has important ethics and values implications. Rather than just being loyal, lawful, and neutral executors of policies, public managers become co-creators of public value (Moore 1995, 2013).

Is such a conception of public managers 'all positive', and do circum-stances actually allow them to co-create value? Views differ. Although politicians and public managers may increasingly share values as they col-laborate across boundaries (Demir and Nyhan 2008; Van der Wal 2014), we may also see more frequent conflict as a result of blurred role concep-tions and the defensive responses they provoke from both sides (Bekker 2009; 't Hart and Wille 2006). Some even argue that political neutrality may be compromised if public managers start to assertively define policy parameters (Rhodes and Wanna 2007). Moreover, horizontal and equal relations are still far from an accepted political reality; loyalty and obedi-ence are all too often eagerly enforced by political masters.

Ethical complexities in three areas

This observation brings us to the second part of this chapter, which deals with 21ˢᵗ century ethical complexities in three key managerial areas. The first is *political-administrative relations*: in an era of adaptiveness, col-laboration, and entrepreneurialism, we expect political astuteness from public managers, yet their operating environment forces political neu-trality upon them. The second cluster of conjectures emerges in *HRM and diversity management* and the pressures that such diversity exerts on already wide-ranging loyalties, obligations, and tolerance.

Third, new types of behaviours spurred by *social media and big data* produce a variety of ethical conjectures, such as managing (online) behav-iour outside of office hours, and updating ethics and privacy guidelines in an era of virtual whistleblowing and increased use of contractors for public sector work. Examples are provided of how various governments have attempted to deal with these complexities.

Typology of unethical behaviour

Before we delve into these three ethics areas, Box 9.2 sets the stage by outlining ten traditional types of unethical conduct in public sector contexts (Huberts and Lasthuizen 2014). These ten types of unethical behaviour serve as a navigational map for the remainder of the chapter. Public managers can encounter these behaviours as recipients, adjudica-tors, mediators, or perpetrators. Many of the behaviours have been with us for centuries and will remain with us for centuries to come. For 21ˢᵗ century public managers, however, the intriguing question is which types will gain importance, how new demands will shape their nature and fre-quency, whether entirely new types will emerge, and how they can be addressed effectively. As social norms change, perceptions of what counts as unethical behaviour change as well. For example, what counted as an innocent joke 20 years ago may now be seen as unethical.

Box 9.2 Ten types of unethical behaviour

1. **Corruption: Bribery**
   Misuse of (public) power for private gain: asking for, offering, accepting bribes.

2. **Corruption: Favouritism (nepotism, cronyism, patronage)**
   Misuse of authority or position to favour family (nepotism), friends (cronyism), or party (patronage).

3. **Fraud and theft of resources**
   Improper private gain acquired from the organization or from colleagues and citizens, with no involvement of an external actor.

4. **Conflict of (private and public) interest through 'gifts'**
   The interference (or potential interference) of personal interest with public/organizational interest because of gifts, services, or assets accepted, or promises made.

5. **Conflict of (private and public) interest through sideline activities**
   The interference (or potential interference) of personal interest with public/organizational interest because of jobs or activities practised outside the organization.

6. **Improper use of authority**
   The use of illegal/improper means or methods to achieve organizational goals (sometimes for 'noble causes').

7. **Misuse and manipulation of information**
   The intended or unintended abuse of (access to) information, such as cheating, violation of secrecy rules, breaching confidentiality of information, or concealing information.

8. **Indecent treatment of colleagues or citizens and customers**
   Unacceptable treatment that includes not only discrimination (based on gender, race, sexual orientation, or other types), intimidation, and sexual harassment but also improper behaviour like bullying, nagging, and gossiping.

9. **Waste and abuse of organizational resources**
   Improper performance, dysfunctional internal behaviour, or failure to comply with organizational standards.

10. **Misconduct in private time**
    Conduct during private time that harms people's trust in the (public) organization.

Source: Huberts and Lasthuizen 2014: 120.

One thing we should also keep in mind is the country and the sector that public managers operate in. Public managers in developing settings are more likely to prioritize systemic, pervasive corruption, nepotism, patronage, and fraud, whereas their counterparts in wealthier, relatively clean countries can devote more time to making sense of sexual intimidation, discrimination, workplace bullying, and (virtual) private time misconduct of public officials (Graycar and Prenzler 2013; Van den Heuvel *et al.* 2010). Depending on the setting, public managers will need to emphasize different elements of integrity management – for example, focusing more on compliance and repression rather than on education and awareness (Karssing and Spoor 2010; Maesschalck 2004; Paine 2000).

Ethics area 1: political-administrative relations

Weberian public administration contends that for public services to be stable, professional, evidence-based, and efficient, they have to be apolitical and professionalized. Traditionally, political neutrality is at the core of public sector ethics (Witesman and Walters 2016). In real life, however, although many public managers may try to remain apolitical, they know it is impossible to get anything done without engaging with politics (Moore 2013; 't Hart 2014a). Indeed, the work of public managers is unquestionably political: 'Processes of reading situations, framing issues, presenting arguments, negotiating, manoeuvring, and exercising influence' are mandatory aspects of a public manager's work (Alford *et al.* 2012: 3).

This work requires political astuteness – that is, 'being able to deploy political skills in situations involving diverse and sometimes competing interests and stakeholders, in order to create sufficient alignment of interests and/or consent in order to achieve objectives' (Hartley *et al.* 2013: 17; Hartley *et al.* 2015). Displaying political astuteness need not imply that public managers do so lightly or for personal gain. Indeed, an important component of being politically astute is the ability to determine political-administrative boundaries and discern to what extent managers can cross boundaries without violating ethical frameworks or jeopardizing their careers (Hartley *et al.* 2013: 73; Hartley *et al.* 2015: 195).

Box 9.3 showcases some of the difficulties public managers face in negotiating and managing the political aspects of their work while serving the public interest.

Indeed, public managers need to display political astuteness to prevent getting entangled in unethical behaviours of type 2 (cronyism) and type 4 (conflicts between public and private interests because of gifts accepted or promises made). In an interview study of senior public managers in Australia, the UK, and New Zealand, the participants indicated they were frequently required to resist pressures from politicians, such as those illustrated in Box 9.3. An oft-mentioned example was the approval of spending in a manner unacceptable to the public or internal audit (Hartley *et al.* 2013). The public managers expounded on the 'personal angst and intellectual energy', and

Box 9.3 Political interference with administrative advice in the UK

Keeping Kids Company, formerly known as Kids Company, is a British charity providing support to about 36,000 vulnerable urban youth. It had always been significantly dependent on public funding. In June 2015, the charity received a £3 million grant from the government despite concerns of mismanagement in the charity. Whitehall officials advised against the payment, but were overruled by ministers. The charity failed only months later.

The Public Administration Committee has since criticized the over-politicization of the charity. Not only did ministers disregard the advice of civil servants in proceeding to provide the grant – according to the committee, they should not have been involved in these decisions in the first place. The head of the charity allegedly garnered the support of high-profile politicians, including the Prime Minister. As a result, impartial judgement did not take place. The committee concluded: 'Ministers should not have allowed charity representatives to exploit their access to government in a way that may have been unethical.' The charity received grant amounts that far exceeded those given to other charities, despite warnings that it was unreliable and ineffective. Ministers nonetheless handed over more than £40 million over a 13-year period without adequate scrutiny.

This case showcases the difficulties that public managers face in their relationships with ministers. How can political astuteness help managers better navigate their relationships with political figures who are not bound by the same values of neutrality? Do codes of conduct adequately draw a boundary beyond which public managers must not trespass in their engagement with politics? What type of skillsets do public managers require to be politically astute? What are the HRM implications? In what context should political astuteness be employed?

Sources: BBC, http://bbc.co.uk; ITV, http://itv.com; *The Guardian*, https://theguardian.com; *The Telegraph*, http://telegraph.co.uk.

the wealth of experience and knowledge they drew on in order to manage political pressure (Manzie and Hartley 2013: 35–39).

In the same vein, Bowman *et al.* (2016) stress how public managers now require political skills more than ever before in order to adequately and creatively negotiate change. New guidelines and training programmes will have to pay attention to such skills, and to the tensions emerging from including an ever-wider range of stakeholders in decision-making. Box 9.4 provides two examples of such guidelines.

Clearly, public managers will have to evolve alongside their political masters to establish a new baseline of understanding about appropriate boundaries in an era of increased stakeholder multiplicity and cross-sectoral collaboration.

Box 9.4 Guidelines on managing political pressure in the UK and Norway

In the UK, recent codes provide guidelines to mitigate conflict of interest scenarios. For instance, public managers are counselled against developing a high level of personal familiarity with individual politicians. They are further advised not to try to influence them based on personal motivations, and to report to the relevant authority any attempts by politicians to press them in manners inconsistent with procedure or policy.

The Norwegian government's guide on administrative leadership similarly provides some direction on managing political conflicts. It stipulates that public managers must ensure that decisions are founded on professionally and legally sound arguments and consider both the current and future needs of the public. And, in managing politicians' short-term political gains and long-term policy goals, public managers are duty-bound to highlight to politicians their potential conflicts that may arise between the two. Further, they are required to conduct critical analyses, offer constructive counter-arguments, examine alternative solutions, and conduct impact assessments.

Sources: Local Government Staff Commission for Northern Ireland, http://lgsc.org.uk; Regjeringen, https://regjeringen.no.

Ethics area 2: HRM and diversity management

A 2015 OECD survey highlights the reality of greater diversity in the public sector. In many EU countries, for instance, women's participation has far surpassed that of men, albeit it is concentrated in certain occupation groups. In the years to come, the workforce will be increasingly diverse in terms of age, gender, ethnic origin, religion, disabilities, and sexual orientation. Ideally, every employee will bring a distinct background, knowledge, skills, and competencies that can add value to the public service if managed well (OECD 2015: 8, 10).

However, managing let alone stimulating diversity will be far from easy. This is because fresh faces, cultures, and customs are adding additional layers to employee relations and ethical obligations. As a result, the public manager now has a much more complicated personnel landscape to manage (Lewis and Gilman 2005: 238–239). Moreover, diversity is one thing, but inclusiveness – of values, concerns, viewpoints, and voices – is another.

Unmanaged diversity issues avert employee focus from performance, resulting in productivity losses and turnover. Greater workforce diversity may lead to ethical gains by increasing workplace fairness, economic opportunity, and social equality (Riccucci 2002, 2009; Wilkins 2006, 2008). At the same time, public managers may have a hard time maintaining clear standards of ethics and professionalism because loyalties of new groups of employees may be ambiguous and multi-layered (Caiden 2001; De Graaf 2010). Tackling this challenge requires additional managerial skills (Lewis and Gilman 2005: 2403; Rabin 2003: 347). Let us take a closer look at the various diversity challenges and the dilemmas they create.

Generational diversity

Ng *et al.* (2012), in a study on managing the new workforce, link certain character traits and behaviours with millennials. This includes greater individualism, narcissism, a sense of entitlement, an inability to take critique well, a lack of group-work skills, and a weaker work ethic. 'While older generations adapt to the workplace, millennials expect the workplace to adapt to them' (Cushman and Wakefield 2014: 5). Some of these character traits seem to go against more altruistic and intrinsic traits long associated with the public service ethos (Van der Wal 2015b). In fact, some scholars have even suggested that the public service ethos is 'in decline' among the newer generation of public servants (Lyons *et al.* 2006: 9).

Managing this new workforce ethically poses a variety of questions to public managers:

- While millennials may be committed to improving the welfare of society, do their character traits undermine their ability to do so within the confines of the public service?
- Are the traditional values of public service in conflict with the individualism of the millennial public servant?
- How can public managers rebrand the public service to attract millennials without undermining the essence of the public sector ethos?

Diversity in gender and orientation

In most countries, the public sector has historically been male dominated and has, with time, developed 'traditional male standards' and expectations when it comes to management (Porfon 2013: 21). Many argue that bureaucratic organizations are innately gendered or masculinized, and disadvantage women in their career advancement (Britton 2000: 430; Kelly and Newman 2001: 20; Williams *et al.* 2014: 53; Acker 1990).

The issues relating to gender in organizations range from limited understanding to varying degrees of inappropriate treatment. This sometimes results in type 8 unethical conduct, noted in Box 9.2 as 'indecent treatment of colleagues or citizens and customers'. More recently, discrimination based on gender identity and sexual orientation has become an issue for public managers, even in seemingly tolerant and liberal contexts (Lambda and Deloitte 2006; Legal Transgender Law Center 2009). Some of the issues include refusal of employment or promotion opportunities, dismissal, and

Box 9.5 LGBTQ public servants in India

In December 2013, Swapna, a 23-year-old Indian transgender woman, was granted the ability to take the provincial Tamil Nadu civil service exam as a result of a court order that enabled her to select a sex of her choice in the exam application. This was an unprecedented feat that took two years of protesting and legal recourse for her to be recognized as a female, as opposed to a third gender. She has since set her sights on joining the central government by pushing for the ability to apply for a public service job at the agency in charge of conducting the civil service exams.

Sources: Al Jazeera, http://aljazeera.com; *The Guardian*, https://theguardian.com.

verbal and physical harassment (Burns *et al.* 2012: 6–8). Public managers must seek to promote an organizational culture that offers a favourable work environment to all, and overcomes structural bias related to gender or sexual orientation in public organizations. Box 9.5 illustrates a recent legal shift in civil service access for transgenders in India.

Religious diversity

Religious discrimination has also emerged as a new managerial ethics issue, with the rate increasing even faster than discrimination based on gender and race. In 2011, the Equal Employment Opportunity Commission in the US revealed that annual religious bias complaints had doubled since 2001. European countries show similar developments (Amnesty International 2012). Many countries in other parts of the world have not even started to adequately register such issues. Whether religious discrimination is overt or covert, or even whether it is 'real', is not the issue; it is the manner in which employees perceive the discrimination that is of significance to public managers. Such perceptions can negatively impact recruitment, organizational culture, compensation, job commitment, and employee relations (Messara 2014: 64, Ensher *et al.* 2001: 56–57; Triana *et al.* 2010).

Moreover, greater religious diversity in the public sector workforce may create additional challenges for public managers in ensuring that staff respond first and foremost to ethical obligations in line with the agency's mission, rather than 'god', family, clan, or personal convictions (think back here to Waldo's 12 ethical obligations).

Indeed, religious beliefs are likely to accompany employees into the work environment, and they may conflict with traditional public service values of neutrality and impartiality. A famous example is the refusal of public servants with orthodox Christian or Muslim backgrounds to execute same-sex marriages even though they are legally mandated to do so.

Box 9.6 Religious holidays for public employees?

New York Mayor Bill de Blasio's move to incorporate two major Muslim holy days, Eid al-Fitr and Eid al-Adha, into school calendars is one way to deal with a hot button issue in many Western countries with large Muslim populations. The move was in consideration of the fact that Islam was the fastest-growing religion in the city. In a tweet, de Blasio explained that it was a change led by an appreciation for the city's diversity.

The move was well received by the likes of the Jamaica Muslim Center, with one of the office coordinators asserting that just as Christian and Jewish holidays are granted, 'they are getting their holiday, we should get our holidays also – everybody should have a holiday'.

However, extending such recognition of non-traditional religious holidays to the workplace is more challenging. Public managers and politicians in many countries struggle with this issue. To what extent should public managers accommodate religious needs and values? How do they ensure fairness towards other faiths without compromising work flows and staffing? One of the countries that has chosen the most inclusive option is multicultural Singapore, which has declared all major Christian, Hindu, and Muslim festive days as public holidays for all, including public servants.

Sources: *The Guardian*, https://theguardian.com; *The Humanist*, https://thehumanist.com.

In many cases, public managers may find ways to internally manage such issues (Menzel 2012). However, assertive individuals are increasingly likely to accommodate personal religious beliefs in the office, creating dilemmas for public managers (Messara 2014: 61). Box 9.6 showcases how Mayor Bill de Blasio of New York has chosen to deal with one such dilemma: the issue of allowing non-traditional religious holidays.

Managing workforce diversity ethically bears all the characteristics of an ethical complexity, as it is impossible to please all the stakeholders and audiences involved – ranging from hardline meritocratists and secularists to the ultra-liberal and progressive – and missteps may have brutal repercussions in the polarized climate characterizing many countries. Box 9.7 discusses two examples of guidelines on workforce diversity management from New Zealand and Australia, countries that have taken a fairly tolerant stance, at least on paper.

Ethics area 3: social media and big data

Technological revolutions create a variety of new ethics issues for public managers: the blurring of public and private domains in the context of social media, privacy concerns related to big data, and the advent of virtual whistleblowing and increasing transparency demands.

Box 9.7 Guidelines for managing diversity in New Zealand and Australia

The Human Rights Commission in New Zealand has developed a guideline for managing religious diversity that offers good practices in various areas: *holidays* – allow employees to apply for leave requests; *dress codes and appearance* – requests to dress in accordance with religious beliefs should be reasonably accommodated; *prayer times and facilities* – employees should consider the provision of facilities in good faith; and *religiously prohibited practices* – such practices should be addressed by the employer and employee and an agreement made during the negotiation of terms of employment.

In Australia, many public agencies nowadays have a workplace diversity coordinator, who is tasked with obtaining understanding of the diversity requirements of employees, advancing the incorporation of workplace diversity matters in HR policies and practices, and facilitating staff awareness of diversity issues. The Public Sector Commission in Western Australia has even developed a workforce diversity and planning toolkit that includes a sample diversity questionnaire (so public managers can collect data to inform policy), a workforce and diversity action plan template (to ensure that certain key elements are included in such plans), and a workforce planning and diversity assessment tool (to assess strengths and areas requiring improvement).

Sources: Commonwealth of Australia 2001; Morris 2011; Public Sector Commission (Western Australia), https://publicsector.wa.gov.au.

Digital media and the blurring of public and private domains

New media have 'turned the public and private domains inside out' (Bratton and Candy 2013: 177; Lewis and Gilman 2005: 91). They expose public servants to increased visibility and vulnerability, not only because public servants are themselves active on social media but also because citizens play the role of journalist and record and post messages of government officials who are perceived to be involved in misconduct (Hoekstra and Van Dijk 2016: 5). As with all perceived unethical behaviour, this 21ˢᵗ century citizen activism has far-reaching consequences even in instances where the accusations turn out to be erroneous. Once online, information is likely to permanently stay in the system, forever accessible by a global audience (Hoekstra and Van Dijk 2016: 5).

The blurred lines between the public and the private create an unavoidable conflict between the public servant's right to privacy versus the public's right to know (Lewis and Gilman 2005: 91). As they increasingly experience conflicts between the right to freedom of speech and 'being bound' (Hoekstra and Van Dijk 2016: 6), public managers need to explain and enforce private time constraints consistently and carefully.

Box 9.8 discusses two recent episodes in which public servants struggle to exercise their civil liberties within the professional constraints implied by the public service ethos.

Surely, legal consequences differ between jurisdictions. However, across countries public servants have been disciplined, fired, or persecuted for their digital slip-ups, suggesting once more that public managers cannot be careful enough in emphasizing and enforcing constraints and increasing awareness towards their staff through collaboratively creating guidelines and analysing real-life cases (see Kaptein 2011, 2013).

Box 9.8 Digital slip-ups in Pakistan and Australia

In recent years, we have witnessed dozens of legal cases against public servants because of their online conduct, in a wide variety of countries and regimes.

In Pakistan in 2015, the then freshly appointed official at the Oil and Gas Regulatory, Mr Noorul Haq, jeopardized his job due to his social media posts. In a range of posts, Mr Haq criticized political parties and the army. A petition was made at the Islamabad High Court for alleged misbehaviour, in terms of violation of his apolitical status with his comments on Twitter and Facebook.

In 2013 an Australian court gave the go-ahead for the dismissal of a public servant for her critical tweets about the country's immigration detention policies. She did not disclose her name or her line of work, and used the Twitter alias @LaLegale. With a Twitter following of 700, she tweeted critical comments related to the department on a regular basis. In court, law graduate Ms Banerji represented herself and argued the following: 'It is evident that they are a simple expression of political opinion, made in my own time away from work, and that any perception of non-compliance by a public servant for conveyance of a political opinion is an infringement of the implicit constitutional freedom of political communication.' Ms Banerji lost her case under the rationale that these rights are not without limit and did not allow her to be in breach of an employment contract. The outcome signifies that public servants do not enjoy identical rights to other citizens, even in their private time.

The cases illustrate that social media indeed present fresh challenges in terms of the ability of public servants to maintain a perception of political neutrality and impartiality. The reach, immediacy, and permanence of social media means a rant can get a public servant into trouble. Further, the anonymity that social media sites such as Twitter grant users still does not give public servants the licence to say as they please, nor are they absolved of their duty of impartiality and non-partisanship.

Sources: *Dawn*, https://dawn.com; Public Service Commission of Canada, http://psc-cfp.gc.ca; *Sydney Morning Herald*, http://smh.com.au.

Various countries have started to produce social media guidelines for public servants, some more detailed and useful than others. For instance, the Dutch National Integrity Office recently produced a detailed policy document, tellingly titled *The Marriage of Heaven and Hell. Integrity and Social Media in the Public Sector* (2016). Also, the UK civil service has a social media guide for civil servants. According to the former Minister for the Cabinet Office, Francis Maude, the benefits that the digital space provides for stakeholder engagement bring with it even greater responsibility. Greater scrutiny requires civil servants to have the same levels of ethical conduct in the digital realm as they do in the 'real world' (Cabinet Office 2014). Box 9.9 shows examples from various countries.

Big data and privacy violations

Public sector-driven innovation initiatives are increasingly facilitated by social media and big data, argued to be a revolutionary, game-changing phenomenon (Gordon 2015: 6; Mayer-Schönberger and Cukier 2013). Big data, 'the enhanced ability to collect, store and analyze previously unimaginable quantitates of data in tremendous speed and with negligible costs', provides significant opportunities for public managers to create value (Tene and Polonetsky 2013). For instance, it facilitates targeted interventions in education and healthcare, and employment opportunities for low-income and under-served segments of society (Ramirez *et al.* 2016: 5–6). Managers increasingly use big-data analysis to spend funds more effectively and uncover fraud while making data available to the public (Gordon 2015).

But what are the ethical complexities for public managers in harnessing these technologies for the public interest? What if innovations lead to violation of individual rights such as privacy? Indeed, the challenge lies in finding a balance between the key values of transparency, accountability, security, accessibility, and privacy. 'Open government' calls for increased disclosure of information to government, as well as significant access to the personal information of citizens (Mulgan 2014). However, this raises serious privacy issues, even when the publication of such data in reusable form may seem to be devoid of personal information or may have been anonymized.

Utilizing such data sets in conjunction with other data creates serious privacy risks. This is because advanced algorithms can be used to match various data sets and recognize specific individuals: re-identification science renders illusory the suggestions of privacy granted by data anonymization (Ohm 2010: 1704; Scassa 2014: 398). The fact that access is provided through corporate-run digital tools makes it an even more complex issue (MacKinnon 2012). For public managers, the dilemma lies in how to show restraint in using information readily entrusted to governments and companies. Box 9.10 highlights some of these privacy concerns.

Box 9.9 Social media guidelines for public servants

In 2010, the Australian government incorporated online media participation guidelines into its code of conduct. The guidelines reiterate that the same principles that govern any other form of public comment apply to online public comments. They emphasize additional factors such as the speed, reach, permanence, and replicability of online communication, the issue of unintended recipients, and the potential for misinterpretation.

Some of the requirements of the guidelines include:

- courteous and respectful behaviour;
- appropriate handling of information and recognizing the need for confidentiality of certain information;
- proper usage of government resources;
- taking measures to mitigate conflicts of interest;
- service provision in a fair, effective, impartial, and courteous manner;
- abiding by public service values and maintaining the integrity and good reputation of the public service;
- desisting from behaviour that may raise concerns about the public servant's apolitical, impartial, and professional nature.

The UK introduced its social media guidelines in 2014. The guidelines recognize the value of digital media tools in enhancing public servants' work while maintaining utmost integrity, and include:

- non-disclosure of information without requisite authorization;
- being wary of making comments regarding government policy and practices in the absence of required authorization;
- desisting from making comments on politically controversial matters;
- desisting from personal attacks or offensive comments.

South Africa, Malta, and Bangladesh introduced social media guidelines in 2011, 2015, and 2016, respectively. In Bangladesh, the following is advised regarding the opening of personal accounts for public servants: display responsible conduct online; exercise caution in the selection and content of material posted; avoid unneeded tagging and referencing.

Sources: Prothom Alo, http://prothom-alo.com; UK Government, https://gov.uk; Australian Public Service Commission, http://www.apsc.gov.au; *The Independent*, https://independent.co.uk.

On the other end of the spectrum, however, public managers may become involved in situations where they have to protect the public's safety by compromising the privacy of individuals, such as in the case of terrorism suspects, an example being the various legal clashes between technology companies and government officials in the US about accessing encrypted communication devices and technologies. How do public managers balance competing interests of transparency, accountability,

Box 9.10 Prying public servants in Australia and the US

Public servants caught prying into citizens' private data showcase some of the potential privacy breaches that can emanate from government's compilation of big data. An ABC news article in 2010 revealed that over 1,000 Medicare employees in Australia had been investigated regarding unauthorized access to the personal data of customers (even though 30 per cent had in fact been snooping on their own files). The Australian Privacy Foundation has since lamented the need for greater measures to ensure that people's privacy is safeguarded, pointing at both legal and ethical reasons for doing so.

Similarly, in the US, a bored former State Department analyst was facing jail time in Virginia in 2008 because he snooped on approximately 200 passport records, including those of Barack Obama, John McCain, and a host of celebrities, athletes, and businessmen. He was able to access the data through the State Department's Passport Information Electronic Records System, which contains the data of millions of US passport holders.

The case illustrated that in a system that can be accessed by around 20,000 workers, but has no policies, procedures, guidelines, or training to guide conduct, there is significant potential for abuse of citizens' personal information. Given incidents like these, questions emerge concerning the measures public managers are expected to take to better protect personal data and to effectively and efficiently detect employee misconduct of this nature. Also, given that politicians often lack the technical skillset – and, sometimes, the patience and interest – to devise and legislate some measures, public managers face increasing responsibilities in assessing system vulnerabilities and pointing out such vulnerabilities to their political masters and legislators.

Sources: ABC News, http://abc.net.au/news/; The Register, http://theregister.co.uk.

and security with privacy rights? Guidelines for usage of big data and big-data analytics protocols are in their early stages. One major issue that public managers already face is how to meaningfully make sense of and use abundant data sources in the first place.

Increased transparency and virtual whistleblowing

The 'new age of transparency' has collided with decreasing public trust in government institutions (Brown *et al.* 2014: 31). One particularly complex development for public managers is the emergence of virtual whistleblowers and 'hacktivists'. Whistleblowing is 'the disclosure by organization members (former or current) of illegal, immoral or illegitimate practices under the control of their employers to people or organizations that might be able to effect action' (Anakin et. *al* 2008: 8).

Whistleblowing – and reporting of alleged unethical behaviour more generally – have long created dilemmas for public managers, who must balance collegiality, organizational morale and reputation, and decision-making prudence with transparency, accountability, and the need to pursue reports of unethical conduct (Brewer and Selden 2000; De Graaf 2010, 2016; Miceli *et al.* 2008). Some contend that whistleblowing itself may be unethical (Davis 1996; Hoffman and Schwartz 2015; Lowry *et al.* 2013). Others see it as the most important mechanism for unveiling wrongdoing in the public realm.

In recent years, technology has simultaneously lowered the cost and complexity of disclosing information and significantly enhanced anonymity (Reitman 2011). Previously, whistleblowers were required to identify a news outlet or reporter that they hoped would safeguard their identity. Further, even when information was successfully and anonymously disclosed, broad dissemination would often fail (Joyce *et al.* 2010). Now, WikiLeaks, LocalLeaks in the US, Rospil in Russia, or Al Jazeera's Transparency Unit, and a range of 'stateless news organizations' (Lang 2010) allow for *virtual whistleblowing* that no longer requires whistleblowers to carefully seek out reporters, and worry about broad dissemination.

All this has significant implications for public managers in terms of managing staff relations with media and access to information (Brown *et al.* 2014). The concerns are even more pressing if the employees are (temporary) contractors or part-time employees, each falling within different legal employment regimes. The famous Snowden case in Box 9.11 captures some of the value conflicts confronting public managers as a result of virtual whistleblowing.

Most governments have whistleblowing policies and provisions in place, including reporting procedures and portals, and confidentiality officers (usually independent and external), and grant legal protection to whistleblowers during the course of disciplinary and criminal investigations (Tak 2013). However, with few exceptions, such policies are 'paper tigers' that do not fully protect whistleblowers against various types of retaliation, perhaps with the exception of the Sarbanes–Oxley Act in the US (Miceli *et al.* 2008).

The various 21st century challenges and the initial regulatory and behavioural responses by governments illustrate the increasing difficulties involved for public managers in leading ethically and in ensuring that employees and stakeholders display appropriate conduct. The final part of this chapter addresses the question of how public managers can manage and mitigate ethical complexities and promote ethical behaviour.

Effective ethics management

As shown in previous sections of this chapter, coming up with tailored, effective solutions for ethics management is far from easy. Yet there is ample evidence out there on what works and what hurts. Indeed, a massive body

Box 9.11 America's Most Wanted Whistleblower

Edward Snowden has made history as one of America's most famous whistleblowers next to the likes of Daniel Ellsberg (the Pentagon Papers) and Bradley Manning (WikiLeaks). Often referred to as 'America's Most Wanted', Snowden was an infrastructure analyst at Booz Allen Hamilton on contract for the National Security Agency (NSA). In June 2013, he disclosed to *Guardian* journalists classified information regarding NSA surveillance activities – in Snowden's words, 'the largest program of suspicion-less surveillance in human history', surpassing that of 'even the most totalitarian states'. Snowden feared he would have received a jail sentence had he taken the information to Congress.

Members of Congress have branded him a defector who should face the full brunt of the law, while his supporters contend that his revelations have ignited a global conversation about the balance between security and privacy. Meanwhile, in a watershed decision in 2015, a US court of appeals ruled unlawful the mass compilation of telephone metadata. This move has opened the door for legal action against the NSA.

Barbara Redman (2014), at the Harvard Center for Ethics, highlights two moral issues of the case. First, since a public servant's duty is to serve the public and safeguard its freedoms, its interests, and the common good as a whole, he should be loyal to the public first and foremost. Second, Snowden's 'civil disobedience' may be deemed by some as a moral right within constraints. According to Snowden, 'there are moral obligations to act when the law no longer reflects the morality of the society it governs'. Should public servants blow the whistle if their organization's actions cease to reflect society's moral fabric?

The case also illustrates a concern for public managers regarding the increasing use of contractors. An *NBC News* report argues that Snowden's security clearance was too high and 'his actions were largely unaudited'. Several questions and dilemmas remain. How can public managers strengthen internal whistleblowing mechanisms so that their organizations can avoid the embarrassment and the loss of face that accompanies external whistleblowing? How do public managers strike a balance between secrecy and transparency? What implications does the Snowden case have in terms of recruitment and management of staff?

Sources: *The Guardian*, https://theguardian.com; Business Insider, https://businessinsider.com; *The Telegraph*, http://telegraph.co.uk; ZDNet, https://zdnet.com; Harvard University Center for Ethics, https://ethics.harvard.edu; *Stanford Daily*, https://stanforddaily.com; Whistleblowing Today, https://whistleblowingtoday.org.

of literature has developed about corruption control, integrity management, ethical leadership, ethical climate, and ethical performance (Bowman and West 2015; Cooper 2012; Huberts 2014; Kaptein and Wempe 2002; Klitgaard 1998; Lawton *et al.* 2013; Menzel 2012; Paine 2000; Treviño *et al.* 2000). Here, we focus on what is most relevant to public managers in light of the emergent ethics issues detailed in this chapter.

Managing ethics effectively: combining hard and soft controls

Research on ethics and integrity management contrasts two possible managerial strategies managers can pursue: the 'compliance-based approach' versus the 'integrity-based approach' (Maesschalck 2004; Paine 1994). The *compliance-based approach* emphasizes (top-down) imposition of rules and regulations intended to prevent non-compliant behaviour and promote norm-compliant behaviour – for example, internal and external supervision, control, and sanctioning. This 'hard' strategy assumes that employees cannot be trusted and their behaviour needs to be regulated and enforced. Instruments include rules for declaring assets, activities, and interests; screening of employees; penal codes on corruption; and a wide range of disciplinary sanctions and procedures (Van der Wal *et al.* 2016: 3).

The *integrity-based approach* emphasizes joint (bottom-up) formulation, internalization of organizational aspirations and values, and promotion of ethical behaviour by strengthening the moral competence and moral reasoning of employees. The strategy is based on a more positive image of employees. It is a 'soft' approach characterized by joint formulation of codes of ethics, ethics education, and awareness training together with 'values jams' (Van der Wal *et al.* 2016: 5).

As discussed before, many governments are in the process of revamping existing guidelines and codes, or developing new ones, to manage emerging ethics challenges. However, we know from evidence that codes, rules, and guidelines can only do so much (Huberts 2014; Kaptein 2011), particularly in settings characterized by pervasive, systemic unethical behaviour. Indeed, awareness, 'discussability', training, and leadership are crucial for strengthening moral competence in light of the new types of dilemmas and violations, and of entirely new expectations of ethical behaviour discussed in this chapter.

Experiences from successful agencies in countries such as Australia, New Zealand, Singapore, Hong Kong, and the Netherlands suggest that combining both strategies is most effective (Huberts 2014; Lawton *et al.* 2013; Quah 2015). In this vein, Karssing and Spoor (2010) propose that public managers adopt a sedimentary view on ethics management where one approach provides the foundation for the other, visualized in Figure 9.3. Managers need to ensure that integrity 1.0 (the basic compliance-inspired infrastructure) is in place before they can move on to master integrity 2.0 (ethical consciousness and awareness). Ultimately, they should aim to reach the end state of integrity 3.0, where integrity is engrained throughout the organization as a self-evident professional responsibility (Van der Wal *et al.* 2016: 1).

Managing issues and stages of implementation

Public managers in developing countries with rampant corruption issues should first get their house in order by implementing integrity 1.0 before

FIGURE 9.3   Integrity 1.0, integrity 2.0, and integrity 3.0

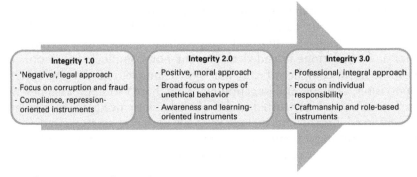

Based on: Karssing and Spoor 2010.

they can expect training and awareness to yield high returns. In highly unethical climates, punishing a number of high-profile figures is effective for acquiring the required buy-in for a more structural mindset change related not only to the *frequency* of violations but also to their societal *acceptability* (Huberts 2014). Public managers in developed settings with different types of ethics issues should prioritize continuous conversations on values, dilemmas, and grey areas. Indeed, success stories from relatively corruption-free countries show that setting and phasing matter (Demmke 2002; Heywood 2012; Lawton *et al.* 2013; Quah 2015).

However, in moving from 1.0 to 3.0, public managers should keep in mind that the various types of training programmes offered by the 'ethics industry' have limited effect unless they are targeted, repetitive, and part of a larger cluster of measures (Menzel 1997; Van Montfort *et al.* 2013). Moreover, it is naïve to assume that many agencies ever reach the stage at which their managers do not need to explicitly label integrity policies and officers anymore. In more than a decade of teaching ethics workshops around the world, I have never met a manager who testified to her agency being at the 3.0 level. As such, integrity as a self-evident, fully achieved professional standard for all employees may be a *desirable* rather than an *attainable* condition.

Clearly, public managers have a key role to play in translating and implementing broad political and societal mandates to 'do something about ethics'. In doing so, they have to mitigate four key implementation issues (Hoekstra 2016; Van der Wal *et al.* 2016):

- *Fragmentation* due to isolated rather than integrated policies developed in response to a particular scandal and insufficient collaboration between key players (Heywood 2012). At the same time, experiences with powerful centralized anti-corruption bodies – often suggested as the 'optimal' approach – vary widely across countries (Quah 2011, 2015).

- *Implementation deficiency* because ethics programmes are not subject to the same rigour, evaluation or follow-up as other programmes or policies (Demmke and Moilanen 2012; Huberts 2014; Transparency International 2012).
- *Misbalance between the strategies* outlined as strategies come into and out of favour over time (Hoekstra and Kaptein 2014). In developed countries, a related problem is that risk analysis and enforcement are used less as the focus has shifted to the integrity 2.0 approach.
- *Austerity measures resulting in more integrity risks* (Transparency International 2012). Attention to integrity fluctuates. For instance, the high-profile UK Standards Boards, made up of various stakeholders to scrutinize the conduct of local government officials (Cowell *et al.* 2011; Lawton and Macaulay 2014), were scrapped when a new government came to power on the wave of austerity. More generally, risks increase as budget cuts and reforms give rise to feelings of anxiety, resentment, and job insecurity (Hoekstra 2016).

Managing institutionalization: informal versus formal approaches

How, then, can public managers institutionalize and implement structures and cultures promoting ethics and integrity? Essentially, they can choose any combination of two routes: informal or formal institutionalization (Brenner 1992; Van der Wal *et al.* 2016). The more implicit and indirect informal approach includes the creation of shared values and rewarding of 'good' behaviour through appraisal. Advocates of this approach label formal policy as an empty shell that is mainly symbolic (Sims and Brinkmann 2003). Moreover, the fact that many organizations often devote limited attention and resources to formal programmes has led some to emphasize the necessity of a more culture-oriented, informal approach (Vitell and Singhapakdi 2008; Weaver *et al.* 1999). Some studies even establish a relation between 'forced', top-down ethics training and increased unethical conduct, suggesting that employees who receive training and are being told to be of high moral calibre feel 'morally licensed' to behave unethically (Roberts 2009; Yam *et al.* 2014).

The formal approach is explicit, direct, and visibly aimed at promoting ethical behaviour (Heres 2014; Hoekstra 2016; Tenbrunsel *et al.* 2003). This approach stresses the development of sustainable structures and standards for supporting and embedding ethical conduct (Sims 2003). According to Berman *et al.* (1994), the formal strategy has the advantage of being more recognizable and easy to explain to employees. Others emphasize that formalization, which should include regular measurement of the effectiveness of instruments together with central registration of violations and investigations, improves the effectiveness of integrity policies (Van den Heuvel *et al.* 2012).

In reality, just as with the hard and soft controls, public managers will have to pursue smart combinations of formal and informal institutionalization rather than a skewed approach. Table 9.2 lists the advantages and disadvantages associated with informal and formal approaches, and suggests behaviours and strategies to maximize the advantages of both approaches.

TABLE 9.2 Managing and institutionalizing ethics: informal versus formal approaches

Approach	Advantages	Disadvantages	Managerial behaviours and strategies
Informal	• Tends to enhance involvement, buy-in, and commitment. • Emphasizes ethical leadership, climate, and competence without suggesting employees are prone to behave unethically. • May promote 'discussability' and sharing of dilemmas and grey areas.	• May create randomness, vagueness, and favouritism in the way management treats unethical conduct and explains expectations. • May create conflicting ethical subcultures within organizations. • May create complacency due to the suggestion that guidelines and sanctions are unnecessary.	• Managers should not refrain from repetitively communicating and informally enforcing standards. • Managers should consistently manage expectations in all parts of the organization. • Managers should involve various types of employees in drafting and discussing codes and value statements.
Formal	• Is likely to create clarity and draw attention from employees. • Helps to ensure transparency, consistency, and fairness. • Enables both internal (disciplinary) and external (judicial) sanctioning.	• May create disincentives to develop ethical competence for the sake of being a good professional. • May create unintended, counterproductive, complacent, and 'gaming' behaviour. • May create a culture of fear and retaliation.	• Managers should provide clear explanation of the 'why' of new policies. • Managers should pursue rigorous evaluation every few years and update if effectiveness is insufficient. • Managers should institutionalize external oversight to prevent opportunistic use of rules by senior leadership.

Effective ethical leadership

In their combined and dynamic pursuit of harder and softer strategies, public managers will sometimes have to follow a 'good cop, bad cop' approach: they need to be flexible if it serves policy objectives without violating basic norms, while being clear and consistent in communicating those norms at the same time. In doing so, they run the risk of being perceived as hypocritical or 'neutral' ethical leaders (Heres and Lasthuizen 2012; Treviño *et al.* 2000: 137; Treviño *et al.* 2003). Indeed, the way in which public managers themselves behave – the 'tone at the top' – will greatly affect the ethical climate in their organizations. As they are seen as transmitting values, behaviours, and expectations (Ciulla 2004; Heres 2016; Schwartz *et al.* 2005), their actions may often be more important than any formal guideline or policy (Downe *et al.* 2016).

Studies show that ethical leadership at the very least limits counterproductive employee behaviour and fosters an ethical climate (Avey *et al.* 2012; De Hoogh and den Hartog 2008; Lasthuizen 2008). Different styles of ethical leadership affect different behaviours: ethical role modelling is effective in minimizing inappropriate interpersonal behaviour – type 8 in Box 9.2 – while enforcement through rewards and punishments is more effective in preventing violations related to organizational resources, such as types 3 and 9 – fraud, waste, abuse, and improper performance (Huberts *et al.* 2007; Lasthuizen 2008). How can public managers develop their own ethical leadership style and ensure they will be perceived as good examples, or even role models taken seriously by employees and stakeholders?

In a seminal piece, Treviño and colleagues (2000) argue that managers, in order to be perceived as ethical leaders, need to be more than just *moral persons*; they need to be *moral managers*. Indeed, in addition to being fair, honest, caring, and just, managers need to be tough, consistent, and clear in frequently communicating, emphasizing, and reinforcing organizational standards and norms. In practice, moral management has three key elements: role modelling through visible action; rewards and discipline; and communication about ethics and values (Brown *et al.* 2005; Lawton *et al.* 2013). Public managers have to be sensitive to the fact that the signals they send may be perceived very differently than was intended – and once set, bad examples are almost impossible to get rid of. As Lawton *et al.* (2013: 161) assert: 'if unethical behavior, unintentionally or not, is left unpunished, facilitated, or even rewarded it might be perceived as acceptable behavior and continue in the future'.

As trivial as this may sound, public leaders in particular often seem to assume that just because they have devoted their life to public service and believe they demonstrate high moral values, their stakeholders and subordinates will automatically perceive them as ethical leaders. In some instances, this may indeed be the case; just think about larger-than-life characters such as Mahatma Gandhi, Martin Luther King Jr, or Nelson Mandela. Although public managers do not operate in the spotlight as such political and civic leaders do, they will be seen as role models in their agencies and beyond. Moreover, as a result of the demands described in this book they will increasingly be scrutinized by the public as well.

If public managers do not go beyond developing high personal moral standards, they may at best be seen as ethically neutral leaders. Conversely, if they act tough on ethics by telling others what to do without 'walking the talk' themselves, followers will view them as hypocritical and may feel empowered to behave unethically themselves (Lawton *et al.* 2013: 161; Treviño *et al.* 2000: 134).

Figure 9.4 visualizes the four types of leader perceptions produced by the interactions between strong and weak actions on the moral manager and moral person dimension. For public managers to become and remain ethical leaders, they will have to build and project the key values and traits discussed in this chapter while communicating values, norms, and standards through the policies they implement, and most importantly, enforce such policies with an eye for consistency and proportionality.

FIGURE 9.4   Ethical leadership: moral manager and moral person

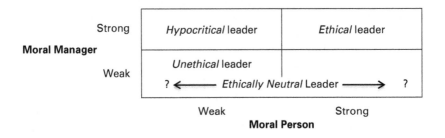

Source: Treviño *et al.* 2000: 137.

What lies ahead

Following this discussion of the various ethical complexities created by 21st century developments, and the managerial strategies and behaviours to address them, chapter 'Managing Short Versus Long Time Horizons' discusses another 21st century demand: *managing short versus long time horizons*. Increasingly, public managers will have to balance never-ending news and election cycles and the short-termism they produce against the long-term horizons required for programmes and policies to mitigate megatrends like ageing, climate change, and urbanization. In doing so, they will have to reconcile various competing logics and behaviours, ensuring both political responsiveness and institutional resilience. How public managers can use foresight methods effectively while acting as improvisers and crisis managers will become clear in the next chapter.

Chapter 10

Managing Short Versus Long Time Horizons

No battle plan survives contact with the enemy.

(Helmuth von Moltke the Elder, German Field Marshal)

Who cares about the long term?

Imagine being a senior public manager in Brussels tasked with coordinating a joint response to the biggest-ever inflow of asylum seekers into the European Union (EU). Spurred by civil war in Syria and accelerated by the alleged 'open invitation' from German Chancellor Angela Merkel, more than a million asylum seekers entered Germany in 2015 alone. The sheer number took EU member state governments and EU agencies by surprise, overwhelming administrative capacity on all levels: the security procedures *at* the southern and eastern borders, with Greece being the major destination for the rickety boats carrying refugees; the processing methodologies *in* individual member states; and the (re)distribution processes *between* member states. In addition, political collaboration is put to the test like never before with countries deciding to 'go it alone' while ignoring treaties and political mores. This is occurring in a context of already severely stretched political ties, with the sovereign debt crisis and the near expulsion of Greece from the eurozone.

Across the EU you have witnessed a surge of anti-migrant movements, some of them violent, fuelled by incidents of some asylum seekers engaging in criminal and subversive activities. Both traditional and new media eagerly reported on such behaviours and the backlash they provoked. Clearly, public resentment and administrative capacity breakdowns could be linked with the sudden explosion in the number of refugees seeking asylum.

However, was this explosion really so 'sudden' or 'unexpected? Events in the Middle East and elsewhere in recent years offered premonitions. Did your agency, staffed with highly educated and well-paid public managers and policy experts, not prepare scenarios and 'battle plans' years ahead? Could such long-term products have helped in mitigating short-term emergencies and sensationalist pressures from media and populist forces? Certainly, the fact that such a developed continent with a reputation for good governance appeared so surprised, in turn surprised many experts across the globe.

The EU refugee crisis illustrates various dilemmas and demands in managing short-term pressures, crises, and expectations while simultaneously keeping the 'long view', trying to plan ahead and turn crises into long-term opportunities. Such demands and dilemmas emerge at various stages of high-impact events. In the *preparatory phase*, public managers engaging in foresight activities and scenario-building have to display astuteness in 'making the case' to their masters. Moreover, they have to convincingly sell how their predictions will help those masters – immediately or further down the line – while knowing all too well that they are actually not interested in what happens five years from now. Would it have been politically expedient to communicate doomy predictions of millions of people arriving from the Middle East in 2013, when the EU economy showed minimal signs of recovery, with consumer confidence at an all-time low? Political trade-offs had to be made there, and stakeholders can only handle so many crises at one time. Ironically, the European Commission adopted an 'Action Plan for Resilience in Crisis Prone Countries' in that same year.

In the *urgent response phase*, public managers have to deal with political logics, media logics, and emergency logics. 'Blame games', accountability pressures, ad-hoc negotiations and mid-term solutions dominate the agenda. No one cares about earlier scenarios unless they help in fending off assaults from stakeholders and sensationalist media, but this is unlikely given the low probability that decision-makers actually acted upon the scenarios.

In the *evaluation and learning phase*, committees, stakeholders, and media wonder why no one had seen this coming. Reports are produced and recommendations implemented. Most likely, agencies and their managers will beef up procedures for horizon-scanning, scenario-planning, and information-sharing, while consultants come and go. In addition, short-term pains during the urgent response phase may start to be perceived and framed as long-term gains, shedding a different light on how political and administrative forces overreacted or underreacted to certain features of the crisis event. In this case, it may turn out that the influx of a young workforce provides not just economic costs but also future benefits for European countries. After all, many of them are ageing rapidly, and face dramatic employee shortages in sectors such as healthcare and education as locals are increasingly unwilling to work in such sectors. However, attempts to frame the refugee issue in these terms hardly resonate amid the polarized crisis discourse.

Clearly, the demand of *managing short versus managing long time horizons* creates a variety of tough questions for public managers. If your commissioner asks you to build a set of plausible scenarios for the next refugee crisis, which may happen three years from now, or ten years from now, or never, where will you start? What skills will you look for? Who will be your target audience? What method(s) will you employ for which topics, contexts, and timeframes? What signals, events, evidence, and cues will you look for? Will you go back in time, and how will you tap into institutional memory? How will you secure funding and justify redundancy and reservoirs? And most important, how do you disseminate and deliver your findings in a way that ensures attention, buy-in, and commitment from administrative and political masters eager for visible results and quick pay-offs? More fundamentally, how will you create processes and programmes that are more robust, adaptive, and resilient so you will be less overwhelmed when a future crisis hits?

Contrasting time horizons

The case highlights many issues that public managers will encounter when managing short-term pressures while keeping in mind long-term policy objectives that transcend election cycles. As such, the tension between managing short-term and long-term objectives is not new. In 1532, Machiavelli argued in his classic *Il Principe* (translated by Machiavelli 1532: 11):

> The Romans were simply doing what all wise rulers must: not restricting themselves to dealing with present threats but using every means at their disposal to foresee and forestall future problems as well. Seen in advance, trouble is easily dealt with; wait until it's on top of you and your reaction will come too late, the malaise is already irreversible.

What makes the tension between 'acting now' and 'anticipating the future' even more acute today is the increased short-termism, exacerbated by never-ending news cycles in a multi-polar media environment seeking scoops ('24/7 news' already seems an outdated term here). At the same time, assertive stakeholders produce their own diagnoses online, creating multiple, increasingly competing arenas for scrutinizing public sector activities (Bertot *et al.* 2012: 78). Such scrutiny increases pressure on governments to take immediate action – or at least create an impression of constant action.

Short-termism – 'the enemy of true strategic thinking' (Bilgin 2004: 177) – is driven by the need to earn points imposed by politicians caught in election cycles and stakeholder demands for something to be done here and now. Meeting such needs and demands is not just easily explained by *opportunism*; it is as much a matter of *timing*. In his memoires, failed candidate for Prime Minister of Canada and renowned Harvard professor Michael Ignatieff beautifully contrasts being right on content with being right on timing (2013: 43):

> An intellectual may be interested in ideas and policies for their own sake, but a politician's interest is exclusively in the question of whether an idea's time has come. When politicians blame their fate on bad

luck, they are actually blaming their timing. I thought content mattered. I thought the numbers in a platform should add up. Ours did and theirs didn't. But none of it mattered.

Meeting short-term pressures and demands will be a key feature in the lives of 21ˢᵗ century public managers and their masters, whether they like it or not. At the same time, megatrends discussed in this book such as 'more with less', 'forever young', 'ultra-urbanization', and 'more from less' necessitate that public managers plan ahead, sometimes decades, to mitigate emerging fiscal, demographic, and environmental pressures.

This chapter will first discuss the various competing pressures and logics that public managers face in balancing short-term and long-term objectives. They have to 'look back' and 'look forward' at the same time, by using personal experience, educated guesses, standard operating procedures (SOPs), and narratives constructed by media (Brändström and Kuipers 2003). Then, it discusses how public managers can build more resilient agencies and policies. In doing so, they will have to manage various tensions and paradoxes between bureaucracy and standardization on the one hand, and adaptiveness and flexibility on the other hand. Public managers may have to act as 'bricoleurs' (Freeman 2007; Van de Walle 2014; Weick 1993) who improvise and experiment while building on institutional memory and knowledge networks.

The final part of the chapter focuses on managing foresight practices and methods, discusses various types and forms of foresight and their pros and cons, and examines how public managers can overcome barriers to foresight, particularly from impatient, pressured political masters.

The tyranny of the present

Public managers used to complain about the politician's unwillingness to look beyond four-year election cycles. Increasingly, however, four years will seem like a lifetime. Even in traditionally stable, predictable democracies, administrations increasingly fail to complete their terms, with elections held every two to three years as a result. Alongside these developments, a mushrooming industry of public affairs, reputation management, and media training has emerged. There is an increasing presence and prominence of political advisors and spin-doctors in government departments, often putting pressure on the traditional position and authority of public managers (Noordegraaf *et al.* 2013; Rhodes 2011).

At the same time, however, wicked problems such as the EU refugee crisis urge public sector leaders to look ahead and make long-term investments and commitments, often beyond their national borders, requiring transboundary crisis management capacity and planning (see Boin and Lodge 2016). In this vein, recent years have seen a proliferation of 'strategy 2030' and 'strategy 2050' documents, often co-produced with eager consultants and think tanks. Indeed, public managers will constantly have to look back, using summative evaluations, historical analogies, institutional legacies, norms, and memories, and legal commitments – as well as look forward, using scenarios, plans, and formative evaluations (Brändström 2016; Brändström and Kuipers 2003).

In short, in managing pressures, stakeholders, and tools associated with the short-term versus the long-term, public managers have to balance a variety of competing logics. Figure 10.1 lists some of the logics justifying and necessitating responses to immediate or long-term demands.

At first glance, these different logics simply seem to require different types of public managers. For example, in addressing the media-driven sensationalist logic, public managers need good communication skills and a well-developed ability to read 'tomorrow's mood' to anticipate shifts in public opinion. To address the politician-driven scoring logic, on the other hand, public managers need to be on the lookout for signs and opportunities to gain favourable reactions from the electorate, and translate such opportunities into 'scoring moments' for political masters that allow them to shine on stage.

However, as policy and managerial work becomes more interlinked and solutions more contested, *all* public managers need to increasingly master communication and political management skills along with foresight capabilities. Scrutinizing publics do not discriminate between institutional boundaries, silos, and programmes, and lack the patience to wait for the 'right' department or communications director to respond. Moreover, we should not overemphasize, let alone caricature, the short-termism of politicians versus the long-termism of public managers. Indeed, Van der Steen and Van Twist (2012: 484) argue that politicians 'do not principally neglect the future, but find the future "difficult" to apply in their day-to-day processes'. At the same time, urgent deadlines give public managers 'the sense of achieving a goal' that more far-off goals cannot provide, creating somewhat of an 'imbalance between present and future interests' (Moshe 2010: 320).

On the one hand, public managers tasked with producing such long-term visions have unlimited opportunities to collect, distribute, and frame

FIGURE 10.1   Immediate versus long-term logics

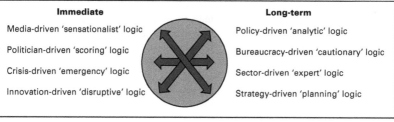

Immediate	Long-term
Media-driven 'sensationalist' logic	Policy-driven 'analytic' logic
Politician-driven 'scoring' logic	Bureaucracy-driven 'cautionary' logic
Crisis-driven 'emergency' logic	Sector-driven 'expert' logic
Innovation-driven 'disruptive' logic	Strategy-driven 'planning' logic

information, and use increasingly sophisticated yet accessible planning, foresight, and scenario-building methodologies. On the other hand, unprecedented pressures confront public managers from media and stakeholders – who, increasingly, operate in tandem – competing for the 'right' information as discussed in chapter 'Managing Authority Turbulence'. Such pressures may drive public managers into exercising caution rather than implementing reforms that make sense from a long-term perspective (van Wart 2013: 558). Moreover, they need to engage in continuous *rhetorical* reform and leadership: they have to appear to be 'on top of things'.

Table 10.1 contrasts key pressures, stakeholders, and managerial strengths and skills associated with managing short versus managing long.

Indeed, rather than externalizing blame for increased short-termism towards 'others', public managers should themselves be mindful of opportunism. They, too, are tempted to measure performance over too brief a period while failing to invest in long-term concerns and organizational causes, resulting in decreasing organizational trust and institutional memory and expertise (Laverty 1996, 2004). This process has been exacerbated by an almost blindsided focus on cutbacks and austerity measures

TABLE 10.1 Managing short versus managing long time horizons

	Pressures	Key stakeholders	Managerial strengths and skills needed
Managing short	• To be 'on top of things' • To come up with solutions and statements • To defuse tensions and crises • To render account to accountability forums	• 24/7 media • Netizens • Political and dministrative bosses • Opposition forces • Voters	• Communication and media strategies • Spinning and framing • Crisis management • Political astuteness • Ability to maximize quick wins
Managing long	• To 'know where things are going' • To produce optimal designs, plans, and models • To be prepared for future crises	• Investors • Partners in industry, academia, and transnational governance networks • Future generations • Planet	• Foresight methods and instruments • Plans and scenarios • Institutional memory • Anti-cyclical budgeting • Bricolage, resilience, and slack resources

in recent years in many developed countries, in the context of economic uncertainty and public debt.

The refugee crisis in the EU serves as an example here. Some of the countries that had been subjected to austerity programmes after various economic crises lacked any capacity to deal with the sudden explosion of asylum seekers. Moreover, even the more developed EU member states that built up great policy expertise and operational credibility during earlier refugee crises in the 1990s had got rid of their expertise and capacity in the relatively quiet years in between these two major crises. The way the crisis unfolded and the public outcry it generated are a case in point for public managers to advocate for more spare capacity to preserve institutional memory. Institutional memory loss is a serious threat to long-term organizational survival. It undermines a manager's ability to accumulate experience and avoid making the same mistakes in the future (Coffey and Hoffman 2003; Covington 1985; Pollitt 2009). Box 10.1 lists six methods for preserving institutional memory.

Managing resilience

Preserving institutional memory and routines is just one aspect of the broader 21st century managerial challenge to create agencies and systems that are 'resilient'. Resilience as a concept was first used in postwar psychological studies about how individuals managed to withstand shocks and stress (de Bruijne *et al.* 2010), and later to assess engineering structures and ecosystems (Holling 1973; Hollnagel *et al.* 2006). It has

---

Box 10.1 Methods of preserving institutional memory

- knowledge acquisition methods: collecting information from existing employees;
- conducting exit interviews with departing employees (and preventing high turnover in the first place);
- implementing archiving systems and methodologies;
- knowledge modelling and knowledge elicitation: analysing tasks performed by experts, interviews, and experimental or semi-experimental manipulations of familiar expert tasks;
- organizing and stimulating organizational learning through mentorship and coaching of newcomers;
- keeping internal knowledge management systems up to date; enforcing record-keeping regulations.

Sources: Coffey and Hoffman 2003; Covington 1985; Pollitt 2000, 2009.

become more prominent in public management in the aftermath of the global financial crisis of 2008 and in debates about climate change mitigation and adaptation, and is now an established concept in crisis management studies (see for instance OECD 2015; Boin and Lodge 2016). Given the volatile operating environment public managers now face – with a high likelihood of crises, shocks, and unexpected high-impact events – scholars and practitioners grapple with how public managers can make their agencies, processes, and people more adaptive, flexible, and robust.

At first glance, creating and managing resilient agencies and systems seems at odds with some of the traditional Weberian qualities and values discussed earlier in this book, such as predictability, and with the recurrent emphasis on austerity and efficiency that produces ever 'leaner and meaner' public agencies (Duit 2016; Van de Walle 2014). In fact, resilience thinking propagates systems that not only are able to 'bounce back' efficiently in the context of rapid or unexpected change but also can continuously adapt to dynamic operating environments (Gundersen 2003). As we discussed in chapter 'Managing Innovation Forces', bureaucratic structures have proven to be highly successful at absorbing turbulence without really allowing radical change or reform (Ansell *et al.* 2010; Comfort *et al.* 2010). Such *adaptive capability* is a key feature of resilience (Stark 2014). In a way, this is nothing new. Eminent organizational scientist James March (1991) emphasized more than a quarter of a century ago that organizations will always face a choice between acting on immediate needs – driven by innovation or crisis – and on future demands, and will be stimulated by the need to develop new strategies, approaches, and sectors.

However, it is clear that the relentless focus on efficiency, cutbacks, and outsourcing across the globe in recent decades has made public management systems less robust and adaptive. Counterintuitively, some argue that resilience is an attractive concept for politicians and public managers in an age of austerity precisely because it promises more robust agencies with 'no redistributive and few regulatory demands' (Duit 2016: 3). Just like with innovation, the risk of 'rhetorical resilience' seems immanent here.

At the same time, the buzzwords of resilience and innovation are two sides of the same coin in terms of what they have to offer to public managers: if they manage to create adaptive and somewhat flexible structures and cultures, it becomes more feasible to adapt to changing circumstances without pursuing radical reform (Davidson 2010). Box 10.2 identifies the key characteristics of resilient public management systems.

Let us turn back to the EU refugee crisis now. Were the public management systems dealing with the massive inflow of asylum seekers at the national and supranational levels insufficiently resilient? The answer may depend on the stage of the process under scrutiny. In fact, the three different phases distinguished in the introductory example – preparatory, urgent response, and evaluation and learning – require public managers

> ## Box 10.2 Characteristics of resilient public management systems
>
> - They consist of multiple organizational units in non-hierarchical networks with overlapping jurisdictions, functions, and expertise.
> - They establish, maintain, and promote cross-scale and cross-sectoral linkages between managers, professionals, and their warning systems and routines.
> - They advocate and budget for spare or 'slack' capacity – in terms of funds, expertise, infrastructure, and manpower – to use in times of crisis.
> - They actively organize and activate multiple, deliberately *competing* types of knowledge and sources of information (scientific, experience, and stakeholder based).
> - They devise mechanisms to encourage stakeholder participation, including participation from adversarial stakeholders.
> - They value trial-and-error experiments and social learning.
> - They regularly organize emergency and disaster simulations and system robustness checks.
>
> *Sources*: Boin et al. 2010; Duit 2016; Van de Walle 2014.

to pursue different types of resilience (Boin *et al.* 2008; Boin and van Eeten 2013; Duit 2016).

Table 10.2 illustrates three different types of resilience related to these three phases – characterized by Duit as a 'ladder of resilience' (2015: 4) – and suggests managerial skills for each phase. It is important, however, not to overstate the analytical distinctiveness between the three phases, given the messy and ambiguous nature of crises and emergencies: preparation and coordination may perpetuate during the evaluation and learning phase, which, in turn, feeds back into future preparations (see Boin *et al.* 2008).

Public managers as bricoleurs

So, how can public managers make their agencies, programmes, and processes more resilient across these various stages? Some argue they should allow a certain amount of redundancy and 'waste' rather than relentlessly trying to get rid of it (Van de Walle 2014: 12). Many public sectors nowadays have overly streamlined, standardized, and lean organizational structures. Such structures function very effectively until changes in the environment occur (Thompson 1965); at this point, when complexity and uncertainty increase, they may fail public managers dramatically (Aldrich 1999; Hood 2000). In short, public managers need to advocate for and create 'slack' (Cyert and March 1963: 36),

TABLE 10.2 Managing resilience across crisis response phases

Phase	Resilience type	Managerial skills
Preparatory	*Precursor* – prepare and handle Boin and van Eeten 2013; Duit 2016.	• Preparing, testing, scenario-building • Being open to 'think the unthinkable' • Engaging adversarial stakeholders and expertise
Urgent response	*Recovery* – coordinate and bounce back Aldrich 2012; Boin *et al.* 2008; Duit 2016.	• Crisis and emergency leadership, coordination and collaboration, communication • Leading forward-looking processes of healing and restoration
Evaluation and learning	*Adaptive* – learn and change Berkes *et al.* 2003; Duit 2016.	• Instigating processes of double-loop learning and reform, and rethinking standard operating procedures • Viewing mistakes as opportunities

redundancy and overlap (Chrisholm 1992; Landau and Chrisholm 1995) rather than emphasize 'lean', a private sector manufacturing concept that sits uncomfortably with some of the demands of public service delivery (Radnor and Osborne 2013: 267). Ultimately, a one-sided focus on 'lean' may even lead to agencies becoming 'anorexic' (Radnor and Boaden 2004).

Still, however, standard operating procedures (SOPs) and formalization provide public managers with reassurance and control, and help them confront accountability pressures (Kassel 2008; Schillemans 2015). They also serve to manage employee expectations, and assist in rewarding employee performance in fair and transparent ways. Moreover, in talking about organizational amnesia and 'organizational forgetting', prominent public management scholar Christopher Pollitt (2000, 2009) argues that formalized, bureaucratic organizations have better memories and well-defined routines and storage locations for information, including long-term employees. He suggests that public agencies and their managers have lost their adaptive capacity over time, with pervasive processes of deskilling, outsourcing, and the devaluation of domain expertise. Clearly, public managers face a number of paradoxes and dilemmas in balancing the advantages of standardization and reliability with the advantages of anticipation and improvisation in creating greater resilience.

In this vein, Van de Walle (2014: 10) has provocatively argued that public managers should act as 'bricoleurs'. Bricolage, a concept introduced to the management domain by Weick (1993), refers to non-linear, non-planned, and non-direct ways of thinking: 'the invention of resources from the available materials to solve unanticipated problems' (Pina e Cunha 2005: 6). Bricoleurs, unlike rational planners and traditional bureaucrats, improvise using available material rather than waiting for optimal conditions (Van de Walle 2014: 10). This does not imply that public managers acting as bricoleurs do just anything. Effective improvisation requires (tacit) expertise, active participation in knowledge networks, and active investment in and nurturing of individual and organizational memory.

Thus, bricolage requires partly different skillsets and mindsets than innovation. Improvisation is not the same as creativity and novelty, but rather recombines or tries out old knowledge and traditional behaviour in untested contexts (Weick 2005). Bricolage thinking reemphasizes the importance of managing institutional and managerial memory in events such as the EU refugee crisis. Indeed, seemingly irrelevant or outdated units, practices, and knowledge may all of a sudden become highly relevant again when managers and their agencies are 'faced with new challenges or external threats' (Van de Walle 2014: 13) that call for maintenance of back-up systems (Hood 1991: 14).

So, 21st century public managers have to be able to encourage, practise, and control bricolage by promoting a view of improvisation as 'contributing to maintenance and preservation of the system' (Brans and Rossbach 1997: 420) rather than being deviant from a Weberian perspective. An oft-mentioned example here are high-reliability organizations (HROs), such as air-traffic control centres, that focus on reliable performance yet refuse to accept simplifications by anticipating the unexpected (Noordegraaf 2015; 't Hart 2014; Weick and Sutcliffe 2001).

Still, as compelling as resilience may appear to public managers, the megatrend of 'more with less' may render justifications for organizational slack unrealistic and even obstructive in the eyes of political masters and voters. As a result, public managers need to become skilled at *anticipating* VUCA events and fine-tuning plans, predictions, and scenarios in order to advocate *why* they need future reservoirs of staff, skills, and budget. In addition, the more skilled they become at anticipation, the less they may have to improvise when VUCA events actually occur.

Strategic planning, foresight, and scenario-planning

Three related yet different sets of instruments, rituals, and procedures may aid public managers in anticipating and managing long-term challenges and ensure 'feed-in' to daily public sector activities: strategic planning, foresight, and scenario-planning (e.g., Bryson 2010; Coates 2010; Hartmann and Stillings 2014). Strategic planning checks the 'short term plans of yesteryear' against current performance and the potential need for change in the short term, but it is not necessarily future-oriented (Coates 2010: 1429).

Foresight and scenario-planning, on the other hand, analyse both plausible future outcomes and their possible effects on actions and decisions, with scenario-planning usually considered as one of the methods in the foresight toolbox (Solem 2011; Varum and Melo 2010; Van der Steen and Van Twist 2012; Wilkinson and Kupers 2013). Figure 10.2 contrasts the three concepts. Scholars use strategic foresight and foresight intertwined; we just use foresight here.

The remainder of this chapter focuses on how foresight and its various tools and techniques can help public managers in keeping the long view, and how public managers can produce foresight that fits the agendas of decision-makers (Van der Steen and Van Twist 2012). Increasingly, public managers may themselves need to become skilled at assessing, selecting, applying, and strategically communicating and leveraging foresight methods, rather than just hiring a consulting firm to run a few scenarios. Being skilled at foresight may not only provide public managers with a competitive advantage in terms of acquiring policy wisdom and building administrative capacity reservoirs before they are really needed (the EU refugee case painfully shows what happens if this is not the case). It may also provide them with ammunition when they face multiple accountability pressures and regimes, either during or after crisis events (Koppell 2003; Schillemans 2015).

Indeed, public managers may use foresight methods and tools for a variety of reasons – for instance, because their increasingly networked environment necessitates more adaptive capacity, or because they want to build resilience and ensure long-term organizational survival. Table 10.3 shows how foresight helps each of these drivers.

It is important to highlight the difference between *planning* and *plans* here. Careful planning practices will aid public managers only if they are adaptive, flexible, and subject to continuous scrutiny. The history of governance provides us with numerous examples of how holding on to rigid, outdated plans produces policy failures and cost overruns.

FIGURE 10.2   Strategic planning, foresight, scenario-planning

Strategic planning	Foresight	Scenario planning
Backward	Ahead	Possible outcomes
Short-term	Plausible future	Likely
Snap-shot	Insightful	Perception
Reactive	Systemic	Proactive, adaptive

TABLE 10.3 Five key foresight drivers and functions

Key driver	How foresight helps managers
Ill-structured, wicked problems	• Provides flexible and insightful responses • Produces policy solutions, tests them, finds evidence, and mitigates path dependency issues Amankwah-Amoah and Zhang 2015: 530; Solem 2011: 22; UNDP 2014: 10; Van der Steen and Van Twist 2012: 484.
Networked governance, stakeholder multiplicity	• Stimulates 'networked thinking', agility, and adaptability UNDP 2014: 10–11.
Entrenched short-termism	• Promotes a broad outlook on long-term goals, helping to engage stakeholders and the public 'as part of a broader democratic process' Dreyer and Stang 2013: 25.
Political dimension of policy-making	• Provides evidence to support policy agendas and claims, develops solutions to political issues, predicts new issues that might emerge in the future, and identifies risks • Stimulates inter-organizational learning – the ability of policy networks to exchange ideas and best practices to avoid 'chronic policy failure' Ferlie et al. 2011: 309; Van der Steen and Van Twist 2012: 483.
Very rapid ('hyper') change	• Helps in coping with unexpected, uncertain events, and assists in reacting rapidly and mitigating failure • Changes existing assumptions and deep-seated beliefs that undermine success, and thus widens alternatives • Stimulates creative thinking and innovation Amankwah-Amoah and Zhang 2015: 530; Coates 2010: 1435; UNDP 2014: 11.

Making foresight work

Once public managers have established drivers and goals, they have to decide on the exact type of foresight they need to employ to meet their specific objectives. A multitude of methods, tools, techniques, and approaches feature in the mushrooming foresight industry and the literature supporting that industry. To start with, public managers need to think about three issues in particular (Goulden and Dingwall 2012: 20–22):

• What is the level of *expertise* needed? Depending on the level of expertise needed, public managers may opt to use a classical Delphi exercise, which uses panel experts, or an exercise that relies heavily on public engagement, 'crowdsourcing', and 'citizen judgements', also discussed in chapter 'Managing Authority Turbulence'.

- What is the number of *knowns* and *unknowns*? Two key approaches here are forecasting and back casting. Forecasting extrapolates current trends into the future whereas back casting projects a desired future and then constructs its way back by identifying key events and actions needed to create such an envisioned future.

- How do they need to *communicate results to stakeholders*? Here, trade-offs concern methodology and design. Quantitative approaches claim 'empirically derived legitimacy' (2012: 21), which public managers can easily communicate to media and academic communities. Qualitative methods are less precise but produce futures that are more accessible to a diverse set of stakeholders. Designs range from dialogical and collaborative, if stakeholders involved are expected to be reliable and committed, to top-down, when groupthink, capture, and lack of reliability are concerns (Weigand *et al.* 2014).

Box 10.3 illustrates how even a careful foresight exercise can backfire. In this case, public managers and their political masters appear to have underestimated a particular response from the public following a stakeholder consultation.

Clearly, various foresight types and methodologies each present their own contextual advantages and drawbacks for public managers. The method they opt to use will depend on the setting, timeframe, and objective. Table 10.4 outlines seven key foresight methods public managers can employ, along with their advantages and drawbacks, and the settings in which they are most likely to generate success.

Overcoming barriers in using foresight

However, any public manager will recognize that both fairly simplistic and advanced foresight practices can only be effective if administrative and political masters *buy in to* their perceived value and *actually incorporate* outcomes and predictions in daily policy realities. Public managers need to use and communicate foresight strategically to overcome a range of barriers: organizational silos, unrealistic expectations, lack of buy-in, and overall resistance to change. Scholars emphasize clear lines of communication and accessible language (Solem 2011; Waehrens and Riis 2010). Clearly, foresight is 'not just a managerial pursuit ... it involves interplay between members of staff, their practices and technologies, as well as the organisational context' (Waehrens and Riis 2010: 336). Once more, the EU example is a case in point. As various EU agencies had substantively beefed up their foresight capabilities in the years prior to the crisis (Kuosa 2011; May 2009), the key issue wasn't the lack of capability and programmes but how such programmes found their way to decision-makers and affected procedural reforms.

Box 10.3 Critical citizens versus careful planners: Singapore's *Population White Paper*

Many Singaporean public managers will remember 1 January 2013 as the date when the National Population and Talent Division released *A Sustainable Population for a Dynamic Singapore: Population White Paper*, known thereafter as the *Population White Paper*. The white paper itself is memorable for its projection of the country's population as 6.9 million in 2030, implying an annual increase of 100,000 people from 2013. The paper, which was the product of a range of consultation exercises between various government agencies involved and a variety of stakeholders, argued that up to 30,000 new permanent residents and 25,000 naturalized citizens were needed annually to sustain a healthy demographic build-up and continued economic growth.

Coming at a time of tangible tensions following the recent influx of immigrants, who were blamed for a range of issues such as the rising cost of living, stagnation of wages, and overcrowding in public transport, many Singaporeans interpreted the white paper as a plan set in stone rather than a prognosis. The report was met with a widespread public outcry, including a rare organized protest with thousands of angry participants, many social media posts, and criticism from expert communities.

The government quickly responded by reiterating that the figure of 6.9 million was merely a 'worst case scenario', and one of many projections rather than a policy plan, let alone a 'desired outcome'. However, the damage was already done – it did not help that the government had already budgeted the projected housing and transport expansions up to 2030. Ultimately, the parliament adopted the paper on 8 February 2013 with a clear amendment that 6.9 million was not a target.

Still, for many years to come, this figure will continue to dominate policy and planning discussions, and the projections that public managers will have to work with. The example shows that 21st century public managers and their political masters must be exceedingly careful in explaining the objective, value, and relative factualness of a scenario. In this case, stakeholders had been consulted extensively but the general public perceived the communication of the final scenarios as final plans, perhaps understandably so given how the country's governance context had historically developed.

Sources: National Population and Talent Division, http://nptd.gov.sg/portals/0/news/population-white-paper.pdf; Yahoo! News, https://sg.news.yahoo.com/fury-over-6-9-million-population-target-for-singapore-103503070.html.

One approach, comparable to the notion of collaborative innovation described in chapter 'Managing Innovation Forces', is to involve decision-makers and key stakeholders early on. Here, however, the same dilemma emerges for public managers as in processes of innovation: early involvement ensures buy-in and legitimacy, but requires that stakeholder involvement be carefully managed to prevent chaos and indecisiveness. Moreover,

TABLE 10.4 Seven key foresight methods

Method	Premise and product	Strengths	Potential drawbacks	Best used
1. *Forecasting, trends analysis* Solem 2011; Samet 2012	Quantified forecast based on trends with error margins	• Statistical and modelling tools to draw on	• Ignores 'discontinuities' • Quantitative focus	When there is a model and enough data to extrapolate
2. *Scenario-planning* Coates 2010; Jackson 2013	Narratives that offer a range of plausible futures	• Expands mode of thinking • Includes discontinuities • Fast, scalable, and tailored	• Requires facilitation and expertise, and extensive stakeholder engagement • Vague and present-bound	In situations with real uncertainty, ambiguity, and possible diverse and divergent outcomes
3. *Delphi technique* Coates 2010; Dreyer and Stang 2013	Forecasts from a structured panel of experts given in several rounds as consensus answers, often ranked	• Minimizes 'follow the leader' dynamics • Transparent • Flexible and reliable	• Time-consuming • Reinforces 'middle of the road' consensus • Costly • Only as good as the precision of wording	For combining expert insights on a well-defined question; effective at the start of foresight initiative
4. *Environment and horizon scanning* Dreyer and Stang 2013	Systematic examination of potential threats and opportunities	• Filters out what is constant and what changes • Provides reality check • Multiple viewpoints	• May create false hope and reinforce linear view of change • Can become an end in itself • Costly • Can be dominated by existing norms	At the front end and as an integral element of a comprehensive foresight approach involving several methods

TABLE 10.4 Continued

Method	Premise and product	Strengths	Potential drawbacks	Best used
5. *Road mapping* Smith and Saritas 2011	A detailed blueprint for future actions (contains both narrative and technical elements)	• A concrete plan of getting 'from here to there' • Builds expert network	• Costly and lengthy • Plan may not be robust for future developments • Tends to produce safer assessments	When results seem apparent but changes are uncertain; needs other methods too
6. *Crowdsourcing* Masum et al. 2010	New types of outputs and engagement; 'wisdom of the crowds'	• Promising prototypes • Improvement of existing tools • Inexpensive • Scalable	• Difficult to change entrenched social habits • Tacit knowledge and expert input needed • Can turn into 'battleground'	When there is a need to leverage collaborations; good first start to solicit broader reactions
7. *Back casting* Goulden and Dingwall 2012	Defines a desirable future and then works backwards to identify major events and decisions that would generate this future	• Opportunities for tailoring steps to pace of change and timeframe • Participants can intuitively relate to their own experience	• Strong dependence on good scenarios and foresight • Complex because of many variables • Requires discipline for institutionalization	For planning and resource management; hardly ever used alone, most effective as a reality check

involving stakeholders early on is no guarantee of success, as the *Population White Paper* example in Box 10.3 shows; just as important is how governments communicate predictions, being mindful of past expectations and rituals and how these will affect stakeholder expectations.

A common dilemma for public managers emerges here once more. To make sure that foresight is not burdened by political interests, it may have to be situated 'at a certain distance from the intrusiveness of day-to-day politics and administrative interference' (Solem 2011: 28). This mode of thinking harks back to the long-standing debate on 'distancing' advisory systems from the core operations of government agencies (Owens 2015; Peters and Barker 1993). Indeed, former head of the Singapore Civil Service Peter Ho (2010: 4) promotes the idea of having a small group of people dedicated to thinking about the future, as the skills needed for long-term planning are different from those needed to address situations of 'more immediate volatility and crisis'. Ho advises against creating an environment whereby 'those charged with thinking about the future … [get] bogged down in day-to-day routines' (2010: 4). At the same time, foresight will only produce public value if it is *of direct political value* to policy formulation and adjustment, which may be harder if activities are too distant.

Figure 10.3 outlines individual, institutional, and cultural barriers to effective foresight practices, and suggests ways to overcome such barriers.

FIGURE 10.3   **Overcoming barriers to foresight**

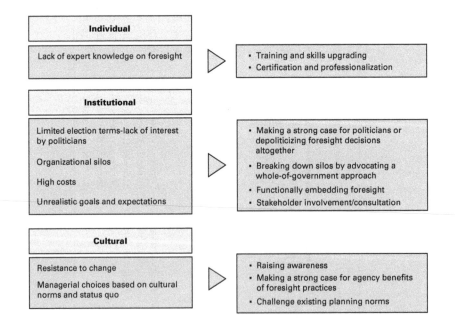

Individual barriers to the practice of foresight include lack of training facilities; management practices leading to conflicting goals and the absence of a shared outlook on agency mission; and high costs of conducting foresight. Coates (2010: 1429) argues that training is the primary instrument for enhancing competence in and use of foresight. Various OECD countries have started to offer modules to public officials on foresight and scenario-building, even though there is not one universally accepted method (OECD 2015).

Limited election terms pose *institutional* challenges, as most politicians are driven by short-term interests and goals that need to be achieved and are less concerned with a far-off future, leading some politicians to insist on practising foresight within pre-fabricated external frameworks (Coates 2010: 1435). In the same vein, Van der Steen and Van Twist (2012: 482) point out that 'swift action tends to outweigh more long-term oriented strategies, as clever and robust as they may be'. They argue that organizational 'rules of the game' and political cues have little tolerance for uncertainty, producing a situation where foresight is 'a disturbing factor in the institutional order of things' (2012: 482).

Cultural barriers include resistance to change or lack of motivation to introduce change – a 'fat and happy culture' (Jackson 2013: 21). Managers' own cultural norms and values may also mean that they assign little importance to foresight, or they may fear a potential decline of influence, status, and trust as a result of choosing new approaches to planning.

Van der Steen and Van Twist (2012) have developed an evaluation framework to measure the potential impact of foresight according to its ability to fit both political and organizational cues, summarized in Figure 10.4. The authors claim their framework is capable of bridging 'the gap between policy and foresight' (2012: 485).

Their argument is that foresight practices have a higher chance of affecting daily practices if they respond to the cues to which organizations and politicians are sensitive, given how foresight results compete for attention

FIGURE 10.4   Foresight that fits political and organizational cues

Political cues	Organizational cues
• Winning political battles	• Falsifying/amending existing policy theory
• Resolving present-day political issues	• Providing new policy theory for existing or emerging issues
• Putting issues on the agenda	• Providing politicians with arguments and advice on how foresight can serve their policy objectives
• Pointing at emergent political issues	• Allowing reflection on and reframing of current organizational paths
• Identifying potential political risks	

Source: Van der Steen and Van Twist 2012: 483–485.

from public managers with the abundance of other types of research reports and advice that comes to their desk (Arnold *et al.* 2005). As Figure 10.4 shows, many of the political cues correspond to the short-term logics and scoring logics identified earlier in this chapter, whereas many of the organizational cues align with resilience and adaptiveness. In both cases, they seem to argue against foresight being a strictly 'distant', expert activity.

Box 10.4 provides two examples of inclusive foresight programmes impacting innovation and technology policy, in indirect and non-linear

---

Box 10.4 Impactful foresight in Hungary and Sweden

The Hungarian Technology Foresight Programme (TEP) ran from 1997 to 2001. TEP's key objective was to instil long-term, yet flexible thinking about the economic future of the transition economy in policy-makers and politicians to move away from rigid, centralized planning. It was a nationwide foresight programme covering all sectors of the economy through thematic panels that included many stakeholders. Years later, TEP results still feature in various strategic documents and policy recommendations across ministries. It took some time for a 'reservoir of knowledge' (Georghiou *et al.* 2004: 5) to materialize and appear in policy-making circles, and personal networks played a strong role here. Moreover, the exercise is now seen as having been very influential in changing overall economic mindsets of decision-makers. Finally, subsequent science, technology, and innovation (STI) policy strategies have been inspired by TEP's approach and outcomes.

Sweden's Second Technology Foresight (TF2) programme ran from 2002 to 2004. A few years after the evaluation by an international team in 2005, direct policy impact appeared to be little. The main users and beneficiaries from the foresight results were research organizations, consultants, and non-profits rather than public agencies (Arnold *et al.* 2005). However, various policy initiatives and bills produced near the end of TF2 showed considerable overlap. So, the impact here may have been less direct but considerable nonetheless in terms of facilitating policy reform proposals. Public managers used the programme as a vehicle to pursue plans in cognate areas, and ample cross-fertilization and cross-referencing ensured political attention.

Clearly, foresight programmes and practices can impact policy-making and public management in various ways. Havas *et al.* (2010) distinguish three types or functions of foresight impact: a *policy-informing* function, a *policy-facilitating* function, and a *policy advisory* function. Clearly, in the case of Hungary, there seemed to have been more direct influence in policy advisory terms. However, in the case of Sweden, impacts on public policy may be more indirect and show more lag time. Both matter, but getting foresight results directly in the key document guiding decision-making will remain the most direct measure of success for public managers.

Sources: Arnold *et al.* 2005; Georghiou *et al.* 2004; Havas 2003; Havas *et al.* 2010.

ways, and with considerable time lags. It shows how foresight can *inform, advise,* and *facilitate* public management practices and policy programmes (Havas *et al.* 2010).

Foresight skills for public managers

So, will all public managers have the time and interest to become skilled at foresight? Most likely not. Indeed, some argue that formalization and professionalization is needed to ensure that foresight does not fall into the hands of amateurs and lead to failure, scepticism, and a lack of credibility (Van der Steen and van der Duin 2012: 493; Coates 2010: 1435). Recently, experts have even advocated for certification of foresight specialists – as opposed to hiring futures studies graduates or requiring current employees to take graduate programmes in foresight – emphasizing that on-the-job training provides public managers with flexibility and adaptability (Gary and von der Gracht 2015: 143; Rhisiart *et al.* 2015: 89).

Dreyer and Stang (2013) already observe a shift from foresight being an activity pursued by external experts to one being practised in foresight divisions across government departments, comparable to how 'strategy' has evolved from being a separate, external activity to one that is practised actively by specialized in-house departments (Lusk 2014 and Bircks 2013). The authors put together a checklist of good foresight practices to secure effectiveness, shown in Box 10.5.

Based on the examples and research discussed in this chapter, Box 10.6 outlines a hands-on public manager's guide to foresight structured around three key issues: making the case for foresight to decision-makers, avoiding common pitfalls, and fostering skills and attributes needed to effectively pursue foresight activities.

Box 10.5 Checklist of good foresight practices

☑ Well-identified target audience
☑ Inclusion of input from target audience in agenda-setting and other stages
☑ Clear communication with the audience in accessible language
☑ Close ties with the top decision-makers and policy-makers
☑ Clear links between foresight and current policy agenda
☑ Internal and external cooperation
☑ Consistent, long-term sources of funding
☑ Feedback loops
☑ Programmes rather than one-off projects
☑ New scenarios based on feedback and testing

Source: Dreyer and Stang 2013: 28.

Box 10.6 Public manager's guide to foresight

How do you make the case to political decision-makers?

- Find a selling point according to the needs of the politician
- Demonstrate successful, proven examples, countries, or governments ('policy-based evidence' rather than 'evidence-based policy')
- Use clear, emotion-based, aspirational language to produce an attractive visioning package
- Follow 'foresight – insight – action' discourse
- Promise continuity

What are the common pitfalls?

- Poor delivery and dissemination
- No feedback or consultation
- Too much uncertified knowledge and too little expert knowledge
- Fragmentation due to policy stovepipes and silos
- No building of knowledge pool
- Lack of supporting allies

What skills and attributes do you need to effectively practise foresight?

- Policy entrepreneurship
- Curiosity
- Ability to manage networks and bring together people of different backgrounds and skills
- Openness to feedback, criticism, and alternative viewpoints
- Political astuteness and antennae for weak signals

Change-ready countries and their foresight practices

A final question to be addressed here is what public managers can learn from countries that have managed to successfully institutionalize foresight in their public sector operations, aiding them in providing best practices to their political masters. Governments of different types, statures, and cultures have adopted extensive foresight programmes and units in recent years. It is no coincidence that many of these countries rank highly in international innovation, policy effectiveness, and 'change-readiness' rankings (Everest-Philips 2015; KPMG 2015; Van der Wal 2016). Indeed, some of the public sectors that are considered frontrunners in foresight practices belong to a small pocket of successful, small countries dominating global rankings: Denmark, Estonia, Hong Kong, Ireland, the Netherlands, New Zealand, Singapore, and

Switzerland, to name a few. Experts have credited these countries for being agile, adaptive, and resilient, allowing them to 'punch above their weight' (Skilling 2012; Van der Steen *et al.* 2016; Van der Wal 2016). The quick recoveries of Ireland and Estonia after the global financial crisis, compared with, for example, Greece and Portugal, are a case in point here. However, some larger countries have also made great waves in establishing foresight programmes.

Two oft-mentioned examples of successful foresight are the UK and Singapore; Box 10.7 illustrates their foresight structures and practices.

Both countries have successfully implemented foresight programmes in the sense that foresight is not just an innovative tool used for the sake of trying out what technology and data have to offer – it actually informs and, in some cases, underpins policy design and implementation (Habegger 2010: 56). In addition, foresight processes are formalized and clearly linked to budgeting, feedback, and impact evaluation (although such exercises are no clear recipe for success, as the *Population White Paper* example has shown us). Although both countries share a Westminster tradition, with Singapore's civil service modelled on the British one, in Singapore, political discourse, electoral dynamics, and institutional memory are more stable than in the UK. Arguably, foresight can produce similarly successful results for public managers in different contexts.

Keenan and Popper (2008) conducted research in Europe, the US, and Asia to test the hypothesis that differences in foresight styles are influenced by 'contextual landscapes', including economic conditions, political agendas, and traditions (2008: 17). They find that the diversity of such landscapes is linked with various dimensions of foresight such as domain coverage, time horizon, and methods, but not as closely linked with the involvement of non-state actors and funding sources (Keenan and Popper 2008: 33). The authors confirm that the use of foresight relates positively to countries' change-readiness.

Box 10.7 Foresight in different political contexts: the UK and Singapore

The UK Foresight Programme started in December 2004 and employs three types of activities: horizon scans, futures projects, and public outreach programmes:

- Two complementary annual *horizon scans*, the Delta Scan and the Sigma Scan, provide cross-sectoral data that informs all foresight activities. These ongoing scans look ahead up to 50 years to identify ambiguities and trends. They result in issue papers that provide a basis for a more detailed analysis in subsequent stages.

→

→
- The *futures projects*, usually three or four at any given time, create in-depth problem overviews and develop a vision of meeting future challenges. Prognosis covers at least ten years in areas where change is rapid and trends are uncertain. The ultimate goal is to produce comprehensive and comprehensible reports to influence policy and funding decisions: these are followed by publicly available action plans to which the ministerial sponsor must agree. Public managers hold follow-up meetings with key stakeholders a year after the results are published, to assess the use and impact of project findings.
- The broad *public outreach* aims to build cross-sectoral networks of futures thinkers and practitioners. The Horizon Scanning Centre (HSC) established the Futures Analysts' Network (FAN Club) as a platform for exchanging ideas and sharing best practices.

The HSC is a key institutional part of the program. In addition, different government departments have their own programmes.

In Singapore, foresight also emerged in the early 2000s as a response to serious national security challenges such as terrorism cells and the outbreak of SARS. The government established the Risk Assessment and Horizon Scanning (RAHS) Programme Office, which is part of the National Security Coordination Secretariat within the Prime Minister's Office. Its approach is also three-pronged, and includes:

- horizon scanning, research, and analysis of emerging risks and opportunities (RAHS Think Centre);
- foresight capacity building and skill enhancement for policy practitioners (RAHS Solutions Centre);
- new tools and technologies to back foresight (RAHS Experimentation Centre).

The system provides end-to-end capabilities to collect and classify data, analyse and understand relationships, and anticipate as well as discover emerging issues that could have a strategic impact on Singapore. The Experimentation Centre tests novel concepts and technologies in operational contexts, and participates in case study exercises with government agencies. The RAHS Programme Office also extends foresight to bodies outside of government. It organizes an acclaimed biennial foresight conference, drawing large international crowds. In addition, the Civil Service College ensures all 60,000 civil servants receive foresight and scenario training in some shape or form at least once.

Sources: Habegger 2010: 49–58; UK Government – Foresight Projects, https://gov.uk/government/collections/foresight-projects; RAHS, http://nscs.gov.sg/public/content.aspx?sid=191.

What lies ahead

Managing short versus managing long will become a demand of increasing importance as a result of various megatrends and the improbable, unpredictable high-impact events they produce, such as the EU refugee crisis or the 3/11 disaster in Japan discussed in chapter 'Trends and Drivers'. Foresight methods and resilient systems will support public managers in dealing with such events, at least to some extent, but convincing sceptical politicians and publics to invest in such practices will continue to be difficult. Public managers can strengthen their case by showing that public sectors of countries that are considered successful, competitive, and innovative increasingly integrate foresight capabilities into policy-making and outreach.

In many ways, the seventh and final managerial demand, discussed in the next chapter – *managing cross-sectoral collaboration* – brings together many of the previous six demands and their reinforcing trends. Indeed, the need for public managers to increasingly engage in collaborative practices and display collaborative behaviour throughout programmes and processes has emerged across the various chapters so far.

However, 'being collaborative' is easier said than done. Potential partners and co-producers have different capabilities, agendas, and styles. In addition, accountability norms dictate that when things go wrong, stakeholders point their finger at public sector partners rather than their nonprofit or private sector counterparts. Which types of partnerships exist, what kind of collaborations work in which contexts, and what types of behaviours and skills public managers have to display to manage various partners and pressures is discussed in the next chapter.

Chapter 11

Managing Cross-sectoral Collaboration

I think there should be collaboration, but under my thumb.

(Elia Kazan, acclaimed American film director)

Co-produce, co-create, and co-complain?

Imagine you are a public manager running a large-scale municipal redevelopment project involving the integration of housing, healthcare, and community services in a historically troubled neighbourhood. The neighbourhood has a plethora of civil society organizations and small local enterprises, along with high-profile citizens who keenly articulate their aspirations for the area and place demands on local government bodies. Redevelopment has been on various local agendas for many years, and all stakeholders involved have expressed their views and preferences about the issue in a series of recent hearings organized by your project organization. It is evident that a project of this scale – with high stakes for all who are affected and involved – can succeed only if it is organized and implemented collaboratively. In accordance with current trends, your director has expressed his expectation that you 'co-create' and 'co-produce' the project together with stakeholders.

Where do you start and who do you involve? It will be impossible to do justice to the interests and agendas of each of the key stakeholders – elderly and disabled tenants who are often of moderate means, small shop owners and entrepreneurs, long-time residents and their families, and housing corporations eager to upgrade and monetize social housing units. You will somehow have to prioritize, yet such a selection cannot just be a government-dominated exercise like in the old days. Moreover, some key stakeholders possess expertise, contacts, and local legitimacy that the project could benefit from. You want them 'inside the tent'. But how does one design an appropriately inclusive collaborative structure that discourages preferential treatment of some partners while avoiding unworkable, chaotic proceedings at the same time?

You also struggle with aligning the views of various senior colleagues from other city departments. Some advocate proceeding cautiously and seem more concerned with protecting turf and managing reputational risk than with effectively integrating procedures, timelines, and workflows to ensure integrated service packages for stakeholders. How can you bring them along, and give them some skin in the game? So far, you have had more success with external actors. You have partnered up with a local religious charity and a well-respected non-profit to provide a variety of welfare services for the elderly, largely financed through municipal funds supplemented by small co-payments from prospective service users. You have also managed to sign a contract with two large construction companies to engage in a public-private partnership (PPP) to co-finance, develop, maintain, and service two brand new-school facilities. Initial construction will start soon, assuming your new partners manage to secure a large loan as agreed in the contract. Now that you're thinking about it, however, they haven't come back to you for some time now ...

Impressed as you are with the passion and drive of their many long-time volunteers, you feel they need to become more skilled, consistent, and professional to offer the level of services the municipality is willing to certify and finance. Also, they will need to hire additional staff to ensure continuity of service. If demand exceeds supply and service provision is halted, this particularly vulnerable constituency will reflexively point their finger at the local government rather than at the actual service providers. Talks and negotiations went fine, but you doubt whether you or your colleagues have the communication and facilitation skills to enthusiastically and sustainably manage partners whose backgrounds and working styles differ substantially from yours.

Clearly, *managing cross-sector collaboration* raises yet another set of distinctive questions and challenges for public managers. Which types of partners should be engaged for which reasons, and at what stage? How should trust and voluntary collaboration be balanced with contracts and incentives? How can public managers ensure that partnerships stay productive and dynamic, and how 'definitive' should they be anyway? How do public managers become skilled network managers? How can clear lines of accountability be established? And, most importantly, how do public managers share responsibilities and powers with other collaborators while remaining 'in charge' of their own agendas and objectives?

The need for collaboration

The introductory case illustrates a cluster of developments that have been emerging for some time now in the operating environment of public managers. Indeed, outsourcing and privatization of core government functions, cutbacks in welfare provisions, service delivery through various partnerships, and the accompanying discourse on networks, governance, participation, and collaboration all point to a world in which government can no longer 'go it alone' (Agranoff 2006; Alford and O'Flynn 2012; Ansell and Gash 2008; Bryson *et al.* 2015).

Increasingly, authority and decision-making discretion will not lie with just one person, office, or sector, or be located exclusively at the top of an organization (Andrews *et al.* 2016: 3). In a VUCA world, public managers are *forced* to closely collaborate within different networks consisting of state and non-state actors – citizens, NGOs, businesses, charities, and social enterprises. Clearly, the various trends and demands highlighted in this book put collaboration front and centre for the 21st century public manager.

This is not to say public managers and their political masters whole-heartedly embrace more horizontal governance. In fact, the urge to simplify, reduce, monopolize, and bureaucratize wicked problems is still omnipresent. However, such urges will turn out to be counterproductive in a VUCA world. On the contrary, fostering collaborative relationships allows managers to pool resources with those available to other actors. Clearly, most 21st century demands outlined in this book require public managers to engage, pool, and leverage the widest possible range of resources.

Collaborative public management: drivers and features

This chapter discusses the managerial roles, values, and competencies needed to effectively manage such cross-sectoral collaboration. It addresses some of the common challenges involved, such as selecting the type of partner and partnership, and ensuring trust, mutual accountability, and aligned incentives. We first discuss drivers and features of collaborative public management, along with different types of partners and partnerships and how and when they suit public managers. Then, we examine managerial activities associated with collaboration, including co-design, co-creation, and co-production, alongside skills and attitudes of successful collaborators. We conclude with an overview of challenges in achieving cultures and structures of shared accountability, and suggest managerial strategies to overcome such challenges.

Table 11.1 outlines seven key drivers for public managers to pursue collaboration and the challenges and opportunities that each of these drivers presents. This list of drivers derived from various studies is far from exhaustive, but it captures the diversity of motives for engaging in collaboration, ranging from acquiring additional financial resources to empowering citizens. The introductory example shows how various drivers may simultaneously urge public managers to reach out to collaborators.

Indeed, collaboration implies more access to different types of resources, as external actors – the private sector partners, local religious charity, NGO, and individual citizens in the case – may have more advanced skills, knowledge, and technologies, as well as more financial resources, than the public sector (Kelman and Hong 2016: 147). At the same time, effective collaboration requires managers to bring together widely divergent agendas, norms, working styles, world views, and opportunistic motives of partners from other sectors.

As such, distributing both risk and responsibility through collaboration creates a double-edged sword for public managers. Unclear lines of

TABLE 11.1 Seven managerial drivers for collaboration

Driver	Challenges	Opportunities
1. *Leveraging outside expertise and ideas*	• Protection of commercial and intellectual property • Unrealistic expectations • Translating and tailoring expertise • Ensuring continuous expert oversight Alford and O'Flynn 2012: 83.	• Access to otherwise unavailable knowledge sources, technology, ideas, and procedures • Mutual learning Koppenjan and Klijn 2004: 108.
2. *Tapping into extended financial resources*	• Risk transfers • Low trust • Hidden 'transactional' costs • Highly dependent on negotiation and contracting skills Brown *et al.* 2006: 326.	• Cost savings and flexibility • Additional investment • Efficiency • More attractive rates and timelines Brown *et al.* 2006: 323–324.
3. *Outsourcing (or sharing) responsibility*	• Unclear lines of accountability • Transparency and communication struggles • Non-aligned public perceptions Agranoff 2006: 61.	• Shifting responsibility for tough, unpopular projects • Increased credibility for highly technical, complex projects Alford and O'Flynn 2012: 83–110.
4. *Empowering citizens*	• Lack of expertise • Unrealistic expectations and pressures Brandsen and Honingh 2016: 429.	• Increasing civic duty • Knowledge transfer • Direct responsiveness Brandsen and Honingh 2016: 433.
5. *Gaining stakeholders' trust*	• Lack of expertise • A multitude of interests and agendas, often difficult to reconcile Koppenjan and Klijn 2004: 147.	• Inclusion and participation • Greater transparency • Shared vision Bryson *et al.* 2015: 656.
6. *Reconciling diverging interests*	• Conflicting motivations and agendas • Requires conflict resolution skills Koppenjan and Klijn 2004: 147.	• Stabilizing of power relations • Leveraging future support • Recognition of authority shifts Agranoff 2006: 61.
7. *Distributing activities according to expertise and resources*	• Management of task dispersal • Need to employ more staff for better oversight and control Alford and O'Flynn 2012: 110.	• Easier to ensure expert leadership • Cost reduction • Culture of collaboration Alford and O'Flynn 2012: 83–110.

accountability may lead to situations in which citizens are caught in a stand-off between government and their partner and end up not receiving what has been promised (Forrer *et al.* 2010: 478). When that happens, stakeholders will often reflexively blame the government, as highlighted in the introductory case. However, publicly shifting the blame to non-state actors is a no-go for public managers: doing so will brand them as incompetent evaders of accountability and responsibility obligations.

In such a precarious context, public managers may also be reluctant to engage the general public for fear that their – sometimes amateur – contributions may degrade service quality (Alford and O'Flynn 2012: 132–133). Yet public managers who do choose to follow the path of collaboration cite shared policy vision, effective multi-level planning, and cultural change as the added value of equal engagement with non-state actors, and citizens in particular (Brandsen and Honingh 2016; Howes *et al.* 2013). Whether such added value is achieved depends on public managers choosing partners and partnerships that fit their objectives and management style. What different types can we distinguish and which behaviours do they require?

Types of partnerships and partners

To answer this question, we first have to organize the wide array of interchangeably used concepts such as networks, partnerships, collaboration, externalization, cooperation, and contracting. Figure 11.1 structures this array of collaborative arrangements as a 'ladder' around four key questions for public managers:

- What is the level of intensity of involvement and connectivity between partners?
- Who produces the product or service?
- Where does the decision-making power lie?
- What are the required managerial behaviours and activities?

The 'three Cs' of coordination, cooperation, and collaboration describe the varying degrees of connection and intensity of interdependence between the members of governance networks (Mischen 2015: 381). In this framework, coordination is characterized by the lowest level of connectivity and intensity, and collaboration by the highest.

As shown in Figure 11.1, various sets of managerial skills, competencies, and behaviours are associated with different types of collaboration. These stem from the level of interdependence and decision-making discretion of partners involved in such arrangements. Public managers need to employ control, compulsion, and negotiation to manage interactions of lower equality between partners; they need to build consensus and create an atmosphere conducive to dialogue and compromise if partner

FIGURE 11.1   Ladder of collaborative arrangements

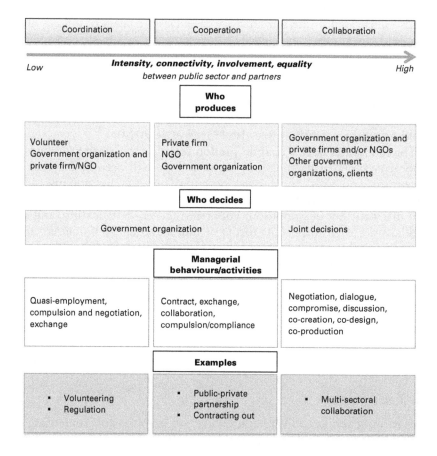

Based on: Mischen 2015: 381; Alford and O'Flynn 2012: 20–22.

autonomy is higher and roles and responsibilities are more evenly distributed (Agranoff 2006; McGuire and Agranoff 2011).

One important issue that is sometimes overlooked in the vast literature on collaborative management is worth mentioning here: public managers struggle first and foremost with getting collaboration going *within* government. Indeed, when I teach executive programmes on stakeholder collaboration and networks to audiences of senior public managers, somewhat strikingly and counterintuitively much of the discussion evolves around the immense difficulties and challenges of collaborating with colleagues from other public agencies.

As public managers assume that interests and agendas from non-governmental partners differ from theirs, their expectations for these partners may be lower but also more easily exceeded. However, many appear to struggle immensely with overcoming deeply siloed mentalities, disjointed agendas, and opportunistic behaviour from their governmental colleagues, as also illustrated in the introductory case. Despite years of talking about 'whole of government' and 'joined up government' (see Christensen and Lae-greid 2006; Christensen *et al.* 2007), this is still not yet a reality, even more so for collaboration in supranational, multi-level, and cross-national settings such as the UN or the EU. As such, many of the challenges and competencies discussed in this chapter apply just as much to realizing intra-governmental and inter-governmental collaboration – a key precondition for successful multi-sectoral partnerships (see also Howes *et al.* 2014).

The remainder of this chapter predominantly focuses on the most col-laborative types of partnerships because these will become increasingly important and yield the largest potential benefits for solving super-wicked problems, yet present considerable challenges to public managers that merit further examination. Volunteering, self-certification, and self-regulation are all important forms of non-state actors pursuing public purpose, but have been extensively examined elsewhere (Groenleer *et al.* 2010; Lodge and Wegrich 2012).

We will briefly discuss contracting out and PPPs, two more traditional forms of non-governmental service provision, before going into multi-sectoral collaboration in greater detail. On the spectrum of 'intensity, connectivity, involvement, and equality' between the public sector and external partners, these two forms of collaboration are situated in the mid-dle, with contractually enforced cooperation as the key mode of interaction.

Contracting out

This form of service delivery externalization involves governments enter-ing into contracts with private or non-profit organizations; the partner carries out the externalized activity, but the government retains respon-sibility. Arguments used in favour of these approaches are that they address inefficient resource allocation that bureaucracies are notorious for, and may be conducive to cost reduction and higher quality (Alford and O'Flynn 2012: 86). Selsky and Parker (2005) suggest that a contract-ing framework applies to managers seeking to externalize their services through 'specific organizational characteristics and/or distinctive contri-butions ... to fulfil predetermined ends and means' (862). In short: public managers may seek to enter contracting out arrangements when they aim to realize cost reductions, higher efficiency and responsiveness to stake-holder requirements, and higher quality of services.

Public-private partnerships (PPPs)

The ambiguity of this outsourcing arrangement lies in the use of the term 'partnership', which usually implies some degree of collaboration. In most

PPPs, however, the service production or other activities are usually not shared by the government and the external actor. Although differing levels of cooperation intensity and interdependence exist, the common role of public managers is to define the scope of the task, set priorities and performance targets, and monitor and oversee the contractual arrangements, intervening only when things go wrong (Alford and O'Flynn 2012: 89; Hodge *et al.* 2010; Reynaers 2014).

Advocates of PPPs cite two main advantages of such arrangements: structured incentives for private partners, and focused targets and risk transfer (Alford and O'Flynn 2012: 91). However, numerous global successes *and* failures show that PPPs only deliver what they promise if contracts are both enforceable and flexible, public managers involved are topic experts and skilled negotiators, and realistic opt-outs are agreed on before partnerships commence (Boyer *et al.* 2015; Eversdijk 2013; Hodge *et al.* 2010; Klijn and Teisman 2003).

A key question for public managers in both types is when engaging private sector partners will ensure better service delivery compared with implementing projects in-house. However, how can they meaningfully assess pros and cons beforehand? An example of a potentially helpful tool is the Public-Private Comparator Manual (PPC) described in Box 11.1, which aims to assist public managers in comparing public, private, or mixed implementation scenarios.

Partnerships straightjacketed by fairly static 20-year or 30-year contracts may work wonderfully well in areas such as infrastructure and housing. Indeed, as various public managers involved in such long-term partnerships happily profess in a large-scale interview study into PPPs, the space for political intervention or changes to the terms of reference is limited (Reynaers 2015: 9).

> This is infrastructure and it lasts about 100 years: You should not want to change our decisions every 5 years. Normally everyone wants to have their say. But we have made our decision in 2003 to last until 2033. Thirty years of little political intervention. I think that is good for the continuity of the project.

However, such structures may not work at all in tackling super-wicked problems such as mitigating climate change, fighting global terrorism, or fairly distributing massive amounts of refugees. When dealing with such contentious issues that require dialogue to ensure legitimate outcomes (Agranoff 2006), public managers will need to use traditional partnerships in conjunction with, or replace them entirely by, organic and bottom-up types of collaboration with more differentiated external involvement. Rather than relying on contracts and financial motives, such partnerships require mutual trust, shared vision and motivations, and a deep-seated belief in the value-add of the partners' involvement. As a consequence,

Box 11.1 The Public-Private Comparator Manual (PPC)

In 2013, the Ministry of Finance in the Netherlands released the PPC, a 75-page English-language manual covering many dimensions of service delivery implementation across four modules – from initiation to evaluation – aimed at supporting public managers across the Dutch government. The manual pays attention to a wide range of relevant project management, financial, and HRM-related topics. It primarily aims to assist the assessment phase in between the initial phase and the preparation phase. Conducting a PPC is mandatory for bigger projects exceeding €25 million (housing) and €60 million (infrastructure), but can be used to improve assessments of smaller projects as well.

The manual is quite specific in proposing methodologies for comparing various implementation scenarios – in-house, mixed, or outsourced – including historical analysis, sensitivity analysis, primary data collection, and international benchmarking. Public managers are advised to include realistic inflationary expectations and transition expenses, in case implementation scenarios may change in the future. Interestingly, the manual also mandates public managers to pay attention to non-financial considerations, such as consequences of the partnership for the organization's identity, ensuring that cultural and managerial dimensions are not neglected.

Do public managers find the PPC useful? Experiences are largely positive, as interview studies show. Public managers use the PPC to draft reports they share within their departments. Evidently, if calculations result in an advice to outsource implementation, responses from colleagues in facility and support roles are not always positive: 'Are we not doing a good job? This means some of us will have to start working for a private consortium.' In addition, some departments with considerable in-house expertise about large-scale projects prefer their own measures and methods to the PPC.

The manual is comprehensive and innovative. Still, various key questions remain for public managers. How can they obtain all the necessary information for their assessment in a context of information asymmetry and potential lack of in-house expertise? If they engage external actors in some of the calculations and assessments, how can public managers be sure these actors will be neutral in their advice? How can public managers factor in future innovations that will make technologies and materials cheaper? Or foresee how political instability and corporate bankruptcies may lead to projects being delayed, postponed, or cancelled? Should the career prospects of their colleagues be included in the advice to outsource or not?

Sources: Government of the Netherlands, https://government.nl/documents/directives/2013/03/01/public-private-comparator-manual-2013; Reynaers 2014.

they require a different type of risk assessment and a different range of behaviours from public managers.

Multi-sectoral collaboration

Multi-faceted, dynamic partnerships between actors from two or more sectors are referred to as multi-sectoral or cross-sectoral collaborations and partnerships, with the 'tri-sector' type involving government, business, and civil society actors gaining increasing traction (Brandsen and Pestoff 2006; Easter 2016; Eggers and Macmillan 2013; Selsky and Parker 2005). Indeed, public managers aiming to effectively tackle super-wicked problems – or get things done at all in a context of assertive, tech-savvy stakeholders – may benefit from involving citizens, private sector players, and NGOs, the latter particularly in less-developed settings.

Box 11.2 identifies benefits, and struggles, experienced by managers in multi-sectoral campaigns in developing contexts, driven by local and international donors in tandem with local governments, who in turn actively engage communities and professionals on the ground.

Clearly, engaging non-profit actors and communities opens up a reservoir of highly passionate, increasingly well-connected and supported networks of employees with eyes and ears on the ground and deep ties with various local constituencies. At the same time, however, public managers shouldn't be naïve in assuming that highly passionate and driven civil society partners will necessarily effectively co-produce their objectives. Among the biggest potential risks are so-called 'mission stickiness', occurring when NGOs desperately hold on to their initial mission and donor base even though changing operating environments render them obsolete and meaningful collaboration necessitates change (Moore 2000: 192). Equally, public managers need to be mindful of the opposite 'mission creep' or 'mission drift', in which NGOs quickly and opportunistically abandon key missions to secure new financial support when continuity is threatened (Oster 1995: 28).

The multi-sectoral partnerships displayed in Box 11.2 hardly included private sector actors. As mentioned, however, tri-sectoral collaboration involving actors from the domains of government, business, and civil society is being applauded as an effective mode to address wicked problems, not in the least by large, global multinationals and private sector academic circles (Lovegrove and Thomas 2013; Porter and Kramer 2006; Rodriguez *et al.* 2015). Such collaborations expand existing discourse on corporate social responsibility (CSR) and social enterprise (Ridley-Duff and Bull 2015; Smith *et al.* 2013; Skagerlind *et al.* 2015). Box 11.3 provides an example of how multinational companies set up charities to run large-scale CSR activities in close collaboration with local NGOs and governments, creating public value or rather compensating negative externalities resulting from private value creation.

234 The 21st Century Public Manager

Box 11.2 Cross-national and multi-sectoral collaboration in Africa and Asia

Large, government-funded development agencies such as the United States Agency for International Development (USAID) engage on a daily basis in collaborations in complex settings. One widely documented example is USAID's long-term involvement in improving education quality in Malawi. Local donors aiming to fund a social mobilization campaign engaged USAID project staff to interview teachers, parents, and education officials about their thoughts on education quality. The project staff also asked local stakeholders how they could best assist with creating action plans, and providing both teacher training and train-the-trainer training to support quality improvements.

Managers from USAID and the Ministry of Education in Malawi collaborated closely to create an environment in which local stakeholders had a real say in determining the project's shape and scope. Although these efforts did not create full – or equal – partnerships, they provided mechanisms through which local ideas and concerns reached policy-makers. This strengthened local support for the project, improved sentiment concerning the state's performance on education, and improved effectiveness by identifying problems of which public managers had been unaware. Various evaluations report long-term educational improvements.

At the same time, evaluations of other collaborative projects on biodiversity and revitalization in post-conflict Cambodia and post-tsunami Indonesia identify various struggles for managers: international and NGO-initiated efforts were seen as obtrusive and irrelevant by officials in the host country, there was a lack of base-level data and analysis on the collaborative objective(s), and efforts to make mutual interests and benefits explicit happened too late in the process. As one project manager involved noted: 'Don't assume anything about the perceptions of others; expect to be surprised and expect not to learn everything in the first meeting.' Still, all participants stressed collaborative structures are essential rather than optional to get anything done

What can public managers take away from these examples? Useful lessons for collaboration include:

- Maximize strong interpersonal relationships while developing institutional relationships as well, to ensure continuity in case of staff turnover or 'personal relationships turned sour'.
- Recognize power imbalances and work around them rather than trying to correct them.
- Do not impose frames on local stakeholders but treat them as full collaborators; equity may – and arguably should – trump efficiency in such cases.
- Start with collectively identifying common objectives and interests while realizing that some will inevitably conflict.

Sources: USAID, https://pdf.usaid.gov/pdf_docs/Pnadg024.pdf; Fauna & Flora International, http://www.fauna-flora.org.

Box 11.3 Corporate social responsibility (CSR) in India

Suzlon Energy is a large wind power company active across the globe. Despite the company's vision to only impact positively on society, communities close to its farms and sites have experienced negative impacts, mainly through land expropriation and damage to the local infrastructure and environment. This resulted in mistrust against the company and in clashes between local communities and Suzlon Energy staff.

To run business operations more effectively and build lasting relationships with all stakeholders, Suzlon Energy established Suzlon Foundation in 2007. The foundation heads CSR initiatives as a separate organization, structurally isolated from the business units of the company, reflecting a trend among multinational corporations to set up separate foundations to deal with CSR and charitable projects. Projects are implemented in communities surrounding the company's wind farms: by 2010, Suzlon Foundation had implemented 125 different projects, in close collaboration with 32 NGOs and 13 government partners.

One particularly interesting take-away for public managers is how projects implemented through tri-sector partnerships can help build the – often volatile and underdeveloped – capacities of NGOs. NGOs experienced the Suzlon partnership as flexible and characterized by knowledge exchange and learning. Similarly, public managers involved felt that tri-sector collaboration in enhancing CSR considerably added value to the quality of life in local communities as well as resource utilization and capacity-building.

Source: Skagerlind *et al.* 2015: 245–275.

Clearly, engaging private sector players carries risks as well as providing benefits. Particularly if tri-sectoral collaborations are initiated by business, as in the CSR example, public managers through their participation may unintentionally legitimize corporate activities whose ultimate intent may be nebulous at best. Indeed, public managers will have to prevent roles and responsibilities from becoming blurred to the extent that collaboration produces 'regulatory capture' of legislative agendas by private sector players through skilled lobbying and negotiating (Laffont and Tirole 1991; Stigler 1971), or acts as 'window-dressing' or 'greenwashing' of harmful private sector activities (Delmas and Burbano 2011; Laufer 2003).

Still, engaging private sector partners opens up enormous potential in helping to address aforementioned super-wicked problems. The private sector's ability to scale up, finance, innovate, and make operations more efficient may well be unparalleled if it sees a business case. Clearly, engaging private sector and civil society actors may create enormous value-add while posing common risks as well.

FIGURE 11.2   Cross-sectoral collaboration: managerial considerations

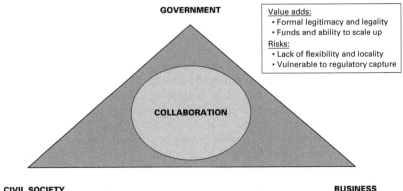

In this vein, Figure 11.2 displays a tri-sector triangle (Pestoff 1995; Van de Donk 2001) that points out key value-adds and risks that public managers should contemplate when engaging potential partners from the three sectors, including government. Effective collaborative managers invest in getting to know the cultures, mores, and workings of the other sectors so they can maximize the potential that partners from other sectors bring to the table while minimizing some of the common risks.

Box 11.4 presents a case of multi-sectoral collaboration in Australia. Here, in contrast to the previous three examples, a private company takes the lead in collaborating with the state government and an academic institution to create public and private value – but this time without explicitly pursuing CSR objectives. The case illustrates a stakeholder engagement framework through which partners deliver mutually beneficial services (Alford and O'Flynn 2012). In this case, the public managers involved 'lead from behind' rather than actively 'take charge', while providing guidance, long-term stability, and assistance in removing legal and procedural barriers. To provide a complete picture, the specific case example is contextualized within the broader context of collaboration and collaborative public management in Australia, illustrating how many public managers still wrestle with 'becoming more collaborative'.

Different partnerships; varying motives and space for involvement

To synthesize: while contracting out and PPPs employ a high degree of involvement from private sector partners, the nature of the outsourcing

Box 11.4 Multi-sectoral collaboration in Australia

In 2010, Boeing Aerostructures Australia (BAA), an international manufacturer of Boeing civilian and defence aircraft, relocated its New South Wales operation to Victoria and began preparations for a significant increase in production to meet global demand. The sophisticated manufacturing process used by BAA required skills and competencies beyond the traditional ones. As the existing certificate in Manufacturing was no longer meeting its needs, Boeing approached the Department of Education and Early Childhood Development (DEECD) of Victoria to co-design a new certificate in Aviation Manufacturing (Composites).

A collaborative project was established to design the new certificate, also involving the Box Hill Institute of TAFE, Australia's largest vocational education provider. Regular meetings were held, and a cross-sectoral working group was created, with the Department helping to simplify procedures. Through the co-design of the certificate in Aviation Manufacturing (Composites), BAA and other sectors now have a fully customized qualification to ensure future workforce development. Up-skilling of 300 new and existing Boeing staff commenced in 2012. In the years that followed, Boeing significantly increased its research and development spending and manufacturing presence in various parts of Australia. Both sides saw a business case and choose to explore it.

Intriguingly, for a long time Australia ranked worst in the OECD in terms of collaboration between public sector (funded) researchers and private industry, according to former Minister for Innovation, Industry, Science and Research Kim Carr. A key issue was collaboration with domestic industry. Various tax credit schemes and innovation supporting projects have been implemented to kick-start more 'home-grown' multi-sectoral collaboration. Future years will show whether they make a long-term difference.

However, while collaboration has been a buzzword in the Australian public sector for some time – some even speak of a 'collaboration cult' (O'Flynn 2009: 112) – public managers still experience many inhibiting factors, as recent workshops and roundtables illustrate. In addition to issues of culture, uncertainty, and procedures, they emphasize territorialism and 'protecting your patch' as main obstacles. Such issues range from egos and fears that credit from the collaboration may go to others, to a lack of understanding of what potential partners are doing and *are capable of*. As supporting factors, managers corroborate issues emphasized in this chapter such as common goals and role clarity, while adding common pools of 'new' resources devoted to collaboration as an incentive, together with access to information, enough time, and coffee.

Sources: Victoria State Government, http://education.vic.gov.au/Documents/about/programs/partnerships/stakeholderengagement11.pdf; Australian Government, https://innovation.govspace.gov.au/2014/08/11/collaboration-whats-the-magic-ingredient-for-working-across-agencies/; O'Flynn 2009.

process, specifically designed terms of reference (ToRs), and contractual arrangements leave little space for innovation. Additionally, private partners are often motivated by financial incentives rather than public value creation. In contrast, multi-sectoral collaborations in which actors jointly co-design and co-produce services are characterized by the highest levels of external partner involvement. As such, they provide greater space for innovation and initiative. Taking shared public value creation as a starting point, public managers have opportunities to direct the motives of external partners towards the creation of value for mutual constituencies rather than private or donor-led wealth creation.

To conclude this section, Figure 11.3 maps various types of collaboration across a 'collaboration cube' for public managers. The cube serves as a decision support tool for public managers in deciding which type of non-state actor involvement is most suitable given the space for initiative and innovation allowed by the project in question, the assumed motivation of the partner to collaborate, and the extent of involvement desired by the public manager.

Collaborative activities, skillsets, and mindsets

When public managers have decided to set up and enter a partnership, weighed pros and cons, and assessed opportunities, the actual 'managerial work' of collaborating commences. Collaboration can occur across various stages of policy-making, implementation, and service delivery. Three increasingly used concepts covering many multi-sectoral

FIGURE 11.3   The collaboration cube: a decision support tool

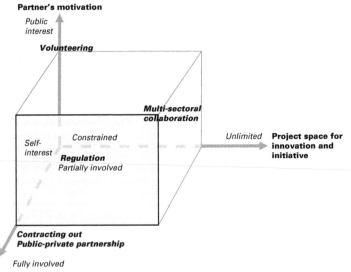

collaborative management activities are co-design, co-creation, and co-production (see also Figure 11.1).

Co-design, co-creation, co-production

These concepts have emerged fairly recently and go hand in hand with the emerging role of public sector innovation, the age of budget austerity, and the rise of social entrepreneurship (Frow *et al.* 2015: 464; Voorberg *et al.* 2015: 1334). Indeed, Freire and Sangiorgi (2010), who study co-design, co-creation, and co-production in the context of healthcare reform, attribute their emergence to a general move 'from centralised and sequential models of value creation to more distributed and open paradigms, where citizens are looked at as co-creators of their own wellbeing' (2010: 2–3).

Table 11.2 defines these three collaborative management activities and lists key efforts, roles, and behaviours associated with each of them. As always, the reality of collaborative policy-making and management is not as neat as this analytical distinction would suggest, and design, creation, and production activities and behaviours will overlap.

TABLE 11.2 Co-design, co-creation, and co-production as collaborative activities

	Co-design	*Co-creation*	*Co-production*
1. Structure Brandsen and Honingh 2016: 428; Freire and Sangiorgi 2010: 3.	Various partners working together in the idea initiation and design development process, with the final solution implemented and led by professionals.	Arrangements in which users not only design services, but also generate their content and shape their continuous development.	Equal and reciprocal relations between professionals and clients that leverage community capacities to deliver public services.
2. Focus and efforts Frow *et al.* 2015: 464; Torfing *et al.* 2012; Voorberg *et al.* 2015: 1334.	Design and idea generation – co-initiation, crowdsourcing, focus groups, discussion, brainstorming.	Initiative and learning – engagement platforms and networks for continuous oversight, learning, and development.	Implementation and delivery – access to resources, self-service, (semi) outsourcing, do-it-yourself (DIY).
3 Managerial roles and behaviours Hartley *et al.* 2013; Meijer 2014; Voorberg *et al.* 2015: 1345.	• Steering • Facilitating • Stimulating	• Dialogue • Negotiating • Prioritizing • Persuading	• Mediating • Compromising • Monitoring • Overseeing • Intervening

Public managers engaged in co-production activities will have to find ways to address active input by citizens who will not necessarily be the end users of the services (Brandsen and Honingh 2016: 428). The citizen co-production example from Scotland in Box 11.5 shows how public managers can involve the widest possible range of citizens by allowing community groups to take the lead in local redevelopment efforts and reach out to citizens who are less eager to partake.

Like many of the projects that public managers in Scotland have recently implemented using a co-production approach (Connolly 2016), the case illustrates how involving communities and forging partnerships with third-sector organizations can help design and deliver services that better meet citizens' needs. In such projects, the public manager simultaneously acts as a coordinator overseeing the overall operations;

Box 11.5 Citizen co-production in Scotland

In 2012, local residents from the Lochside area identified a need for a more coordinated, meaningful approach to involving local people in improving the neighbourhood. At the same time, the South Ayrshire Council committed to designing services together with locals and third-sector organizations. The partnership adopted community development principles in its development. A community-led group was established in which locals identified interest and concern, and also the skills, knowledge, and strengths present within the community.

Based on those priorities, the group developed a number of small projects and initiatives. They carried out wider community engagement activities with citizens who initially were less eager to participate, before developing a community action plan based on what locals said mattered to them. Through a series of workshops, the group co-designed a new play area with local children and families, with wide-ranging positive feedback as a result. Also, after consulting with locals, architects revised plans for a new housing development, improving its design and appearance.

Improvements in community safety, with a 35 per cent reduction in youth-related anti-social behaviour since 2012, resulted from positive diversionary activities. Community Safety officers helped to set up the Lochside Girls Group, whose members have been learning about the dangers of alcohol with their parents. Lochside Church has also provided activities for children and young people from more than 100 families through weekly children's clubs. Increased community involvement continued via email, word of mouth, meetings, one-to-one interviews, focus group discussions, Facebook updates, and events involving over 1,000 households including 210 local children.

Source: Scottish Co-production Network, http://coproductionscotland.org.uk/files/7513/8728/4017/Lochside_case_study.pdf.

a mediator helping to capture and explain the community's needs to the executor of the idea; and a co-creator, investing time and ideas.

Managerial skillsets and mindsets

The managerial work of collaboration requires specific skillsets and mindsets, some of which have been listed throughout this chapter. Indeed, the literature dealing with wicked problems stresses they demand collaborative strategies and skills that are 'in limited supply' (Christie *et al.* 2009; Head and Alford 2015). Collaboration can easily end in disappointment – dialogue can turn into conflict, hardened positions, and stalemate. Successful collaboration thus demands that all partners bring relevant skills and personal attributes to the table. Public managers have to think beyond their own skillsets and mindsets. Once they enter a partnership they are part of something bigger; *developing the skillsets of their partners* and affecting their mindsets become equally important. Consultative and participatory competencies are vital here.

In addition, effective collaboration between networks of potentially divergent actors also requires communication and conflict management skills from public managers, as they need to 'persuade and seduce' initially sceptical stakeholders. Figure 11.4 synthesizes specific attitudes, values, and skills needed for effective collaboration in various types of partnerships, both one-sided and multi-sectoral. These different types of collaboration require somewhat different attitudes and skills from public managers, given their modes of work, the level of non-state partner involvement, and the goals pursued both by the public manager and the partners.

FIGURE 11.4   Mindsets and Skillsets of the collaborative public manager

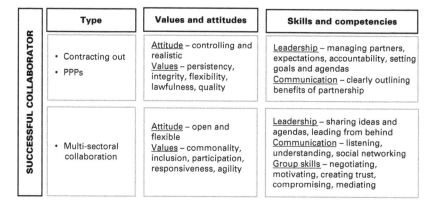

	Type	Values and attitudes	Skills and competencies
SUCCESSFUL COLLABORATOR	• Contracting out • PPPs	Attitude – controlling and realistic Values – persistency, integrity, flexibility, lawfulness, quality	Leadership – managing partners, expectations, accountability, setting goals and agendas Communication – clearly outlining benefits of partnership
	• Multi-sectoral collaboration	Attitude – open and flexible Values – commonality, inclusion, participation, responsiveness, agility	Leadership – sharing ideas and agendas, leading from behind Communication – listening, understanding, social networking Group skills – negotiating, motivating, creating trust, compromising, mediating

Based on: O'Leary *et al.* 2012: 572–573.

Public managers as boundary-spanners

One specific skill or role for public managers that will become increasingly important is that of the *boundary-spanner* – a programme specialist involved in networks who is highly aware of the need to collaborate across sectors and agency boundaries (Noordegraaf 2015; Stamper and Johlke 2003; Williams 2002, 2010, 2013). Governments slowly but surely move towards creating job descriptions geared for full-time engagement in boundary-spanning (Beck Jørgensen and Rutgers 2014; Guarneros-Meza and Martin 2016).

Boundary-spanning is based on the premise that 21ˢᵗ century demands and challenges 'transcend traditional procedural, professional and organizational boundaries' (Guarneros-Meza and Martin 2016: 239), therefore calling for a new breed of public managers who can work across sectors, organizations, fields, cultures, and missions. In a seminal study, Paul Williams (2002) identified four key factors that define effective boundary-spanning, each involving different roles, competencies, and personal characteristics. In his later work, he re-emphasized and refined some of these roles and competencies (Williams 2010, 2013), while others use a slightly different vocabulary when building on his work (e.g., Guarneros-Meza and Martin 2016). The four key factors and their roles and competencies, derived through a number of studies among public managers, are illustrated in Figure 11.5.

To illustrate what boundary-spanners look like, Box 11.6 presents a success story of a 'tri-sector athlete' (Lovegrove and Thomas 2013: 1) – a manager with a strong set of skills gained from two or more different sectors who is able to creatively apply those skills to deliver collaborative

FIGURE 11.5   Public managers as boundary-spanners

1. **Building sustainable relationships**
   - *Communicating and listening* – avoiding jargon to engage partners from other areas.
   - *Understanding, empathizing, and resolving conflict* – be willing to move on after fallout.
   - *Personality* – displaying an inviting personality and the ability to divest from baggage.
   - *Trust* – requiring reciprocal risk taking with initial trust being established in 1 – 2 days.
2. **Managing through influencing and negotiation**
   - *Brokering solutions* – requiring expertise and perceived legitimacy from all to fulfil role.
   - *Networking* – undertaken most effectively outside formal structures, with key nodal actors.
3. **Managing complexity and interdependencies**
   - *Inter-organizational experience* – producing invaluable insider knowledge and understanding.
   - *Transdisciplinary, technical knowledge* – creates a 'passport of legitimacy' to engage partners.
   - *Cognitive capacity* – being able to mobilize new resources and seek windows of opportunity.
4. **Managing roles, accountabilities, and motivations**
   - *Delicate judgment* – empowering others to act while respecting institutional mandates.
   - *Hegemony, resource opportunity, and mandate* – recognizing collaboration as the only viable way to address wicked issues and an opportunity to access new resources and policy options.

Source: Williams 2002: 115–121.

Box 11.6 Tri-sector athletes: characters and characteristics

In a 2013 *Harvard Business Review* article, Nick Lovegrove and Matthew Thomas outline the character and characteristics of tri-sector athletes by describing the role of former public manager Jeff Seabright in revamping Coca-Cola's water sustainability initiatives. The Coca-Cola Company has a stake in contributing to creation of sustainable sources of fresh water, as it uses over two litres of water to make one litre of product.

A lack of collaboration in the past resulted in local protests and the banning of production in South India. Coca-Cola hired Jeff Seabright, an outsider and relative newcomer to the private sector, to help design a practical response and engage with partners across sectors. Seabright had previous experience in the US Foreign Service, the Senate, USAID, and the White House Task Force on Climate Change.

He started by translating the issue of water scarcity into business language for his colleagues. Seabright found that expansion of production margins coincided with areas where water pressures would be most intense. Impressed with his analytical capabilities, Coca-Cola managers gave him the budget to fund several water sustainability initiatives. He built effective partnerships with governments and NGOs, using his USAID experience to create a $20 million partnership with the World Wildlife Foundation. As a result, Coca-Cola is on the way to meeting its 2020 target for water neutrality and is regarded as an industry leader in this area.

According to the authors, tri-sector athletes have six characteristics in common:

- **balanced motivations** – a desire to create public value wherever they work, combining their motivations to *exert influence* (often in government), have *social impact* (often in non-profits), and *generate wealth* (often in business);
- **transferable skills** – a set of distinctive skills valued across sectors: quantitative analytics, strategic planning, and stakeholder management;
- **contextual intelligence** – a deep understanding of the differences within and across sectors, especially those of language, culture, and performance indicators;
- **integrated networks** – a set of relationships across sectors to draw on when advancing their careers, building teams, or bringing together decision-makers;
- **prepared mind** – a willingness to pursue an unconventional career that zigzags across sectors, and the readiness to take potential pay cuts from time to time;
- **intellectual thread** – holistic subject matter expertise on a particular tri-sector issue, gained by understanding it from the perspective of each sector.

Source: Lovegrove and Thomas 2013.

results. Because of actual multi-sectoral experience, tri-sector athletes know from the inside out what drives agencies and managers in various sectors, and how their various constituencies may be best persuaded to participate in collaborative partnerships. They gain most of their skills from professional experience, however, and this raises intriguing questions: to what extent current degree programmes in our field can successfully teach future public managers tri-sectoral qualities, and which competencies and values merit more attention.

Managing shared accountability and performance

As far back as 1993, in their famous book on effective teams, Katzenbach and Smith identified shared responsibility and accountability as key preconditions for successful partnerships. They also identified them as one of the hardest objectives for managers to achieve. Accountability is a particularly complex and tricky issue in collaboration because very often lines, subjects, and objects of accountability may be unclear, thus complicating managerial responsibilities of compliance, control, and quality assurance. Managers involved may have competing views on targets, outcomes, and implementation stages (Clarke and Fuller 2010: 86; Williams 2002: 120), particularly if partnerships are not driven by strict, enforceable contracts (but even if they are).

Further, different types of collaborations will vary in their collective legitimacy as experienced by the partners involved, and the rhetoric they use in justifying and framing collaboration (Koschmann *et al.* 2012: 343). All such issues come on top of the multitude of accountability pressures and challenges that public managers already face in responding to legally mandated queries from various forums, even in non-collaborative settings (Bovens *et al.* 2008; Bovens *et al.* 2014; Koppell 2005; Schillemans 2015; Sinclair 1995). Not only do they need to manage multiple accountabilities, they have to do so *across* sectors and institutions, with partners pursuing their *own* multiple accountabilities.

Here, key questions for public managers are:

- Who is in charge, and when, and who decides?
- Who is to blame if things go wrong? Or, rather: how do we prevent the question of blame from dominating and potentially poisoning dialogue about genuine responsibility sharing?
- And, from an HRM perspective, how can performance assessment structures be devised such that (cross-sectoral) teamwork is genuinely part of KPIs, rewards, and promotions for managers and staff?

Indeed, most of the management literature on teamwork suggests common goals and motivations, and the collective energy and passion they evoke are most likely to generate the reciprocal willingness to accept responsibility for failure and success. Such micro-level incentives may be much more effective for public managers to pursue than multi-year attempts to change and design institutional coordination mechanisms, as often happens in the wake of scandals involving formal networks, as shown by the Hurricane Katrina inquiries in the US, to name a prominent example (Boin and Nieuwenburg 2013; Helsloot *et al.* 2012; Koliba *et al.* 2011).

A meaningful example is provided by Page *et al.* (2015), who review a range of collaborative projects aimed at reducing traffic congestion. They stress that public managers should organize collaborative accountability around actual public value creation by defining tangible and intangible outcomes that speak to the various partners involved. Examining both *vertical accountability* – being legal and responsive to various political and financial 'authorizers', and *horizontal accountability* – being responsive and constructive towards various collaborative partners, the authors identify instances where preferences of individual stakeholders conflicted with the objectives of the collaboration as a whole. In such cases, solutions lie in designing a process in which authorization from elite stakeholders is sufficient in most stages, while endorsement and support from citizens, legislators, or special interest groups is only required at the early stages and towards the end (2015: 723).

While collaborative settings exacerbate existing value trade-offs for public managers – for instance, between achieving maximum performance, procedural fairness, or democratic accountability (Provan and Kenis 2008) – they also provide opportunities for engaging stakeholders directly in speaking out about such trade-offs. However, if broad and collectively endorsed public value objectives are set at an early stage, public managers have more leeway to sacrifice value preferences of individual stakeholders later in the process, as long as they make sure such sacrifices are distributed fairly among partners (Page *et al.* 2015: 729)

Still, even in a context of clearly defined and widely supported public value creation, the question remains why actors in partnerships would *at all be incentivized to accept responsibility and accountability for collective action* without negatively oriented sanctions in place, and how public managers should get them there. Indeed, Bryson *et al.* (2015: 663), listing accountability as a key collaborative success criterion in their collaborative checklist, emphasize how collaborations need to build on individual *and* organizational self-interest. Box 11.7 provides insights about how managers can stimulate and reward collective behaviour.

Based on the observations outlined in this chapter, public managers can achieve shared accountability among partners with at least three important caveats.

- First, it is important to define the subjects and the objects of accountability – who is responsible for what. This should be done based on the resources, expertise, powers, and networks each of the actors have

Box 11.7 How managers can effectively reward collaborative behaviour

The importance of teamwork for achieving managerial goals has been emphasized for decades. Intriguingly, most performance appraisal systems used by public managers are still highly individualistic. This was one of the reasons why consulting giant Deloitte decided in 2015 to do away with them altogether, a move that generated widespread debate about how organizations enforce one-sided behaviour. In the context of collaboration, achieving shared accountability and responsibility requires smart incentives backed up by supportive managerial behaviour.

There is, however, meaningful work that shows which incentives and behaviours are effective, such as the practice-based books *X-Teams* by Ancona and Bresman (2007) and *Decide and Deliver* by Blenko *et al.* (2010), and scholarly articles by Scott and Tiessen (1999) and Stevens and Campion (1994). This diverse set of studies shows how collective performance targets set by partners themselves, which carry considerable weight in assessing individual performance, result in better collaborative performance. Recent evidence from China suggests that well-targeted individual rewards can also elevate team performance, but only if they are perceived as fair, managers award them transparently, and members central to the team performance (informal leaders) are the recipients of such rewards (Li *et al.* 2016).

In an overview piece, Amy Gallo (2013) identifies six effective ways to manage and reward collective performance. Translated to the audience of this book, they suggest that public managers:

- **Set clear objectives** by bringing partners together before their collaborative journey begins to jointly define what success looks like. This creates value objectives and has a motivational effect.
- **Check in on progress** by regularly evaluating whether collective goals are being achieved, both in person and anonymously. Team members can grade progress through surveys, allowing managers to set actionables.
- **Use the full arsenal of rewards** by changing monetary rewards to substantively include collective performance. If they don't have that influence, public managers can use non-monetary rewards like awards, public recognition, and exposure to senior leadership.
- **Get to know their team** by spending time with individual members and the team as a whole, with the aim of finding out what they value and what drives them. Make an effort online and offline.
- **Focus on collaborative efforts** by addressing the team and their successes and drawbacks collectively. Public managers should reward collaborative behaviours such as helping others with their tasks.
- **Evaluate team performance** by conducting team reviews, for instance every six months, in addition to individual performance reviews. In such exercises, public managers should focus on team efforts only.

Sources: Ancona and Bresman 2007; Blenko *et al.* 2010; Gallo 2013; Li *et al.* 2016; Stevens and Campion 1994.

at their disposal. Institutional and legal frameworks and mandates help public managers, but they should not dominate. Establishing a collective drive for excellence and success is much more powerful.

- Second, targets, results, and outcomes have to be developed and established jointly, and continuously, if shared accountability is to be attained. Public managers play an important role here as drivers of collectiveness, sustained energy, fairness, and frequent interaction, in good times and in bad times.
- Third, timing is key. Public managers have to ensure that conditions, roles and responsibilities are laid out and agreed upon prior to the start of the process in order to avoid confusion and potential backing down by partners. For the partners to honour the arrangement, it has to be firmly in place and jointly embraced. This does not mean, however, that public managers should hammer out arrangements that are set in stone; circumstances may require that targets and outcomes are frequently reassessed.

As discussed in this chapter, in order to become effective collaborators, public managers need to possess and develop various skills and values, and display behaviours that are not necessarily taught in degree programmes, let alone incentivized in the organizational environments in which they are socialized. Negotiation, mediation, consultation, and communication are crucial skills for reconciling differing views, languages, and interests. It is the public manager's job to act as a bridge between partners in collaborative arrangements. This is why the case for tri-sector champions is strong. The 21st century public manager has to draw on the experiences of all three sectors, leverage on their strengths, and exert genuine and concerted effort to bring parties to the table who speak completely different languages and have historically pursued partly competing objectives.

What lies ahead

This chapter concludes our discussion on specific 21st century demands for public managers. Having discussed in detail seven of the key demands and the roles, values, and competencies they require, in the next and final chapter this book synthesizes its key observations to sketch a profile of the 21st century public manager. In addition, it outlines a roadmap for aspiring 21st century public managers to acquire that profile, and also for HR officers seeking to recruit, develop, and nurture such managers. The universalism of such a profile is critically assessed amid the key characteristics of governance regimes in different parts of the world. Finally, it sketches how public agencies and organizational environments enable 21st century public managers to flourish. After all, managers are only as strong as their environment allows them to be.

Chapter 12

The 21st Century Public Manager

This concluding chapter outlines the profile of the 21st century public manager – someone who has the ability to turn complex, emerging challenges into opportunities for public value creation. Even though this book is global in scope and ambition, and many 21st century trends and demands are global in nature, it is important to realize that such a profile can never be entirely universal.

The space for two-way stakeholder communication and horizontal networking behaviours may be more limited in authoritarian regimes than in vibrant democracies. In some contexts, traditional, conservative, and hierarchical traits of public managers may be more appreciated – and much harder to change – than in others. Major events may temporarily shift expectations towards public managers and re-emphasize qualities that seemed to have gone out of fashion.

Still, the overall trends detailed in this book all point towards the need for public managers to become more adaptive, networked, communicative, entrepreneurial, innovative, smart, and agile. These traits increasingly apply to public managers in all functions and roles. However, some managers will be more hardwired with these traits than others, or have more ability or talent to quickly learn and adapt to their changing environments.

With this in mind, smart recruitment, training, and management development practices will become even more important than they already are. Across the globe, public sectors aim to develop more strategic HRM practices while future-proofing their leadership programmes and competency frameworks (e.g., ABD 2016; PSD 2016). Such programmes and frameworks emphasize how practices and ideas from past decades will prove to be relevant in new ways, and need not all be devaluated and replaced (cf. Dickinson and Sullivan 2014: 54; Rhodes 2016).

This chapter is organized around three central questions:

- What does a 21st century public manager look like?
- How does one become, develop, and train a 21st century public manager?
- What do enabling organizational environments for such managers look like?

In formulating answers to these questions, various new questions emerge. After all, the journey of profiling, becoming, and producing 21st century public managers starts rather than ends with the final pages of this book. One thing is important for that journey to be a meaningful and successful one: (aspiring) public managers need a serious voice and 'agency' in shaping their own futures and the future of the public sector workforce, as studies from various countries show they feel left out of that conversation so far (Dickinson and Sullivan 2014; Needham and Mangan 2014). Let's now start our final conversation, and strive towards making it an inclusive one.

Five characteristics of a 21ˢᵗ century public manager

Many roles, skills, competencies, and values of a 21ˢᵗ century public manager have been discussed, contextualized, and contrasted in the various chapters of this book. I focus here on five key characteristics of 21ˢᵗ century public managers who are ready to face a VUCA world, displayed in Figure 12.1. In outlining these characteristics, I realize they are

FIGURE 12.1   Five key characteristics of 21ˢᵗ century public managers

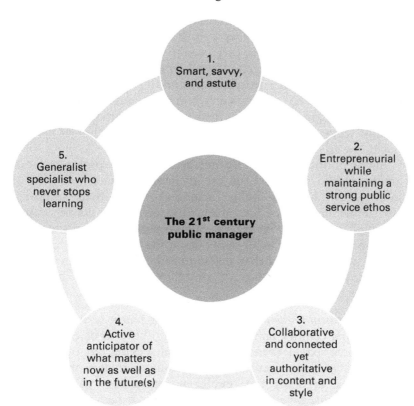

beleaguered with tensions, dilemmas, and questions. I list some of these questions at the end of each section.

I also take inspiration from other recent works on the 21st century public service and the future public sector workforce, some of which identify fairly similar or overlapping areas (Dickinson and Sullivan 2014; Hamidullah 2016; KPMG 2013; Needham and Mangan 2014, 2016; Noordegraaf 2015; 't Hart 2014b).

In order to readily engage a VUCA world, 21st century public managers will have to be all of the following.

1. *Smart, savvy, and astute*
   Twenty-first century public managers will not thrive in a VUCA world because of seniority, or because they were designated as important or powerful in the past. They cannot simply command respect and authority from their environment. They will only continue to gain such respect and authority by being *smart* – at least as smart as their various counterparts; *savvy* – in leveraging opportunities and technologies to outperform competitors and convince masters; and *astute* – in strategically securing support and funding from their various authorizing environments.

   Such public managers realize they are only as good as their environments allow them to be, so they have to 'mould' and 'play' their environments as well as they can. Rather than using either hard power or soft power skills, they need to use 'smart power' as Joseph Nye (2010: 147) has suggested, combining IQ (intelligence quotient), EQ (emotional intelligence quotient), and CQ (contextual intelligence quotient) (2010: 85). Smart, savvy, and astute public managers establish and maintain antennae in their various operating environments; in knowledge networks, peer institutions, and stakeholder networks (including adversarial ones); and in industries.

   But if political masters do not accept such a pro-active stance among public managers, or are themselves smarter, savvier, and more astute, how do public managers extend their authorizing environments and not just obediently serve their masters? Active sabotage is hardly to be praised. Should public managers temporarily de-prioritize their other networks at the risk of being 'out of the loop' later? Or should they invest considerable energy in confronting their political masters to demand the space needed to adequately co-create public value?

2. *Entrepreneurial while maintaining a strong public service ethos*
   Twenty-first century public managers also have to be entrepreneurial, to some extent even commercial, in seeking out opportunities and starting ventures across sectors to enhance their problem-solving capabilities. In doing this, public managers have to walk a fine line. They *must be entrepreneurial but cannot become full-blooded*

entrepreneurs chasing a limited group of profitable or 'easy' clients. Instead, they must smartly target certain segments of stakeholders in the early stages of new projects, pilots, and idea generation – early adaptors – without losing sight of accessibility for all segments of society at a later stage. Public managers need to be competent in differentiating between stakeholders to optimally achieve various objectives, and can emulate sophisticated marketing, survey, and sales techniques from their private sector counterparts.

By displaying entrepreneurial behaviour, 21st century public managers also leverage opportunities provided by cross-sectoral collaboration. They constantly seek out, recruit, and entice potential partners from within and outside government that may be able to add value to the problem-solving process. In doing so, they honestly and critically identify skills gaps that potential partners can fill, contributing to more diverse and effective teams.

How do public managers balance long-appreciated administrative virtues and values (of neutrality, stability, impartiality, and lawfulness) with entrepreneurial virtues and values (of innovation, profit, courage, and risk-taking) without crossing ethical lines or disadvantaging certain stakeholder segments? Which types of private sector behaviours can or should they emulate, and how should they translate these behaviours to adapt them to their own environments? Should public agencies increase recruitment from the private sector, especially at senior positions, given the mixed experiences in many countries so far?

3. *Collaborative and connected, yet authoritative in content and style*
    Twenty-first century public managers realize they won't get anything done by being hierarchical, siloed, protectionist, and monopolistic about defining problems and conceiving solutions. They have to be able to 'let go': to invite, enable, and allow others to participate in processes of public problem-solving, increasingly including regular citizens ('laymen'). At the same time, as long as we have formal government structures and elections, the formal authority, responsibility, and accountability for addressing social issues will largely remain with public managers and their political masters. Public managers can only successfully command *formal authority* and fulfil the obligations and mandates such authority entails if they are granted *informal authority* and legitimacy by their various partners. Informal authority and legitimacy have to be continuously earned through excellent performance; through enabling and energizing leadership; and through a sufficient display of expertise and content knowledge.
    It is far from easy to maintain a certain degree of control while simultaneously letting go. Stakeholders' expectations towards public managers will also be ambiguous and inconsistent. Convincing and genuine collaborative behaviours may be more powerful than

ever-tighter contracts and institutional accountability arrangements. To develop such behaviours, 21st century public managers invest in getting to know the structures, cultures, and worldviews of other sectors through exchanges, training, internships, and career switches.

How can public managers remain 'in charge' and 'let go' at the same time? How do they earn respect from partners they engage for skills and expertise they themselves so apparently lack? Which managerial styles will be most effective, and how much time do public managers have to find out what works and what doesn't?

4. *Active anticipator of what matters now and in the future(s)*
    On a daily basis, 21st century public managers must simultaneously manage the 'political scoring logic' in an era of never-ending news cycles while building multiple long-term scenarios and analytical models to anticipate VUCA events and super-wicked problems. They have to convincingly operate on various stages, both in the spotlight and behind the scenes. To retain respect and legitimacy from political masters, media, and stakeholders, they act decisively in the now and show to the outside world they are 'on top of things'. At the same time, they are constantly preparing for and anticipating multiple futures – through scenarios, simulations, and experimentations, and by advocating the need for reservoir capabilities in order to improve resilience.

    Twenty-first century public managers will find ways to connect both logics and timelines. They do so by showing political masters and other key stakeholders how investing in long-term planning and anticipation *will also help them to do better* in the 'now', to address and account for crises and scandals. In addition, they make the process of conducting foresight exercises accessible, meaningful, and inclusive, and tap into the opportunities that technology and crowdsourcing provide. They recognize and appreciate the differences between amateur and expert contributions, and communicate transparently about such differences to various stakeholders.

    What are the optimal amounts of staff and financial resources that public managers should dedicate to the 'present' versus the 'future'? How do they balance expert and amateur advice, and how do they translate highly technical, abstract, and 'far away' scenarios for impatient and pressured publics?

5. *Generalist specialist who never stops learning*
    Twenty-first century public managers have *both generic and specialist skills and competencies*. They are able to rapidly and frequently switch between roles, sectors, projects, networks, and issues. They go in-depth when necessary, mastering a dynamic set of skills such as developing social media platforms and campaigns, designing apps for service delivery that improve user experience, and designing and negotiating complex partnership contracts with a range of stakeholders. Mastering such a wide and dynamic range of skills

requires a mindset attuned to lifelong learning. This learning can take place through frequent executive courses (managerial and technical), internships, exchanges, and cross-sectoral job rotation.

'Generalist specialists' realize that their initial training will only partly determine where they will end up and how their careers will unfold. Twenty-first century public managers can start out as specialists while acquiring management and leadership skills through executive training during their careers, or can get a generalist degree that prepares them for a wide range of roles and then acquire technical skills through on-the-job modules. Despite fierce debates among HR specialists and public and private sector leaders in recent years, there is no consensus as to what is a more fruitful or strategic route. With the right mindset, both will be viable.

How do public managers negotiate substantial space and budget for learning and growth while also creating an enabling learning environment for others? How can they allow employees to make mistakes and learn from those mistakes in a pressured, performance-oriented operating environment?

Are the characteristics of the 21st century public manager universal?

Will public managers be able to acquire and enact these characteristics, regardless of whether they operate in the West, the Middle East, Asia, Africa, Latin America, or the Pacific? It is difficult to answer that question because no one knows how individual countries and regions will continue to develop, how their public sectors will respond to megatrends, and whether their responses will converge.

It is likely that public managers in liberal democratic environments will be more enabled to create space for collaboration, open innovation, and genuine stakeholder participation and crowdsourcing. Meanwhile, public managers in a context of traditional authority and respect (or fear) of seniority, and of government in general, may have considerably more leeway to swiftly execute much-needed reforms and scale up and roll out large-scale innovations. Such large-scale implementation and reform will also be more straightforward in centralized, unitary systems than in decentralized, federal systems, regardless of the specific political regime (Pollitt and Bouckaert 2011).

Still, it is hard to imagine that countries and regimes will be able – and allowed – to isolate themselves altogether from the trends and demands outlined in this book, given the speed at which they travel in an interconnected, globalized world. Even if they do, this may ultimately lead to suboptimal government performance. Consistent good performance, in turn, ultimately provides the legitimacy for public managers in any kind of system and regime.

Becoming, developing, training

How does one become a 21st century public manager? Are some people more talented or hardwired than others? And how do public sector organizations recruit, train, and develop 21st century public managers? These questions matter to ambitious (aspiring) public managers who seek to upgrade themselves; public managers who need to upgrade their teams or think strategically about their own succession and the staffing of their organizations; and HR managers who want to bring in and continue to develop 21st century public managers.

The design of training and management development (MD) programmes needs to take into account that a decade from now, typical public service careers will look dramatically different from today (Dickinson and Sullivan 2014: 17). Sector-switching and job-switching will increase, with five years in one organization considered a lifetime to younger generations (Lyons *et al.* 2015). While retaining and incentivizing high-potential employees ('high-potentials'), organizations will need to continuously invest just as much, or maybe even more, in senior employees who have to stay employed into their late 60s while staying motivated to walk the extra mile.

Thus, to produce maximal return on investment, training and development programmes need to smartly target both junior and senior high-potentials. This is even more important as newer generations consider investment in their future-readiness and career development through training programmes an increasingly important incentive for performing well and committing to their employer – in fact, for staying around at all (Hamidullah 2016). Trainee programmes and 'candidacy training' are important (Van Wart *et al.* 2015: 18), but organizations must also become more inventive in retaining high-potentials. Experience in various countries shows that many of these individuals leave within their first few years on the job for better opportunities elsewhere, or because of disappointment with a system that is not as 'new' and 'cool' as it brands itself.

In a comparative global study of senior civil servant training, Van Wart *et al.* (2015) note that expectations towards senior executives have risen in recent years. Public sectors are increasingly concerned with formulating key competencies and designing various types of training. Getting into the higher managerial echelons without a graduate degree is more or less impossible now, and a degree from an elite institution is no longer sufficient to rise through the ranks as it was one or two decades ago. To become 21st century public managers, let alone 'tri-sector athletes' (Lovegrove and Thomas 2013), employees need to pursue exchanges with other organizations, sectors, and networks, and upgrade both generic and specific skills and competencies based on frequent, critical assessments. To meet such dynamic lifelong learning demands, public management education has to evolve as Box 12.1 argues.

Box 12.1 The future of public management education

Do we need to drastically reform graduate and executive education programmes for public managers, or is the way in which they currently take shape sufficient for producing 21st century skills, competencies, and values? In my view, as argued throughout the book, we should aim to further update and upgrade existing frames, tools, and assumptions as times progress, and make the learning we offer more experiential *and* experimental.

For instance, the readings and frameworks we use all propagate 'collaboration' – but do we actually teach future managers *how* to collaborate, beyond the mandated group work so dreaded by most students? Similarly, do we optimally utilize opportunities for students to mix with their future counterparts from other sectors, by offering exciting combined modules, projects, and internships with programmes in business administration, law, social work, economics, computer science, marketing, and engineering?

Do we pay sufficient attention to 'skills' in general – sometimes looked down upon in academic environments – let alone specific new skills such as designing social media campaigns, video-editing, prototyping policies and services derived through open innovation, and big-data analytics? No school or programme can do everything, but given the rapidly changing environment of public managers and of higher education itself, public management education also needs to become 21st century proof.

Indeed, while *training is important, experience is king*. Inspired by Van Wart *et al.* (2015: 17), who distinguish five key factors in enhancing experience, I suggest that aspiring 21st century public managers take into account the following:

- The amount of time spent in the field or in a specific agency remains key (with the average time spent in the same function, role, or agency likely to continuously decrease).
- While experience may be a good teacher in itself, this is not so much the case in dysfunctional systems, creating serious issues for HR managers in such systems (see Box 12.2).
- (Reverse) mentoring provides hands-on opportunities to experience how systems operate, and identify skills gaps and training and development needs of individuals and teams.
- Rotational opportunities and experiences – including (overseas) study trips, 'secondments' to the political, private sector, or non-profit domain, and participation in peer networks and long-term experiential training programmes – all widen the views of (aspiring) public managers, challenge current assumptions, and provide exposure to potential collaborators, competitors, or adversaries in other sectors and countries.

Box 12.2 Can aspiring managers gain 'good' experience in a 'bad' environment?

What do you do when you're ambitious but your bosses and subordinates are incompetent, lazy, and perhaps even unethical? Or when you and your team members are passionate about creating value, and believe you have the skills to do so, but operate in a dysfunctional institutional and political environment? Do you adjust your ambitions and motivations downwards, do you 'run' (if you have realistic options to pursue something better), or do you simply give up? Do you try to bring in external consultants, the World Bank or OECD, or a development aid agency? Or do you lobby for training, support, and advice?

There are no easy answers to these questions, but they come up all too often when I teach executive programmes, graduate classes, or induction training to talented, passionate new hires to a public agency in developing settings. For some, getting a week of attention, reassurance, and exposure to new ways of thinking and some practical tools may provide the necessary nourishment to continue to fight their uphill battle. Also, providing a contrasting environment and an image of 'how things could be' may strengthen their resolve to persistently address dysfunctionalities back home.

At the same time, these thoughts may very well be naïve and somewhat self-congratulatory. Changing dysfunctional systems and institutions takes decades and requires a critical mass of public managers, political leaders, and stakeholders. Still, one has to start somewhere. Planting the seeds of change and future possibilities contributes to changing mindsets, one at a time. HR managers and personnel directors are particularly important players in such contexts. Most likely, their room to manoeuvre will be constrained by impermeable tenure systems that were established a long time ago. Thus, in addition to training high-potentials, it may be particularly effective to invest their energy in those senior employees who can still be motivated to challenge and improve themselves.

- Critical, transparent, and high-quality feedback and appraisal systems that combine qualitative and quantitative assessment, and include individual and collective exercises and indicators, produce more competent and conscious managers.

Clearly, it is hard to provide meaningful, stimulating experiences to develop better public managers in dysfunctional, chaotic, and corrupt environments. In such settings, training and development of individuals will often be less of a priority than improving institutional features. Still, managers in such settings have much to gain from investing in their high-potentials, as long-term change will come from individual employees and their mindsets at least as much as from externally enforced and overly generic structures and templates, albeit incrementally.

Enabling organizations

These observations bring us to the final question of this book. Managers do not operate in isolation from the organizations and collaborations that employ, enable, and direct them, so what do enabling environments of 21st century public managers look like? What are the characteristics of high-performing, '21st century-proof' public organizations? Logically, such characteristics would mirror many of the characteristics managers need to be able to flourish: producing public service excellence requires excellence in both people and institutions.

In a recent essay, 't Hart (2014b: 33–34) outlined '10 golden characteristics' of the 21st century public organization, shown in Box 12.3. These characteristics align well with the profile of the 21st century public manager as construed throughout this book. They should be viewed as desirable, rather than easily attainable, traits, as each public organization is subject to its own unique constraints and conditions. Demands and expectations will continue to increase, and no organization is static, let alone settled and perfected.

Looking ahead

A little over a decade ago, Hugh Compston published a book titled *King Trends and the Future of Public Policy*. Compston (2006) outlined a number of big global trends and sketched how they would affect the practice of public policy in Europe in the years to come. Some of the trends Compston included resemble the megatrends central to this book: information and communication technology, increasing mobility, population ageing, climate change, and rising levels of education. Other, more specific trends that Compston examined are more implicitly featured in this book, while still others – biotechnology, military technology, sexual liberalization – are not immediately relevant for the broad audience of public managers I intend to reach.

As with many books that aspire to look ahead, some of Compston's predictions were more accurate and relevant than others for the present day. Of course, nobody knows exactly what the future will hold. Moreover, the past two centuries teach us that futurologists and scenario planners are sometimes very accurate in predicting key trends but often less accurate in detailing the responses and behaviours from individuals and organizations. Given these caveats, how will public managers view this book five or ten years from now? Most likely, the trends and drivers detailed here – and the demands they put on public managers – will indeed turn out to play a role in their professional lives. Will they play *the* most important role? Perhaps not always, or for everyone.

Most importantly, though, I hope that the rich reservoir of cases and examples, and the critical, sometimes unorthodox, views of roles,

Box 12.3 Ten golden characteristics of the 21st century public organization

1. **Value-driven:** it articulates what it stands for and ensures its public value proposition is supported by political-administrative principals, public accountability forums, and societal stakeholders.
2. **Process-conscious, results-oriented:** it systematically targets fulfilment of its societal goals while complying with judicial process norms and principles of integrity. When these two value clusters *compete*, it arrives at transparent choices through consultation with principals and forums.
3. **Cost-conscious:** it is conscious of the fact it is working with public money, and continuously builds efficient and transparent processes while keeping control functions proportional: the mission is central, and internal bureaucracy is monitored and mitigated.
4. **Self-consciously serving:** it serves democratically legitimized actors, and service delivery meets the needs, contexts, and interaction preferences of clients. At the same time, it is conscious of its own responsibilities in safeguarding public interests and quality of governance.
5. **Time sensitive:** it communicates in 'real time' with clients and society, and delivers 'just in time' when principals need them to. At the same time, it ensures that 'looking back' and 'looking ahead' – and middle and long-term considerations – feature consistently in policy deliberations.
6. **Smart:** it has adequate knowledge management structures, has content knowledge as well as process knowledge, and acquires and shares knowledge wherever it is available.
7. **Learning:** it has a culture in which evaluation and (self-)reflection are central, it continuously focuses on improvement, and it considers errors as data and discussion points. Management stimulates and protects that culture, particularly when the agency faces external (accountability) pressures.
8. **Flat:** its operational structure is as flat as possible, aimed at maximizing latitude for its professional members. The managerial structure serves operational processes as much as possible and ensures that decision-making powers are located alongside the relevant expertise.
9. **Porous:** it creates as few 'walls' as possible between 'inside' and 'outside', it actively conducts boundary-spanning, and it is a desired and reliable partner for other organizations within and beyond the public sectors. It is transparent, accessible, and interactive.
10. **Able to separate 'bulk' from 'tailored' tasks:** it has a thought-through framework to separate 'simple' from 'complex' tasks and activities, and uses advanced IT capabilities to produce optimal client experiences in simple activities while prioritizing professional judgement and effectiveness in complex activities. Management accounts for the framework and its effects on an annual basis.

Source: 't Hart 2014b: 33–34.

competencies, and values featured in this book will prove helpful to public managers trying to make sense of a VUCA world, and will assist aspiring public managers in preparing for an unknown future. As I've tried to convey throughout, I don't believe in easy answers or ready-made, 'cookie-cutter' solutions. Public managers will have to take from this book what they find most useful, and experience the excitement and discomfort of viewing existing issues differently or being confronted with entirely new issues and perspectives. I've done my part. The rest is up to you. The journey starts here.

Bibliography

Aberbach, J. D., Putnam, R. D., & Rockman, B. A. (1981). *Bureaucrats and politicians in western democracies*. Cambridge: Harvard University Press.

ABD (2016). *Nieuw Publiek Leiderschap*. Den Haag: Algemene Bestuursdienst.

Acker, J. (1990). Hierarchies, jobs, bodies: A theory of gendered organizations. *Gender & Society*, 4(2), 139–158.

Adams, G. B., & Balfour, D. L. (2009). *Unmasking administrative evil*. London: SAGE.

Adams, S. J. (2000). Generation X: How understanding this population leads to better safety programs. Professional Safety, 45, 26–29.

2011). *Asian Development Outlook – 2011 Update: Preparing for Demographic Transition*. Available at: http://www.adb.org/publications/asian-development-outlook-2011-update-preparing-demographic-transition

ADB (2013). *Asian Development Outlook – 2013: Asia's Energy Challenge*. Available at: http://adb.org/sites/default/files/pub/2013/ado2013.pdf

Agranoff, R. (2006). Inside collaborative networks: Ten lessons for public managers. *Public Administration Review*, 66(s1), 56–65.

Alford, John & O'Flynn, Janine (2012). *Rethinking public service delivery: Managing with external providers*. New York: Palgrave Macmillan.

Allen, T. D., Poteet, M. L., & Russell, J. E. (1998). Attitudes of managers who are more or less career plateaued. *The Career Development Quarterly*, 47(2), 159–172.

Amankwah-Amoah, Joseph & Zhang, Hongxu (2015). "Tales from the grave": What can we learn from failed international companies? *Foresight*, 17(5), 528–541.

Anakin L, Brown A. J., Cassematis P. (2008). *Whistleblowing in the Australian public sector: Enhancing the theory and practice of internal witness management in public sector organisations*. Canberra: The Australian National University E Press.

Ancona, D.G. and H. Bresman (2007). X-Teams: How to Build Teams that Lead, Innovate, and Succeed. Boston, MA: Harvard Business School Press.

Andersen, L. B., Eriksson, T., Kristensen, N., & Pedersen, L. H. (2012). Attracting public service motivated employees: How to design compensation packages. *International Review of Administrative Sciences*, 78(4), 615–641.

Andrews, Matt, Pritchett, Lant, & Woolcock, Michael (2016). 'Managing Your Authorizing Environment in a PDIA Process' Centre for International Development at Harvard University Working Papers. Available at: http://bsc.cid.harvard.edu/files/bsc/files/authorizing_environ_cid_wp_312.pdf

Andrews, Matt (2013). *The limits of institutional reform*. Cambridge: Harvard University Press.

Andrews, R. (2013, January). 'Performance feedback and incremental organizational learning: Does social capital make a difference?' in *Academy of management proceedings*. Academy of Management, Vol. 2013, No. 1, p. 16191.

Angira, Z. (2013). 'Kenya Launches e-center to cut red tape on services', see: http://www.africareview.com/News/Kenya-launches--e-centre-to-cut-red-tape/-/979180/2065020/-/q9hofuz/-/index.html

Ansell, C., A. Boin, & A. Keller (2010), Managing Transboundary Crises: Identifying the Building Blocks of an Effective Response System. 18 (4): 195–207.

Ansell, C. and Gash, A. (2007) Collaborative Governance in Theory and Practice. Journal of Public Administration Research and Theory, 18: 534–571.

Ansell, C. and Jacob, T. (Ed). 2014. Public Innovation through Collaboration and Design. London, UK: Routledge.

Arendt, H. (1963). Eichmann in Jerusalem. A Report on the Banality of Evil. New York: Penguin.

Arestis, Philip, Georgios Chortareas, Evangelia Desli and Theodore Pelagidis (2012). Cambridge Journal of Economics, 36, 481–493.

Arestis, P. (2012). Fiscal policy: a strong macroeconomic role. *Review of Keynesian Economics*, 1(1), 93–108.

Armstrong-Stassen, M., & Ursel, N. D. (2009). Perceived organizational support, career satisfaction, and the retention of older workers. *Journal of Occupational and Organizational Psychology*, 82(1), 201–220.

Argyris, C. 1982. Reasoning, Learning, and Action: Individual and Organizational. San Francisco: Jossey-Bass.

Argyris, C., Schön, D.A. 1978. Organizational Learning: a Theory of Action Perspective. Reading, Mass.: Addison-Wesley.

Argyris, C., Schön, D.A. 1996. Organizational Learning II: Theory, Method and Practice. Reading, Mass.: Addison-Wesley.

Asad M. (2015). 'Facebook Posts Land Civi Servant in Trouble', *DAWN* see: http://www.dawn.com/news/1198494

Austin, Tom (2012). 'Viewpoint: Gartner on the changing nature of work' *BBC News*. Available at: http://www.bbc.com/news/business-16968125

Gillard, J. (2012). *Australia in the Asian Century: White Paper*. Australian Government.

Australian Government (2015). Australian public service better practice guide for big data. *Commonwealth of Australia*

Australian Public Service Commission (2012). 'Guidance on Making Public Comment and Participating Online', *Australian Government* see: http://www.apsc.gov.au/publications-and-media/circulars-and-advices/2012/circular-20121

Avey, J.B., Wernsing, T.S., & Palanski, M.E. (2012). Exploring the process of ethical leadership: The mediating role of employee voice and psychological ownership. Journal of Business Ethics, 107, 21–34.

Avey, J. B., Palanski, M. E., & Walumbwa, F. O. (2011). When leadership goes unnoticed: The moderating role of follower self-esteem on the relationship between ethical leadership and follower behavior. *Journal of Business Ethics*, 98(4), 573–582.

AXS (2016). 'AXS Station', see: http://www.axs.com.sg/help_axsStationFAQ.php

Badaracco, J. L. (1997). *Defining moments. When managers must choose between right and right*. Cambridge: Harvard Business School Press.

Baetens, T. (2013). De ambtenaar als 'frontlijnwerker' [The civil servant as frontline worker]. *Academie voor overheidscommunicatie*, April, 1–4.

Baldissin, N., Bettiol, S., Magrin, S., & Nonino, F. (2013). *Business game-based learning in management education*. Lulu.com.

Balia B., Bertok J., Turkama A., Van Delden S. J., & Lewis C. W. (2007). Reality check: Practitioners' Take on institutionalising public service ethics. *Public Integrity*, 10(1), 53–64.

Banks A., Bayliss J., Hipkiss S., & Jones S. (2014). 'Government Whistleblowing Policies', *National Audit Office*

Barber, B. R. (2013). *If mayors ruled the world: Dysfunctional nations, rising cities*. New Haven: Yale University Press.

Barber M., Lvey A., & Mendonca L. (2007). 'Global Trends Affecting the Public Sector', *Deloitte*

Barber, M., Moffit, A., & Kihn, P. (2010). *Deliverology 101: A field guide for educational leaders*. Thousand Oaks, CA: Corwin Press.

Barber, M. (2015). *How to run a government. So that citizens benefit and taxpayers don't go crazy*. London: Penguin.

Barrett, K., & Greene, R. (2008). Grading the states: The mandate to measure. *Governing, 21*(6), 24–95.

Barry D. (2015). 'Government to Issue New Guidelines on Social Media Use by Civil Servants, PN Reacts', *The Malta Independent* see: http://www.independent.com.mt/articles/2015-12-10/local-news/Government-to-issue-new-guidelines-on-social-media-use-by-civil-servants-6736150219

Bason, C. (2010). *Leading public sector innovation: Co-creating for a better society*. Bristol: Policy Press, pp. 1–17.

Batey, M. (2008). *Brand meaning*. London: Routledge

Bauerlein, M. (2008). The Dumbest Generation: How the Digital Age Stupefies Young Americans and Jeopardizes Our Future(Or, Don 't Trust Anyone Under 30). New York: Penguin Group.

BBC (2013). 'Kenya Launches Huduma e-Center to Cut Bureaucracy', see: http://www.bbc.com/news/world-africa-24855993

BBC News (2016). 'Kids Company Closure: What Went Wrong', see: BBC http://www.bbc.com/news/uk-33788415

Beechler, Schon, and Ian C. Woodward (2009). The global "war for talent". Journal of International Management 15 (3): 273–285

Behn, R.D. (2008). Measurement is Rarely Enough. *Behn's Public Management Report*: 5(9).

Behn, R.D. (2014). What Performance Management is and is not. *Behn's Public Management Report* 12(1).

Bekkers, V. (2009). Flexible information infrastructures in Dutch e-government collaboration arrangements: Experiences and policy implications. *Government Information Quarterly, 26*(1), 60–68.

Benington, J., & Moore, M. H. (2011). *Public Value: Theory and Practice*, Basingstoke: Palgrave.

Bennett, N., & Lemoine, J. (2014). What VUCA really means for you. *Harvard Business Review, 92*(1/2).

Bertot, John Carlo, Jaeger, Paul T., & Grimes, Justin M. (2012). Promoting transparency and accountability through ICTs, social media, and collaborative e-government. *Transforming Government: People, Process and Policy, 6*(1), 78–91.

Berman, E., J. West and A. Cava. 1994, Ethics management in municipal governments and large firms, Administration & Society, Vol. 26 No. 2, pp. 185–203.

Bessant, T.J. and Pavitt, K. (2005): Managing Innovation. London: Wiley and Sons. 3rd edition.

Biggs (2016), web source: https://www.gpstrategies.com/blog/reverse-mentoring

Bilgin, Pinar (2004). From 'rogue' to 'failed' States? The fallacy of short-termism. *Politics, 24*(3), 169–180.

Blenko, M. W., Mankins, M. C., & Rogers, P. (2010). Decide & deliver: 5 steps to breakthrough performance in your organization. Boston: Harvard Business School Press.

Bode, Ingo & Brandsen, Taco (2014). State-third sector partnerships: A short overview of key issues in the debate. *Public Management Review*, 16(8), 1055–1066.

Boin, A., & t' Hart, P. (2000). 'Institutional crises and reforms in policy sectors' in *Government institutions: Effects, changes and normative foundations*. Netherlands: Springer, pp. 9–31.

Boin, A., t' Hart, P. & McConnell, A. (2009). Crisis exploitation: Political and policy impacts of framing contests. *Journal of European Public Policy*, 16(1), 81–106.

Boin, A., McConnell, A. & 't Hart P. (2008). *Governing after crises. The politics of investigation, accountability, and learning*. Cambridge: Cambridge University Press.

Boin, A., & Lodge, M. (2016). Designing resilient institutions for transboundary crisis management. A time for public administration. *Public Administration*, 94(2), 289–298.

Boin, A., & Van Eeten, M. J. G. (2013). The resilient organization. *Public Management Review*, 15(3), 429–445.

Boin, A., 't Hart, P., McConnell, A., and Preston, T. (2010) "Leadership style, crisis response and blame management: the case of hurricane Katrina." Public Administration. 88 (3): 706 – 723.

Boin, A., McConnell, A. and 't Hart, P. (2008) Governing after Crisis: The Politics of Investigation, Accountability and Learning. Cambridge, UK: Cambridge University Press.

Borgatti, S. P., & Cross, R. (2003). A relational view of information seeking and learning in social networks. *Management Science*, 49(4), 432–445.

Borins, S. (2006). 'The Challenge of Innovating in Government', *IBM Center for The Business of Government*.

Borins, S. F. (2014). *The persistence of innovation in government*. Washington, D.C.: Brookings Institute Press.

Bouckaert, G., & Halligan, J. (2008). *Managing performance. international comparisons*. London: Routledge.

Bourgon, J. (2011). *A new synthesis of public administration: serving in the 21st century*. Montréal: McGill-Queen's Press-MQUP, Vol. 81.

Boutellier, H. (2004). *The safety utopia*. Netherlands: Springer.

Bovens, M. (1996). The integrity of the managerial state. *Journal of Contingencies and Crisis Management*, 4(3), 125–132.

Bovens, M., Goodin, R. & Schillemans, T. (2014). *Oxford Handbook of Public Accountability*. Oxford: Oxford University Press.

Bovens, M., & Wille, A. (2010). The education gap in participation and its political consequences. *Acta Politica*, 45(4), 393–422.

Bovens, M., Schillemans, T., & t' Hart, P. (2008). Does public accountability work? An assessment tool. *Public Administration*, 86(1), 225–242.

Bowman, J. S., West, J. P., Berman, M., & Van Wart, M. (2016). *The professional edge: Competencies in public service*. London: Routledge.

Bowman, J. S., & West, J. P. (2015). Ethics Management and Training. In N. M. Ricucci (Ed.) *Public personnel management*. London and New York: Routledge, pp. 213–227.

Boyd, Danah (2011). Dear voyeur, meet flâneur ... sincerely, social media. *Surveillance and Society*, 8(4), 505–507.

Boyer, Eric, David M. Van Slyke, & Juan Rogers (2016). An empirical examination of public involvement in public-private partnerships: Qualifying the benefits of public involvement in PPPs. *Journal of Public Administration, Research and Theory*, 26(1), 45–61.

Boyer, Eric J., David M. Van Slyke, and Juan D. Rogers. 2016. An Empirical Examination of Public Involvement in Public–Private Partnerships: Qualifying the Benefits of Public Involvement in PPPs. 26(1): 45–61.

Bozeman, B. and G. Kingsley. 1998. "Risk culture in public and private organizations", Public Administration Review, Vol. 58, 393–407.

Bozeman, B. (2004). All Organizations are Public. Bridging Public and Private Organizational Theories. 2nd ed. Frederick: Beard Books.

Bozeman, B., & Feeney, M. K. (2007). Toward a useful theory of mentoring a conceptual analysis and critique. *Administration & Society*, 39(6), 719–739.

Bozeman, B., & Feeney, M. K. (2008). Mentor matching: A "goodness of fit" model. *Administration & Society*, 40 (5): 465–482.

Bozeman, B., & Feeney, M. K. (2009). Public management mentoring: What affects outcomes? *Journal of Public Administration Research and Theory*, 19(2), 427–452.

Bozeman, B., & Ponomariov, B. (2009). Sector switching from a business to a government job: Fast-Track career or fast track to nowhere? *Public Administration Review*, 69(1), 77–91.

Beser, S. G. (2011). Pocket primer of comparative and combined foresight methods. *Foresight*, 13(2), 79–96.

Brandsen, T., Boogers, M., & Tops, P. (2006). Soft governance, hard consequences: The ambiguous status of unofficial guidelines. *Public Administration Review*, 66(4), 546–553.

Brandsen, Taco & Honingh, Marlies (2016). 'Distinguishing different types of coproduction: a conceptual analysis based on the classical definitions' *Public Administration Review*, 76(3), 427–435.

Brandsen, Taco & Pestoff, Victor (2006). Co-Production, the third sector and the delivery of public services: an introduction. *Public Management Review*, 8(4), 493–501.

Brandsen, Taco, van de Donk, Wim & Putters, Kim (2007). Griffins or chameleons? Hybridity as a permanent and inevitable characteristic of the third sector. *International Journal of Public Administration*, 28(9–10), 749–765.

Brans, M., & Peters, B. G. (Eds.). (2012). *Rewards for high public office in Europe and North America*. London: Routledge.

Brändström, A. (2016), Crisis, Accountability and Blame Management Strategies and Survival of Political Office-Holders. Utrecht: USBO.

Brändström, A. and Kuipers, S. (2003) "From 'Normal Incidents' to Political Crisis: Understanding the Selective Politicization of Policy Failures." Government and Opposition 38 (3): 279–305.

Bratton, D., & Candy, V. (2013). Federal government ethics: Social media. *International Journal of Management & Information Systems (Online)*, 17(3), 175.

Braun, L. (2012). Social media and public opinion. *Master's Thesis, Universitat de València, Valencia*.

Brecher, J. (1993). Global village or global pillage. *The Nation*, 257, 685–688.

Brenner, S.N. 1992, Ethics programs and their dimensions, Journal of Business Ethics. 11 (5): 391–399.

Breslauer, G. W. (2002). *Gorbachev and Yeltsin as leaders.* Cambridge: Cambridge University Press.

Brewer, G. A., & Selden, S. C. (2000). Why elephants gallop: Assessing and predicting organizational performance in federal agencies. *Journal of Public Administration Research and Theory*, 10(4), 685–712.

Briscoe, J. P., & Hall, D. T. (2006). The interplay of boundaryless and protean careers: Combinations and implications. *Journal of Vocational Behavior*, 69(1), 4–18.

Briscoe, J. P., Hall, D. T., & DeMuth, R. L. F. (2006). Protean and boundaryless careers: An empirical exploration. *Journal of Vocational Behavior*, 69(1), 30–47.

Britton, D. M. (2000). The epistemology of the gendered organization. Gender and Society, 14(3), 418–434.

Kharas, Homi & Geoffrey, Gertz (2010). The New Global Middle Class: A Cross-Over from West to East, In: Li, C (Ed.) "China's Emerging Middle Class: Beyond Economic Transformation", Washington, DC: Brookings Institution Press

Brooks, J. (2014). 'Uber, Lyft Fallout: Taxi Rides Plunge in San Francisco', *KQED News* see: http://ww2.kqed.org/news/09/17/2014/taxi_rides_san_francisco

Brown, A. J., Vandekerckhove, W., & Dreyfus, S. (2014). The Relationship between Transparency, Whistleblowing, and Public Trust. In Research Handbook on Transparency (pp. 30–58). United Kingdom: Edward Elgar.

Brown M. (2014). 'Edward Snowden - the True Story Behind the NSA Leaks', *The Telegraph* see: http://www.telegraph.co.uk/culture/film/11185627/Edward-Snowden-the-true-story-behind-his-NSA-leaks.html

Brown, M. E., Treviño, L. K., & Harrison, D. A. (2005). Ethical leadership: A social learning perspective for construct development and testing. *Organizational Behavior and Human Decision Processes*, 97(2), 117–134.

Brown, Trevor L., Matthew Potoski, & David M. Van Slyke (2016). Managing complex contracts: A theoretical approach. *Journal of Public Administration, Research and Theory*, 26(2), 294–308.

Brown, Trevor L., Potoski, Matthew, Van Slyke, David M. (2006). Managing public service contracts: Aligning values, institutions, and markets. *Public Administration Review* 66(3), 323–331.

Brownlow, L., Merriam, C. E., & Gulick, L. (1937). Report of the president's committee on administrative management. In Hyde, AC, Parkers, SJ, & Shafritz, JM and Russell (eds), *Classics of public administration*. Boston: Cengage Learning, pp. 99–103.

Bruijn, H. D., & Dicke, W. (2006). Strategies for safeguarding public values in liberalized utility sectors. *Public Administration*, 84(3), 717–735.

Bryson, J. M. (2004). What to do when stakeholders matter: Stakeholder identification and analysis techniques. *Public Management Review*, 6(1), 21–53.

Bryson, J. M., Crosby, B. C., & Stone, M. M. (2015). Designing and implementing cross-sector collaborations: Needed and challenging. *Public Administration Review*, 75(5), 647–663.

Bryson, John M. (2010). The future of public and non-profit strategic planning in the united states. *Public Administration Review*, 70(1), 255–267.

Bryson, John M., Crosby, Barbara C., Stone, Melissa Middleton (2015). Designing and implementing cross-sector collaborations: Needed and challenging. *Public Administration Review*, 75(5), 647–663.

Buelens, M., & Van den Broeck, H. (2007). An analysis of differences in work motivation between public and private sector organizations. *Public Administration Review*, 67(1), 65–74.

Burke, R. J., & Cooper, C. L. (2006). The human resources revolution. Oxford: Elsevier.

Burke, R. (2006). Why leaders fail: Exploring the dark side. *International Journal of Manpower*, 27(1), 91–100.

Burmeister, K. (2008). *Megatrends*. Köln: Z_Punkt GmbH The Foresight Company.

Burns, C., Barton, K., and Kerby, S. (2012). The State of Diversity in Today's Workforce. As Our Nation Becomes More Diverse So Too Does Our Workforce. Washington DC: Center for American Progress.

Bushman, B. J., Baumeister, R. F., Thomaes, S., Ryu, E., Begeer, S., & West, S. G. (2009). Looking again, and harder, for a link between low self-esteem and aggression. *Journal of Personality*, 77(2), 427–446.

Bysted, R., & Jesperson, K. R. (2013). Exploring managerial mechanisms that influence innovative work behaviour: Comparing private and public employees. *Public Management Review*, 16(2), 217–241.

Cabinet Office (2014): https://www.gov.uk/government/publications/social-media-guidance-for-civil-servants/social-media-guidance-for-civil-servants

Cabinet Office and Civil service (2014). Social Media Guidance for Civil Servants: October 2014', see: https://www.gov.uk/government/publications/social-media-guidance-for-civil-servants/social-media-guidance-for-civil-servants

Caiden, G. E. (2001). Administrative reform. *Public Administration and Public Policy*, 94, 655–668.

Caillier, J. G. (2016). Do Teleworkers Possess Higher Levels of Public Service Motivation? *Public Organization Review*, 1–16: 461–476.

Caillier, J. G. (2011). Are teleworkers less likely to report leave intentions in the united states federal government than non-teleworkers are? *American Review of Public Administration*. Published online ahead of print. doi:10.1177/0275074011425084.

Caillier, J. G. (2012). Impact of telework on work motivation in a U.S. federal government agency. American Review of Public Administration, 42(4),461–480.

Caluwe, C. D., & Van Dooren, W. (2013, June). Do organizations matter? A multilevel analysis explaining perceptions of organizational performance. In: *11th Public Management Conference, Madison, Wisconsin*, pp. 1–22.

Cameron, K. S., & Quinn, R. E. (1989). *Diagnosing and changing organizational culture: Based on the competing values framework*. San Francisco: Jossey Bass.

Camm, T. W. (2014), "The Dark Side of Leadership: Dealing with a Narcissistic Boss". Mining Engineering. Paper 2. http://digitalcommons.mtech.edu/mine_engr/2

Campbell, D. A., Lambright, K. T., & Wells, C. J. (2014). Looking for friends, fans, and followers? Social media use in public and nonprofit human services. *Public Administration Review*, 74(5), 655–663.

Cankar, S. S., & Petkovsek, V. (2013). Private and public sector innovation and the importance of cross-sector collaboration. *The Journal of Applied Business Research*, 29(6), 1597–1606.

Carlin B. (2009). 'Civil Servants to Get Own Facebook Site So They Can Gossip Without Fear of Public Exposure and Ridicule', MailOnline: http://www.

dailymail.co.uk/news/article-1199089/Civil-servants-1m-Facebook-site-gossip-fear-public-exposure-ridicule.html

Cascio, W. F. (2000). Managing a virtual workplace. *The Academy of Management Executive, 14*(3), 81–90.

Castells, Manuel and Cardoso, Gustavo (2005). eds. The Network Society: From Knowledge to Policy. Washington, DC: Johns Hopkins Center for Transatlantic Relations.

Castells, M., & Cardoso, G. (Eds.). (2006). *The network society: From knowledge to policy.* Center for Transatlantic Relations, Paul H. Nitze School of Advanced International Studies, Johns Hopkins University, pp. 3–23.

Caulkin, S. (2015). Have we created an unachievable myth of leadership? Financial Times, 7 December 2015.

CBC News (2015). 'Donald Trump emphasizes plans to build 'real' wall at Mexico border', see: http://www.cbc.ca/news/world/donald-trump-emphasizes-plans-to-build-real-wall-at-mexico-border-1.3196807

Century Governance. Available at: http://www.undp.org/content/undp/en/home/librarypage/capacity-building/Stewardship.html

Cels, S. and J. Arensman (2007). Dat hoort u mij niet zeggen. Hoe politici u de waarheid voorspiegelen [That's not what you heard me say. How politicians offer you the truth]. Amsterdam: Bert Bakker.

Chao, G. T., Walz, P., & Gardner, P. D. (1992). Formal and informal mentorships: A comparison on mentoring functions and contrast with nonmentored counterparts. *Personnel Psychology, 45*(3), 619–636.

Charles, M. B., W. Dicke, J. Koppenjan, & N. F. Ryan (2007). Public values and safeguarding mechanisms in infrastructure policies: A conceptual and theoretical exploration. Annual Conference of the International Research Society for Public Management. Potsdam.

Charness, N., & Czaja, S. J. (2006). Older Worker Training: What We Know and Don't Know. # 2006–22. *AARP.*

Chaudhuri, S., & Ghosh, R. (2012). Reverse mentoring a social exchange tool for keeping the boomers engaged and millennials committed. *Human Resource Development Review, 11*(1), 55–76.

Chen, Chung-An, & Chih-Wei Hsieh. (2015). Does pursuing external incentives compromise public service motivation? Comparing the effects of job security and high pay. *Public Management Review, 17*(8), 1190–1213.

Cherry M. A. (2012). 'Virtual Whistleblowing', *54 South Texas Law Review, Saint Louis University School of Law Legal Studies Paper No. 2013–19.*

Chesbrough, Henry (2003) Open Innovation: The New Imperative for Creating and Profiting from Technology. Harvard Business School Press, Boston.

Chong, D., & Druckman, J. N. (2007). A theory of framing and opinion formation in competitive elite environments. *Journal of Communication, 57*(1), 99–118.

Christensen, T. (2012). Post-NPM and changing public governance. *Meiji Journal of Political Science and Economics, 1*(1), 1–11.

Christensen, T., & Lærgreid, P. (2001). *New Public Management: the Transformation of Ideas and Practice.* Aldershot: Ashgate

Christensen, T. and P. Lægreid (2007). The Whole-of-Government Approach to Public Sector Reform. Public Administration Review, 67 (6): 1059–1066

Christiansen, J., & Sabroe, R. (2015). 'Innovation Labs as Public Change Agents', *Public Sector Digest.*

Christensen, C. M. (1997). *The innovator's dilemma when new technologies cause great firms to fail.* Cambridge, MA: Harvard Business School Press.

Chun, Y. H., & Rainey, H. G. (2005). Goal ambiguity and organizational performance in US federal agencies. *Journal of Public Administration Research and Theory*, 15(4), 529–557.

Cities Alliance (2014). *Managing systems of secondary systems. Policy responses in international development.* London: Bookworx.

Ciulla, J. B. (2004). The relationship of ethics to effectiveness in leadership. In Sternberg, R. J., Antonakis, J., & Cianciolo, A. T (eds) *The nature of leadership.* Thousand Oaks, CA, London and New Dehli: Sage Publications, pp. 302–27.

CNN (2011). 'Homeland Security Chief Cancels Costly Virtual Border Fence', see: with "long radar and high resolution cameras". Available at: http://edition.cnn.com/2011/US/01/14/border.virtual.fence/

CNN (2015). '5 things to know about China's 'Inconvenient Truth'. Available at: http://edition.cnn.com/2015/03/02/asia/china-smog-documentary/

Coates, Joseph F. (2010). The future of foresight – A US perspective. *Technological Forecasting and Social Change*, 77(9), 1428–1437.

Coffey, John W., & Hoffman, Robert R. (2003). Knowledge modelling for the preservation of institutional memory. *Journal of Knowledge Management*, 7(3), 38–52.

Collins, D. (2011). *Business ethics: How to design and manage ethical organizations.* Hoboken: John Wiley & Sons.

Collm, A., & Schedler, K. (2013). Strategies for introducing organizational innovations to public service organizations. *Public Management Review*, 16(1), 140–161.

Comfort, L.K., A. Boin and C.C. Demchack. 2010. Designing Resilience: Preparing for Extreme Events. Pittsburgh, PA: Pittsburgh University Press.

Commissioner for Public Sector Employment (2009). 'Code of Ethics for the South Australian Public sector', *Government of South Australia.*

Committee on Standards in Public Life (2014). 'Ethical Standards for providers of Public Services'

Commissie Elias (Commission Elias) (2015). Grip op ICT. The Hague: The Netherlands Parliament.

Competence in foresight work. Available at: http://foresightcanada.com/wp-content/uploads/2015/07/A-Glossary-of-Core-Terms-for-Strategic-Foresight-v2.0.pdf

Compston, H. W. (2006). *King trends in public policy.* Basingstoke: Palgrave Macmillan.

Connolly, J., (2016). Contribution analysis as an approach to enable public managers to demonstrate public value: The Scottish context. *International Journal of Public Sector Management*, 29(7), 690–707.

Cook, G., Mathews, M., & Irwin, S. (2009). 'Innovation in the Public Sector: Enabling Better Performance, Driving New Direction', *Australian National Audit Office* see: http://www.anao.gov.au/bpg-innovation/1_introduction.html

Coombs, R., P. Narandren, A. Richards (1996). A literature-based innovation output indicator. Research Policy (25) 3: 403–413.

Cooper, T. L. (2012). *The responsible administrator. An approach to ethics for the administrative role* (6th Ed). San Francisco: John Wiley & Sons.

Cooper, T. L., & Menzel, D. C. (2013). *Achieving ethical competence for public service leadership.* Armonk: M. E. Sharpe.

Courtney, H. (2001). *20/20 Foresight: Crafting strategy in an uncertain world.* Boston, MA: Harvard Business School Press

Covington, C.R. 1985. 'The Development of Organizational Memory in Presidential Agencies', Administration and Society, 17, 171–96.

Cowell, R., Downe, J., & Morgan, K. (2011). The ethical framework for local government in England: Is it having any effect and why? *Public Management Review*, *13*(3), 433–457.

Crandall, W., & Gao, L. (2005). An update on telecommuting: Review and prospects for emerging issues. *SAM Advanced Management Journal*, *70*(3), 30.

Crosby B, Graham K. C., & Menefee-Libey S. (2012). 'Gay and Transgender Discrimination in the Public Sector', *Center for American Progress and AFSCME*.

Crosby, Barbara C., and John M. Bryson. 2010. Integrative Leadership and the Creation and Maintenance of CrossSector Collaborations. Leadership Quarterly 21(2): 211–30.

CSIRO. (2013). CSIRO Annual Report. Retrieved from http://www.csiro.au/en/About/Our-impact/Reporting-our-impact/Annual-reports/13-14-annual-report

Cucciniello, M, and G Nasi (2014). Evaluation of the impacts of innovation in the health care sector: A comparative analysis. Public Management Review 16 (1), 90–116.

Cummings, T. G., & Worley, C. G. (2001). *Essentials of organization development and change*. Cincinnati: South-Western College Publishing.

Curry D. (2014). 'Trends for Future Public Sector Reform: A Critical Review of Future-looking Research in Public Administration', *COCOPS*

Cushman & Wakefield (2014). 'Facing the Millennial Wave'. *A Cushman and Wakefield Global Business Consulting Publication*.

Dalton, R.J. (2004). Democratic Challenges, Democratic Choices: The Erosion of Political Support in Advanced Industrial Democracies. Oxford: Oxford University Press.

Damanpour, F. (1991). Organizational innovation: a meta-analysis of effects of determinants and moderators. Academy of Management, 34(3), 555–590.

Damanpour, F., & Schneider, M. (2009). Characteristics of innovation and innovation adoption in public organizations: Assessing the role of managers. Journal of Public Administration Research and Theory, 19(3), 495–522.

Davidson, D.J. 2010. 'The Applicability of the Concept of Resilience to Social Systems: Some Sources of Optimism and Nagging Doubts', Society & Natural Resources, 23, 12, 1135–49.

Davis, Michael (1996). "Some Paradoxes of Whistleblowing". Business & Professional Ethics Journal, 15 (1): 3–19.

Dean (2014). He is a business correspondent. Reference is URL: http://raconteur.net/technology/4g-vs-5g-mobile-technology

de Bruijne, M., A. Boin and M. van Eeten. 2010. 'Resilience: Exploring the Concept and its Meanings', in L.K. Comfort, A. Boin and C.C. Demchack (eds), Designing Resilience: Preparing for Extreme Events. Pittsburgh, PA: Pittsburgh University Press, pp. 13–32.

De Bruijn, H. (2012) 2nd Ed. *Managing performance in the public sector*. London: Routledge.

De Bruijn, J.A. (2012). 2nd Ed. Managing Performance in the Public Sector. London: Routledge.

De Graaf, G. (2010). A report on reporting: Why peers report integrity and law violations in public organizations. *Public Administration Review*, *70*(5), 767–779.

De Graaf, G., & van Der Wal, Z. (2008). On value differences experienced by sector switchers. *Administration & Society*, *40*(1), 79–103.

De Graaf, G., & Van Der Wal, Z. (2010). Managing conflicting public values: Governing with integrity and effectiveness. *The American Review of Public Administration, 40*(6), 623–630.

De Graaf, G., Van Doeveren, V., Reynaers, A. M., & Van der Wal, Z. (2011). Goed bestuur als management van spanningen tussen verschillende publieke waarden. *Bestuurskunde, 20*(2), 5–11.

De Hoogh, A. H. & Den Hartog, D. N. (2008). Ethical and despotic leadership, relationships with leader's social responsibility, top management team effectiveness and subordinates' optimism: A multi-method study. *The Leadership Quarterly, 19*(3), 297–311.

De Jong, M., Marston, N., & Roth, E. (2015). 'The Eight Essentials of Innovation', *McKinsey &Company* see: http://www.mckinsey.com/insights/innovation/the_eight_essentials_of_innovation?cid=other-eml-ttn-mip-mck-oth-1512

De Vries, M. (2002). Can you afford Honesty? Administration & Society 34 (3): 309–334.

De Vries, H. D., Bekkers, V., & Tummers, L. (2016). Innovations in the public sector: A systematic review and future research agenda. *Public Administration, 94*(1), 146–166.

Deiser, R., & Newton, S. (2013). Six social-media skills every leader needs. *McKinsey Quarterly, 1*, 62–67.

Delmas, M. A., & Burbano, V. C. (2011). The drivers of greenwashing. *California Management Review, 54*(1), 64–87.

Deloitte. (2010). Unlocking government: How data transforms democracy. Retrieved from http://www2.deloitte.com/content/dam/Deloitte/nl/Documents/public-sector/deloitte-nl-ps-govlab-unlocking-government.pdf

Deloitte. (2016). Global Human Capital Trends 2016. The New Organization: Different by Design. Deloitte University Press.

Demir, T., and R.C. Nyhan (2008). The Politics – Administration Dichotomy: An Empirical Search for Correspondence between Theory and Practice. Public Administration Review 69 (1): 81–96.

Demmke, C. (2002). Undefined boundaries and grey areas: The evolving interaction between the EU and national public services. *Eipascope, 2002*(2), 1–8.

Demmke, C., & Moilanen, T. (2012). Effectiveness of public? service ethics and good governance in the central administrations of the EU? 27. *Frankfurt am Main, Peter Lang*.

Denmark, A.M. and Kaplan, R.D. (2010). Contested Commons: The Future of American Power in a Multipolar World. Washington DC: Center for a New American Security.

Dente, B., Bobbio, L., Spada, A. (2005), "Government o governance per l'innovazione metropolitana? Milano e Torino a confront", Studi organizzativi, 2, pp. 29–47.

Dickinson, Helen & Needham, Catherine (2012). 'Twenty-first century public servant: Summary of roundtable discussion' University of Birmingham Public Service Academy Roundtable. Available at: http://www.birmingham.ac.uk/Documents/college-social-sciences/public-service-academy/21c-ps-paper.pdf

Dickinson, H., & Sullivan, H. (2014). *Imagining the 21st century public service workforce*. Melbourne School of Government: University of Melbourne.

Dill, K. (2015, November 6). 7 Things Employers Should Know About the Gen Z Workforce. Forbes. Retrieved from http://www.forbes.com/sites/

kathryndill/2015/11/06/7-things-employers-should-know-about-the-gen-z-workforce/-23b24db32188

Dobbs, R., J. Manyika en J. Woetzel (2015). *No ordinary disruption. The four forces breaking all the trends.* New York: Public Affairs.

Dobel, P.J. (2005). Public Integrity. Baltimore: Johns Hopkins University Press.

DOE (2014). 'Draft Revised Code of Conduct for Local Government Employees', *Local Government Reform Joint Forum.*

Doorn, J.A.A. van (2002) Gevangen in de tijd: Over generaties en hun geschiedenis. Amsterdam: Boom.

Downe, J., Cowell, R., & Morgan, K. (2016). What determines ethical behavior in public organizations: Is it rules and/or leadership? *Public Administration Review*, 76(6): 898–909.

Doz, Y., & Kosonen, M. (2014). Governments for the future: Building the strategic and agile state. *Sitra Studies*, 80.

Dreyer, Iana & Stang, Gerald (2013). 'Foresight in governments – practices and trends around the world' Yearbook of European Security. Available at: http://www.iss.europa.eu/fileadmin/euiss/documents/Books/Yearbook/2.1_Foresight_in_governments.pdf

Dreyfus S. (2012). 'Whistleblowers: gagged by those in power, admired by the public', The Guardian: http://www.theguardian.com/media-network/media-network-blog/2012/oct/19/whistleblowing-survey

Droll Peter (2013). ' Powering European Public Sector Innovation: Towards a New Architecture' European Commission.

Duit, Andreas & Galaz, Victor (2008). Governance and complexity – emerging issues for governance theory. *Governance: An International Journal of Policy, Administration, and Institutions*, 21(3), 311–335.

Duit, Andreas, Galaz, Victor, Eckerberg, Katarina, Ebbesson, Jonas (2010). Governance, complexity and resilience. *Global Environmental Change*, 20, 363–368.

Dunleavy, P., Margetts, H., Bastow, S., & Tinkler, J. (2006). New public management is dead—long live digital-era governance. *Journal of Public Administration Research and Theory*, 16(3), 467–494.

Durose, C., Mangan, C., Needham, C., & Rees, J. (2013). Transforming local public services through co-production.

Duit, A. (2016). RESILIENCE THINKING: LESSONS FOR PUBLIC ADMINISTRATION. Public Administration 94 (2): 364–380.

Durkin, D. (2010). Managing generational diversity. Baseline, (105), 14.

Earle (2011), websource: http://blogs.cisco.com/diversity/how-we-plan-to-use-cisco%E2%80%99s-reverse-mentoring-programme-to-encourage-inclusion-and-diversity

Easter, S. and M.Y. Brannen (2016). Merging Institutional Logics and Negotiated Culture Perspectives to Help Cross-Sector Partnerships Solve the World's Most Wicked Problems. AnthroSource 1 (1): 36–56.

Eby, L. T., & Allen, T. D. (2002). Further investigation of protégés' negative mentoring experiences patterns and outcomes. *Group & Organization Management*, 27(4), 456–479.

The Economist (2014). 'A troubling trajectory'. Available at: http://www.economist.com/news/finance-and-economics/21636089-fears-are-growing-trades-share-worlds-gdp-has-peaked-far

Eddy S.W. Ng, Charles W. Gossett, Samuel Chinyoka, Isaac Obasi, (2016) "Public vs private sector employment: An exploratory study of career choice among graduate management students in Botswana", Personnel Review, Vol. 45 Iss: 6, pp.1367–1385

Eggers, W. D., & Singh, S. K. (2009). 'The Public Innovator's Playbook: Nurturing bold ideas in government', *Deloitte.*

Eggers, W., Baker, L., Gonzalez, R., & Vaughn, A. (2012). 'Public Sector Disrupted, How Innovation Can Help Government Achieve More for Less'

Eggers, W. D. & Macmillan, P. (2013, October 3). Five cross-sector partnerships innovating to solve social problems. The Guardian. Retrieved from http://www.theguardian.com/public-leaders-network/2013/oct/03/five-ways-develop-solution-economy

Ehrich, L. C., & Hansford, B. C. (2008). Mentoring in the public sector. *Practical Experiences in Professional Education*, 11(1), 1–16.

Ehrich, Lisa C., & Brian C. Hansford. (2008). Mentoring in the public sector. *Practical Experiences in Professional Education*, 11(1), 1–16.

Eisenberger, R., Huntington, R. H., & Sowa, S. (1986). D. (1986). Perceived organisational support. *Journal of Applied Psychology*, 71, 31.

Elkins (2015), web source: http://www.businessinsider.sg/experts-predict-that-one-third-of-jobs-will-be-replaced-by-robots-2015–5/?r=US&IR=T#ohUidYtBJKjIzRXM.97

Emerson, K., Nabatchi, T., & Balogh, S. (2012). An integrative framework for collaborative governance. *Journal of Public Administration Research and Theory*, 22(1), 1–29.

Ensher, E. A., Grant-Vallone, E. J., & Donaldson, S. I. (2001). Effects of perceived discrimination on job satisfaction, organizational commitment, organizational citizenship behavior, and grievances. *Human Resource Development Quarterly*, 12(1), 53–72.

Erickson D. (2015). 'Top US Cities by Smart Phone Penetration', *E-Strategy Marketing Trends* see: http://trends.e-strategyblog.com/2015/05/01/top-us-cities-by-smart-phone-penetration/24887

Eshuis, J., & Edelenbos, J. (2009). Branding in urban regeneration. *Journal of Urban Regeneration & Renewal*, 2(3), 272–282.

Eshuis, J., & Klijn, E. H. (2012). *Branding in governance and public management.* Routledge.

Etzioni, Amitai (2010). Is Transparency the Best Disinfectant? The Journal of Political Philosophy 18 (4): 389–404.

Evans, G. (2003). Hard-branding the cultural city–from Prado to Prada. *International Journal of Urban and Regional Research*, 27(2), 417–440.

Eversdijk, A. (2013). Choosing Public-Private Partnerships in Dutch Infrastructure Projects. Rotterdam: Erasmus University.

Fang, R., Duffy, M.K., & Shaw, J.D., 2011. The organizational socialization process: Review and development of a social capital model. *Journal of Management*, 37 (1): 127–152.

Fauna & Flora International. Relationship in crisis: Lessons from cross-sectoral collaboration to conserve biodiversity and rebuild livelihoods following natural disaster and human conflict. Retrieved from http://povertyandconservation.info/sites/default/files/20100428-Poster_Abstracts.pdf

Feeney, M. K., & Bozeman, B. (2008). Mentoring and network ties. *Human Relations*, 61(12), 1651–1676.

Felipe Monteiro, Michael Mol, Julian Birkinshaw (2016). Ready to Be Open? Explaining the Firm-Level Barriers to Benefiting from Openness to External Knowledge. *Long Range Planning*. http://dx.doi.org/10.1016/j.lrp.2015.12.008

Ferlie, Ewan, Fitzgerald, Louise, McGivern, Gerry, Dopson, Sue and Bennett, Chris (2011). Public policy networks and 'wicked problems': a nascent solution? *Public Administration, 89*(2), 307–324.

Ferrazzi. K. (2012). How to build trust in a virtual workplace. Harvard Business Review. Retrieved from https://hbr.org/2012/10/how-to-build-trust-in-virtual/

Ferrera, M., & Hemerijck, A. (2003). in J. Zeitlin and D. Trubeck (eds), Governing Work and Welfare in a New Economy: European and American Experiments, Oxford, Oxford University Press, pp. 88–128.

Ferris, G. R., Treadway, D. C., Kolodinsky, R. W., Hochwarter, W. A., Kacmar, C. J., Douglas, C., & Frink, D. D. (2005). Development and validation of the political skill inventory. *Journal of Management, 31*(1), 126–152.

Finkelstein, L. M., Allen, T. D., & Rhoton, L. A. (2003). An examination of the role of age in mentoring relationships. *Group & Organization Management, 28*(2), 249–281.

Fiol, C. M., & O'Connor, E. J. (2005). Identification in face-to-face, hybrid, and pure virtual teams: Untangling the contradictions. *Organization Science, 16*(1), 19–32.

Flood, R.L. & Romm, N.R.A. (1996). Plurality revisited: Diversity management and triple loop learning. Systems Practice. 9 (6): 587–603.

Florida, (2012). 10th Ed. The Rise of the Creative Class. New York: Basic Books.

Foresight Canada (2015). *A Glossary of core terms for strategic foresight and three levels of Competence in Foresight Work.* Canada: Foresight Canada: 1–7.

Foroohar, R. (2015, May 12). Here's the Secret Truth About Economic Inequality in America. TIME. Retrieved from http://time.com/3855971/us-economic-inequality/

Foroohar, R. (2016). *Makers and takers: The rise of finance and the fall of American business.* New York: Crown Business.

Forrer, J., Kee, J., Newcomer, K., Boyer, E., 2010. Public-private partnerships and the public accountability question. Public Adminstration Review 70 (3): 475–484.

Foster, J. D., Campbell, W. K., & Twenge, J. M. (2003). Individual differences in narcissism: Inflated self-views across the lifespan and around the world. *Journal of Research in Personality, 37*(6), 469–486.

Fox News (2014). Arizona Lawmakers Advance $30 M "Virtual Fence" Proposal For US-Mexico Border. Retrieved from: http://www.foxnews.com/politics/2014/02/18/arizona-lawmakers-advance-30m-virtual-fence-proposal-for-us-mexico-border.html

Fox, R. L., & Schuhmann, R. A. (2001). Mentoring experiences of women city managers are women disadvantaged?. *The American Review of Public Administration, 31*(4), 381–392.

Francois, J., Manchin, M., Norberg, H., Pindyuk, O., & Tomberger, P. (2013). *Reducing transatlantic barriers to trade and investment: An economic assessment* (No. 20130401). Institue for International and Development Economics.

Frederickson, D. G., & Frederickson, H. G. (2006). *Measuring the performance of the hollow state.* Washington, D.C.: Georgetown University Press.

Frederickson, H. G., & Matkin, D. S. (2007). Public leadership as gardening. In SR Morse, TF Buss, & CM Kinghorn (eds), *Transforming public leadership for the 21st century.* Armonk: M. E. Sharpe, Inc., pp. 34–46.

Frederickson, H.G. (2005). Public ethics and the new managerialism: An axiomatic theory. In *Ethics in public management,* ed. H.G. Frederickson and R.K. Ghere, 165–183. New York & London: M.E. Sharpe.

Freeman, R. 2007. Epistemological bricolage: How practitioners make sense of learning. Administration and Society, 39(4): 476–496.

Freidson, E. (1994). *Professionalism reborn: Theory, prophecy, and policy.* Chicago: University of Chicago Press.

Freire, Karine, Sangiorgi, Daniela (2010). 'Service design and healthcare innovation: from consumption to co-production and co-creation' *Nordic Service Design Conference Paper.* Available at: file:///C:/Users/E0001110/Desktop/servdes2010_freiresangiorgi.pdf.

Frey, C. B., & Osborne, M. A. (2013). The future of employment: how susceptible are jobs to computerisation. *Retrieved September, 7,* 2013.

Friess S. (2015). 'Revealed: Clinton's Office Was Warned Over Private Email Use', *Aljazeera America* see: http://america.aljazeera.com/articles/2015/3/3/govt-cybersecurity-source-clintons-office-warned-private-email-use.html

Frow, Pennie, Nenonen, Suvi, Payne, Adrian, Storbacka, Kaj (2015). Managing co-creation design: A strategic approach to innovation. *British Journal of Management, 26*(3), 463–383.

Fry, B. R., & Raadschelders, J. C. (2013). *Mastering public administration: From Max Weber to Dwight Waldo: From Max Weber to Dwight Waldo.* Washington, D.C.: CQ Press.

Freeman, R. 2007. Epistemological bricolage: How practitioners make sense of learning. Administration and Society, 39(4): 476–496.

FS-UNEP (2016). GLOBAL TRENDS IN RENEWABLE ENERGY INVESTMENT 2016. Frankfurt: Frankfurt School of Finance & Management.

Fukuyama, F. (2013). What is governance? *Governance, 26*(3), 347–368.

Fuller, R. B. (1982). *Critical path.* Basingstoke: Palgrave Macmillan.

Fung, A. (2006). Varieties of participation in complex governance. *Public Administration Review, 66*(s1), 66–75.

Fung, A. (2015). Putting the public back into governance: The challenges of citizen participation and its future. *Public Administration Review, 75*(4), 513–522.

Gaiman, N., & Pratchett, T. (2006). *Good omens: The nice and accurate prophecies of Agnes Nutter, Witch.* New York: Harper Collins.

Gallo, A. (2013). How to Reward Your Stellar Team. Harvard Business Review. Retrieved from https://hbr.org/2013/08/how-to-reward-your-stellar-tea/

Gandz, J., & Murray, V. V. (1980). The experience of workplace politics. *Academy of Management Journal, 23*(2), 237–251.

Gary, Jay E., & von der Gracht, Heiko A. (2015). The future of foresight professionals: Results from a global Delphi study. *Futures, 71,* 132–145.

Gauld, R., S. Goldfinch and S. Horsburgh. 2010. 'Do they want it? Do they use it? The 'Demand-Side' of e-Government in Australia and New Zealand.' Government Information Quarterly 27: 177–186

Gentile, B., Twenge, J. M., & Campbell, W. K. (2010). Birth cohort differences in self-esteem, 1988–2008: A cross-temporal meta-analysis. *Review of General Psychology, 14*(3), 261.

Godshalk, V. M., & Sosik, J. J. (2003). Aiming for career success: The role of learning goal orientation in mentoring relationships. *Journal of Vocational Behavior, 63*(3), 417–437.

Goldfinch, S. Gauld, R. and N. Baldwin. 2011. 'Information and Communications Technology Use, E-Government, Pain and Stress Amongst Public Servants'. New Technology, Work and Employment. 26(1): 39–53.

Goli, S., Doshi, R., & Perianayagam, A. (2013). Pathways of economic inequalities in maternal and child health in urban India: A decomposition analysis. *PLoS One, 8*(3), e58573.

Gordon, J. (2015). The dawn of marketing's new golden age. McKinsey Quarterly, February 2015. http://www.mckinsey.com/business-functions/marketing-and-sales/our-insights/the-dawn-of-marketings-new-golden-age

Goulden, Murray & Dingwall, Robert (2012). Chapter 2 managing the future: Models, scenarios and the control of uncertainty. In Tim Ryley & Lee Chapman (eds) *Transport and climate change*. Emerald Group Publishing. Available at: http://www.emeraldinsight.com/doi/abs/10.1108/S2044-9941%282012%290000002005

Government Merit Systems Protection Board (MSPB) (2011). TELEWORK: Weighing the Information, Determining an Appropriate Approach. Washington DC.

Government of Canada' Canada Public Service Agency; Canada Public Service Commission (2007). 'Key Leadership Competencies'.

Government Office of Personnel Management (2011). Guide to Telework in the Federal Government. Washington DC.

Graaf, G. de (2016). What works: The role of confidential integrity advisors and effective whistleblowing. International public management journal. doi: 10.1080/10967494.2015.109416.

Graham H. May (2009). Foresight and futures in Europe: an overview. *Foresight, 11*(5), 57–67, (EU Commission website)

Gratton, L. (2011). *The shift. The future of work is already here*. London: HarperCollins.

Gratton, L. and Scott, A. (2016). The 100-year life. Living and working in an age of longevity. London: Bloomsbury.

Graycar, A., & Prenzler, T. (2013). *Understanding and preventing corruption*. Basingstoke: Palgrave Macmillan.

Green, D. D., & Roberts, G. E. (2010). Personnel implications of public sector virtual organizations. *Public Personnel Management, 39*(1), 47–57.

Greenleaf, R. K., & Spears, L. C. (2002). *Servant leadership: A journey into the nature of legitimate power and greatness*. New York: Paulist Press.

Greenwald G., MacAskill E., Poitras L. (2013). 'Edward Snowden: the Whistleblower behind the NSA Surveillance Revelations', *The Guardian* see: http://www.theguardian.com/world/2013/jun/09/edward-snowden-nsa-whistleblower-surveillance

Grimmelikhuijsen, S. G., & Meijer, A. J. (2015). Does twitter increase perceived police legitimacy? *Public Administration Review, 75*(4), 598–607.

Groenleer, M., Kaeding, M., & Versluis, E. (2010). Regulatory Governance through EU Agencies? The Implementation of Transport Directives. Journal of European Public Policy. 17 (8): 1212–1230.

Gronn, P. (2002). Distributed leadership as a unit of analysis. *The Leadership Quarterly, 13*(4), 423–451.

Guardian Public Leaders Network (2014). 'Civil Service Global Round up: India Transgender Woman Fights for Right to Apply for the Civil Service', *The Guardian* see: http://www.theguardian.com/public-leaders-network/2014/mar/08/israel-discrimination-women-workplace-civil-service

Guarneros-Meza, Valeria & Martin, Steve (2016). Boundary-spanning in local public service partnerships: Coaches, advocates or enforcers? *Public Management Review, 18*(2), 238–257.

Gunderson, L.H. 2003. 'Adaptive Dancing: Interactions between Social Resilience and Ecological Crises', in F. Berkes, J. Colding and C. Folke (eds), Navigating Social-Ecological Systems: Building Resilience for Complexity. Cambridge: Cambridge University Press, pp. 33–52.

Habegger, B. (2010). Strategic foresight in public policy: Reviewing the experiences of the UK, Singapore, and the Netherlands. *Futures*, 42, 49–58.

Hage, J., & Aiken, A. (1967). The Relationship of Centralization to Other Structural Properties, Administrative Science Quarterly, 12, 72 – 92.

Haldenby A. (2015). 'After the Kids Company Scandal, Ministers Must Realize They Can Turn off the Spending Tap', see: The Telegraph http://www.telegraph.co.uk/news/politics/11970089/After-the-Kids-Company-scandal-ministers-must-realise-they-can-turn-off-the-spending-tap.html

Hall, David (2014). 'Why public-private partnerships don't work. The many advantages of the public alternative' Public Services International Research Unit (PSIRU) University of Greenwich. Available at: http://www.world-psi.org/en/publication-why-public-private-partnerships-dont-work

Hamidullah, M.F. (2016). Managing the Next Generation of Public Workers. A Public Solutions Handbook. London: Routledge.

Han, Kirsten (2013). 'Singapore's Population Debate Grows Heated' The Diplomat. Available at: http://thediplomat.com/2013/02/singapores-population-debate-grows-heated

Hansen, J. R. (2014). From public to private sector: Motives and explanations for sector switching. *Public Management Review*, 16(4), 590–607.

Haq S. (2011). Ethics and leadership in the public service. *Procedia Social and Behavioural Sciences*, 15, 2792–2796.

Hargittai, E. (2002). Beyond logs and surveys: In-depth measures of people's web use skills. *Journal of the American Society for Information Science and Technology*, 53(14), 1239–1244.

Hargadon, A. B. (2002) "Knowledge brokering: A network perspective on learning and innovation," Research in Organizational Behavior, B. Staw and R. Kramer (Eds), JAI Press, 21: 41–85.

Hargrove, R. (2008), 'Creating creativity in the design studio: Assessing the impact of metacognitive skill development on creative abilities', Doctoral dissertation, North Carolina: North Carolina State University, College of Design.

't Hart, P. (1993). Symbols, rituals and power: The lost dimensions of crisis management. Journal of contingencies and crisis management 1 (1), 36–50.

t Hart, P. (2013). After Fukushima: Reflections on risk and institutional learning in an era of mega-crises. *Public Administration*, 91(1), 101–113.

t' Hart, P. (2014a). *Understanding Public Leadership*. Basingstoke: Palgrave Macmillan.

t' Hart, P. (2014b). *Ambtelijk Vakmanschap 3.0. De zoektocht naar het handwerk van de overheidsmanager.* The Hague: VOM.

t' Hart, P. (2014c). Collaborating to manage: A primer for the public sector. *Public Administration*, 92(3), 763–764.

t' Hart, P., & Wille, A. (2006). Ministers and top officials in the Dutch core executive: Living together, growing apart? *Public Administration*, 84(1), 121–146.

Hartley, J. (2005). Innovation in governance and public services: Past and present. Public Money & Management, 25(1), 27–34.

Hartley, J., and Benington, J. (2006). Copy and paste, or graft and transplant? Knowledge sharing through inter-organizational networks Public Money and Management, 26(2): 101–108.

Hartley, J., and Downe, J. (2007). The shining lights? Public service awards as an approach to service improvement. Public Administration, 85(2): 329–353.

Hartley, J., Sørensen, E., & Torfing, J. (2013). Collaborative innovation: A viable alternative to market competition and organizational entrepreneurship. Public Administration Review, 73(6),821–830.

Hartley J., Alford J., & Hughes O. (2012). 'Political Astuteness as an Aid to Discerning and Creating Public Value', *Paper for Conference on Creating Public Value in a Shared-Power, Multi-Sector World, Center for Integrative Leadership, University of Minnesota.*

Hartley J., Alford J., Hughes O., & Yates S. (2015). Public value and political astuteness in the work of public managers: The art of the possible. *Public Administration 93*(1), 195–211.

Hartley, J. (2015). In: John M. Bryson, Barbara C. Crosby, and Laura Bloomberg, (Eds.) Public Value and Public Administration, 82–94.

Hartley, J., & Fletcher, C. (2008). Leading with political awareness: Leadership across diverse interests inside and outside the organisation. In *Leadership perspectives*. UK: Palgrave Macmillan, pp. 163–176.

Hartley, J., Alford, J., Hughes, O., & Yates, S. (2013). Leading with political astuteness: A study of public managers in Australia, New Zealand and the United Kingdom. *Australia and New Zealand School of Government and the Chartered Management Institute.*

Hartmann, David & Stillings, Christopher (2015). Using scenarios in multinational companies across geographic distances – a case from the chemical industry. *Foresight, 17*(5), 475–488.

Hatmaker, D. M. (2015). Bringing networks in: A model of organizational socialization in the public sector. *Public Management Review, 17*(8), 1146–1164.

Harvey, M., McIntyre, N., Heames, J. T., & Moeller, M. (2009). Mentoring global female managers in the global marketplace: Traditional, reverse, and reciprocal mentoring. International Journal of Human Resource Management, 20, 1344–1361.

Havas, A. (2003). Evolving Foresight in a Small Transition Economy: The design, use and relevance of foresight methods in Hungary. Journal of Forecasting 22 (2–3), 179–201.

Havas, A, D Schartinger, M Weber (2010). The impact of foresight on innovation policy-making: recent experiences and future perspectives. Research Evaluation 19 (2), 91–104.

Hazell, R. and B. Worthy (2010). Assessing the performance of freedom of information. Government Information Quarterly 27: 352–359.

Head, B.W. and Alford, J. (2015). Wicked Problems: implications for public policy and management. Administration and Society. 47 (6): 711–39.

Heifetz, R. A. (1994). *Leadership without easy answers*. Boston: Harvard University Press.

Heifetz, R. A, M. Linsky en A. Grashow (2009). *The practice of adaptive leadership*. Boston: Harvard Business Press.

Heres, L., & Lasthuizen, K. (2012). What's the difference? Ethical leadership in public, hybrid and private sector organizations. *Journal of Change Management, 12*(4), 441–466.

Heres, L. (2014), One style fits all? The content, origins, and effect of follower expectations of ethical leadership, Enschede: Ipskamp.

Heres, L. (2016). Tonen van de Top. De rol van topambtenaren in het integriteitsbeleid. Utrecht: USBO.

Helsloot I., Boin A., Jacobs B., Comfort L.C. (eds.) (2012). Mega-Crises: Understanding the Prospects, Nature, Characteristics and Effects of Cataclysmic Events. Charles C. Thomas, Springfield, IL.

Heywood, P. M. (2012). Integrity management and the public service ethos in the UK: Patchwork quilt or threadbare blanket? *International Review of Administrative Sciences, 78*(3), 474–493.

Ho, P. (2008). Governance at the Leading Edge: Black Swans, Wild Cards, and Wicked Problems. Retrieved from https://www.cscollege.gov.sg/Knowledge/Ethos/Issue%204%20Apr%202008/Documents/HCS%20Peter%20Ho--Speech%20at%20the%204th%20Strategic%20Perspectives%20Conference.pdf

Ho, Peter (2010). 'Thinking About the Future: What the Public Service Can Do' Ethos 7. Available at: https://www.cscollege.gov.sg/Knowledge/Ethos/Issue%20 7%20Jan%202010/Pages/Thinking-About-the-Future-What-the-Public-Service-Can-Do.aspx

Ho, Peter (2014). 'The Butterfly Effect: speech at the opening of the NTU Complexity Institute'. Available at: https://www.cscollege.gov.sg/Knowledge/Pages/Speech-The-Butterfly-Effect.aspx

Hodge, G., & Greve, C. (2011, June). Theorizing public-private partnership success: A market-based alternative to government. In *Paper for the Public Management Research Conference at Syracuse University*, pp. 2–4.

Hodge, G., C. Greve, and A. Boardman. 2010. International Handbook on Public–Private Partnership. Northampton, MA: Edward Elgar.

Hoekstra A., & Van Dijk M. (2016). 'The Marriage of Heaven and Hell Integrity and Social Media in the Public Sector', *Dutch National Integrity Office*

Hoekstra, A. (2016). Institutionalizing integrity management: Challenges and solutions in times of financial crises and austerity measures. *The Routledge Companion to Ethics and Public Service Organizations.*

Hoekstra, A., & Kaptein, M. (2014). Understanding integrity policy formation processes: A case study in the Netherlands of the conditions for change. *Public Integrity, 16*(3), 243–264.

Hoffman, W. M., & Schwartz, M. S. (2015). The morality of whistleblowing: A commentary on Richard T. De George. *Journal of Business Ethics, 127*(4), 771.

Holling, C.S. 1973. 'Resilience and Stability of Ecological Systems', Annual Review of Ecology and Systematics, 4, 1, 1–23.

Hollnagel, E., D.D. Woods and N. Leveson (eds). 2006. Resilience Engineering: Concepts and Precepts. Aldershot: Ashgate Publishing.

Holmes, L. (2012). Researching Gen Y … do you know how to speak to them.

Hood, C. (1991). A public management for all seasons? *Public Administration, 69*(1), 3–19.

Horton, Sylvia. 2008. History and Persistence of an Idea and an Ideal. In Motivation in Public Management: The Call of Public Service, edited by James L. Perry and Annie Hondeghem, 17–32. Oxford: Oxford University Press.

Houston, D. J. (2000). Public-service motivation: A multivariate test. *Journal of Public Administration Research and Theory, 10*(4), 713–728.

Houston, D. J. (2014). Public service motivation in the post-communist state. *Public Administration, 92*(4), 843–860.

Howes, Michael, Tangney, Peter, Reis, Kimberley, Grant-Smith, Deanna, Heazle, Michael, Bosomworth, Karyn, Burton, Paul Burton (2014). Towards networked governance: Improving interagency communication and collaboration for disaster risk management and climate change adaptation in Australia. *Journal of Environmental Planning and Management* doi:10.1080/09640568.2014.891974

Howlett, M.P. and Ramesh, M. (1995). Studying Public Policy: Policy Cycles and Policy Subsystems. Toronto: Oxford University Press. http://edition.cnn.com/2012/01/26/opinion/mackinnon-sopa-government-surveillance/

HSBC (2015). Trade Winds: shaping the future of international business. London: HSBC Commercial Banking.

Huberts L. W. J. C., Van Den Heuvel H., Punch M. (2000). 'Public and Business Ethics: Similar or Different?' *International Institute for Public Ethics Conference.*

Huberts, L. W., Kaptein, M., & Lasthuizen, K. (2007). A study of the impact of three leadership styles on integrity violations committed by police officers. *Policing: An International Journal of Police Strategies & Management*, 30(4), 587–607.

Huberts, L., & Lasthuizen, K. (2014). *The integrity of governance. What it is, what we know, and where to go.* Basingstoke: Palgrave Macmillan.

Huberts, L.W.J.C. 2014, The Integrity of Governance, Basingstoke: Palgrave Macmillan.

Hunter, S. T., Cushenbery, L., & Friedrich, T. (2012). Hiring an innovative workforce: A necessary yet uniquely challenging endeavour. *Human Resource Management Review*, 22(4), 303–322.

IBM. (2013). Bringing big data to the enterprise. Retrieved from https://www-01.ibm.com/software/data/bigdata/what-is-big-data.html

ILO. (2013). Global Employment Trends for Youth 2013. Retrieved from http://www.ilo.org/wcmsp5/groups/public/---dgreports/---dcomm/documents/publication/wcms_212423.pdf

IMF (2013). Global Trends in Public Pension Spending and Outlook. Available at: https://www.imf.org/external/np/seminars/eng/2013/oapfad/pdf/clements.pdf

IMF (2014). 'April 2014 Fiscal Monitor ' "Public Expenditure Reform—Making Difficult Choices'. Available at: https://www.google.com.sg/url?sa=t&rct=j&q=&esrc=s&source=web&cd=1&cad=rja&uact=8&ved=0ahUKEwjej92Bqe HOAhVoCcAKHe_FBhQQFggaMAA&url=https%3A%2F%2Fwww.imf.org%2Fexternal%2Fpubs%2Fft%2Ffm%2F2014%2F01%2Fdata%2Ffmdata.xlsx&usg=AFQjCNGi4_V_vJC0tUFg7Aww4VvQOsVpZg&sig2=rCyFdbNb qw6MSzra9rycgg&bvm=bv.131286987,d.bGg

INIA (International Institute on Ageing) (2013). World Population Ageing 2013. Malta: United Nations.

ITV Report (2013). 'Kids Company: Scathing Report Attacks Ministers for Treating Charity as a £46m 'Special Case", *ITV* see: http://www.itv.com/news/2015-11-13/kids-company-scathing-report-attacks-ministers-for-treating-charity-as-a-46m-special-case/

Jacobs, J. (1992). *Systems of survival. A dialogue on the moral foundations of commerce and politics.* New York: Random House Inc.

Jacobs, Kerry, and Cuganesan, Suresh (2014). Interdisciplinary accounting research in the Public Sector: Dissolving boundaries to tackle wicked problems. Accounting, Auditing & Accountability Journal 27 (8): 1250–1256.

Jacoby, William G. (2000). Issue framing and public opinion on government spending. American Journal of Political Science 44: 750–767.

Jackson, Michael, *Practical Foresight Guide* (2013). Available at: http://www.shapingtomorrow.com/media-centre/pf-complete.pdf

Jacques, M. (2009). *When China rules the world: The end of the western world and the birth of a new global order.* New York: Penguin.

Johansen, Bob (2007). *Get there early: Sensing the future to compete in the present.* San Francisco: Berrett-Koehler Publishers.

Johnson, J. McGinnis, en E. S. Ng. (2015). Money talks or millennials walk. The effect of compensation on nonprofit millennial workers sector-switching intentions. *Review of Public Personnel Administration, 36*(3), 283–305.

Johnson, M. (2010, October 31). Telework boosts productivity, decreases carbon footprint. Federal Times. Retrieved from http://www.federaltimes.com/article/20101031/ADOP06/10310307/

Jomo Kenyatta University of Agriculture and Technology (2015). 'Huduma Center Services', see: http://www.jkuat.ac.ke/directorates/iceod/huduma-centre-services/

Jones, S. E. (2013). *Against technology: From the Luddites to neo-Luddism.* Routledge.

Jordan, S. R. (2013). The innovation imperative: an analysis of the ethics of the imperative to innovate in public service delivery. *Public Management Review,* 16 (1): 67–89.

Jørgensen, T. B., & Rutgers, M. R. (2015). Public values core or confusion? Introduction to the centrality and puzzlement of public values research. *The American Review of Public Administration, 45*(1), 3–12.

Joshua P. Meltzer (2014). The Importance of the Internet and Transatlantic Data Flows for U.S. and EU Trade and Investment. Washington DC: Global Economy and Development Program at Brookings.

Kanter, Rosabeth M. (1984). The Change Masters: Innovation for Productivity in the American Corporation. New York: Simon & Schuster

Kaptein, Muel (2006). De Integere Manager [Managing with Integrity]. Assen: Koninklijke Van Gorcum.

Kaptein, M., & Wempe, J. F. D. B. (2002). *The balanced company: A theory of corporate integrity.* Oxford; New York, USA: Oxford University Press.

Kaptein, S. P. (2011). Towards effective codes: Testing the relationship with unethical behavior. *Journal of Business Ethics, 99*(2), 233–251.

Kaptein, S. P. (2013). *Dienaren van het Volk: Over de macht van integriteit.* Internet: Free E-book.

Karens, R., Eshuis, J., Klijn, E. H., & Voets, J. (2015). The impact of public branding: An experimental study on the effects of branding policy on citizen trust. *Public Administration Review,* 76 (3): 486–494.

Karssing, E., & Spoor, S. (2010). Integriteit 3.0. *Jaarboek Integriteit.* BIOS: The Hague.

Kassel, D.S. 2008. Performance, accountability and the debate over rules. Public Administration Review, (March/April): 241–252.

Katzenbach, J. R., & Smith, D. K. (1993). *The discipline of teams.* Harvard business review, 1993 Mar-Apr, 71 (2): 111–120.

Kaufman, H. (1960). *The forest ranger: A study in administrative behavior.* Resources for the Future.

Keeler, J. T. (1993). Opening the window for reform mandates, crises, and extraordinary policy-making. *Comparative Political Studies, 25*(4), 433–486.

Keenan, Michael and Popper, Rafael (2008). Comparing foresight "style" in six world regions. *Foresight, 10*(6), 16–38.

Keene J. (2006). Age discrimination. In Greenhaus J. H., Callanan G. A. (Eds.), Encyclopedia of career development (Vol. 1, pp. 10–14). Thousand Oaks, CA: SAGE.

Kellar, E. (2015). The Uberizing of the Government Workforce. Retrieved from http://www.governing.com/columns/smart-mgmt/col-government-workforce-temporary-contract-employees-millennials-flexibility.html

Kelly R. M., & Newman M. (2001). The gendered bureaucracy. *Women and Politics, Taylor and Francis Online, 22*(3), 1–33.

Kelman, Steven, and Sounman Hong. ""Hard," "Soft," or "Tough Love" Management: What Promotes Successful Performance in a Cross-Organizational Collaboration?" International Public Management Journal 19.2 (2016): 141–170.

Kets de Vries, M. F. R. (2003). Leaders, fools and imposters: Essays on the psychology of leadership. New York: iUniverse.

Khojasteh, M. (1993). Motivating the private vs. public sector managers. *Public Personnel Management, 22*(3), 391–401.

Kim, S., Vandenabeele, W., Wright, B. E., Andersen, L. B., Cerase, F. P., Christensen, R. K., ... & Palidauskaite, J. (2013). Investigating the structure and meaning of public service motivation across populations: Developing an international instrument and addressing issues of measurement invariance. *Journal of Public Administration Research and Theory, 23*(1), 79–102.

Kingdon, John W. 1995. Agenda, alternatives, and public policies (2nd ed.). New York: HarperCollins.

Kingston, 2014, web source: http://www.macleans.ca/society/life/get-ready-for-generation-z/

Kirkpatrick, L. O. (2007). The two "logics" of community development: Neighborhoods, markets, and community development corporations. *Politics & Society, 35*(2), 329–359.

Kjeldsen, A. M., & Jacobsen, C. B. (2013). Public service motivation and employment sector: Attraction or socialization? *Journal of Public Administration Research and Theory, 23*(4), 899–926.

Klijn, E.H., en G.R. Teisman (2003). Institutional and strategic barriers to Public-Private partnership: an analysis of Dutch cases. Public Money and Management 23 3: 137–146

Klijn, E. H., Steijn, B., & Edelenbos, J. (2010). The impact of network management on outcomes in governance networks. *Public Administration, 88*(4), 1063–1082.

Klitgaard, R. (1998). *Controlling corruption.* California: University of California Press.

Koliba, C., Meek, J. W. and Zia, A. (2011) Governance Networks in Public Administration and Public Policy, Boca Raton, FL: CRC Press.

Koppell, J.G.S. 2005. "Pathologies of Accountability: ICANN and the challenge of multiple accountabilities disorder." Public Administration Review 65 (1): 94–108.

Koppenjan, J. (2008). Creating a playing field for assessing the effectiveness of network collaboration by performance measures. *Public Management Review, 10*(6), 699–714.

Koppenjan, J., Charles, M. B., & Ryan, N. (2008). Editorial: Managing competing public values in public infrastructure projects.

Koppenjan, Joop & Klijn, Erik-Hans (2004). *Managing uncertainty in networks: a network approach to problem solving and decision making.* New York: Routledge

KPMG. (2013). Future State 2030. Retrieved from https://www.kpmg.com/ID/en/IssuesAndInsights/ArticlesPublications/Documents/Future-State-2030.pdf

Koschmann, M. A., Kuhn, T. R. and Pfarrer, M. D. (2012). 'A communicative framework of value in cross-sector partnerships'. Academy of Management Review, 37, 332–54.

Kossek Ellen Ernst and Thompson Rebecca. (2015). Workplace flexibility: Integrating employer and employee perspectives to close the research to practice implementation gap. In: Allen Tammy D, Eby Lillian T., editors. The Oxford Handbook of Work and Family. Oxford: Oxford university Press.

Kramer, M. R. (2011). Creating shared value. *Harvard Business Review*, 89(1/2), 62–77.

Kroft, S. (2010). 'Watching the Border: the Virtual Fence', *CBS News* see: http://www.cbsnews.com/news/watching-the-border-the-virtual-fence/2/

Kuah, A. W. J. (2013). Foresight and policy: Thinking about Singapore's future(s). *Social Space*, 104–109.

Kuah, A. W. J. (2015). Stories matter in how we think about the future. *Straits Times*, 29 December 2015.

Kurbjuweit, D. (2010). Der Wutbürger. Der Spiegel, 11 October 2010.

Kyle (2009), web source: http://www.canada.com/Business/Millennials+know+what+they+want/1494997/story.html

Laffont, J. J., & Tirole, J. (1991). The politics of government decision-making: A theory of regulatory capture. *The Quarterly Journal of Economics*, 106(4), 1089–1127.

Lambda Legal, & Deloitte Financial Advisory Services LLP. (2006). 2005 workplace fairness survey. New York, NY: Lambda Legal.

Lancaster, L. C., & Stillman, D. (2002). *When generations collide: Who they are. Why they clash. How to solve the generational puzzle at work*. New York City: HarperCollins Publishers.

Landau, M. and D. Chisholm. 1995. 'The Arrogance of Optimism: Notes on Failure-Avoidance Management', Journal of Contingencies and Crisis Management, 3, 2, 67–80.

Lang O. (2010). 'Welcome to a New Age of Whistleblowing', *BBC News* see: http://www.bbc.com/news/world-us-canada-10774473

Lasthuizen, K. (2008). Leading to integrity. *Empirical research into the effects of leadership on ethics and integrity*. Amsterdam: Vrije Universiteit Amsterdam.

Laufer, W. S. (2003). Social accountability and corporate greenwashing. *Journal of Business Ethics*, 43(3), 253–261.

Laverty, Kevin J. (1996). Economic 'short-termism': The debate, the unresolved issues, and the implications for management practice and research. *Academy of Management Review*, 21(3), 825–860.

Laverty, Kevin J. Managerial myopia or systemic short-termism? The importance of managerial systems in valuing the long term. *Management Decision*, 42(7/8), 949–962.

Laverty, K.J. 2004. Managerial myopia or systemic short-termism? Management Decision, 42(8): 949–962.

Lavelle, John (2010). TRENDS & CHALLENGES FOR HR MANAGEMENT IN THE BROADER PUBLIC SECTOR IN THE INTERNATIONAL ARENA. Durban: UNPAN.

Laville S., Butler P., & Mason R. (2016). 'Kids Company: Ministers Must Explain Why They Overrode Civil Service', *The Guardian* see: http://www.theguardian.com/uk-news/2016/feb/01/kids-company-ministers-overrode-civil-service-bernard-jenkin

Lawton A. (2004). Public service ethics in a changing world. *Futures, 37,* 231–243 (Elsevier).

Lawton A., Rayner J., & Lasthuizen K. (2013). *Ethics and management in the public sector.* London: Routledge

Lawton, A., & Macaulay, M. (2014). Localism in practice: Investigating citizen participation and good governance in local government standards of conduct. *Public Administration Review,* 74(1), 75–83.

Lazarus, R. J. (2010). Super wicked problems and climate change: Restraining the present to liberate the future. *Land Use Environment Law Review,* 41, 229.

Lee J. A., & Tomer A. (2015). 'Building And Advancing Digital Skills To Support Seattle's Economic Future', *The Brookings Institution* see: http://www.brookings.edu/research/reports/2015/10/23-seattle-digital-skills-lee-tomer

Lekhi, R. (2007). 'Public Service Innovation', *The Work Foundation.*

Lent, D., & Wijnen, P. W. (2007). War for talent. *Alleen bij het grote geld.*

Leon, L. R., Simmonds, P., & Roman, L. (2012). 'Trends and Challenges in Public Sector Innovation in Europe', *Technopolisgroup.*

Levy, F., & Murnane, R. J. (2004). Education and the changing job market. *Educational Leadership,* 62(2), 80.

Lewis C. W., & Gilman S. C. (2005). *The ethics challenge in public service a problem solving guide.* San Francisco: Jossey-Bass (A Wiley Imprint)

Lewis D., Brown A. J., & Moberly R. (2014). *International handbook on whistleblowing research.* Cheltenham; Northampton: Edward Elgar Publishing

Lewis L. (2014). 'Snowden Awarded Alternative Nobel Price', *Whistleblowing Today* see: http://whistleblowingtoday.org/2014/09/snowden-awarded-alternative-nobel-prize/

Lewis, C. W., & Gilman, S. C. (2005). *The ethics challenge in public service: A problem-solving guide.* Hoboken: John Wiley & Sons.

Lewis, G. B., & Frank, S. A. (2002). Who wants to work for the government? *Public Administration Review,* 62(4), 395–404.

Leyden J. (2008). 'Passport Snooping Public Servant Faces Year in the Can', *The Register* see: http://www.theregister.co.uk/2008/09/23/passport_snooping_plea/

Li, Ning; Zheng, Xiaoming; Harris, T. Brad; Liu, Xin; Kirkman, Bradley L. (2016). Recognizing "me" benefits "we": Investigating the positive spillover effects of formal individual recognition in teams. Journal of Applied Psychology 101 (7): 925–939.

Lipsky, M. (1980). *Street level bureaucrats.* New York: Russell Sage Foundation.

Liu, Bangcheng and Thomas Li-Ping Tang. 2011. "Does the love of money moderate the relationship between public service motivation and job satisfaction? The case of Chinese professionals in the Public Sector". Public Administration Review 71 (5): 718–727.

Lodge, M. and K. Wegrich (2012). Managing Regulation. Regulatory analysis, politics, and policy. Basingstoke: Palgrave Macmillan.

LoGuirato B. (2013). 'Why a 29 Year Old Contractor Had Access to Government Secrets', *Business Insider* see: http://www.businessinsider.com/edward-snowden-nsa-leak-booz-allen-hamilton-2013-6?IR=T&r=US&IR=T

Longmire, S. (2015). 'DHS Installs Seven Camera Towers On Border In Fourth Virtual Fence Attempt', *Breitbart* see: http://www.breitbart.com/texas/2015/03/02/

dhs-installs-seven-camera-towers-on-border-in-fourth-virtual-fence-attempt/

Lorenz, E. N. (1969). The predictability of a flow which possesses many scales of motion. *Tellus*, *21*(3), 1–19.

Lovegrove, N. and M. Thomas (2013). Why the world needs tri-sector leaders. *Harvard Business Review*, 13 February 2013.

Low, D., & S. T. Vakadeth (2014). *Hard choices: Challenging the Singapore consensus*. Singapore: NUS Press.

Lowry, P. B., Zhang, D., Zhou, L., & Fu, X. (2010). Effects of culture, social presence, and group composition on trust in technology-supported decision-making groups. Information Systems Journal, 20(3): 297–315.

Lozano E., Joyce A., Schiemann R., Ting A., & Yahyavi D. (2010). 'Wikileaks and Whistleblowing: Digital Information Leakage and its Impact on Society', see: http://cs.stanford.edu/people/eroberts/cs201/projects/2010-11/WikiLeaks/online.html

Luk S. C. Y. (2012). Questions of ethics in public sector management: The case study of Hong Kong. *Public Personnel Management*, *41*(2), 361–378.

Lusk, S. and N. Bircks (2014). Rethinking Public Strategy. Basingstoke: Palgrave Macmillan.

Luxembourgish Ministry of Civil Service and Administrative Reform and OECD (2015). 'Managing a Diverse Public Administration or Effectively Responding to the Needs of a More Diverse Workforce', *European Public Administration Network Survey*

Lynn Jr, L. E. (2006). *Public management: Old and new*. London: Routledge.

Lyons, S., & Kuron, L. (2014). Generational differences in the workplace: A review of the evidence and directions for future research. *Journal of Organizational Behavior*, *35*(S1), 139–157.

Lyons, S. T., Schweitzer, L., & Ng, E. S. (2015). How have careers changed? An investigation of changing career patterns across four generations. Journal of Managerial Psychology, 30(1).

Lyons, S., Ng, E. S., & Schweitzer, L. (2014). Changing Demographics and the Shifting Nature of Careers: Implications for Research and Human Resource Development. Human Resource Development Review, 13 (2),180–205.

Lyons, S. T., Ng, E. S. W., & Schweitzer, L. (2012). Generational career shift: Millennials and the changing nature of careers in Canada, in Ng, E. S. W., Lyons, S. T., & Schweitzer, L. Managing the new workforce: International perspectives on the millennial generation. Northampton, MA: Edward Elgar.

Lyons, S., Urick, M., Kuron, L., & Schweitzer, L. (2015). Generational Differences in the Workplace: There is Complexity beyond the Stereotypes. Industrial and Organizational Psychology: perspectives on science and practice, 8 (3), 346–356, doi:10.1017/iop.2015.48.

Lyons, S.T., Duxbury, L.E. and Higgins, C.A. (2006). A comparison of the values and commitment of private sector, public sector, and parapublic sector employees. Public Administration Review 66 (4): 605–618.

MacAskil E. (2013). 'Edward Snowden: How the Spy Story of the Age Leaked Out', *The Guardian* see: http://www.theguardian.com/world/2013/jun/11/edward-snowden-nsa-whistleblower-profile

MacCarthaigh, Muiris (2008). Public service values. Dublin: Institute of Public Administration.

Machiavelli, Niccolò (1469–1527) translated by Parks, Tim (ed.) The Prince: A new translation by Tim Parks (London, Penguin Classics: 2009). Available at: http://

gateway.proquest.com.libproxy1.nus.edu.sg/openurl?ctx_ver=Z39.88–2003
&xri:pqil:res_ver=0.2&res_id=xri:lion&rft_id=xri:lion:ft:pr:Z001579950:0

Machiavelli, N. (1532). Il Principe. translated by Tim Parks. New York: Penguin Classics, 2009.

Mackinnon R. (2012). 'We're Losing Control of Our Digital Privacy', *CNN* see: http://edition.cnn.com/2012/01/26/opinion/mackinnon-sopa-government-sur-veillance/

Mackinnon R. (2012). 'We're Losing Control of Our Digital Privacy', *CNN*

MacKinnon, R. (2012). The netizen. *Development*, *55*(2), 201–204.

Macnamara J., Sakinofsky P., & Beattie J. (2012). 'Electoral Engagement: Maintaining and Enhancing Democratic Paritcipation through Social Media', *A Report for Australian Electoral Commission*.

Maesschalck, J. (2004). Approaches to ethics management in the public sector: A proposed extension of the compliance-integrity continuum. *Public Integrity*, *7*(1), 20–41.

Mair, Peter (2013). Ruling the Void. The Hollowing Out of Western Democracy. New York: Verso Books.

Mahbubani, K. (2008). *The new Asian hemisphere: The irresistible shift of global power to the East*. New York: Public Affairs.

Mahbubani, K. (2013). *The great convergence and the logic of one world*. New York: Public Affairs.

Mahbubani K. (2015). *Can Singapore survive?* Singapore: Straits Times Press Pte Ltd.

Mahler, J. (2012). The telework divide managerial and personnel challenges of telework. *Review of Public Personnel Administration*, *32*(4), 407–418.

Malatesta, D., and D. Van Slyke. 2015. "Complex Contracting. Government Purchasing in the Wake of the US Coast Guard's Deepwater Program." *Journal of Public Administration Research and Theory* (2015): 655–658.

Mannhelm M. (2013). 'Public Servant Loses Fight Over Twitter Attack on Government', *The Sydney Morning Herald* see: http://www.smh.com.au/national/pub-lic-servant-loses-fight-over-twitter-attack-on-government-20130812–2rsgn.html

Manyika, J., Chui, M., Bughin, J., Dobbs, R., Bisson, P., & Marrs, A. (2013). *Disruptive technologies: Advances that will transform life, business, and the global economy*. New York: McKinsey Global Institute, Vol. 12.

Manzie, Stella and Hartley, Jean (2013). Dancing on Ice: leadership with political astuteness by senior public servants in the UK. The Open University Business School, Milton Keynes, UK.

March, J. G., & Olsen, J. P. (1983). The new institutionalism: Organizational factors in political life. *American Political Science Review*, *78*(03), 734–749.

March, J.G. and Olsen, J.P. (1989). *Rediscovering Institutions*. New York: Maxwell Macmillan International.

March, James (1991). Exploration and exploitation in organizational learning. *Organization Science*, *2*(1), 71–87.

Margetts, H. Z. (2011). Experiments for public management research. *Public Management Review*, *13*(2), 189–208.

Masum, Hassan, Ranck, Jody & Singer, Peter A. (2010). Five promising methods for health foresight. *Foresight*, *12*(1),54–66.

Matmiller M. (2016)'Digital Equity', *Seattle.Gov*. see: http://www.seattle.gov/tech/initiatives/digital-equity

Mayer-Schönberger, V., & Cukier, K. (2013). *Big data: A revolution that will transform how we live, work, and think*. Houghton: Mifflin Harcourt.

Mazuccato, M. (2013). The Entrepreneurial State. Debunking Public vs. Private Sector Myths. London: Anthem Press.

McCann, J. E., & Selsky, J. (1984). Hyperturbulence and the emergence of type 5 environments. *Academy of Management Review, 9*(3), 460–470.

McCarthy T. (2015). 'New York City Adds Two Muslim to Public School Calendar', *The Guardian* see: http://www.theguardian.com/us-news/2015/mar/04/new-york-city-muslim-holidays-public-schools

McCreary, L. (2014). How to handle your first meeting with a new boss. Retrieved from https://hbr.org/2014/12/how-to-handle-your-first-meeting-with-a-new-boss

McGregor S. (2016). 'Apple Isn't Protecting a Shooter's iPhone Data - They're Defending Digital Privacy', *The Guardian* see: http://www.theguardian.com/commentisfree/2016/feb/18/san-bernardino-shooter-iphone-apple-tim-cook-fbi-decrypt-unlock

McGuire, M. (2006). Collaborative public management: Assessing what we know and how we know it. *Public Administration Review, 66*(s1), 33–43.

McGuire, M. and R. Agranoff. 2011. 'The Limitations of Public Management Networks', Public Administration, 98, 2, 265–84.

McKinsey Global Institute (2012). *Urban world: Cities and the rise of the consuming class*. New York: McKinsey Global Institute.

McKinsey Global Institute (2013). *Disruptive technologies: Advances that will transform life, business, and the global economy*. Washington, D.C.: McKinsey Global Institute.

McLuhan, M., & Fiore, Q. (1967). The medium is the message. New York: Random House, Vol. 123, pp. 126–128.

McLuhan, M. (1967). The Medium is the Message. New York: Penguin Books.

Medrano, L. (2014). 'Virtual Birder Fence Idea Revived Another Billion Dollar Boondoggle?', *The Christian Science Monitor* see: http://www.csmonitor.com/USA/2014/0319/Virtual-border-fence-idea-revived.-Another-billion-dollar-boondoggle-video

Meijer, A. (2015). E-governance innovation: Barriers and strategies. *Government Information Quarterly, 32*(2), 198–206.

Meijer, A. J., & Torenvlied, R. (2014). Social media and the new organization of government communications. An empirical analysis of twitter usage by the Dutch police. *The American Review of Public Administration, 46*(2), 143–161.

Meijer, A., t' Hart, P. & Worthy, B. (2015). Assessing government transparency. An interpretive framework. *Administration & Society*. doi:10.1177/0095399715598341.

Meijer, A. J. (2014). From Hero-Innovators to Distributed heroism: An in-depth analysis of the role of individuals in public sector innovation. Public Management Review, 16(2), 199–216.

Melbourne School of Government (2013). *The 21st century civil servant. A discussion paper*. Melbourne: Melbourne School of Government and the Victorian Department of Premier and Cabinet

Menyah D. (2010). 'Ethical Dilemmas and the Public Service', *CAPAM Report*

Menzel, D. C. (1997). Teaching ethics and values in public administration: Are we making a difference? *Public Administration Review, 57* (3), 224–230.

Menzel, D. C. (2012). *Ethics management for public administrators: Leading and building organizations of integrity*. Armonk: M. E. Sharpe.

Mergel, I. (2010). Government 2.0 revisited: Social media strategies in the public sector. Washington, D.C.: IBM Center for the Business of Government.

Mergel, I. (2011). Crowdsourced ideas make participating in government cool again. *PA Times*, *34*(4), 4–6.

Mergel, I. (2012). *Social media in the public sector: A guide to participation, collaboration and transparency in the networked world.* John Wiley & Sons.

Mergel, I. (2014, June). Social media adoption: Toward a representative, responsive or interactive government? In *Proceedings of the 15th Annual International Conference on Digital Government Research.* ACM, pp. 163–170.

Messara L. C. (2014). Religious diversity at work: The perceptual effects of religious discrimination on employee engagement and commitment. *Contemporary Management Research*, *10*(1), 59–80.

Messarra, L. C. (2014). Religious diversity at work: The perceptual effects of religious discrimination on employee engagement and commitment. *Contemporary Management Research*, *10*(1), 59.

Miles, R. E. (1978). The origin and meaning of Miles' Law. *Public Administration Review*, *38*(5), 399–403.

Ministry of Devolution and Planning (2015). 'Huduma Center Wins Public Service Forum Award In Medellin, Columbia', see: http://www.devolutionplanning.go.ke/?post_type=news&p=995

Ministry of Finance (2013). *Public-private comparator manual.* The Netherlands: The Hague.

Mintrom, Michael. 1997. Policy Entrepreneurs and the Diffusion of Innovation. American Journal of Political Science 41: 738–70.

Mischen, Pamela (2015). Collaborative network capacity. *Public Management Review*, *17*(3), 380–403.

Mitchell, R. K., Agle, B. R., & Wood, D. J. (1997). Toward a theory of stakeholder identification and salience: Defining the principle of who and what really counts. *Academy of Management Review*, *22*(4), 853–886.

Montanaro D. (2015). 'Fact Check: Hilary Clinton, Those Emails and the Law', *NPR* see: http://www.npr.org/sections/itsallpolitics/2015/04/02/396823014/fact-check-hillary-clinton-those-emails-and-the-law

Moore, G. (2014). Crossing the Chasm. 3rd Ed. New York: Harper Business.

Moore, M. (2000). Managing for Value: Organizational Strategy in For-Profit, Nonprofit, and Governmental Organizations. Nonprofit and Voluntary Sector Quarterly 29: 183–204.

Moore, M. H. (1995). *Creating public value: Strategic management in government.* Cambridge, MA: Harvard University Press.

Moore, M. H. (2013). *Recognizing public value.* Cambridge, MA: Harvard University Press.

Moore, M. H. and Jean Hartley. 2008. Innovations in governance. Public Management Review, 10(1): 3–20.

Morris P. (2011). *Religious diversity in the workplace: Questions and concerns', Auckland.* New Zealand: Human Rights Commission

Morrison, E. W. (2002). Newcomers' relationships: The role of social network ties during socialization. *Academy of Management Journal*, *45*(6), 1149–1160.

Morse, R. S. (2008). Developing public leaders in an age of collaborative governance. In R. S. Morse & T. F. Buss (Eds), Innovations in public leadership development (pp. 79–100). Armonk, NY: M. E. Sharpe.

Moshe, Mira (2010). It's about time: policy time. *Policy Studies*, *31*(3), 319–330.

Motivaction (2013). Mentaliteitstrends 2013 [Mentality trends 2013]. Amsterdam: Motivaction.

Moulton, S., & Wise, C. (2010). Shifting boundaries between the public and private sectors: Implications from the economic crisis. *Public Administration Review*, 70(3), 349–360.

Moynihan, D. P. & Pandey, S. K. (2010). 'The big question for performance management. Why do managers use performance information?'. *Journal of Public Management Research and Theory*, 20(4), 849–866.

Mulgan, G. (2014). *Innovation in the public sector: How can organizations better create, improve and adapt?* London: Nesta.

Mulgan, R. (2003). *Holding power to account: Accountability in modern democracies*. Basingstoke: Palgrave Macmillan.

Mulgan, R. (2014). *Making open government work*. Basingtoke: Palgrave Macmillan.

Murphy, M., Arenas, D. and Batista, J.M. (2015). Value Creation in Cross-Sector Collaborations: The Roles of Experience and Alignment. Journal of Business Ethics 130 (1): 145–162.

Mutuku, D. (2015). 'How Huduma is transforming public service', *Standard Digital* see: http://www.standardmedia.co.ke/article/2000169141/how-huduma-is-transforming-public-service

Myers, David (2000). American Paradox. New Haven" Yale University Press.

Myers, K. K., & Sadaghiani, K. (2010). Millennials in the workplace: A communication perspective on millennials' organizational relationships and performance. *Journal of Business and Psychology*, 25(2), 225–238.

Nabatchi, T. (2012). *Democracy in motion. Evaluating the practice and impact of deliberative civic engagement*. Oxford: Oxford University Press.

Nabatchi, T. (2014). Deliberative civic engagement in public administration and policy. Journal of Public Deliberation 10 (1): 1–4.

Nabatchi, T., & Leighninger, M. (2015). *Public participation for 21st century democracy*. New York: John Wiley & Sons.

Nabatchi, T., Ertinger, E., & Leighninger, M. (2015). The Future of Public Participation: Better Design, Better Laws, Better Systems. *Conflict Resolutions Quarterly*, 33(s1), 35–44.

Naisbitt, J. (1988). *Megatrends: Ten new directions changing our lives*. New York: Grand Central Publishing.

National Population and Talent Division (2013). A Sustainable Population for a Dynamic Singapore: Population White Paper. Available at: http://population.sg/whitepaper/resource-files/population-white-paper.pdf

Needham, C., & Mangan, C. (2014). *The 21st century public servant*. Birmingham: University of Birmingham.

Needham, C., en C. Mangan (2016). The 21st Century Public Servant. Working at three boundaries of public and private. *Public Money and Management*, 36(4), 265–272.

Neo, Boon Siong & Chen, Geraldine (2007). *Dynamic governance: Embedding culture, capabilities and change in Singapore*. Singapore: World Scientific.

Newman, Janet and Clarke, John (2009). Publics, politics and power: Remaking the public in public services. London: Sage.

Ng D. S., Lyons S., & Schweitzer L. (2012). *Managing the new workforce*. Cheltenham: Edward Elgar Publishing

Ng, E. S., Schweitzer, L., & Lyons, S. T. (2010). New generation, great expectations: A field study of the millennial generation. *Journal of Business and Psychology, 25*(2), 281–292.

Ng, E., Lyons, S. T., & Schweitzer, L. (Eds.). (2012). *Managing the new workforce: International perspectives on the millennial generation.* Cheltenham: Edward Elgar Publishing.

NIA (International Institute on Ageing) (2015). World Population Ageing 2013. Malta: United Nations.

Nieuwenkamp, R. (2001). *De prijs van het politieke primaat: Wederzijds vertrouwen en loyaliteit in de verhouding tussen bewindspersonen en ambtelijke top.* Delft: Eburon.

Ning Li, Xiaoming Zheng, T. Brad Harris, Xin Liu, Bradley L. Kirkman. Recognizing "Me" Benefits "We": Investigating the Positive Spillover Effects of Formal Individual Recognition in Teams. Journal of Applied Psychology, 2016; DOI: 10.1037/apl0000101.

Noe, R. A. (1988). An investigation of the determinants of successful assigned mentoring relationships. *Personnel Psychology, 41*(3), 457–479.

Noordegraaf, M. (2004). *Management in het publieke domein: issues, instituties en instrumenten.* Bussum: Coutinho.

Noordegraaf, M. (2007). From "Pure" to "Hybrid" professionalism present-day professionalism in ambiguous public domains. *Administration & Society, 39*(6), 761–785.

Noordegraaf, M. (2015). *Public Management: Performance, Professionalism and Politics.* Basingstoke: Palgrave Macmillan.

Norwegian Ministry of Government Administration and Reform (2008). 'Leadership in Norway's Civil Service', *Norwegian Ministry of Government Administration* and *Reform*

Nye, Joseph C. (2010). *The powers to lead.* Oxford: Oxford University Press.

Nye, J.C. (2010). *The Powers to Lead.* Oxford: Oxford University Press.

O'Flynn, Janine (2009). The Cult of Collaboration in Public Policy. The Australian Journal of Public Administration (68): 1: 112–116.

'O Leary, R. (2005). The Ethics of Dissent. Managing Guerilla Government. London: CQ Press.

O'Leary, Rosemary and Vij, Nidhi (2012). Collaborative Public Management: Where Have We Been and Where Are We Going? The American Review of Public Administration, 42(5), 507–522.

O'Neill B. (2013). 'The Ethics of Whistleblowing', *Mises Institute* see: https://mises.org/library/ethics-whistleblowing

OECD (2005). 'Managing Conflict of Interest in the Public Sector A Toolkit'

OECD (2010). 'The Emerging Middle Class In Developing Countries' Working Paper No. 285. Available at: https://www.oecd.org/dev/44457738.pdf

OECD (2008). OECD Key Environmental Indicators. Paris: OECD.

OECD (2009). Government at a Glance. Paris. OECD.

OECD (2015). Government at a Glance. Paris. OECD.

OECD (2015). OECD Public Governance Reviews. Estonia and Finland; Fostering Strategic Capacity across Governments and Digital Services across Borders. Paris: OECD.

O' Flynn, J. (2009). The cult of collaboration in public policy. *Australian Journal of Public Administration, 68*(1), 112–116.

Ohm, P. (2010). Broken promises of privacy: Responding to the surprising failure of anonymization. *UCLA Law Review*, *57*(6), 1701.

O'Leary, R. (2010). Guerrilla employees: Should managers nurture, tolerate, or terminate them? *Public Administration Review*, *70*(1), 8–19.

O'Leary, Rosemary, Choi, Yujin & Gerard, Catherine, M. (2012). 'The skill set of the successful collaborator' *Public Administration Review*, *72*(1), 570–583.

Osborne, D. and Gaebler, T. (1992). *Reinventing government. How the entrepreneurial spirit is transforming the public sector.* Reading: Addison-Wesley.

Osborne, S. P. (2009). Debate: Delivering public services: Are we asking the right questions? *Public Money & Management*, *29*(1), 5–7.

Osborne, S. P., and Brown, K. (2005). Managing change and innovation in public service organizations. London and New York: Routledge.

Osborne, S. P., and Brown, L. (2011). Innovation, public policy and public services delivery in the UK. The word that would be king? Public Administration, *89*(4),1335–1350.

Osborne, S. P., and Brown K. (2013). —Introduction: Innovation in Public Services, in S. P. Osborne and K. Brown, eds, Handbook of Innovation in Public Services. Cheltenham, UK: Edward Elgar, pp. 1–14.

Osborne, S. P. (Ed.). (2010). *The new public governance: Emerging perspectives on the theory and practice of public governance.* London; New York: Routledge.

Osborne, S. P., Radnor, Z., & Nasi, G. (2013). A new theory for public service management? Toward a (public) service-dominant approach. *The American Review of Public Administration*, *43*(2), 135–158.

Osborne, Stephen P. (2006). 'The New Public Governance?' *Public Management Review*, *8*(3), 377–388.

Oster, S. M. (1995). Strategic management for nonprofit organizations: Theory and cases. New York: Oxford University Press.

Ostrom, Elinor (1996). 'Crossing the Great Divide: Coproduction, Synergy, and Development' *World Development*, *24*(6), 1073–1087.

Overmyer, S. P. (2011). Implementing telework: Lessons learned from four federal agencies. Arlington, VA: IBM Center for the Business of Government.

Overview of Andhra Pradesh Smartcard Project (2010). Retrieved from http://www.rd.ap.gov.in/smartcard/note_smartcard

Paarlberg, L. E., & Lavigna, B. (2010). Transformational leadership and public service motivation: Driving individual and organizational performance. *Public Administration Review*, *70*(5), 710–718.

Page, E. 2012. Policy without Politicians: Bureaucratic Influence in Comparative Perspective. Oxford: Oxford University Press.

Paine, L. S. (1994). Managing for organizational integrity. *Harvard Business Review*, *72*(2), 106–117.

Paine, L. S. (2000). Does ethics pay? *Business Ethics Quarterly*, *10*(01), 319–330.

Pajo, K., & McGhee, P. (2003). The institutionalisation of business ethics: are New Zealand organisations doing enough? *Journal of Management & Organization*, *9*(01), 52–65.

Parks, Roger B., Paula C. Baker, Larry Kiser, Ronald Oakerson, Elinor Ostrom, Vincent Ostrom, Stephen L. Percy, Martha B. Vandivort, Gordon P. Whitaker & Rick Wilson (1981). Consumers as co-producers of public services: some economic and institutional considerations. *Policy Studies Journal*, *9*(7), 1001–1011.

Parry, E., Unite, J., Chuddzikowski, K., Briscoe, J. P., & Shen, Y. (2012). Career success in the younger generation. In E. S. Ng, S. T. Lyons, & L. Schweitzer (Eds.), Managing the New Workforce: International Perspectives in the Millennial Generation (pp. 242–261). Cheltenham, UK: Edward Elgar Publishing Limited.

Partridge, P. H. (1974). An evaluation of bureaucratic power. *Australian Journal of Public Administration, 33*(2), 99–115.

Pasotti, E. (2010). *Political branding in cities: the decline of machine politics in Bogotá, Naples, and Chicago.* Cambridge; New York: Cambridge University Press.

Peixoto, Tiago. (2014). Participatory Budgeting Map. https://maps.google.com/maps/ms?ie=UTF8&hl=en&msa=0&msid=210554752554258740073.00045675b996d14eb6c3a&t=m&11=40.979898,14.765625&spn=145.175291,298.828125&z=1&source=embed [accessed January 30, 2015]

Penn, Mark, & E. Kinney Zalesne (2009). *Microtrends: The small forces behind tomorrow's big changes.* New York: Twelve.

Perrewé, P. L., & Nelson, D. L. (2004). Gender and career success: The facilitative role of political skill. *Organizational Dynamics, 33*(4), 366–378.

Perrow, C. (1986). Economic theories of organization. *Theory and Society, 15*(1), 11–45.

Perry, J. L., & Wise, L. R. (1990). The motivational bases of public service. *Public Administration Review,* 367–373.

Perry, J. L., Hondeghem, A., & Wise, L. R. (2010). Revisiting the motivational bases of public service: Twenty years of research and an agenda for the future. *Public Administration Review, 70*(5), 681–690.

Perry, J.L. (1996). Measuring Public Service Motivation: An Assessment of Construct Reliability and Validity. *Journal of Public Administration Research and Theory* 6 (1): 5–22.

Perry, James L. 2000. "Bringing society in: Toward a theory of public service motivation", *Journal of Public Administration Research and Theory,* 10 (2): 471–488.

Pestoff, V. (1998). Beyond the market and state: social enterprises and civil democracy in a welfare society. Farnham: Ashgate.

Pestoff, V. (1995). Citizens as co-producers of social services - from the welfare state to the welfare mix. In Pestoff, V., ed., *Reforming social services in central and eastern Europe - An eleven nation overview.* Cracow: Academy of Economics, pp. 29–117.

Peters, B. G., & Barker, A. (1993). Advising West European governments: Inquiries, expertise and public policy. Edinburgh: Edinburgh University Press.

Petersen, J. L. (2000). Out of the Blue: How to Anticipate Big Future Surprises. Lanham: Madison Books.

Pew (2010), web source: http://www.pewresearch.org/2010/03/11/portrait-of-the-millennials/

Pina e Cunha, M. 2005. Bricolage in Organizations. Lisbon: Mimeo.

Pink, Daniel H. (2009). Drive. The surprising truth about what motivates us. New York: Penguin.

Pitts, D. W., & Wise, L. R. (2010). Workforce diversity in the new millennium: Prospects for research. *Review of Public Personnel Administration, 30*(1), 44–69.

Pollitt, C. (2000). Institutional amnesia: A paradox of the 'Information Age'? *Prometheus, 18*(1), 5–16.

Pollitt, C. (2000). How do we know how good public services are? *Governance in the twenty-first century: revitalizing the public service*. Montreal: McGill-Queen's University Press, pp. 119–52.

Pollitt, C. (2010a). Cuts and reforms—Public services as we move into a new era. *Society and Economy*, 32(1), 17–31.

Pollitt, C. (2010b). Simply the best? The international benchmarking of reform and good governance. *Comparative administrative change and reform: Lessons learned*. Montreal; Ithaca: McGill-Queen's University Press, pp. 91–113.

Pollitt, Christopher (2011). '30 years of public management reforms: Has there been a pattern?' *World Bank Blog: Governance for Development*. Available at: http://blogs.worldbank.org/governance/30-years-of-public-management-reforms-has-there-been-a-pattern

Pollitt, C., & Bouckaert, G. (2011). 3rd Ed. *Public management reform: A comparative analysis-new public management, governance, and the Neo-Weberian state*. Oxford; New York: Oxford University Press.

Pollitt, C. (2008). *Time, policy, management: Governing with the past: Governing with the past*. Oxford: OUP.

Pollitt, C. (2009). BUREAUCRACIES REMEMBER, POST-BUREAUCRATIC ORGANIZATIONS FORGET? 87 (2): 198–218

Porfon L. D. (2013). 'Organisational System Gender Bias Within Canadian Public Sector Organisations', *Athabasca University, Master of Arts - Integrated Studies*.

Porter, M.E. and Kramer, M.R. (2006), Strategy and society: the link between competitive advantage and corporate social responsibility. Harvard Business Review 84 (12): 78–92.

Prahalad, C. K., and Venkat Ramaswamy. 2004. "Co-creation experiences: The next practice in value creation". Journal of Interactive Marketing no. 18 (3):5–14.

Provan, K. G., & P. Kenis. (2008). Modes of network governance: Structure, management, and effectiveness. *Journal of Public Administration Research and Theory*, 18(2), 229–52.

Public Sector Commission (2014). 'General Workforce and Diversity Planning', *Government of Western Australia* see: https://publicsector.wa.gov.au/workforce/workforce-planning/toolkit

Public Service Commission of Canada (2014). 'Guidance Document for Participating in Non-Candidacy Political Activities', see: http://www.psc-cfp.gc.ca/plac-acpl/guidance-direction-eng.htm

Public Services Alliance (2015). 'DIY Workforce: Uberization of American Jobs'. Available at: http://publicservicesalliance.org/2015/07/13/diy-workforce-uberization-of-american-jobs/

Putters, K. (2009). *Besturen met duivelselastiek*. Inaugural lecture: Erasmus University Rotterdam.

Public Service Division (2016). http://www.psd.gov.sg/what-we-do/developing-leadership-in-the-service

Puttick, R., Baeck, P., & Colligan, P. (2014). i-teams. The teams and funds making innovation happen in governments around the world: UK: Nesta.

Quah, Jon S. T. (2011). *Curbing Corruption in Asian Countries: An Impossible Dream?* Bingley: Emerald Group Publishing.

Quah, Jon S. T. (2015). Evaluating the effectiveness of anti-corruption agencies in five Asian countries. *Asian Education and Development Studies*, 4(1), 143–159.

Rabin J. (2003). 'Encyclopedia of Public Administration and Public Policy: A-J Decker Encyclopedia Series', *CRC*

Rabin, J. (2003). *Encyclopedia of public administration and public policy: AJ.* Boca Raton: CRC Press, Vol. 1.

Radnor, Z.J. and J. Boaden. 2004. Developing an understanding of corporate anorexia. International Journal of Operations and Production Management, 24(4): 424–440.

Radnor, Zoe, and Stephen P. Osborne. 2013. Lean: A Failed Theory for Public Services? Public Management Review 15(2): 265–87.

Ragins, B. R. (1997). Diversified mentoring relationships in organizations: A power perspective. *Academy of Management Review*, 22(2), 482–521.

Ragins, B. R., & Kram, K. E. (2007). *The handbook of mentoring at work: Theory, research, and practice.* Los Angeles: Sage Publications.

Raile Eric D. (2013). 'Building Ethical Capital: Perceptions of Ethical Climate in the Public Sector' *Public Administration Review*, 73(2) 253–262.

Ramirez E. Brill J., Ohlahausen M. K., & McSweeny T. (2016). Big Data: A Tool for Inclusion or Exclusion? Understanding the Issues', *FTC Report*

Ramirez, Rafael, Mukherjee, Malobi, Vezzoli, Simona, Kramer, Arnoldo Matus (2015). Scenarios as a scholarly methodology to produce "interesting research". *Futures, 71,* 70–87.s

RAND. (2013). Cyber-security threat characterization. Retrieved from http://www.rand.org/content/dam/rand/pubs/research_reports/RR200/RR235/RAND_RR235.pdf

Rayner, J. Williams, H.M., Lawton, A., and C.W. Allinson. 2011. Public Service Ethos: Developing a Generic Measure. *JPART* 21 (1): 27–51.

Rayner, J., Lawton, A., & Williams, H. M. (2012). Organizational citizenship behavior and the public service ethos: Whither the organization? *Journal of Business Ethics, 106*(2), 117–130.

Redman B. (2014). 'Snowden and Institutional Corruption, What Have We Learnt', *Edmond J. Safra Center For Ethics* see: http://ethics.harvard.edu/blog/snowden-and-institutional-corruption-what-have-we-learned

Redman-Simmons L. (2009). 'Bureaucracy vs. the Public Service Ethos: Contemporary Concepts of Public Service', *NYSPSA 63rd Annual Conference*

Rehg, M. T., Miceli, M. P., Near, J. P., & Van Scotter, J. R. (2008). Antecedents and outcomes of retaliation against whistleblowers: Gender differences and power relationships. *Organization Science, 19*(2), 221–240.

Reitman R. (2011). 'Will the Rise of WikiLeaks Competitors Make Whistleblowing Resistant to Censorship?', *Electronic Frontier Foundation* see: https://www.eff.org/deeplinks/2011/02/will-rise-wikileaks-competitors-make

Reynaers, A. (2014). It takes two to tangle: Public Private Partnerships and their impact on Public values, doctoral thesis, VU University Amsterdam. ISBN 978 90 90280912.

Reynaers, A.M. (2015), Public Water in Private Hands: A case study on the safeguarding of public values in the first DBFMO in the Dutch water sector. International Journal of Water Governance 3 (2): 1–16.

Rhisiart, Martin & Poli, Roberto (2015). Ethical issues in futures studies: Theoretical development and applications. *Futures, 71,* 88–90.

Rhodes, R.A.W. (2011). Everyday Life in British Government. Oxford: Oxford University Press.

Rhodes, R. A. W. (1996). The new governance: Governing without government. *Political Studies, 44*(4), 652–667.

Rhodes, R. A. W. (2016). Recovering the craft of public administration. *Public Administration Review, 76*(4), 638–647.

Rhodes, R. A. W. & Wanna, J. (2007). The limits to public value, or rescuing responsible government from the platonic guardians. *Australian Journal of Public Administration*, 66(4), 406–421.

Rhodes, R. A. W. (1994). The hollowing out of the state: The changing nature of the public service in Britain. *The Political Quarterly*, 65(2), 125–233.

Riccucci, N. (2002). *Managing diversity in public sector workforces.* New York: Westview Press.

Riccucci, N. M. (2009). The pursuit of social equity in the federal government: A road less traveled? *Public Administration Review*, 69(3), 373–382.

Riccucci, N. M. (2010). *Public administration: Traditions of inquiry and philosophies of knowledge.* Washington, D.C.: Georgetown University Press.

Ridley-Duff, R. and S. Bull (2015). Understanding Social Enterprise. London: Sage.

Rittel, H. W., & Webber, M. M. (1973). Dilemmas in a general theory of planning. *Policy Sciences*, 4(2), 155–169.

Ritz, A., Brewer, G. A., & Neumann, O. (2016). Public service motivation: A systematic literature review and outlook. *Public Administration Review*, 76(3), 414–426.

Roberts D., Ackerman S. (2015). 'NSA Mass Phone Surveillance Revealed by Edward Snowden Ruled Illegal', *The Guardian* see: http://www.theguardian.com/us-news/2015/may/07/nsa-phone-records-program-illegal-court

Roberts, R. (2009). The rise of compliance-based ethics management: Implications for organizational ethics. *Public Integrity*, 11(3), 261–278.

Roberts, Alasdair S., (2012) Transparency in Troubled Times. Tenth World Conference of the International Ombudsman Institute, November 2012; Suffolk University Law School Research Paper 12–35.

Roberts, B.H. (2014). Managing Systems of Secondary Systems. Policy Responses in International Development. Brussels: Cities Alliance.

Roberts, N.C., and Raymond Trevor Bradley (1991). Stakeholder Collaboration and Innovation: A Study of Public Policy Initiation at the State Level. Journal of Applied Behavioral Science 27 (2): 209–27.

Roberts, Nancy C. and Paula J. King. Transforming Public Policy: Dynamics of Policy Entrepreneurship and Innovation. San Francisco, CA: Jossey-Bass Publishers, 1996.

Rodrigues, R., Huber, M. & Lamura, G. (eds.) (2012). Facts and Figures on Healthy Ageing and Long-term Care. European Centre for Social Welfare Policy and Research: Vienna.

Rodwan J. G. (2015). 'Should Public Schools Close for Christian, Jewish, and Muslim Holidays?', *The Humanist* see: http://thehumanist.com/news/religion/should-public-schools-close-for-christian-jewish-and-muslim-holidays

Roland Berger Strategy Consultants (2011). *Trend Compendium 2030.* Available at: https://www.rolandberger.com/gallery/trend-compendium/tc2030/content/assets/trendcompendium2030.pdf

Romme, A. G. L. & Van Witteloostuijn, A. (1999). Circular organizing and triple loop learning. Journal of Organizational Change Management 12(5), 439–454

Rorh, J. (1992). Ethics for Bureaucrats. An Essay on Law and Values. 2nd Ed. New York: CRC Press.

Rose, R. P. (2013). Preferences for Careers in Public Work: Examining the Government-Nonprofit Divide among Undergraduates through Public Service Motivation. *The American review of Public Administration* 43 (4): 416–437.

Rosen, Yigal (2015). *Handbook of research on technology tools for real-world skill development*. Hershey, PA: Information Science Reference.

Rosenbloom, David (2015). The constitution and a reasonable public servant. In Lily Xiao Hong Lee & David Rosenbloom (eds) *A reasonable public servant: Constitutional foundations of administrative conduct in the United States*. New York: Routledge, pp. 3–18.

Rothkopf, D. (2008). *Superclass: The global power elite and the world they are making*. New York: Macmillan.

Rustin, B. (1955). Speaking truth to power: A Quaker search for an alternative to violence. Retrieved from https://afsc.org/sites/afsc.civicactions.net/files/documents/Speak_Truth_to_Power.pdf

Rutgers, M. (2010). Theory and scope of public administration: An introduction to the study's epistemology. *Public Administration Review. Foundations of Public Administration Series*, 1–45.

Rutgers, M.R. (2005). Retracing Public Administration. Public Administration 83 (1): 243–264.

Rutgers, M. 2008. Sorting Out Pulic Values? On the Contingency of Value Classifications in Public Administration. Administrative Theory & Praxis, 30, 92–113.

Rutgers, M. 2015. As Good as it Gets? On the Meaning of Public Value in the Study of Policy and Management. American Review of Public Administration, 45, 29–45.

Rutgers, M. R., & Beck Jørgensen, T. (2014). Tracing public values change: a historical study of civil service job advertisements. Contemporary Readings in Law and Social Justice, 6(2), 59–80.

Ryde, R. (2012). *Never mind the bosses: Hastening the death of deference for business success*. New York: John Wiley & Sons.

Samet, Robert H. (2014). Complexity science and theory development for the futures field. *Futures, 44*, 504–513.

Scassa, T. (2014). Privacy and Open Government. *Future Internet*, 6(2), 397–413.

Schall, E. (1997). Public-sector succession: A strategic approach to sustaining innovation. *Public Administration Review*, 57(1), 4–10.

Schein, E. H. (1992). *Organizational Culture and Leadership*. San Francisco: Jossey Bass.

Schillemans, T. (2008). Accountability in the Shadow of Hierarchy. The Horizontal Accountability of Agencies in the Netherlands. *Public Organization Review*, 8, 175–194.

Schillemans, T. (2011). Does horizontal accountability work? Evaluating potential remedies for the accountability deficit of agencies. *Administration & Society*, 43(4), 387–416.

Schillemans, T. (2015). Managing public accountability: How public managers manage public accountability. *International Journal of Public Administration*, 38(6), 433–441.

Schmidt, John Michael (2015). Policy, planning, intelligence and foresight in government organizations. *Foresight*, 17(5), 489–511.

Schnabel, P. (2015). Angst voor de toekomst en onvrede spelen Nederland parten. Dossier Sociale Vraagstukken (online publication: http://www.socialevraagstukken.nl/angst-voor-de-toekomst-en-onvrede-spelen-nederland-parten/)

Schooner, S. L., Katzenbach, J. R., Kotter, J. P., & Smith, D. K. (1997). Change, Change Leadership, and Acquisition Reform.

Schrobsdorff (2015), The Millennial Beard: Why Boomers Need Their Younger Counterparts. TIME Magazine, 3 December 2015.

Schumpeter, J. (1942). Creative destruction. *Capitalism, socialism and democracy*. New York: Harper, pp. 82–85.

Schwartz, M. S., Dunfee, T. W., & Kline, M. J. (2005). Tone at the top: An ethics code for directors? *Journal of Business Ethics*, 58(1–3), 79–100.

Scott, T. W., & Tiessen, P. (1999). Performance measurement and managerial teams. *Accounting, Organizations and Society*, 24(3), 263–285.

Scott, W.R. (1992) Organizations: Rational, natural and open systems (3rd ed.), Englewood Cliffs, NJ: Prentice Hall.

Scott, W.R. (2008). Lords of the Dance: Professionals as Institutional Agents. Organization Studies 29(2): 219–238.

Scottish Co-production Network (2013). Case study – Lochside Neighbourhood Group: Making a Difference in Our Neighbourhood. Available at: http://www.coproductionscotland.org.uk/files/7513/8728/4017/Lochside_case_study.pdf

SCP (2015). De Sociale Staat van Nederland [The Social State of the Netherlands]. The Hague: SCP.

Selsky, John W., & Parker, Barbara (2005). Cross-sector partnerships to address social issues: challenges to theory and practice. *Journal of Management*, 31(6), 840–873.

Selsky, J. W. and Parker, B. (2005). Cross-sector partnerships to address social issues: Challenges to theory and practice. Journal of Management, 31:849–873.

Seltzer L. (2013). 'How Snowden Got the NSA Documents', *ZDNet* see: http://www.zdnet.com/article/how-snowden-got-the-nsa-documents/

Senge, Peter M. (1990). The Fifth Discipline: The Art and Practice of the Learning Organization. New York: Doubleday.

Senge, Peter M. (1999). The Dance of Change: The Challenges to Sustaining Momentum in Learning Organizations. New York: Crown Business.

Sevilla I. S. (2014). 'Effectiveness of Whistleblowing - Before and After the Digital Age: An Analysis of the Impact of Whistleblowing on Documents', *MPP Professional Paper*, The University of Minnesota

Shanker V. P. (2013). 'Indian Transgender Passes Test Before Exam', *Aljazeera* see: http://www.aljazeera.com/indepth/features/2013/12/indian-transgender-passes-test-before-exam-2013129145640227933.html

Shaw, S., & Fairhurst, D. (2008). Engaging a new generation of graduates. *Education+ Training*, 50(5), 366–378.

Silverman, R.E. (2011), Performance Reviews Lose Steam. Some Companies Find New Ways to Motivate, Exchange Feedback; A Few Scrap the Practice Altogether. Wall Street Journal, 19 December 2011.

Sims, R. R., & Brinkmann, J. (2003). Enron ethics (or: Culture matters more than codes). *Journal of Business Ethics*, 45(3), 243–256.

Sims, R.R. 2003, Ethics and corporate responsibility. Why giants fall. Westport, CT: Greenwood.

Sinclair, A. (1995). The chameleon of accountability: Forms and discourses. *Accounting, Organizations and Society*, 20(2), 219–237.

Skagerlind Hede H., Westman, M., & Berglund, H. (2015). Corporate Social Responsibility through Cross-sector Partnerships: Implications for Civil Society, the State, and the Corporate Sector in India. Business and Society Review, 120(2), 245–275.

Smith, Jack E., & Saritas, Ozcan (2011). 'Science and technology foresight baker's dozen: a pocket primer of comparative and combined foresight methods. Foresight (13) 2: 79–96.

Smith, W.K., M. Gonin and M. Besharov (2013). Managing Social-Business Tensions: A Review and Research Agenda for Social Enterprise', Business Ehtics Quarterly 23 (3): 407–442.

Solem, Knut Erik (2011). Integrating foresight into government. Is it possible? Is it likely? *Foresight, 13*(2), 18–30.

Sonenshein, Raphael J. 2013. When the People Draw the Lines: An Examination of the California Citizens Redistricting Commission. Sacramento: League of Women Voters of California.

Staff Correspondent (2016). 'Public servants Get Guidelines on Social Media', *Prothom Alo* see: http://en.prothom-alo.com/bangladesh/news/98607/Govt-issues-guidelines-on-using-social-media

Stamper, C. L., & Johlke, M. C. (2003). The impact of perceived organizational support on the relationship between boundary spanner role stress and work outcomes. *Journal of Management, 29*(4), 569–588.

Standard Digital (2015). 'Government to Open 22 Additional Huduma Centers Across the Country', see: http://www.standardmedia.co.ke/business/article/2000148367/government-to-open-22-additional-huduma-centres-across-the-country

Stark, A. (2014). BUREAUCRATIC VALUES AND RESILIENCE: AN EXPLORATION OF CRISIS MANAGEMENT ADAPTATION. Public Administration 92 (3): 692–706.

State of Victoria Department of Education and Early Childhood Development (2012). Stakeholder Engagement Framework. Available at: http://www.education.vic.gov.au/Documents/about/programs/partnerships/stakeholderengagement11.pdf

Steelman, T.A. (2010). Implementing Innovation. Fostering enduring change in environmental and natural resource governance. Washington DC: Georgetown University Press.

Stella M., & Hartley J. (2013). *Dancing on ice: Leadership with political astuteness by senior public servants in the UK*. Milton Keynes UK: The Open University Business School.

Stevens, M. J., & Campion, M. A. 1994. The knowledge, skill, and ability requirements for teamwork: Implications for human resource management. Journal of Management, 20: 503–530.

Stevens M. S. (2013). 'The Facebook Question: Social Media and Local Government HR Practices'

Stewart, J. (2006). Value conflict and policy change. Review of Policy Research, 23(1) 183–195.

Stigler, G. J. 1971. The theory of economic regulation. Bell Journal of Economics and Management Science, 2: 3–21.

Stiglitz, J., Abernathy, N., Hersh, A., Konczal, M., & Holmberg, S. (2015). Rewriting the rules of the American economy. Retrieved from http://rooseveltinstitute.org/rewriting-rules-report/

Storey, Donovan (2014). 'Setting the Scene: The Rise of Secondary Cities' Presentation for the Asia Development Dialogue: Building Resilience and Effective Governance of Emerging Cities in ASEAN. Available at: http://lkyspp.nus.edu.

sg/wp-content/uploads/2014/01/Asia-Development-Dialogue-STOREY-Rev-Final-20140331.pdf

Su, X. & Bozeman, B. (2015). Public service motivation concepts and theory: A critique. *Public Administration Review*, 75(5), 700–710.

Suchman, M. C. (1995). Managing legitimacy: Strategic and institutional approaches. *Academy of Management Review*, 20(3), 571–610.

Su, X. & B. Bozeman (2009). Dynamics of Sector Switching: Hazard Models Predicting Changes from Private Sector Jobs to Public and Nonprofit Sector Jobs. *Public Administration Review* 69 (6): 1106–1114.

Swiering, J., & Wierdsma, A. (1992). Becoming a learning organization: Beyond the learning curve. Addison-Wesley: Reading.

Taleb, N. N. (2007). *The black swan: The impact of the highly improbable*. New York: Random House.

Tamás Gaspar (2015). Strategia sapiens – strategic foresight in a new perspective. *Foresight*, 17(5), 405–426.

Taylor, H. F. (1911). *Principles of scientific management*. New York and London: Harper and Brothers.

Taylor, P., & Urwin, P. (2001). Age and participation in vocational education and training. *Work, Employment & Society*, 15(4), 763–779.

Teisman, G.R. & Klijn, E.H. (2002). Partnership Arrangements: Governmental Rhetoric or Governance Scheme? Public Administration Review, 62 (2), 197–205.

Tenbrunsel, A. E., Smith-Crowe, K., & Umphress, E. E. (2003). Building houses on rocks: The role of the ethical infrastructure in organizations. *Social Justice Research*, 16(3), 285–307.

Tene, O., & Polonetsky, J. (2013). Judged by the tin man: Individual rights in the age of big data. *Journal on Telecommunications and High Technology Law*, 11(2), 351–368.

Tepper, Bennett J. 1995. Upward maintenance tactics in supervisory mentoring and nonmentoring relationships. Academy of Management Journal 38 (4):1191–1205.

Terjesen, S., Vinnicombe, S., & Freeman, C. (2007). Attracting generation Y graduates: Organisational attributes, likelihood to apply and sex differences. *Career Development International*, 12(6), 504–522.

Term Planning Tool for Developing Countries. Available at: http://www.undp.org/content/dam/undp/library/capacity-development/English/Singapore%20Centre/GPCSE_Foresight.pdf

Terry, Larry D. (1995). *Leadership of Public Bureaucracies: The Administrator as Conservator*. Thousand Oaks, CA: Sage

Tevis, Robert E. (2010). Creating the future: Goal-oriented scenario planning. *Futures*, 42, 337–344.

Thacher, D., & Rein, M. (2004). Managing value conflict in public policy. *Governance*, 17(4), 457–486.

Thompson, Dennis. (2008). Who Should Govern Who Governs? The Role of Citizens in Reforming the Electoral System. In Designing Deliberative Democracy: The British Columbia Citizens' Assembly, edited by Mark E. Warren and Hilary Pearse, 20–49. New York: Cambridge University Press.

Tidd, J. and Bessant, J. (2009), Managing Innovation: Integrating Technological, Market and Organizational Change, 5th Edition. New York: Wiley & Sons.

Tideman, T. N., & Tullock, G. (1976). A new and superior process for making social choices. *The Journal of Political Economy*, 1145–1159.

Trevino K. L., Hartman P. L., Brown M. (2000). Moral person and moral manager: How executives develop a reputation for ethical leadership. *California Management Review*, 42(4), 128.

Treviño, L. K., Brown, M., & Hartman, L. P. (2003). A qualitative investigation of perceived executive ethical leadership: Perceptions from inside and outside the executive suite. *Human Relations*, 56(1), 5–37.

Triana M. D., Garcia M. F., & Colella A. (2010). Managing diversity: How organisational efforts to support diversity moderate the effects of perceived racial discrimination on affective commitment. *Personnel Psychology*, 63(4), 817–843.

Trommel, W.A. (2009). Gulzig Bestuur [Greedy Governance]. The Hague: Boom Bestuurskunde.

Tschirhart, M., Reed, K. K., Freeman, S. J., & Anker, A. L. (2008). Is the grass greener? Sector shifting and choice of sector by MPA and MBA graduates. *Nonprofit and Voluntary Sector Quarterly*, 37(4), 668–688.

Tullock, Gordon (1976). *The Vote Motive*. London: IEA.

Tully, Cat (2015). 'Stewardship of the Future Using Strategic Foresight in 21st Century Governance' UNDP Global Centre for Public Service Excellence. Available at: http://www.undp.org/content/dam/undp/library/capacity-development/English/Singapore%20Centre/GCPSE_Stewardship-Foresight2015.pdf

Tuomo Kuosa (2011). Practising Strategic Foresight in Government. The Cases of Finland, Singapore, and the European Union. Singapore: RSIS.

Turkle, S. (2012). *Alone together: Why we expect more from technology and less from each other*. New York: Basic Books.

Twenge, J. M. (2010). A review of the empirical evidence on generational differences in work attitudes. *Journal of Business and Psychology*, 25(2), 201–210.

Twenge, J. M., & Campbell, S. M. (2012). Who are the Millennials? Empirical evidence for generational differences in work values, attitudes and personality. *Managing the new workforce: International perspectives on the millennial generation*. Cheltenham: Edward Elgar, pp. 152–180.

Twenge, J. M., & Kasser, T. (2013). Generational changes in materialism and work centrality, 1976–2007 associations with temporal changes in societal insecurity and materialistic role modeling. *Personality and Social Psychology Bulletin*, 39(7), 883–897.

Twenge, J. M., Campbell, W. K., & Freeman, E. C. (2012). Generational differences in young adults' life goals, concern for others, and civic orientation, 1966–2009. *Journal of personality and social psychology*, 102(5), 1045.

Tosey, P., M. Visser, and M.N.K. Saunders. 2012. The origins and conceptualisations of 'triple-loop' learning: A critical review. Management Learning 43(3): 291–307.

Treviño, L.K., Hartman, L.P. and Brown, M.E. (2000) "Moral person and moral manager: How executives develop a reputation for ethical leadership." California Management Review 42 (4): 128–142.

Twenge, J. M. (2006). Generation Me: Why today's young Americans are more confident, assertive, entitled—and more miserable than ever before. New York, NY: Free Press.

Twenge, J. M., Campbell, W. K., & Gentile, B. (2012). Generational increases in agentic self-evaluations among American college students, 1966 –2009. Self and Identity 11 (4): 409–427.

Twenge, Jean M., Sherman, Ryne A., and Sonja Lyubomirsky. (2016). More Happiness for Young People and Less for Mature Adults: Time Period Differences in Subjective Well-Being in the United States, 1972–2014. Social Psychological and Personality Science 7 (2): 131–141.

UNDP Global Centre for Public Service Excellence (2015). *Using strategic foresight in 21st century*. Singapore: UNDP.

UNDP (2011). *Human Development Report 2011: Sustainability and Equity: A Better Future for All*. Available at: http://hdr.undp.org/sites/default/files/reports/271/hdr_2011_en_complete.pdf

UNDP (2013). *Human Development Report 2013. The Rise of the South: Human Progress in a Diverse World*. Available at: http://hdr.undp.org/sites/default/files/reports/14/hdr2013_en_complete.pdf

UNESCO (2011). *GMR Gender Overview*. Available at: http://www.unesco.org/new/fileadmin/MULTIMEDIA/HQ/ED/pdf/gmr2011-gender-overview.pdf

United Nations Population Division (2013). *World Fertility Report 2013: Fertility at the Extremes*. Available at: http://www.un.org/en/development/desa/population/publications/pdf/fertility/worldFertilityReport2013.pdf

United Nations Population Division (2006) World Urbanization Prospects: The 2005 Revision. New York: United Nations.

USAID (2006). Stakeholder Collaboration: An Imperative for Education Quality. Available at: http://pdf.usaid.gov/pdf_docs/Pnadg024.pdf

Usher, R. and I. Bryant. 1989. Adult Education as Theory, Practice, and Research: The Captive Triangle. London: Routledge.

Vancoppenolle, Diederik, Mirko Noordegraaf and Martijn van der Steen (2011). Politieke ambtenaren? Formele en feitelijke rolverschillen tussen Nederlandse politiek assistenten en vlaamse kabinetsmedewerkers. Bestuurskunde 20 (2): 63–74.

Van de Donk, W. (2001). De gedragen gemeenschap. Den Haag: SDU Uitgevers.

Van de Walle, S., Van Roosbroek, S., & Bouckaert, G. (2008). Trust in the public sector: Is there any evidence for a long-term decline? *International Review of Administrative Sciences*, 74(1), 47–64.

Van de Walle (2014). Building Resilience in Public Organizations: The Role of Waste and Bricolage The Innovation Journal: The Public Sector Innovation Journal, volume 19(2), 2014, article 6.

Van den Heuvel, J.H.J., Huberts, L.W.J.C. and Verberk, S. (2002). *Het morele gezicht van de overheid. Waarden, normen en beleid [The moral face of government. Values, norms and policy]*. Utrecht, The Netherlands: Lemma.

Van der Meer, F. M., Van den Berg, C. F., & Dijkstra, G. S. (2013). Rethinking the 'Public Service Bargain': The changing (legal) position of civil servants in Europe. *International Review of Administrative Sciences*, 79(1), 91–109.

Van der Steen, M. (2015). De gelaagde praktijk van ambtelijk vakmanschap. In: J. J. M. Uijlenbroek (Ed.) *Staat van de Ambtelijke Dienst. De overheid in tijden van verandering*. The Hague: CAOP.

Van der Steen, M., Scherpenisse, J., van Twist, M. (2015). Sedimentatie in sturing- systeem brengen in netwerkend werken door meervouding organiseren. The Netherlands: NSOB

Van der Steen, Martijn & van der Duin, Patrick (2012). Learning ahead of time: how evaluation of foresight may add to increased trust, organizational learning and future oriented policy and strategy. *Futures, 44*, 487–493.

Van der Steen, Martijn & van Twist, Mark (2012). Beyond use: Evaluating foresight that fits. Futures, 44, 475–486.

Van der Steen, M., Z. Van der Wal, and P. Bloemen (2016). Adaptive Capacity and Policy Design in Successful Small Countries. The Delta Works Case in the Netherlands. Paper Presented at GDN Workshop, 26–27 February 2016, Singapore.

Van der Veen, R., & Trommel, W. (1999). Managed liberalization of the Dutch welfare state: A review and analysis of the reform of the Dutch social security system, 1985–1998. *Governance, 12*(3), 289–310.

Van der Voet, J. & Vermeeren (2016). Change management in hard times can change management mitigate the negative relationship between cutbacks and the organizational commitment and work engagement of public sector employees? *The American Review of Public Administration.* doi:10.1177/0275074015625828.

Van der Voet, J., Kuipers, B. S. & Groeneveld, S. M. (2016). Implementing change in public organizations: The relationship between leadership and affective commitment to change in a public sector context. *Public Management Review, 18*(6), 842–865.

Van Der Wal Z, De Graaf G., & Lasthuizen K. (2008). 'What's Valued Most? Similarities and Differences Between the Organizational Values of the Public and Private Sector', *Public Administration,* 86(2) 465–482.

Van der Wal, Z. (2008). *Value solidity. Differences, similarities and conflicts between the organizational values of government and business.* Amsterdam: VU University.

Van der Wal, Z. (2011). The content and context of organizational ethics. *Public Administration, 89*(2), 644–660.

Van der Wal, Z. (2013). Mandarins versus machiavellians? On differences between work motivations of administrative and political elites. *Public Administration Review, 73*(5), 749–759.

Van der Wal, Z. (2014). Elite ethics: Comparing public values prioritization between administrative elites and political elites. *International Journal of Public Administration, 37*(14), 1030–1043.

Van der Wal, Z. (2014b). What drives public managers in tough governance settings? In *Governing Asia: Reflections on a research journey.* Singapore: World Scientific Publishing Company, pp. 197–205.

Van der Wal, Z. (2015a). "All quiet on the non-Western front?" A review of public service motivation scholarship in non-Western contexts. *Asia Pacific Journal of Public Administration, 37*(2), 69–86.

Van der Wal, Z. (2015b). Future Business and Government Leaders of Asia: How Do They Differ and What Makes Them Tick? *Journal of Business Ethics,* 1–14. DOI: 10.1007/s10551-015-2783-1.

Van der Wal, Z. (2016). Small Countries, Big Performers: In Search of Shared Strategic Public Sector HRM Practices in Successful Small Countries. *International Journal of Public Administration,* 1–16. DOI:10.1080/01900692.2015.1122038.

Van der Wal, Z. & L. Yang (2015). Confucius meets Weber or "Managerialism takes all"? Comparing Civil Servant Values in China and the Netherlands. *International Public Management Journal, 18*(3), 411–436.

Van der Wal, Z., Graycar, A. & K. Kelly (2016). See no Evil, Hear no Evil? Assessing Corruption Risk Perceptions and Strategies of Victorian Public Bodies. *Australian Journal of Public Administration, 75*(1), 3–17.

Van der Wal, Z., Nabatchi, T., & De Graaf, G. (2015). From galaxies to universe: A cross-disciplinary review and analysis of public values publications from 1969 to 2012. *The American Review of Public Administration, 45*(1), 13–28.

Van der Wal, Z., G. de Graaf & A. Lawton (2011). Competing Values in Public Management. Introduction to the Symposium Issue. Public Management Review *13*(3): 331–341.

Van der Wal, Z., G. de Graaf & C. van Montfort (2011). Introductie: Goed Bestuur als Management van Spanningen tussen Publieke Waarden. Bestuurskunde *20*(2): 2–4.

Van der Wal, Z., Graycar, A. & K. Kelly (2016). See no Evil, Hear no Evil? Assessing Corruption Risk Perceptions and Strategies of Victorian Public Bodies. Australian Journal of Public Administration *75*(1): 3–17.

Van den Heuvel, J.H.J, Huberts, L.W.J.C., Van der Wal, Z. & K. Steenbergen (2010). Integriteit van het Lokaal Bestuur. Raadsgriffiers en gemeentesecretarissen over integriteit. Den Haag: Lemma.

Van Dijk, J. A. (2005). *The deepening divide: Inequality in the information society*. Thousand Oaks: Sage Publications.

Van Dooren, W., G. Bouckaert & J. Halligan (2015). Performance management in the public sector. London: Routledge.

Van Montfort, A. J. G. M., L. Beck and A. A. H. Twijnstra. 2013. 'Can Integrity be Taught in Public Organizations? The Effectiveness of Integrity-Training Programs for Municipal Officials'. *Public Integrity*, *15*(2):117–132.

Van Rijn, M., & van der Burgt, R. (2012). *Handboek scenarioplanning: toekomstscenario's als strategisch instrument voor het managen van onzekerheid: kijk over de horizon, voorzie, anticipeer en word succesvol*. Deventer: Kluwer.

Van Wart, Montgomery (2013). 'Lessons from Leadership Theory and the Contemporary Challenges of Leaders' *Public Administration Review*, *73*(4), 553–565.

Vandenabeele, W. (2008). Government calling: Public service motivation as an element in selecting government as an employer of choice. *Public Administration*, *86*(4), 1089–1105.

Varum, Celeste Amorium & Melo, Carla (2010). Directions in scenario planning literature – A review of the past decades. *Futures*, *42*, 355–369.

Vielmetter, G., & Sell, Y. (2014). *Leadership 2030: the six megatrends you need to understand to lead your company into the future*. AMACOM Div American Mgmt Assn.

Vitell, S. J., & Singhapakdi, A. (2008). The role of ethics institutionalization in influencing organizational commitment, job satisfaction, and esprit de corps. *Journal of Business Ethics*, *81*(2), 343–353.

Vogel, R., & Frost, J. (2009). Innovating in the German public sector: How a think tank frames the debate on NPM. *The Innovation Journal: The Public Sector Innovation Journal*, *14*(2), 1–21.

Voorberg, W. H., Bekkers,V. J. J. M., & Tummers, L. G. (2015). A systematic review of co-creation and coproduction: Embarking on the social innovation journey. *Public Management Review*, *17*(9), 1333–1357. doi:10.1080/147190 37.2014.930505

Von Hippel, Eric. 2005. Democratizing innovation: the evolving phenomenon of user innovation International Journal of Innovation Science, 1(1): 29–40.

Waehrens, Brian Vejrum & Riis, Jens Ove (2010). Failures to enact the future – A social practice perspective. *Futures*, *42*, 328–336.

Waldmeir, P. (2015). 'China Outlines Regulations for Car-hailing Apps Such As Uber', *The Financial Times* see: http://www.ft.com/intl/cms/s/0/d08338b6-6fde-11e5-ad6d-f4ed76f0900a.html#axzz3x9HLVuVm

Waldo, D. (1988). The Enterprise of Public Administration. A Summary View. Novato, CA: Chandler & Sharp Publishers.

Walker, R. M., Damanpour, F., & Devece, C. A. (2011). Management innovation and organizational performance: The mediating effect of performance management. Journal of Public Administration Research and Theory, 21(2), 367–386.

Wart, van, M., Hondeghem, A. en E. Schwella (2015). *Leadership and Culture. Comparative models of Top Civil Servant Training*. Basingstoke: Palgrave Macmillan.

Wart, van, M., Hondeghem, A. en E. Schwella (2015). *Leadership and Culture. Comparative models of Top Civil Servant Training*. Basingstoke: Palgrave Macmillan.

Watkins, M. (2013). Making virtual teams work: Ten basic principles. *Harvard Business Review*.

Watt, I. (2012). Reflections on My First Year as Secretary of the Department of the Prime Minister and Cabinet and thoughts on the future. Address to the Institute of Public Administration Australia, ACT Division, Great Hall, Parliament House, October, 5.

Wayland, Rebecca (2015). Strategic foresight in a changing world. *Foresight*, 17(5), 444–459.

Weaver, G. R., L. Treviño and P. L. Cochran. 1999. 'Corporate Ethics Programs as Control Systems: Influences of Executive Commitment and Environmental Factors'. *Academy of Management Journal* 42(1):41–57.

Weber, M. (1919). *Wissenschaft als beruf*. Munich & Leipzig: Duncker & Humblot, Vol. 1.

Weber, M. (1921). *The definition of sociology and social action*. Max Weber: Economy and Society, Berkeley, CA: University of California Press, Vol. 1978, pp. 4–26.

Weber, M. (1968). *Politics as a vocation*. Philadelphia: Fortress Press.

Weggeman, M. C. D. P. (2007). *Leidinggeven aan professionals. Niet doen*. Schiedam: Scriptum.

Weick, K.E. 1993. The collapse of sensemaking in organizations: The Mann Gulch Disaster. Administrative Science Quarterly, 38(4): 628–652.

Weick, K.E. 2005. Organizing and failures of imagination. International Public Management Journal, 8(3): 425–438.

Weigand, Kirk, Flanagan, Thomas, Dye, Kevin & Jones, Peter (2014). Collaborative foresight: Complementing long-horizon strategic planning. *Technological Forecasting and Social Change*, 85, 134–152.

Wilkins, V. M. (2006). A mixed bag: The Supreme Court's ruling on the ADEA and disparate impact. Review of Public Personnel Administration, 26, 269–274

Wilkins, V. M., & Williams, B. N. (2008). Black or blue: Racial profiling and representative bureaucracy. Public Administration Review, 68(4): 654–664.

Wilkinson, Angela & Kupers, Roland (2013). Living in the futures. *Harvard Business Review*. Available at: https://hbr.org/2013/05/living-in-the-futures

Williams, A. (2015, September 18). More Over, Millennials, Here comes Generation Z. The New York Times. Retrieved from http://www.nytimes.com/2015/09/20/fashion/move-over-millennials-here-comes-generation-z.html?_r=0

Williams, P. (2002). The competent boundary spanner. *Public Administration*, 80(1), 103–124.

Williams, P. (2013). We are all boundary spanners now? *International Journal of Public Sector Management*, 26(1), 17–32.

Williams, P. (2010). Special Agents: The Nature and Role of Boundary Spanners. Paper to the ESRC Research Seminar Series – 'Collaborative Futures: New Insights from Intra and Inter-Sectoral Collaborations', University of Birmingham, February 2010.

Williams, Christine L., Chandra Muller, and Kristine Kilanski (2012). Gendered Organizations in the New Economy. Gend Soc. 26(4): 549–573.

Wilson, W. (1887). The study of public administration. *Political Science Quarterly* 2 (2): 197–222.

Witesman E., & Walters L. (2016). The public values of political preference. *International Journal of Public Administration*, 39(1), 63–73.

Wolf, Charles (2011). 'China's Next Buying Spree: Foreign Companies' The Wall Street Journal. Available at: http://www.wsj.com/articles/SB100014240527487 04754304576095880533686442

Wood C., Steve T., Knell N., Pittman E., & Mulholland J. (2014). '2014 Digital Cities: Winners Focus on Innovation, Boosting Transparency and Privacy' see: http://www.govtech.com/local/Digital-Cities-Survey-2014.html?page=2

World Bank (2010). *World* Development Report 2010: *Development and Climate Change*. Available at: http://siteresources.worldbank.org/INTWDR2010/Resources/5287678-1226014527953/WDR10-Full-Text.pdf

World Bank (2014). *'Trade (% of GDP)'*. Available at: http://data.worldbank.org/indicator/NE.TRD.GNFS.ZS

World Economic Forum (2016). The Future of Jobs. Geneva: World Economic Forum.

Worstall, T. (2013). More People Have Mobile Phones Than Toilets.

Worstall, T. (2013). More People Have Mobile Phones Than Toilets. Forbes Magazine, 23 March 2013.

Wright, B. E., & Grant, A. M. (2010). Unanswered questions about public service motivation: Designing research to address key issues of emergence and effects. *Public Administration Review*, 70(5), 691–700.

Wu, Xun, Ramesh, M, Howlett, Michael (2015). Policy capacity: a conceptual framework for understanding policy competences and capabilities. *Policy and Society*, 34, 165–171.

Wynen, J., Verhoest, K., Ongaro, E., & Thiel, S. v. (2013). Innovation-Oriented culture in the public sector: Do managerial autonomy and result control lead to innovation? *Public Management Review*, 16(1), 45–66.

Xu V. (2015). "Edward Snowden Talks Ethics of Whistleblowing", *The Stanford Daily* see: http://www.stanforddaily.com/2015/05/18/edward-snowden-talks-ethics-of-whistleblowing/

Yadron D., Ackerman S., & Thielman S. (2016). 'Inside the FBI's Encryption Battle with Apple', *The Guardian* see: https://www.theguardian.com/technology/2016/feb/17/inside-the-fbis-encryption-battle-with-apple

Yates, J. (1989). The emergence of the memo as a managerial genre. *Management Communication Quarterly*, 2(4), 485–510.

Yuthas, Kristi, Jesse F. Dillard, and Rodney K. Rogers. 2004. "Beyond Agency and Structure: Triple-Loop Learning." Journal of Business Ethics 51 (2): 229–43.

YAM, KAI CHI, KLOTZ, ANTHONY C., WEI HE, REYNOLDS, SCOTT J. (2014). TURNING GOOD SOLDIERS INTO BAD APPLES: EXAMINING WHEN AND WHY CITIZENSHIP BEHAVIOR LEADS TO DEVIANCE. Academy of Management Annual Meeting Proceedings, 21516561.

Zhu, X. (2013). Mandate versus championship: Vertical government intervention and diffusion of innovation in public services in authoritarian China. *Public Management Review*, 16(1), 117–139.

Index

In this index *b* indicates box, *f* indicates figure, and *t* indicates table

moral managers, 197–8, 198f
moral obligations, 182
moral persons, 197, 198f
motivations
    job security, 136b
    of public managers, 29t
    public sector workers, 120–3
    public service, 27–9, 29t
Mulgan, Geoff, 165b
multiplicity, of public sector settings, 52
multi-polar world, 43–4
multi-sectorial collaboration, 280–6
    in Australia, 233–6b
    nonprofits and, 228
Musk, Elon, 47, 167

narcissistic employees, 115
National Endowment for Science Tech-
    nology and the Arts (UK), 165b
National Security Agency (NSA), 127b,
    192b
Nature, 167
navigational instructions, 53
navigator role, 21–2b
NBC News, 192b
netizens, 99
networking relation-focused
    collaborator, 17–8
networks
    of innovation, 162
    for managing newcomer
        socialization, 129–30
New Public Governance (NPG), 18
New Public Management (NPM), 14, 17
New York Times, 47
non-governmental organizations
    (NGOs), 233–5b
non-profits, cross-sectoral
    collaboration and, 233–4

Obama, Barack, 76, 100, 145b, 153b,
    156b, 165b, 190b
Observatory of Public Sector
    Innovation (OECD), 165b
Occupy Central, 38, 87
office settings, remote/virtual, 26
open data, 98t
open innovation, 141
open *v.* tailored participation, 104t
opportunism, 201

opportunities
    authority turbulence, 57–8, 57b
    cross-sectoral collaboration, 63b
    innovation forces, 60b
    new workforce, 58–9, 59b
    short- *v.* long-term horizons, 63b
    stakeholder multiplicity, 56, 57b
Organisation for Economic Co-operation
    and Development (OECD), 20
organizational adaptation, 158b
organizational capabilities, 81
organizational cues, foresight and, 217f
organizational drivers, public sector
    innovation, 164–6f
organizational features, that attract
    innovators, 165b
organizational forgetting, 208
organizational information networks, 130
organizational outcomes, PSM and, 124f
organizations, enabling, 257–8
organizing professionalism, 110b
Osborne, David, 17
outsourcing, public-private
    partnerships and, 230–1

paradigm shift, 34b
parental leave, 130
participation
    designing to exchange legitimacy,
        open *v.* tailored, 104t
    tailoring, authority turbulence and,
        100–7
participatory policy-making *v.*
    traditional, 102
partnerships, collaborative, 213–4
    contracting out, 214
    corporate social responsibility (CSR),
        India, 235b
    motives/space for involvement, 236–8
    multi-sectoral collaboration, 233–6
    public-private comparator manual
        (PPC), 232b
    public-private partnerships (PPPs),
        236–7
    skillset/mindset development, 241–5f
party loyalties/membership, 159b
peer feedback systems, 138
Pentagon Papers, 192b
performance, manage shared
    accountability and, 226–34

Lightning Source UK Ltd.
Milton Keynes UK
UKHW021412101022
410237UK00009B/1619